DANCE THEORY

Dance Theory

Source Readings from Two Millennia of Western Dance

A Critical Anthology by Tilden Russell

OXFORD
UNIVERSITY PRESS

Oxford University Press is a department of the University of Oxford. It furthers
the University's objective of excellence in research, scholarship, and education
by publishing worldwide. Oxford is a registered trade mark of Oxford University
Press in the UK and certain other countries.

Published in the United States of America by Oxford University Press
198 Madison Avenue, New York, NY 10016, United States of America.

© Oxford University Press 2020

Library of Congress Cataloging-in-Publication Data
Names: Russell, Tilden A., editor. | Oxford University Press.
Title: Dance theory : source readings from two millennia of
Western dance / edited by Tilden Russell.
Other titles: Source readings from 2 millennia of Western dance
Description: New York : Oxford University Press, 2020. |
Includes bibliographical references and index.
Identifiers: LCCN 2019035560 (print) | LCCN 2019035561 (ebook) |
ISBN 9780190059750 (Hardback) | ISBN 9780190059767 (Paperback) |
ISBN 9780190059774 (UPDF) | ISBN 9780190059781 (ePub)
Subjects: LCSH: Dance—Philosophy—History. | Dance notation—History. |
Choreography—History. Classification: LCC GV1588 .D35 2020 (print) |
LCC GV1588 (ebook) | DDC 792.8—dc23
LC record available at https://lccn.loc.gov/2019035560
LC ebook record available at https://lccn.loc.gov/2019035561

9 8 7 6 5 4 3 2 1

Paperback printed by Marquis, Canada
Hardback printed by Bridgeport National Bindery, Inc., United States of America

To Dominique
and to the memory of the four Finneman sisters:
my mother Stella, and aunts Gertrude, Rose, and Blanche

Contents

Illustrations

Preface

This book began in 2014 as an introduction to the book I was then writing about a small group of dance theorists—five Germans and an Englishman—and their treatises published between 1703 and 1721: obviously a very narrow conspectus in subject and years.[1] The aim of the introduction was to place these largely ignored writers (especially the Germans) in a broad historical context that would demonstrate how essential and pivotal they were. As I read further in dance theory, I found more and more sources on the subject that turned out to be far more interesting and complex than I had originally imagined. The introduction kept getting longer, until it became an albatross on the book's actual text, not only because of its ever-increasing length, but more gravely, because I had assumed it would trace a teleological ascent in dance theory culminating in my authors and their works, followed by a degenerative aftermath. This tendentious viewpoint threatened not only to deter readers from a sympathetic reading of the book as a whole; it turned out, the more I read and learned, to be simply wrong.

The history of dance theory, as I gradually came to realize, is too interesting and important to be exploited for spurious purposes. Also, it's an untold story. Dance historians are familiar with many or most of the authors and titles, but not what they have to say about dance theory. That's the part usually at the beginning of books that is skimmed through in order to get to the more urgent preoccupations of historical dancers and dance historians: performance practice, reconstruction, technique, and repertoire. Viewed superficially, moreover, it can seem as if the same self-evident and obligatory themes keep getting repeated like clichés in these sections under the general rubric of theory: a definition of dance and/or dance theory, or at least a list of their basic components; the relation of dance to the other arts and other areas of knowledge; dance's origin and history; and its utility (i.e., health, social conduct and success, recreation).

Finally, and contrary to what I had long believed, dance theory is not dead. In fact, it is thriving in the twenty-first century. Yes, I was fully aware that something called dance theory was being copiously written and talked about, and that "theory" and "theorizing" and "theorist" had become wildly ubiquitous in dance scholars' lexicon, but I believed that what they were talking about was no genuine dance theory, had no kinship with what was historically accepted as dance theory, and did not meet the criteria of what a theory should be. I was convinced that what I considered dance theory had been swept away in the iconoclastic, irreverent, and nonconformist spirit of postmodernism. Luckily, early readers tactfully convinced me to address my folly. As I wrote, I learned. Writing this book has already served as a textbook in my own learning experience.

There are some excellent compilations of readings in dance history. The common format is to devote each chapter to a historical period, with an introductory essay followed by relevant readings. The number of readings tends to increase as history marches on, peaking in the nineteenth century. A sampling of such compilations follows. Each book differs from this one in different ways, but in general, and by intent, none of them does everything this book sets out to do: treat theory in depth and as a discrete topic; treat theatrical and social dance equally; include readings dating from classical Antiquity to the twenty-first century; and link the readings, through brief introductory essays, from end to end by a narrative thread based on salient topics as seen from evolving perspectives.

Selma Jeanne Cohen's *Dance as a Theatre Art: Source Readings in Dance History from 1581 to the Present* is the classic scholarly compilation.[2] It was designed for use in college dance history classes, for which no such textbook yet existed, and is still useful and relevant. It includes twenty-seven readings, from the Renaissance to Meredith Monk. While Cohen pays some attention to dance theory, composition, and criticism, her principal focus, as indicated in the title, is on theatrical dance performance.

Five compilations published between the 1980s and now exemplify the different target audiences, time frames, and thematic emphases of the present book's more recent predecessors.[3] Jack Anderson's reader is intended for "students and inquisitive dancegoers" (p. xii); the time frame is from Homer to Pina Bausch (d. 2009); and the emphasis is on theatrical dance, classical ballet, and modern dance performance. Elizabeth Aldrich's entertaining reader aims at a general audience; her content is limited to "ballroom dance in the United States during the 1800s, with an emphasis on the Northern states" (xviii). Allison Thompson's intended audience is both scholarly and generalist; her time frame is ca. 1600 to the mid-twentieth century; and her focus is on social dance, with readings taken mostly from nondance, literary sources. Maureen Needham focuses mainly on the nineteenth and twentieth centuries and predominantly on vernacular dance as practiced in different social contexts and cultures in the United States; only her section on modern dance deals with dance as a creative, high-culture, artistic endeavor. Marie-Joëlle Louison-Lassabliere's sources come from a period of approximately two and a half centuries; they are all of French origin, written in Latin and French; they represent many genres: treatises, dictionaries, histories, drama, poetry, and memoirs, and they are not presented in strictly chronological order.

Two other books—neither of them selections of readings—have been especially inspirational to me in the conception of this book.

Vom "Affect" zur "Action", by Stephanie Schroedter, is the first study to present the early eighteenth-century French, German, and English theoretical sources in their proper historical and intellectual context.[4] Though not a book of readings, its generous and lengthy quotations could easily have been collected as such, had the author not provided such a wealth of history, commentary, and insight within which to situate them.

Gustave Reese's *Fourscore Classics of Music Literature* is really just a ninety-one-page booklet in a category quite different from the preceding titles.[5] Its topic is music, not dance, and it contains "thumbnail sketches" (about one per page), not readings. Its subtitle sums up its focus and format: "A Guide to Selected Original Sources on Theory and Other Writings on Music Not Available in English, with Descriptive Sketches and Bibliographical References." As a work devoted to the history of music theory, it provided me with an intellectual template for a similar approach to dance theory.

Like Cohen's *Dance as a Theatre Art*, Reese's book is written for advanced college students—graduate musicology students, in his case. Reese describes eighty works dating from Greek antiquity to 1927. With the exception of four sources in a chapter on "Islam and the Orient," all the works are European in origin and are described in chronological order. Aside from very brief and general introductory statements, there is no narrative thread connecting one source to another. In inverse relation to the collections of dance readings, the number of sources diminish as they approach the nineteenth century, with only eight sources after 1800; the reason is not that there were fewer sources, but that the number of sources written in or translated into English has radically increased in the last two hundred years.

In sheer numbers, *Fourscore Classics* hints at the wealth of music-theoretical sources, especially considering how many hundreds or thousands of additional sources had to be excluded by Reese's criteria. It is easy to deduce that music theory's historical development benefited from continuous dialogue and the steady accretion of knowledge—an observation highly pertinent to the work that follows.

NOTES

1. Tilden Russell, *Theory and Practice in Eighteenth-Century Dance: The German-French Connection*, Studies in Seventeenth- and Eighteenth-Century Art and Culture (Newark, DE: University of Delaware Press, 2017).

2. New York: Harper & Row, 1974.

3. Jack Anderson, *Ballet & Modern Dance: A Concise History*, 2nd ed. (Princeton, NJ: Princeton Book Company, 1992 [1st ed. 1986]); Elizabeth Aldrich, *From the Ballroom to Hell: Grace and Folly in Nineteenth-Century Dance* (Evanston, IL: Northwestern University Press, 1991); Allison Thompson, *Dancing Through Time: Western Social Dance in Literature, 1400–1918: Selections* (Jefferson, NC: McFarland & Company, Inc., 1998); *I See America Dancing: Selected Readings, 1685–2000*, ed. Maureen Needham (Urbana: University of Illinois Press, 2002); Marie-Joëlle Louison-Lassabliere, *Feuillets pour Terpsichore: La danse par les textes du XVᵉ au XVIIᵉ siècle* (Paris: L'Harmattan, 2007).

4. Stephanie Schroedter, *Vom "Affect" zur "Action"; Quellenstudien zur Poetik der Tanzkunst vom späten Ballet de Cour bis zum frühen Ballet en Action* (Würzburg: Königshausen & Neumann, 2004).

5. Gustave Reese, *Fourscore Classics of Music Literature*, The Library of Liberal Arts (Indianapolis: The Bobbs-Merrill Co., 1957).

Acknowledgments

Linda Tomko, the first reader and editor of this material when it was still form-less and raw as an unlicked bear cub, guided and encouraged me through the first awkward, unsteady steps.

Thanks to Norman Hirschy (Oxford University Press), every phase of publishing this book has been a pleasure: by far the most committed, intelligent, supportive, and frustration-free experience I have known in my entire modest publishing career. He sagely counseled me to raise my head out of the sand to examine crucial areas that I had felt inadequately equipped to confront—an empowering and liberating experience.

I deeply appreciate the trenchant and sensitive comments of my anonymous readers, who allowed me to see the book as others will see it, and to reflect in time on how to improve it.

Thank you, Kent De Spain, Susanne Franco, Flavia Pappacena, and Robert Farrar Thompson for personally granting me permission to use your work, and to Marie Glon, Sandra Noll Hammond, Flavia Pappacena, and Stephanie Schroedter for contributing source material. Thanks also to the Rudolf Laban Archive and to the Merce Cunningham Trust.

For permission to use the cover photograph, my thanks and awe-struck *Baselmanus* to Anne Teresa De Keersmaeker; also to Hans Galle of Rosas, and photographer Max Vadukul.

I am grateful to those who helped in many different ways: Irene Brandenburg, Kathryn Dickason, Hans Galle, Claudia Jeschke, William Lepowsky, Suzanne Eggleston Lovejoy, Ed Mormon, Marie-Thérèse Mourey, Mali Skotheim, Sandra Stelts and the staff of the Eberle Family Special Collections Library (Pennsylvania State University), Jennifer Thorp, Hanna Walsdorf, and Susan L. Wiesner.

And a big thank you, Harry Weintraub, for treating me to my first "Agon" and "Apollo."

To Dominique Bourassa, my partner in wedlock and "unlocking collections" and the minuet: blissful gratitude.

Introduction
Dance Theory as a Problem in Dance History

> ... the Muse who has assumed everything rejected by
> the higher Muses of philosophy and art, everything unfounded in truth,
> everything which is merely contingent but which also reveals other laws:
> the Muse of history!
>
> —MARCEL PROUST, *The Fugitive*
> (trans. Peter Collier [London: Penguin Books, 2003]), 640

In 1852, dancer, choreographer, and theorist Arthur Saint-Léon envisioned a dance theory that would be "indestructible, immutable, respected like laws."[1] Seldom if ever in the dance world has a more futile wish been uttered. In the second decade of the twenty-first century, as this is being written, the concept of dance theory is more elusive than ever. There is no article titled "dance theory" in the *International Encyclopedia of Dance,* a valuable and authoritative scholarly source in the field of dance studies, and the first and still only publication of its kind in our time.[2] A full-length history of dance theory as a discrete subject, from Plato to the present, has yet to be written.

Dance theory does have a history, albeit disjunct and short of memory because the writers in every age theorized prescriptively, according to their own needs and ideals. It is hard to detect a continuous discursive tradition between sources through commentary, translation, innovation, and refutation. Brilliant episodes found few successors to build upon and surpass their achievements. Moreover, a definitive break in dance-theory discourse occurred in the late eighteenth and early nineteenth centuries, when, thanks chiefly to the ideas of Jean-Georges Noverre, dance theory underwent a complete U-turn in terms of its ideals, fundamental principles, and goals. The situation around 1870 is eloquently lamented by G. Léopold Adice:

Sadly, traditions lacking a methodology are soon lost, and an art such as ours that moves forward randomly, deprived of a method and theory, and abandoned to caprice, can only fall into ruin, the sad results of which are already evident.[3]

Indeed, like a *Leitmotif* recurring in every century since the sixteenth, theorists have continually asserted the lack of any pre-existing dance theory.[4]

There is a broad spectrum of definitions of the word *theory* and its cognate words. The Greek root has to do with observation or contemplation. In modern English, the most casual usage can express illogic, improbability, guesswork—"Theoretically, anything can happen"—giving the impression that theory can validate anything one wants it to. Science demands the more methodical interpretation of starting from a plausible *hypothesis*, which at least must be proved or disproved. In this book we take a position between the original Greek definition and St.-Léon's understanding of the word: theory is an open-minded way of observing something analytically in order to grasp its essential and eternal nature. Wherever a clear distinction exists between the theory and practice of an art form, theory will deal with the constituent elements and principles common to all manifestations of that art. Music theory will serve as our model for dance theory.

Music is the art most intimately related to dance—according to legend, either by a sibling or filial relationship. Aristides Quintilianus (dated vaguely between the first century BCE and the fourth century CE) is said to be the first writer to observe the theory-practice distinction in music, in his *Peri mousikes* (or *De musica*).[5] Melody, harmony, meter, and rhythm are the basic elements of music theory. They have been the subject of numerous treatises produced continually since the early Middle Ages and have remained a constant, no matter what style of composition or notation was in use in any given period. Modern academic programs in music offer degrees in three specialized areas: music theory, music history (musicology), and performance.[6] Professional music theorists teach in graduate programs, present their research before learned organizations like the Society for Music Theory, and publish analytical studies and treatises of their own on theory topics both historical and contemporary. Few such academic, scholarly, and professional institutions have existed for dance theory.

Why did writers on dance never succeed in establishing a permanent set of elements upon which a theory could be based? Several hypotheses come to mind. Historiographically speaking, dance lacks music's compelling creation stories and founding heroes—including theorists like Pythagoras with his anvil and hammers, as well as musicians like Orpheus, King David, and Saint

Cecilia—who throughout its history have imparted a sense of tradition, purpose, and continuity. As John Weaver wrote of Pythagoras in *The Spectator* in 1712, and was quoted 120 years later by E. A. Théleur:

> By these Steps, from so mean a Beginning, did this great Man reduce, what was only before Noise, to one of the most delightful Sciences, by marrying it to the Mathematicks; and by those means caused it to be one of the most abstract and demonstrative of Siences [*sic*]. Who knows therefore but Motion, whether Decorous or Representative, may not (as it seems highly probable it may) be taken into consideration by some Person capable of reducing it into a regular Science, tho' not so demonstrative as that proceeding from Sounds, yet sufficient to entitle it to a Place among the magnify'd Arts.[7]

Weaver implies that without theory, dance cannot be considered on a par with the other "magnify'd Arts." In contrast to music, dance in Weaver's time was not yet formally recognized as belonging to the liberal arts except, at best, as music's inferior offspring. Dance's ambivalent relationship to religion—its reputation of sinfulness *versus* its various biblical justifications—also mitigated against it.

The historical discontinuity of dance theory is surely due, in part, to the various walks of life from which its writers approached it. In the course of this *Reader*, we will encounter philosophers and historians, a Jesuit scholar, encyclopedists and lexicographers, dancing masters and ballet masters, choreographers and professional dancers, anthropologists and art historians, and most recently—almost as if coming full circle—dance-studies academics obsessed with the philosophical currents *du jour*. The most crucial reason, however, may be dance's inability to develop a single, generally accepted, continuously evolving notation system in which theoretical ideas are signified and applied to practice. Musical notation, with its four basic elements in full array, is such a system.[8]

The purpose of this book is to revive and reintegrate dance theory as a field of historical dance studies, and to present a coherent reading of the interaction of theory and practice during two millennia of dance history. The first hurdle in this undertaking is to establish what sources, what ideological threads, to follow. This is not just a book about books with "theory" in the title, but it is that, too. Dance sources used the term "theory" only discontinuously and inconsistently, so a history of the term by itself will exclude much pertinent material. Indeed, in the course of this book we will meet genuine theorists who never used the word "theory," as well as writers for whom the word "theory" meant precisely its opposite: practice. Some writers merely flaunt the word in their title to hint at a degree of intellectual profundity that is absent from their content.

If our aim is to model a working definition of dance theory on music theory's core functional principles of melody-harmony-meter-rhythm, it becomes immediately apparent that many twentieth-century discussions of dance have relied on taxonomies that theorize *about* dance but are not *of* dance, being based, rather, on standards or categories such as aesthetics, modality, and genre. By aesthetics I mean subjective standards of taste and beauty, which mutate unceasingly with the times. By modality I am referring to categories like mimetic, expressive, and formalistic dance.[9] By genre I mean theatrical, social, national, folk, religious dance, and so on. These taxonomies, according to André Levinson, are contingent and extraneous to theory, or associated with theory but not essential parts of it:

> It seems as though everyone had piled upon this art mistaken attributes or supplementary burdens in his efforts to redeem—if only in a small way— the actual movements of the dance.
>
> I cannot think of anyone who has devoted himself to those characteristics which belong exclusively to dancing, or who has endeavored to formulate specifically the laws of this art on its own ground.[10]

Dance's essential constituent is human motion, and its unique manifestation or artifact is ephemeral: a living, moving, present human body. How, then, is one to abstract its principles from one's own physical experience? "Nothing is more difficult than to reduce the essential esthetic realities of the dance to verbal formulas," Levinson writes, because it is "so peculiarly inarticulate." Practical works (manuals, choreographies, *recueils*), on the other hand, are based on "empirical laws which rule the execution of their elements."[11] They are the "how-to" books: how to make steps, how to dance current dances, and so forth. As such, they have easily cast a shadow of superfluousness over the very idea of a dance theory, and as a result, practical works have played a disproportionately large role in our modern reconstruction of the performance and ethos of early dance.

If practice is the "how" of dance, theory is the no less basic "what" and "why": what is it, and why do we do it? Historically, the earliest theoretical writing predates the earliest practical sources, and until around 1800, dance writers gave theory priority. They placed statements on dance principles and ideals at the head of their treatises, and many insisted that one cannot learn to dance without first acquiring a respectful understanding of its theory. They believed that theory consists of principles governed by rational laws; that practice begins when works embodying these principles and laws are created; and that notation is developed from dance works as a means of pedagogy, performance, and preservation. However, by the second half of the eighteenth century the edifice was beginning to fall apart, and dance theory failed to evolve toward Saint-Léon's idealistic vision. What follows is a tale of inverted priorities, redefinition of basic terms, brand-new epistemologies, and even an ending *in medias res*, as it were, and more optimistic than I could have expected.

This is a typical book of collected readings, and as such, a history of an idea from one generation to another. The book is divided into nine chapters organized chronologically by historical era and predominant intellectual and artistic currents. Each chapter begins with an introduction, of varying length, that serves as a transition through the interstices of time, ideologies, and zeitgeist. The individual source readings that follow have their own introductions. My job as a historian was to follow the wayward path of dance theory wherever the sources led. This means that certain imbalances are inevitable; for example, Antiquity and the Middle Ages (a span of ca. 1800 years) are covered in one chapter, while the eighteenth century is spread over three. The Appendix: Table of Dance Periodization should help sort out the chronological structure of the book.

A graver issue: no women theorists before the twentieth century, a situation endemic in all the arts, but even more pronounced in dance because of its unmediated physicality. The absence of women in dance theory until the twentieth century is a by-product of a sexist mind-body dualism, according to which women should be voiceless (dumb in common parlance) and beautiful, and should let men do all the thinking. As dancers, however, women have been feted, idolized, and idealized for centuries. Classical ballet is the pinnacle of this glorification of the female form and movement; it was George Balanchine, after all, who said: "Woman is still first in ballet. Man is an attendant to a queen. He is a consort, he is noble, brilliant, but, finally merely *good enough* to be her partner. Ballet is a woman."[12] Of the pre-1900 sources included here, only two refer even glancingly to a female dancing master or teacher of dance, whereas in Chapters 8 and 9 there are nearly twice as many women theorists as men.[13]

Probably the most sensitive issue of all is the way I have organized African American dance theory readings in clusters in Chapters 8 and 9. I would very much regret if this procedure were perceived as a kind of ghettoization—it would be the opposite of my intention. I decided to cluster African American Dance Theory I because even though the readings cover a seventy-year time span, they trace the establishment of basic principles in a close, coherent sequence, the impact of which would have been lost, I felt, if the five readings had been scattered in strict chronological order. The current placement also draws attention to the synergistic relation between African American dance movement and modernist dance as exemplified by Martha Graham. African American Dance Theory II is a small essay in its own right, covering only fourteen years and showing how this field maintains its historical roots and principles while spreading globally and embracing the theory and methodology of poststructuralism.

The readings comprise a corpus that addresses a circumscribed dance repertoire conveniently referred to as "Western" dance because it originated in the area now known as Western Europe. It remained within this area until the ages of exploration and colonization, when it gradually was exported to the Western hemisphere and began to confront—or be confronted by—native dance traditions and the dance styles brought by African slaves. Even in this period, however, the theoretical treatises were written by Europeans in Europe, who were concerned only with their own dance culture. The only real exception to this state of affairs is found in encyclopedias and other reference works, or books that aim in length and breadth at encyclopedic inclusiveness. Charles Compan, for example, has articles on "CHINOIS (Danses des)" and "KALUMET, ou CALUMET. Danse des Othagras & des Sakis, Sauvages du Canada" in his *Dictionnaire* (1787); Gottfried Taubert's *Rechtschaffener Tantzmeister* (1717), nearly 1,300 pages long, takes all the space needed to expound at leisure on the entire universe of dance knowledge.

Only in the twentieth century did "Western" dance theory begin to open up to non-Western influences. In the United States this broadening of scope was encouraged by immigration, which increased demographic diversity; by advanced study programs in anthropology, ethnology, and especially ethnomusicology; by the civil rights movement, the growth of African and African American studies programs, and, in particular, the vitality and popularity of African American dance itself; and by the interdisciplinarity, intertextuality, and global reach of twenty-first century poststructuralist dance studies. However, to understand what the dance theorists in this collection are saying, the reader requires no background in the basics of, say, Brazilian, Japanese, Ghanaian, or Hopi dance. I hope that the principles and criteria—the working definition—of dance theory adumbrated earlier and, ideally, as "immutable" as Saint-Léon wished it to be, will suffice as a standard, uniformly applicable to every reading.

Above all, my aim is to keep the story focused and connected. A weighty and costly encyclopedic tome (that will never be global enough to satisfy all tastes) is the last thing needed in a dynamic learning environment in which supplemental material is readily available for further reading, research, and discussion.

This book makes no claim to cite every source; nor does it assume an all-knowing or *ex cathedra* authority. The corpus is not a canon. Indeed, readers should not hesitate to interrogate my choices, criteria, and opinions—to say nothing of my presumptuousness as an interloper in the dance world. The book will succeed to the extent that it provides readers with a solid intellectual basis for independent critical thinking about dance theory and how it relates to experiencing dance performance.

In traversing the different eras, nationalities, mentalities, and priorities of the different authors, readers are encouraged to detect and follow a skein of connective threads that trace a coherent and, one hopes, fair narrative of the evolution of dance theory as a concept in Western culture. The way is signposted by numerous cross-references from one reading to another, going both backward and forward in time, and increasing as the book progresses. These threads include definitions of dance theory and the names and significance of its essential elements; theory's relation to practice; its relation to ethics; to humanism; to linguistic issues; to choreography, gymnastics, and pedagogy; to sciences (especially anatomy, physics, and the social sciences); to other arts (especially music and painting); and to the liberal arts.

Note: Some of the readings originally contain annotations of various sorts (footnotes, endnotes, etc.). To include these annotations in the readings would confusingly encumber the book with dual footnote systems, without adding any essential information. Therefore, all readings are transcribed without their footnotes/endnotes, etc., if present, unless otherwise indicated.

All translations are by the author unless otherwise indicated. All transcriptions follow the orthography, punctuation, and accentuation of the source text.

NOTES

1. Arthur Saint-Léon, *La Sténochorégraphie* (Paris: author and Brandus & Cie., 1852), 13.
2. *International Encyclopedia of Dance*, ed. Selma Jeanne Cohen, 6 vols. (New York: Oxford University Press, 1998).
3. G. Léopold Adice, "Grammaire/et/Théorie chorégraphique/Composition de la gymnastique/de la danse théâtrale" (ms.: Paris, Bibliothèque-Musée de l'Opéra, cote B61(1), [1868–1871]), Gallica 311742, "Des Bras," 599: "Malheureusement les traditions sans la methode se perdent bientôt, et un art qui marche à l'aventure comme la [*sic*] notre privé de methode et de théorie et abandonnée [*sic*] au caprice, ne peut que tomber bientôt en ruine, nous en voyons déjà les tristes effets."

4. Sixteenth century: Arbeau; seventeenth century: De Lauze, Menestrier; eighteenth century: Behr, Cahusac, Noverre, Compan; nineteenth century: Blasis, Adice, Zorn; twentieth century: Laban, Levinson; twenty-first century: Foster. All these authors (except André Levinson) are represented in the readings that follow.

5. See Thomas J. Mathiesen, "Aristides Quintilianus," *Grove Music Online*, http://www.oxfordmusiconline.com/subscriber/article/grove/music/01244?q=Aristides+Quintilianus&search=quick&pos=1&_start=1#F010731, who dates the treatise most likely in the second or third century CE; also Egon Wellesz, "Musicology," *Grove's Dictionary of Music and Musicians,* 3rd ed., ed. H. C. Colles, *Supplementary Volume* (New York: The Macmillan Company, 1940), 456.

6. Many departments have broadened their offerings in recent decades to include ethnomusicology and other areas of specialization.

7. John Weaver, *The Spectator* 334 (March 24, 1712), 60; quoted by E. A. Théleur, *Letters on Dancing* (London: Sherwood & Co., 1831; facs. ed. *Studies in Dance History* II/1 [Society of Dance History Scholars, 1990]), vii. Théleur (v) incorrectly attributes the passage to Richard Steele.

8. This explanation has been previously advanced by Fernau Hall, "Dance Notation and Choreology," *What Is Dance? Readings in Theory and Criticism,* ed. Roger Copeland and Marshall Cohen (Oxford: Oxford University Press, 1983), 394–395.

9. See Roger Copeland and Marshall Cohen, eds., *What Is Dance?* (Oxford: Oxford University Press, 1983), 1–9; Noël Carroll, "Dance," *The Oxford Handbook of Aesthetics,* ed. Jerrold Levinson (Oxford: Oxford University Press, 2003), 583–593, misleadingly (in my view) describes as aesthetics what I call modality.

10. Levinson, "The Spirit of the Classic Dance," *Reading Dance,* ed. Robert Gottlieb (New York: Pantheon Books, 2008), 413. The essay originally appeared in *Theatre Arts Monthly* (March 1925).

11. Ibid., 412–413.

12. Undated quotation, from Robert Gottlieb, "Balanchine's Dream," *Vanity Fair* (December 1998), https://www.vanityfair.com/culture/1998/12/george-balanchine-new-york-city-ballet-history.

13. Gottfried Taubert (Reading 4.3) states that there were *Tantzmeisterinnen* in Antiquity (34, not quoted in this reading); Eugène Giraudet (Reading 7.6a) says a woman can be an effective dance teacher.

Dance Theory to ca. 1300

Around 1,660 years passed between Plato, the first reading in this chapter, and Johannes de Grocheio, the last. During this millennium-and-a-half, "dance theory" did not exist. Its founding documents are not dance treatises, but parts of larger works on subjects in which dance is implicated, by authors whose knowledge of dance was based more on observation than participation. While the attitude of the classical authors (Plato, Aristotle, Plutarch, Lucian) was positive, based primarily on popular theatrical pantomime and choric dance, the prevailing attitude during the Middle Ages (ca. 450–1450) was negative because of ecclesiastic objections to dance's sensuality and reputation of immorality.

Three distinct approaches to dance theory emerge from our readings of the four classical theorists:

1. the ethics of dance: dance's ethical and civic function (Plato);
2. the raw materials of dance: the physical components of organized human movement, thus the theoretical basis of dance practice (Aristotle and Plutarch); and
3. the culture of dance: how dance fits into the life of a civilized society; its history, its utilitarian, aesthetic, and moral benefits, and its relation to other arts and disciplines (Lucian).

None of the theorists who follow will fail to emphasize one or more of these themes.

I.I. PLATO (428/427 OR 424/423–348/347 BCE)
Laws (written 360 BCE), trans. R. G. Bury, Loeb Classical Library 187 (Cambridge, MA: Harvard University Press, 1984), Book II.

The earliest purely theoretical writing on dance—sparse though it may be—predates the first practical dance treatises by almost two millennia.

Book II of Plato's *Laws* deals with music and dance together. Plato says that all living creatures have an inborn impulse to move, but only humans can do so in an organized way because only they can perceive rhythm and harmony. Harmony is the order of song, and rhythm is the order of dance; both together form the basis of choric dance. Plato defines "choric performances" as "representations of character, exhibited in actions and circumstances of every kind." Education is given through Apollo and the nine Muses (not exclusively through Terpsichore, the muse of dance). To be well educated is to dance and sing well, and that which is sung or danced must also be good. "Education is the process of drawing and guiding children towards that principle which is pronounced right by the law and confirmed as truly right by the experience of the oldest and the most just." Therefore, laws should compel poets (i.e., creative artists) to compose works that teach virtue. Plato establishes themes that will reappear continually in dance theoretical writing: dance as a divine gift that can be received and enjoyed only through the medium of human rationality; dance's power to instill virtue; its educative mission to foster ethical behavior in a civilized society; and its mimetic nature.

READING 1.1
Plato (trans. Bury)

PP. 88–113

Athenian Stranger. In the next place, we probably ought to enquire, regarding this subject, whether the discerning of men's natural dispositions is the only gain to be derived from the right use of wine-parties, or whether it entails benefits so great as to be worthy of serious consideration. What do we say about this? Our argument evidently tends to indicate that it does entail such benefits; so how and wherein it does so let us now hear, and that with minds attentive, lest haply we be led astray by it.

Clinias of Crete. Say on.

Ath. I want us to call to mind again our definition of right education. For the safe-keeping of this depends, as I now conjecture, upon the correct establishment of the institution mentioned.

Clin. That is a strong statement!

Ath. What I state is this,—that in children the first childish sensations are pleasure and pain, and that it is in these first that goodness and badness come to the soul; but as to wisdom and settled true opinions, a man is lucky if they come to him even in old age; and he that is possessed of these blessings, and all that they comprise, is indeed a perfect man.

I term, then, the goodness that first comes to children "education." When pleasure and love, and pain and hatred, spring up rightly in the souls of those who are unable as yet to grasp a rational account; and when, after grasping the rational account, they consent thereunto through having been rightly trained in fitting practices:—this consent, viewed as a whole, is goodness, while the part of it that is rightly trained in respect of pleasures arid pains, so as to hate what ought to be hated, right from the beginning up to the very end, and to love what ought to be loved,—if you were to mark this part off in your definition and call it "education," you would be giving it, in my opinion, its right name.

Clin. You are quite right, Stranger, as it seems to us, both in what you said before and in what you say now about education.

Ath. Very good. Now these forms of child-training, which consist in right discipline in pleasures and pains, grow slack and weakened to a great extent in the course of men's lives; so the gods, in pity for the human race thus born to misery, have ordained the feasts of thanksgiving as periods of respite from their troubles; and they have granted them as companions in their feasts the Muses and Apollo the master of music, and Dionysus, that they may at least set right again their modes of discipline by associating in their feasts with gods. We must consider, then, whether the account that is harped on nowadays is true to nature? What it says is that, almost without exception, every young creature is incapable of keeping either its body or its tongue quiet, and is always striving to move and to cry, leaping and skipping and delighting in dances and games, and uttering, also, noises of every description. Now, whereas all other creatures are devoid of any perception of the various kinds of order and disorder in movement (which we term rhythm and harmony), to us men the very gods, who were given, as we said, to be our fellows in the dance, have granted the pleasurable perception of rhythm and harmony, whereby they cause us to move and lead our choirs, linking us one with another by means of songs and dances; and to the choir they have given its name from the "cheer" implanted therein. Shall we accept this account to begin with, and postulate that education owes its origin to Apollo and the Muses?

Clin. Yes.

Ath. Shall we assume that the uneducated man is without choir-training, and the educated man fully choir-trained?

Clin. Certainly.

Ath. Choir-training, as a whole, embraces of course both dancing and song.

Clin. Undoubtedly.

Ath. So the well-educated man will be able both to sing and dance well.

Clin. Evidently.

Ath. Let us now consider what this last statement of ours implies.

Clin. Which statement?

Ath. Our words are,—"he sings well and dances well": ought we, or ought we not, to add,—"provided that he sings good songs and dances good dances"?

Clin. We ought to add this.

Ath. How then, if a man takes the good for good and the bad for bad and treats them accordingly? Shall we regard such a man as better trained in choristry and music when he is always able both with gesture and voice to represent adequately that which he conceives to be good, though he feels neither delight in the good nor hatred of the bad,—or when, though not wholly able to represent his conception rightly by voice and gesture, he yet keeps right in his feelings of pain and pleasure, welcoming everything good and abhorring everything not good?

Clin. There is a vast difference between the two cases, Stranger, in point of education.

Ath. If, then, we three[1] understand what constitutes goodness in respect of dance and song, we also know who is and who is not rightly educated; but without this knowledge we shall never be able to discern whether there exists any safeguard for education or where it is to be found. Is not that so?

Clin. It is.

Ath. What we have next to track down, like hounds on the trail, is goodness of posture and tunes in relation to song and dance; if this eludes our pursuit, it will be in vain for us to discourse further concerning right education, whether of Greeks or of barbarians.

Clin. Yes.

Ath. Well then, however shall we define goodness of posture or of tune? Come, consider: when a manly soul is beset by troubles, and a cowardly soul by troubles identical and equal, are the postures and utterances that result in the two cases similar?

Clin. How could they be, when even their complexions differ in colour?

Ath. Well said, my friend. But in fact, while postures and tunes do exist in music, which deals with rhythm and harmony, so that one can rightly speak of a tune or posture being "rhythmical" or "harmonious," one cannot rightly apply the choirmasters' metaphor "well-coloured" to tune and posture; but one can use this language about the posture and tune of the brave man and the coward, and one is right in calling those of the brave man good, and those of the coward bad. To avoid a tediously long disquisition, let us sum up the whole matter by saying that the postures and tunes which attach to goodness of soul or body, or to some image thereof, are universally good, while those which attach to badness are exactly the reverse.

Clin. Your pronouncement is correct, and we now formally endorse it.

Ath. Another point:—do we all delight equally in choral dancing, or far from equally?

Clin. Very far indeed.

Ath. Then what are we to suppose it is that misleads us? Is it the fact that we do not all regard as good the same things, or is it that, although they are the same, they are thought not to be the same? For surely no one will maintain that the choric performances of vice are better than those of virtue, or that he himself enjoys the postures of turpitude, while all others delight in music of the opposite kind. Most people, however, assert that the value of music consists in its power of affording pleasure to the soul. But such an assertion is quite intolerable, and it is blasphemy even to utter it. The fact which misleads us is more probably the following—

Clin. What?

Ath. Inasmuch as choric performances are representations of character, exhibited in actions and circumstances of every kind, in which the several performers enact their parts by habit and imitative art, whenever the choric performances are congenial to them in point of diction, tune or other features (whether from natural bent or from habit, or from both these causes combined), then these performers invariably delight in such performances and extol them as excellent; whereas those who find them repugnant to their nature, disposition or habits cannot possibly delight in them or praise them, but call them bad. And when men are right in their natural tastes but wrong in those acquired by habituation, or right in the latter but wrong in the former, then by their expressions of praise they convey the opposite of their real sentiments; for whereas they say of a performance that it is pleasant but bad, and feel ashamed to indulge in such bodily motions before men whose wisdom they respect, or to sing such songs (as though they seriously approved of them), they really take a delight in them in private.

Clin. Very true.

Ath. Does the man who delights in bad postures and tunes suffer any damage thereby, or do those who take pleasure in the opposite gain therefrom any benefit?

Clin. Probably.

Ath. Is it not probable or rather inevitable that the result here will be exactly the same as what takes place when a man who is living amongst the bad habits of wicked men, though he does not really abhor but rather accepts and delights in those habits, yet censures them casually, as though dimly aware of his own turpitude? In such a case it is, to be sure, inevitable that the man thus delighted becomes assimilated to those habits, good or bad, in which he delights, even though he is ashamed to praise them. Yet what blessing could we name, or what curse, greater than that of assimilation which befalls us so inevitably?

Clin. There is none, I believe.

Ath. Now where laws are, or will be in the future, rightly laid down regarding musical education and recreation, do we imagine that poets will be granted such licence that they may teach whatever form of rhythm or tune or words they best like themselves to the children of law-abiding citizens and the young men in the choirs, no matter what the result may be in the way of virtue or depravity?

Clin. That would be unreasonable, most certainly.

Ath. But at present this licence is allowed in practically every State, with the exception of Egypt.

Clin. How, then, does the law stand in Egypt?

Ath. It is marvellous, even in the telling. It appears that long ago they determined on the rule of which we are now speaking, that the youth of a State should practise in their rehearsals postures and tunes that are good: these they prescribed in detail and posted up in the temples, and outside this official list it was, and still is, forbidden to painters and all other producers of postures and representations to introduce any innovation or invention, whether in such productions or in any other branch of music, over and above the traditional forms. And if you look there, you will find that the things depicted or graven there 10,000 years ago (I mean what I say, not loosely but literally 10,000) are no whit better or worse than the productions of to-day, but wrought with the same art.

Clin. A marvellous state of affairs!

Ath. Say rather, worthy in the highest degree of a statesman and a legislator. Still, you would find in Egypt other things that are bad. This, however, is a true and noteworthy fact, that as regards music it has proved possible for the tunes which possess a natural correctness to be enacted by law and permanently consecrated. To effect this would be the task of a god or a godlike man,—even as in Egypt they say that the tunes preserved throughout all this lapse of time are the compositions of Isis. Hence, as I said, if one could by any means succeed in grasping the principle of correctness in tune, one might then with confidence reduce them to legal form and prescription, since the tendency of pleasure and pain to indulge constantly in fresh music has, after all, no very great power to corrupt choric forms that are consecrated, by merely scoffing at them as antiquated. In Egypt, at any rate, it seems to have had no such power of corrupting,—in fact, quite the reverse.

Clin. Such would evidently be the case, judging from what you now say.

Ath. May we confidently describe the correct method in music and play, in connexion with choristry, in some such terms as this: we rejoice whenever we think we are prospering, and, conversely, whenever we rejoice we think we are prospering? Is not that so?

Clin. Yes, that is so.

Ath. Moreover, when in this state of joy we are unable to keep still.

Clin. True.

Ath. Now while our young men are fitted for actually dancing themselves, we elders regard ourselves as suitably employed in looking on at them, and enjoying their sport and merry-making, now that our former nimbleness is leaving us; and it is our yearning regret for this that causes us to propose such contests for those who can best arouse in us through recollection, the dormant emotions of youth.

Clin. Very true.

Ath. Thus we shall not dismiss as entirely groundless the opinion now commonly expressed about merry-makers,—namely, that he who best succeeds in giving us joy and pleasure should be counted the most skilful and be awarded the prize. For, seeing that we give ourselves up on such occasions to recreation, surely the highest honour and the prize of victory, as I said just now, should be awarded to the performer who affords the greatest enjoyment to the greatest number. Is not this the right view, and the right mode of action too, supposing it were carried out?

Clin. Possibly.

Ath. But, my dear sir, we must not decide this matter hastily; rather we must analyse it thoroughly and examine it in some such fashion as this: suppose a man were to organize a competition, without qualifying or limiting it to gymnastic, musical or equestrian sports; and suppose that he should assemble the whole population of the State and, proclaiming that this is purely a pleasure-contest in which anyone who chooses may compete, should offer a prize to the competitor who gives the greatest amusement to the spectators,—without any restrictions as to the methods employed,—and who excels all others just in doing this in the highest possible degree, and is adjudged the most pleasure-giving of the competitors: what do we suppose would be the effect of such a proclamation?

Clin. In what respect do you mean?

Ath. The natural result would be that one man would, like Homer, show up a rhapsody, another a harp-song, one a tragedy and another a comedy; nor should we be surprised if someone were even to fancy that he had the best chance of winning with a puppet-show. So where such as these and thousands of others enter the competition, can we say who will deserve to win the prize?

Clin. An absurd question; for who could possibly pretend to know the answer before he had himself actually heard each of the competitors?

Ath. Very well, then; do you wish me to supply you with the answer to this absurd question?

Clin. By all means.

Ath. If the tiniest children are to be the judges, they will award the prize to the showman of puppets, will they not?

Clin. Certainly they will.

Ath. And older lads to the exhibitor of comedies; while the educated women and the young men, and the mass of the people in general, will award it to the shower of tragedies.

Clin. Most probably.

Ath. And we old men would very likely take most delight in listening to a rhapsode giving a fine recitation of the Iliad or the Odyssey or of a piece from Hesiod, and declare that he is easily the winner. Who then would rightly be the winner of the prize? That is the next question, is it not?

Clin. Yes.

Ath. Evidently we three cannot avoid saying that those who are adjudged the winners by our own contemporaries would win rightly. For in our opinion epic poetry is by far the best to be found nowadays anywhere in any State in the world.

Clin. Of course.

Ath. Thus much I myself am willing to concede to the majority of men,—that the criterion of music should be pleasure; not, however, the pleasure of any chance person; rather I should regard that music which pleases the best men and the highly educated as about the best, and as quite the best if it pleases the one man who excels all others in virtue and education. And we say that the judges of these matters need virtue for the reason that they need to possess not only wisdom in general, but especially courage. For the true judge should not take his verdicts from the dictation of the audience, nor yield weakly to the uproar of the crowd or his own lack of education; nor again, when he knows the truth, should he give his verdict carelessly through cowardice and lack of spirit, thus swearing falsely out of the same mouth with which he invoked Heaven when he first took his seat as judge. For, rightly speaking, the judge sits not as a pupil, but rather as a teacher of the spectators, being ready to oppose those who offer them pleasure in a way that is unseemly or wrong; and that is what the present law of Sicily and Italy actually does: by entrusting the decision to the spectators, who award the prize by show of hands, not only has it corrupted the poets (since they adapt their works to the poor standard of pleasure of the judges, which means that the spectators are the teachers of the poets), but it has corrupted also the pleasures of the audience; for whereas they ought to be improving their standard of pleasure by listening to characters superior to their own, what they now do has just the opposite effect. What, then, is the conclusion to be drawn from this survey? Is it this, do you suppose?

Clin. What?

Ath. This is, I imagine, the third or fourth time that our discourse has described a circle and come back to this same point—namely, that education is the process of drawing and guiding children towards that principle which is pronounced right by the law and confirmed as truly right by the experience of the oldest and the most just. So in order that the soul of the child may not become habituated to having pains and pleasures in contradiction to the law and those who obey the law, but in conformity thereto, being pleased and pained at the same things as the old man,—for this reason we have what we call "chants," which evidently are in reality incantations seriously designed to produce in souls that conformity and harmony of which we speak. But inasmuch as the souls of the young are unable to endure serious study, we term these "plays" and "chants," and use them as such,—just as, when people suffer from bodily ailments and infirmities, those whose office it is try to administer to them nutriment that is wholesome in meats and drinks that are pleasant, but unwholesome nutriment in the opposite, so that they may form the right habit of approving the one kind and detesting the other. Similarly in dealing with the poet, the good legislator will persuade him—or compel him—with his fine and choice language to portray by his rhythms the gestures, and by his harmonies the tunes, of men who are temperate, courageous, and good in all respects, and thereby to compose poems aright.

I.2. ARISTOTLE (384–322 BCE)

Poetics (written ca. 335 BCE), ed. and trans. Stephen Halliwell, Loeb Classical Library 199 (Cambridge, MA: Harvard University Press, 1995), 27–141.

Aristotle takes an entirely different approach to dance from Plato's. While Plato is concerned with dance's political and social usefulness, Aristotle's interest is scientific and analytic: he wants to know what dance is, not what it is for.

The poetry that is the subject of the *Poetics* is by definition mimetic. It is divided into four genres: epic, tragic, comic, and dithyrambic. All of these are mimetic, or imitative of nature, in some manner or form. Mimesis is produced by rhythm, language, and melody. Since dance is part of the performance of dramatic poetry in ancient Greece, it is mimetic by definition, meaning that it includes pantomime.

What is confusing in this definition is that Aristotle states that the three elements—rhythm, language, and melody—may be employed "separately or in combinations," meaning that we cannot be certain as to what pantomime dance looked or sounded like. The most problematic sentence, and the most challenging for translators, is this: "rhythm on its own, without melody, is used by the art of dancers (since they too, through rhythms translated into movements, create mimesis of character, emotions, and actions)."[2] On its surface, this sentence seems to contradict abundant iconographic and written evidence of dancers accompanied by musicians playing melody instruments.[3] Anastasia-Erasmia Peponi proposes a convincing reinterpretation of this passage, focusing on the phrase *dia ton schematizomenon rhythmon* ("through rhythms translated into movements"), which contains the words *schema* and *rhythmos*. Peponi offers a more literal though awkward translation: "articulation-ly rhythmicized," supported by the writing of Aristotle's pupil Aristoxenus, who associates the word *schema* (interpreted as shape) with *soma* (the body), and *rhythmos* (rhythm) with *chronos* (time). *Schema* therefore gives shape to shapeless time. To be perceived or felt, melody must be rhythmicized or articulated by pauses or rests. According to Peponi's interpretation, Aristotle conceives of dance as "an aural property in the course of being turned into a visible one."[4] Music is implicitly present in this interpretation.

The inherent difficulties in this text may explain why it is not widely cited or quoted by later dance theorists who were primarily concerned with social dance, which has nothing to do with mimesis. Only Claude-François Menestrier (Reading 3.2), with his overriding interest in theatrical dance, gives it some detailed attention. More frequently Aristotle's name is grouped with that of other ancient authors, without any specific reference to his writings (Sulzer, Reading 6.3; Compan, Reading 6.5). Certain theorists, however, found wisdom in a wider, curious, and erudite reading of Aristotle's works. Domenico da Piacenza (Reading 2.1) refers to the *Nicomachean Ethics* on the subjects of locomotion and the virtue of moderation; and to the *Physics* on the three types of motion. Menestrier (and later writers) receives the concept of quality versus quantity from Aristotle's *Categories*, a division of his *Organon*. Johann Pasch (Reading 4.2) refers to the *Metaphysics* on the difference between practical and speculative knowledge. Gottfried Taubert (Reading 4.3) refers to the *Physics* on the four types of causation.[5] And Bartholome Ferriol Y Boxeraus (Reading 5.2) quotes from the *Posterior Analytics*.

READING 1.2
Aristotle (trans. Halliwell)

PP. 28–33 (I. 1447A–1447B)

We are to discuss both poetry in general and the capacity of each of its genres; the canons of plot construction needed for poetic excellence; also the number and character of poetry's components, together with the other topics which belong to the same enquiry—beginning, as is natural, from first principles.

Now, epic and tragic poetry, as well as comedy, dithyramb, and most music for aulos and lyre, are all, taken as a whole, kinds of mimesis. But they differ from one another in three respects: namely, by producing mimesis in different media, of different objects, or in different modes. Just as people (some by formal skill, others by a knack) use colours and shapes to render mimetic images of many things, while others again use the voice, so too all the poetic arts mentioned produce mimesis in rhythm, language, and melody, whether separately or in combinations.

That is, melody and rhythm alone are used by music for aulos and lyre, and by any other types with this capacity, for example music for panpipes; rhythm on its own, without melody, is used by the art of dancers (since they too, through rhythms translated into movements, create mimesis of character, emotions, and actions); while the art which uses either plain language or metrical forms (whether combinations of these, or some one class of metres) remains so far unnamed. [...] There are also some arts which use all the stated media—rhythm, melody, metre—as do dithyramb and nomes, tragedy and comedy.[6] They differ in that some employ all together, others use them in certain parts. So these are the distinctions between the arts in the media in which they produce mimesis.

I.3. PLUTARCH (LUCIUS MESTRIUS PLUTARCHUS)
(46–AFTER 119 CE)

Moralia, vol. IX, Loeb Classical Library LCL 425, trans. Edwin L. Minar, Jr., F. H. Sandbach, and W. C. Helmbold (Cambridge, MA: Harvard University Press, 1961), 288–299.

Plutarch's two most important works are the famous *Parallel Lives* of major Greek and Roman figures, and the series of essays collected under the title *Moralia.* Like his fellow classical theorists, he was no dance specialist, and his short statement on dance is no more than a fragment, an incidental bit of erudite postprandial conversation ("Table Talk") at a symposium, apropos of a dance contest just witnessed by the interlocutors. Whereas Plato rationalizes the educational and civic virtues of dance, Plutarch resembles Aristotle in presenting a concise analysis of dance movement and gesture.

The speaker, Ammonius, names and interprets three elements of dance. The first element, *phora*, commonly translated as "phrase," refers to movement itself. The second, *schema*, is translated as "pose," or position.[7] Movements end in poses. The third element, *deixis*, is translated as "pointing"—not literally pointing at someone or something, but rather a way of attaching meaning to the movement, which Ammonius equates with the functions of onomatopoeia and metaphor in poetry. These terms are somewhat vague and need to be understood in the sense in which they were used in Greek dance around the time of the early Roman Empire. Lillian B. Lawler explains that *phora*, defined by Plutarch as *kinesis*, refers to any step or gesture made by the whole body or any part of it. *Schema* is too rich in meanings to be pinned down conclusively, though the connotations of form, shape, or figure (as in speech or geometry) seem to predominate; Lawler says: "It would seem that the *schemata* were really brief, distinctive patterns which were visible in the course of a dance, some of them lasting but a few seconds, others longer." Anastasia-Erasmia Peponi, as we have seen in her interpretation of Aristotle (Reading 1.2), further refines the definition to refer to the articulating pauses or silences that delineate rhythm. *Deixis* refers to the portrayal of a character or thing. Lawler says: "Obviously gesture or *cheironomia* [hand gesticulation] would play a part in such portrayal."[8] Peponi associates *deixis* with *semeion* (a sign or gesture), the root from which we get the words *semiotics* and *semiology.*[9]

Ammonius makes an analogy between the way a dancer moves from one position to another and the way a melody moves from one note to another. Beside alluding to the intimate, primordial connection between dance and music, this analogy is more specifically significant in pointing out that melodies move both by "note" and by "interval," that is, conjunctly (do-re) or by a leap of two or more scale steps (do-mi, etc.); "phrases," therefore, are of varying description. While "pose" and "phrase" seem applicable to all dance, "pointing" applies specifically to pantomime dance, which Ammonius calls *hyporchema*, the combination of poetry and dance to convey meaning.[10]

The analogy to poetry leads to discussion of a saying of the Greek lyric poet Simonides of Ceos (ca. 556–ca. 468 BCE): painting is unspoken poetry and poetry is a speaking painting. Through the voice of Ammonius, Plutarch revises this aphorism by replacing painting with dance: dance is wordless poetry and poetry is a dance of words. Plutarch, in fact, became the principal conduit through which the aphorism, in this form, was received by later dance theorists.[11] The analogic association between dance and painting remained a powerful trope in dance theory of the second half of the eighteenth century, particularly in the writing of Jean-Georges Noverre (see Reading 6.1c).

To Plato's ideological concept of dance theory, Plutarch juxtaposes a complementary theory based on the action and signification of dance kinetics: a theory, that is, of dance practice. Subsequent sources will deal with both these approaches to various extents, only rarely achieving a balanced appreciation of both.

READING 1.3
Plutarch (trans. Minar, Sandbach, and Helmbold)

Table Talk IX
Question 15

PP. 289–291

After this, cakes were brought in, to be the prize for dancing by the boys. My brother Lamprias was appointed, along with Meniscus the trainer, to be judge, as he gave a convincing performance of the pyrrhic dance and had been thought better at shadow-fighting than any of the boys in the wrestling-schools. Many boys now danced with more zest than art: there were two who gained approval, attempting to preserve gracefulness throughout; some of the company demanded that these two should dance phrases alternately.

Thrasybulus inquired the meaning of the word "phrase," and gave Ammonius the opportunity of giving at some length an exposition of the elements of dancing, which he said were three in number: the phrase, the pose, and pointing. "Dancing," he explained, "consists of movements and positions, as melody of its notes and intervals. In the case of dancing the rests are the terminating points of the movements. Now they call the movements 'phrases,' while 'poses' is the name of the representational positions to which the movements lead and in which they end, as when dancers compose their bodies in the attitude of Apollo or Pan or a Bacchant, and then retain that aspect like figures in a picture. The third element, pointing, is something that does not copy the subject-matter, but actually shows it to us. Poetry provides a parallel. Poets employ the proper names of things to indicate or denote them, using the words 'Achilles,' 'Odysseus,' 'earth,' and 'heaven' exactly as they are used by the ordinary man, but employ onomatopoeia and metaphor in their pursuit of imitative representation and vivid suggestion."

P. 293

"Similarly in dancing the pose is imitative of shape and outward appearance. The phrase again is expressive of some emotion or action or potentiality. By pointing they literally indicate objects: the earth, the sky, themselves, or bystanders. If this is done with precision, so to say, and timing, it resembles proper names in poetry when they are uttered with a measure of ornament and smoothness."

P. 295

"In short, one can transfer Simonides' saying from painting to dancing, [rightly calling dance] silent poetry and poetry articulate dance. There seems to be nothing of painting in poetry or of poetry in painting, nor does either art make any use whatsoever of the other, whereas dancing and poetry are fully associated and the one involves the other. Particularly is this so when they combine in that type of composition called *hyporchema*, in which the two arts taken together effect a single work, a representation by means of poses and words."

I.4. LUCIAN OF SAMOSATA (CA. 125 CE–AFTER 180 CE)
"The Dance," *Lucian*, vol. 5, trans. A. M. Harmon, Loeb Classical Library 302 (Cambridge, MA: Harvard University Press, 1936), 209–289.

Peri Orcheseos or *De saltatione* (On Dance), by Lucian of Samosata, is written in dialogue format, like Plato's *Laws*. Lucian's interlocutor, Lycinus, defends dance (Gr. ὄρχησις, orchesis) for the edification of his doubting companion Crato, on the grounds of its utility, pleasure, and beauty; its combination of the intellectual and the physical, and of strength and suppleness; and its salutary moral influence. He also describes its primordial origin (traced back to the movements of heavenly bodies), history, ethnology in various cultures, and complementary relationship with music. Much of Lucian's wealth of anecdotes and lore is passed on by later theorists, especially his remarks on pantomime dancing, which would be widely cited in support of *ballet d'action*

in the eighteenth century. However, although his comments principally address theatrical dance, his ideas were received and repeated as of equal relevance to the theory of social dance. He is the first writer on dance to list
areas of knowledge or competence that should inform a pantomime dancer's
preparation: music, philosophy, rhetoric, history and mythology, painting and
sculpture (¶35); this may be his most influential contribution to dance theory,
reflected in references up to the early nineteenth century (Blasis), if not later.
The dancer should cultivate the art of memory (¶36–37) and be true to nature
(¶65, 76). Lucian mentions Plato's authoritative approval of dance, but instead
of repeating Plato's reasoning, he supplements it with additional theoretical
justifications: dance's utilitarian, aesthetic (i.e., in the general sense of dance's
grace, elegance, and pleasure to behold), and moral benefits, and its historical
as well as mythological precedents.

READING 1.4
Lucian (trans. Harmon)

PP. 218–223

¶6

Lycinus. Then are you willing to leave off your abuse, my friend, and hear me
say something about dancing and about its good points, showing that it brings
not only pleasure but benefit to those who see it; how much culture and instruction it gives; how it imports harmony into the souls of its beholders, exercising
them in what is fair to see, entertaining them with what is good to hear, and
displaying to them joint beauty of soul and body? That it does all this with the
aid of music and rhythm would not be reason to blame, but rather to praise it.

Crato. I have little leisure to hear a madman praise his own ailment, but if
you want to flood me with nonsense, I am ready to submit to it as a friendly
service and lend you my ears, for even without wax I can avoid hearing rubbish.
So now I will hold my peace for you, and you may say all that you wish as if
nobody at all were listening.

¶7

Ly. Good, Crato; that is what I wanted most. You will very soon find out whether
what I am going to say will strike you as nonsense. First of all, you appear to me
to be quite unaware that this practice of dancing is not novel, and did not begin
yesterday or the day before, in the days of our grandfathers, for instance, or in
those of their grandfathers. No, those historians of dancing who are the most
veracious can tell you that Dance came into being contemporaneously with the

primal origin of the universe, making her appearance together with Love—the love that is age-old. In fact, the concord of the heavenly spheres, the interlacing of the errant planets with the fixed stars, their rhythmic agreement and timed harmony, are proofs that Dance was primordial. Little by little she has grown in stature and has obtained from time to time added embellishments, until now she would seem to have reached the very height of perfection and to have become a highly diversified, wholly harmonious, richly musical boon to mankind.

¶8

In the beginning, they say, Rhea, charmed with the art, ordered dances to be performed not only in Phrygia by the Corybantes but in Crete by the Curetes, from whose skill she derived uncommon benefit, since they saved Zeus for her by dancing about him; Zeus, therefore, might well admit that he owes them a thank-offering, since it was through their dancing that he escaped his father's teeth. They danced under arms, clashing their swords upon their shields as they did so and leaping in a frantic, warlike manner. Thereafter, all the doughtiest of the Cretans practised it energetically and became excellent dancers, not only the common sort but the men of princely blood who claimed leadership. For example, Homer calls Meriones a dancer, not desiring to discredit but to distinguish him; and he was so conspicuous and universally known for his dancing that not only the Greeks but the very Trojans, though enemies, were aware of this about him. They saw, I suppose, his lightness and grace in battle, which he got from the dance. The verses go something like this: "Meriones, in a trice that spear of mine would have stopped you/Good as you are at the dance." Nevertheless, it did not stop him, for as he was well versed in dancing, it was easy for him, I suppose, to avoid the javelins they launched at him.

PP. 242–249

¶34

At this point I should like to defend the numerous omissions in my account, that I may not create an impression that I lack sense or learning. I am not unaware that many before our time who have written about the dance have made it the chief matter of their essays to enumerate all its forms and list their names, telling what each is like and by whom it was discovered, thinking to make a display of wide learning thereby. But for my own part, first and foremost, I think that to be zealous about these things is tasteless, pedantic, and as far as I am concerned, out of place, and for that reason I pass them over. Besides, I want you to understand and remember that the topic which I have proposed for myself at present is not to give the history of every form of the dance, and I have not taken it upon myself as the aim of my discussion to enumerate names of dances, except for the few that I mentioned at the outset, in touching upon the more characteristic of them. No, at present anyhow, the chief object of my discussion is to praise the dance as it now exists and to show how much that is pleasurable and profitable it comprises in its embrace, although it did not begin to attain such a height of beauty in days of old, but in the time of Augustus, approximately.

Those early forms were roots, so to speak, or initial stages, of the dance; but the flowering of it and the consummate fruition, which precisely at this moment has been brought to the highest point of perfection—that is what our discussion treats of, omitting the Tongs and the Crane-dance and so forth as no longer having anything to do with the dancing of today. And as to that "Phrygian" form of the dance, the one that accompanied wine and revelry, performed amidst drunkenness, generally by peasants who executed, to the music of flutes played by women, violent and trying gambols still prevalent in the country districts, that too I have not omitted out of ignorance but because those gambols have nothing to do with our present dance. As you know, Plato in the Laws praises certain forms of the dance, but strongly condemns certain others, dividing them with reference to what is pleasurable and profitable and rejecting the more unseemly sorts, but valuing and admiring the rest.

¶35

About the dance itself, let this suffice; for it would be tasteless to prolong my discussion by taking up everything. What qualifications the dancer on his part ought to have, how he should have been trained, what he should have studied, and by what means he should strengthen his work, I shall now set forth for you, to show you that Dance is not one of the facile arts that can be plied without pains, but reaches to the very summit of all culture, not only in music but in rhythm and metre, and especially in your own favourite, philosophy, both physics and ethics. To be sure, Dance accounts philosophy's inordinate interest in dialectics inappropriate to herself. From rhetoric, however, she has not held aloof, but has her part in that too, inasmuch as she is given to depicting character and emotion, of which the orators also are fond. And she has not kept away from painting and sculpture, but manifestly copies above all else the rhythm that is in them, so that neither Phidias nor Apelles seems at all superior to her.

¶36

Before all else, however, it behoves her to enjoy the favour of Mnemosyne and her daughter Polymnia, and she endeavours to remember everything. Like Calchas in Homer, the dancer must know "what is, and what shall be, and was of old," so thoroughly that nothing will escape him, but his memory of it all will be prompt. To be sure, it professes in the main to be a science of imitation and portrayal, of revealing what is in the mind and making intelligible what is obscure. What Thucydides said of Pericles in praising the man would also be the highest possible commendation of a dancer, "to know what is meet and express it"; and by expressing I mean the intelligibility of his postures. [. . .]

PP. 270–281

¶68

Moreover, the other performances that appeal to eye and ear contain, each of them, the display of a single activity; there is either flute or lyre or vocal music or tragedy's mummery or comedy's buffoonery. The dancer, however, has everything at once, and that equipment of his, we may see, is varied and comprehensive—the flute, the pipes, the tapping of feet, the clash of cymbals, the melodious voice of the actor, the concord of the singers.

¶69

Then, too, all the rest are activities of one or the other of the two elements in man, some of them activities of the soul, some of the body; but in dancing both are combined. For there is display of mind in the performance as well as expression of bodily development, and the most important part of it is the wisdom that controls the action, and the fact that nothing is irrational. Indeed, Lesbonax of Mytilene, a man of excellent parts, called dancers "handiwise," and used to go to see them with the expectation of returning from the theatre a better man.[12] Timocrates, too, his teacher, one day, for the sole and only time, came in by chance, saw a dancer ply his trade and said: "What a treat for the eyes my reverence for philosophy has deprived me of!"

¶70

If what Plato says about the soul is true, the three parts of it are excellently set forth by the dancer—the orgillous part when he exhibits a man in a rage, the covetous part when he enacts lovers, and the reasoning part when he bridles and governs each of the different passions; this last, to be sure, is disseminated through every portion of the dance just as touch is disseminated through the other senses. And in planning for beauty and for symmetry in the figures of the dance, what else does he do but confirm the words of Aristotle, who praised beauty and considered it to be one of the three parts of the chief good? Moreover, I have heard a man express an excessively venturesome opinion about the silence of the characters in the dance, to the effect that it was symbolic of a Pythagorean tenet.[13]

¶71

Again, some of the other pursuits promise to give pleasure and others profit, but only the dance has both; and indeed the profit in it is far more beneficial for being associated with pleasure. How much more delightful it is to see than young men boxing, astream with blood, and other young men wrestling in the dust! Why, the dance often presents them in a way that is less risky and at the same time more beautiful and pleasurable. As to the energetic movement of the dance, its twists and turns and leaps and back-flung poses, they are really not only pleasurable to the spectators, but highly healthful for the performers themselves. I should call it the most excellent and best balanced of gymnastic exercises, since besides making the body soft, supple and light, and teaching it to be adroit in shifting, it also contributes no little strength.

¶72

Then why is not dancing a thing of utter harmony, putting a fine edge upon the soul, disciplining the body, delighting the beholders and teaching them much that happened of old, to the accompaniment of flute and cymbals and cadenced song and magic that works its spell through eye and ear alike? If it is felicity of the human voice that you seek, where else can you find it or what can you hear that is more richly vocal or more melodious? If it is the high-pitched music of the flute or of the syrinx, in the dance you may enjoy that also to the full. I forbear to mention that you will become better in character through familiarity with such a spectacle, when you see the assembly detesting misdeeds, weeping over victims of injustice, and in general schooling the characters of the individual spectators.

¶73

But let me tell you in conclusion what is particularly to be commended in our dancers: that they cultivate equally both strength and suppleness of limb seems to me as amazing as if the might of Heracles and the daintiness of Aphrodite were to be manifested in the same person.

¶74

I wish now to depict for you in words what a good dancer should be like in mind and in body. To be sure, I have already mentioned most of his mental qualities. I hold, you know, that he should be retentive of memory, gifted, intelligent, keenly inventive, and above all successful in doing the right thing at the right time; besides, he should be able to judge poetry, to select the best songs and melodies, and to reject worthless compositions.

¶75

What I propose to unveil now is his body, which will conform to the canon of Polyclitus. It must be neither very tall and inordinately lanky, nor short and dwarfish in build, but exactly the right measure, without being either fat, which would be fatal to any illusion, or excessively thin; for that would suggest skeletons and corpses.

¶76

To illustrate, I should like to tell you about the cat-calls of a certain populace that is not slow to mark such points. The people of Antioch, a very talented city which especially honours the dance, keep such an eye upon everything that is done and said that nothing ever escapes a man of them. When a diminutive dancer made his entrance and began to play Hector, they all cried out in a single voice, "Ho there, Astyanax! where is Hector?" On another occasion, when a man who was extremely tall undertook to dance Capaneus and assault the walls of Thebes, "Step over the wall," they said, "you have no need of a ladder!" And in the case of the plump and heavy dancer who tried to make great leaps, they said, "We beg you, spare the stage!" On the other hand, to one who was very thin they called out: "Good health to you," as if he were ill. It is not for the joke's sake that I have mentioned these comments, but to let you see that entire peoples have taken a great interest in the art of dancing, so that they could regulate its good and bad points.

¶77–¶78

In the next place, the dancer must by all means be agile and at once loose-jointed and well-knit, so as to bend like a withe as occasion arises and to be stubbornly firm if that should be requisite. That dancing does not differ widely from the use of the hands which figures in the public games—that it has something in common with the noble sport of Hermes and Pollux and Heracles, you may note by observing each of its mimic portrayals.

¶79

Herodotus says that what is apprehended through the eyes is more trustworthy than hearing; but dancing possesses what appeals to ear and eye alike. Its spell, too, is so potent that if a lover enters the theatre, he is restored to his right mind by seeing all the evil consequences of love; and one who is in the clutch of grief leaves the theatre in brighter mood, as if he had taken some potion that brings forgetfulness and, in the words of the poet, "surcease from sorrow and anger." An indication that each of those who see it follows closely what is going on and understands what is being presented lies in the fact that the spectators often weep when anything sad and pitiful reveals itself. And certainly the Bacchic dance that is especially cultivated in Ionia and in Pontus, although it is a satyr-show, nevertheless has so enthralled the people of those countries that when the appointed time comes round they each and all forget everything else and sit the whole day looking at titans, corybantes, satyrs, and rustics. Indeed, these parts in the dance are performed by the men of the best birth and first rank in every one of their cities, not only without shame but with greater pride in the thing than in family trees and public services and ancestral distinctions.

I.5. JOHANNES DE GROCHEIO (CA. 1300)
"De musica" ([ms. H] London, British Library, codex Harley 281; [ms. D] Darmstadt, Hessische Landesbibliothek, codex 2663).[14]

There is plenty of proof that people danced during the Middle Ages, but the documentary evidence, consisting of iconography, a small repertoire of dance tunes, and anti-dance fulmination, is not highly informative about the dancing itself; for about one thousand years, scarcely anyone seems to have seen fit to intellectualize about it. The corpus of medieval treatises on music theory, on the other hand, produced during the same period, is vast. Thousands of manuscripts were written and handed down in Latin, largely by monastic clerics and scribes concerned almost exclusively with music for the Church. Most if not all of these manuscripts, moreover, were bound together in compendia of several such treatises, and copies of the most important treatises are bound into numerous compendia, each copy, or apograph, containing its own unique textual variations and interpretive marginalia.[15] This robust scribal tradition may come as a revelation to dance historians. Certainly with respect to music theory, the so-called Dark Ages were far from dark.

The "De musica" of Johannes de Grocheio is testimony to the paucity—really a vacuum—of dance theoretical writing in the Middle Ages. Grocheio's treatise is the unique exception: "the single surviving medieval theoretical treatise to deal with the subject of secular music in any detail."[16] He "gave a treatment of vernacular monody unparalleled in any other Latin treatise, and surpassed any other writer before the 16th century in his sense that the musical forms in use could be systematically correlated with the different human groups who cultivated them."[17] The "vernacular monody" he investigated was dance music as practiced by the "human group" he identifies as "the people of Paris."

Monophony is the musical texture characterized by unaccompanied—that is, unharmonized—pure melody or monody, which means "one song." Monophonic melody can be purely instrumental, purely vocal, or vocal with instrumental accompaniment, and it can be performed by one person or many at once, as long as everyone is playing or singing in unison. Singing and dancing at the same time is choric dance. Grocheio shows familiarity with monophonic secular songs by the titles that he cites, but what interests him is not the words so much as the purely musical elements that accompany dance: rhythm and form. The beat of an untexted dance melody "stimulates men's spirits to move gracefully according to the art known as dance, and especially to the measured motion of *ductiae* and choral dances."[18] The concept of a natural human impulse to move in an organized way is derived from, though not attributed to, Plato. Grocheio discusses dance forms according to the various dance types (*rotundellus, ductia, carola, stantipes* [*estampie*]), which in vocal music also correspond to poetic verse-and-refrain patterns.

Boethius, in the first century CE, divided music into a three-part hierarchy.[19] The lowest level is *musica instrumentalis*, music produced by instruments made from inanimate materials. Above that is *musica humana*, music emanating from the soul and body of human beings, that is, vocal music, specifically chant or other music sung to praise God. The highest level is *musica mundana*, the (inaudible to humans) Music of the Spheres. Under the Boethian system, dance, a subcategory of monophonic secular vocal and instrumental music, would be a subject of lowest priority in a strict religious community.

Grocheio proposes his own three-part system, divided not by cosmic orbit but, more simply, by practice: who in "the different human groups" sings what. The lowest level is *musica civilis*, which includes monophony with "vulgar," or vernacular, texts; dance music falls under this rubric by its association with secular songs. Above that is *musica canonica*, or polyphonic music performed by or for clerics, in other words, music learned in style and performed by and for those who can appreciate it. The highest level is *musica ecclesiastica*, monophonic chant sung in church. Though Grocheio was not a churchman, his system conforms to the religious standards of his time. Dance is still in the lowest category, but it is justified by its social context and moral benefits.

The fact remains that if medieval dance tunes had been *only* nonvocal, they would have been even less worthy of scholarly interest than that evinced by Grocheio. Only in the Renaissance would dance be liberated from the constraints of the medieval religious value system and emerge as an artistic activity worthy of serious study and cultivation.

READING 1.5
Grocheio (trans. Russell after the German of Rohloff, and Seay)

H 42R, D 59R COL. A

Let us say, then, that the music used by the people of Paris can be divided into three main parts. One part we name simple or city music, which we call vulgar or people's music. The second is composed or regulated or canonic music, which we call measured music. The third type is that which is made by arranging the other two into something better. It is called ecclesiastic and its purpose is to praise the Creator.

H 43R–V, D 60R COL. B

Let us say, then, that the musical forms or categories contained in the first part, which we called vulgar, are organized so that their mediation will mitigate the inborn ills of mankind, about which we have written in more detail in the sermon to Clement, the *exequiarius*.[20] These [forms] are of two types. They are performed either by human voices or handmade instruments. Of those performed by human voices, there are two types: we speak either of *cantus* or *cantilena*, each of which is divided three ways. We call *cantus* either *gestualis* or *coronatus* or *versiculatis*; and *cantilena* either *rotunda* or *stantipes* or *ductia*.

H 43V–44R, D 60V COL. B–61R COL. A

Therefore the way in which *cantus* is described will now be shown.

Rotunda or *rotundellus* is called by many *cantilena*, because it turns back on itself in circular fashion, and begins and ends in the same way. However, we give the name *rotunda* or *rotundellus* only to those that have no melody that differs from that of the response or refrain. They are sung, like *cantus coronatus*, in a slow rhythm, as in the French "Toute sole passerai le vert boscage."[21] This kind of *cantilena* comes from the west, say, Normandy, and is sung by girls and youths to enhance festivals and great feasts.

The *cantilena* called *stantipes* is that in which the parts and the refrain differ with respect to both their rhymes and melodies, as in the French "A l'entrant d'amors" or "Certes mie ne cuidoie." Their complexity requires the concentration of young men and maids, which distracts them from bad thoughts.

The *ductia* is a light and swift *cantilena* with a rising and falling melody, sung by youths and girls while dancing [*in choreis*], like the French "Chi encor querez amoretes." It draws the hearts of girls and youths away from frivolity and is said to counteract amorous or erotic passion.

H 44V, D 6IV COL. A–B

A good artist generally plays every *cantus* and every *cantilena* and all musical forms on the vielle. But those that are usually played at the feasts and games of the wealthy are generally of three types: the *cantus coronatus*, the *ductia*, and the *stantipes*. Having earlier spoken of the *cantus coronatus*, it is thus now time to speak of the *ductia* and *stantipes*.

The *ductia* is an untexted musical work measured with a fitting percussive beat. I say untexted because, while it may be sung by the human voice and represented in writing with notes, it cannot be written in letters since it has no letters or words. But when I say "with a fitting beat," [I mean that] it measures the movements of the performers and stimulates men's spirits to move gracefully according to the art known as dance, and especially to the measured motion of *ductiae* and choral dances.

The *stantipes* is an untexted musical work with divisions called *puncta* whose concordances are difficult to distinguish. I say "difficult, etc." Precisely due to this difficulty, the mind of the performer as well as of the observer must concentrate, and often the spirit of the wealthy is turned away from depraved thoughts. I also say "divisions called *puncta*" because the percussive beat heard in the *ductia* is lacking, so that only the difference between *punctae* can be distinguished.

NOTES

1. There is a third character, Megillus of Lacedaemon, who does not speak in this passage.—Ed.
2. Anastasia-Erasmia Peponi, "Aristotle's Definition of Dance," *Choreutika: Performing and Theorising Dance in Ancient Greece*, ed. Laura Gianvittorio (Pisa: Fabrizio Serra Editore, 2017), 233–234, offers eight different translations, each unsatisfying in some way, in addition to the one quoted in this reading.
3. Peponi, "Aristotle's Definition of Dance," 218–219.
4. Peponi, "Aristotle's Definition of Dance," 224–233.
5. Taubert (see Reading 4.3), 70, referring to the *Physics* II.3.
6. "Nomes were traditional styles of melody, for string or wind instrument, to which various texts could be set; by Ar.'s time the term covered elaborate compositions closely related to dithyramb."—Halliwell's note.
7. This interpretation is not inconsistent with Aristoxenus's association of *schema* with *soma* (see Reading 1.2).
8. The word comes from the Greek χείρ, hand.

9. Lillian B. Lawler, *The Dance in Ancient Greece* (London: Adam & Charles Black, 1964), 24–27. Peponi, "Aristotle's Definition of Dance," 225.

10. Henry George Liddell and Robert Scott, *An Intermediate Greek-English Lexicon*, 7th ed. (Oxford: Oxford University Press, 1961), 846.

11. See, for example, Menestrier (Reading 3.2), 82; Pasch (Reading 4.2), 168–169; and Taubert (Reading 4.3), 490 and 525.

12. "Handiwise" (Greek χειρισοφους, hand knowledge) referring to the use of gesture, especially manual.—Ed.

13. Pythagorian philosophy valued the eloquence of silence over that of speech.—Ed.

14. Grocheio's "De musica" survives in two manuscripts. For an authoritative introduction, facsimile, annotated transcription of both mss., and German translation, see Ernst Rohloff, *Die Quellenhandschriften zum Musiktraktat des Johannes de Grocheio* (Leipzig: VEB Deutscher Verlag für Musik, 1972), 124–137 (facs. 66–77). See also Johannes de Grocheo, *Concerning Music*, 2nd ed., trans. Albert Seay (Colorado Springs, CO: Colorado College Music Press, 1974), 11–20.

15. The *Répertoire international des sources musicales* (*RISM*), Series B III, *The Theory of Music*, vols. I–VI (Munich-Duisberg: G. Henle Verlag, 1961–2003), is an inventory of Latin manuscripts dating from the Carolingian period to ca. 1500 (i.e., around seven hundred years). There is no official count of these documents. (I am grateful to Suzanne Eggleston Lovejoy for her insight on this subject.) In addition, there are separate *RISM* volumes representing ancient Arabic, Hebrew, Persian, and Greek music theory.

16. Timothy J. McGee, "Medieval Dances: Matching the Repertory with Grocheio's Descriptions," *The Journal of Musicology* VII,/4 (Fall 1989), 498.

17. Christopher Page, "Grocheio [Grocheo], Johannes de," *Grove Music Online*, https://doi.org/10.1093/gmo/9781561592630.article.14359 (2001).

18. Grocheio, [H] 44v, ll. 27–33; [D] 61 v, ll. a31–b8: "Sed *cum recta percussione, eo quod ictus eam mensurant et motum facientis et excitant animum hominis ad ornate movendum secundum artem, quam ballare vocant, et eius motum mensurant in ductiis et choreis.*" Translation based on Rohloff, 137, and Seay, 20.

19. Anicius Manlius Severinus Boethius (ca. 480–ca. 525 CE), "De institutione musica."

20. A monastic official in charge of funerals.—Ed.

21. The meaning of *coronatus* in this context is unclear. "Slow rhythm" follows McGee, "Medieval Dances," 500, for Grocheio's "longo tractu."—Ed.

| 2 |

The Renaissance

From the Renaissance on, periodization in the arts is generally divided into one- or two-century chunks. This is not done merely for convenience's sake. The approach to and experience of the turn of a century seem to evoke a heightened anticipation and awareness of change and transition, and sensitivity to this change is particularly reflected in the arts. As with all the names given to periods, the name "Renaissance" was not adopted spontaneously by the people of the fifteenth and sixteenth centuries as a synonym of "the present." It was adopted centuries later, with the wisdom of historical hindsight, even though it eloquently expresses the spirit of rebirth (after the Middle Ages) that characterizes its time. The Renaissance in dance begins before the mid-fifteenth century and ends around 1600; these dates correspond very closely to the dates of the earliest and latest treatises discussed in this chapter.

The concept and name of dance theory were invented in Renaissance Italy and France. The concept comes first, with four closely related mid-fifteenth-century Italian sources (Readings 2.1, 2.2, and 2.3). These four sources treat dance as an autonomous art for the first time. They are the first to separate dance into the two areas of theory and practice, and the first to name and define the elements of dance theory. Whenever in this book we refer to "traditional dance theory," we are referring to a body of written work based on the principles first enunciated by these early Italian Renaissance theorists. The term "theory" itself was not introduced until around 150 years after them, in the third edition of Thoinot Arbeau's *Orchesographie* (Reading 2.4), on the cusp of the Baroque.

2.1. DOMENICO DA PIACENZA (1390–1470)
De arte saltandi & choreas ducendi/Dela arte di ballare et danzare (between 1452 and 1465), Ms.: Paris, Bibliothèque nationale, fonds Ital. 972.[1]

2.2. ANTONIO CORNAZANO (1430–1484)
Libro dell'arte del danzare (dated 1455 on the basis of its dedicatory poem), Ms.: Rome, Biblioteca Apostolica Vaticana, Capponiano 203.[2]

2.3. GUGLIELMO EBREO OF PESARO (CA. 1420–AFTER 1484)

De pratica seu arte tripudii (1463)/*On the Practice or Art of Dancing*, trans. Barbara Sparti (Oxford: Oxford University Press, 1993).[3]

GIOVANNI AMBROSIO

De pratica seu arte tripudii (1463), Ms.: Paris, Bibliothèque nationale, fonds Ital. 476.[4]

After the near-vacuum in the Middle Ages, one can truly speak of a literal renaissance in dance-theoretical writing in Italy around 1450. No fewer than ten manuscript treatises survive from this time up to the early sixteenth century. At the head of the group are four works: *De arte saltandi & choreas ducendi/Dela arte di ballare et danzare*, by Domenico da Piacenza; the *Libro dell'arte del danzare*, by Antonio Cornazano; and *De pratica seu arte tripudii*, by Guglielmo Ebreo (1463). The fourth source, by Giovanni Ambrosio, is actually a later version, with additions, of Guglielmo's *De pratica*, but written under the name he assumed after converting from Judaism to Christianity in 1465. Domenico is the source upon which the others are based. Both Cornazano and Guglielmo/Ambrosio express deep respect for him as a teacher and master of their art.[5] Derived from these sources are six anonymous treatises, all showing the influence of Domenico and Guglielmo/Ambrosio.[6]

These sources collectively establish a two-part format with introductory sections on the principles of what would become dance theory, followed by longer practical sections on steps and dances. Each theoretical section begins by succinctly listing the elements of dance, followed by explanatory material. Guglielmo/Ambrosio begins the theoretical section with a quasi-historical narrative that demonstrances how music is the progenitor of dance.[7] He also commences his Book II with a recapitulatory explanation and justification of the elements of dance, in dialogue form.[8]

With their clear and consistent delineation of the elements of dance, these Renaissance writers come as close to the basic premises of music theory as dance theory would ever get. Domenico lists nine essential elements, five of which are repeated—in slightly varying sequence, terminology, and orthography—by the subsequent writers: *misura* (measure or mensuration, according to the music); *memoria* (memory); *maniera* (manner); *misura, compartimento,* or *partire di terreno* (orientation within the dance space and with respect to other dancers); and *aire* (air). (Cornazano differentiates between *maniera*, referring to aptitude, skill, and suavity, and *aire*, having to do with grace and radiating joy to observers through one's movements.[9]) To these five elements, Domenico adds *agilitade* (agility); *fantasmate* (hair-trigger reflexes); *porzendose aiuto* (accommodation to one's partner); and *acidentia* (translated tentatively, "a mysterious something whose virtue lies in its happening by chance"—possibly a description of insoucience or improvisation).[10] *Agilitade, fantasmate,* and *acidentia* are found in no other source. *Porzendose aiuto* is found again (as *porgere adiuto*) in an anonymous manuscript in Siena. *Diversita di cose* (variety of steps) is found only in Cornazano. *Movimento corporeo* (the movement of a healthy and well-formed body) is introduced by Guglielmo Ebreo and found again in Giovanni Ambrosio and the Sienese source, the last of which presents two additional elements found nowhere else: *seguitare alla fila* (following in a line) and *passeggiare misurato con arte* (moving rhythmically from place to place).[11]

Barbara Sparti points out the parallelism between the lists of elements in the dance treatises and in contemporary Italian books on the theory of painting and architecture, disciplines that, like dance, were not then included in the liberal arts: "[Leon Battista] Alberti and Guglielmo [Ebreo] were surely concerned to enlarge the scope of the *arte liberali* to embrace art on the one hand and the dance on the other."[12] The Italians revealed dance's connection to the quadrivium in the liberal arts through its use of number and measurement. Domenico in particular links *misura* to the quadrivium through musical meter and through the measurements that determine the dancer's placement in the dance space. A third parameter is measured movement *through* that space (*passeggiare misurato*), introduced in the Sienese manuscript. Thus, even while dance *practice* existed through the Middle Ages, only theory could raise dance to the status of, in Guglielmo/Ambrosio's words, "a liberal art and virtuous science."[13] Guglielmo/Ambrosio, furthermore, may be the first theorist to call dance "an outward manifestation of the movements of the soul"—a definition that will re-echo in dance writing through the centuries.[14]

Domenico cites two of Aristotle's treatises. The *Nicomachean Ethics* (350 BCE) treats of virtue, moderation, health and beauty, motion, and pleasure.[15] He also cites the *Physics* (VII.2), where Aristotle writes about motion and its causes,[16] as the source of the nine natural and three incidental dance movements (*motti*) named in the passage that directly follows the reading here (i.e., paragraph [8] ff.). These *motti* are actually steps used in Renaissance dance: *sempio, doppio, ripresa, continentia,* and so on, and ornaments, and therefore cannot have been the steps Aristotle was referring to. In general, Domenico's prominent citations of Aristotle offer our first example of Renaissance humanism, meaning the revival of interest in, and creative emulation of, the cultural inheritance of classical Antiquity.

READING 2.1
Domenico da Piacenza (trans. Smith, rev. Russell)

fols. 1r–2v in orig.; pp. 10–15 in Smith trans.

ON THE ART OF DANCING

Thanks be to the great and mighty God by whose grace are instilled, and to Him alone are due, the honor and glory of all practices both intellectual and moral. And the worthy and noble knight Sir Domenico of Piacenza, desiring to write about the movement of the body with utmost reverence in his breast, [offers thanks] to the One who always, with His holy humanity, has deigned to assist said practitioner and author in the success of this work. And even though many object to this agile and *pelegrino* motion, made with great subtlety and difficulty, as being immoral and a waste of time, the author responds by citing the second [book] of the *Ethics*, saying to him that all things are corrupted or spoiled if they are practiced or malpracticed excessively.[17] Moderation is protection.[18] And wise Aristotle writes quite a lot about motion in the tenth [book] of *Ethics*. Yet in other parts, even with his perspicacity, he is never able to tease apart the subtleties of the body's various motions from one place to another by means of *mexura, memoria, agilitade*, and *maniera*, [and by] *mexura de terreno* helping to carry or impel the body with *fantaxmate*.[19] [The author] states, arguing well and truthfully, that this art is a refined demonstration of as much intellect and difficulty as can be found. And note that I say, to whoever performs this motion in such a way that it does not lead to extremes, that in practice, this refined art is full of natural goodness and unexpected delight [*azidenzia*].

Note that no creature who has a genetic defect is capable of this refined motion.[20] [The author][21] states that those who are lame, hunch-backed, or cross-eyed can learn all fields [*ministerii aprensin*] but this one, in the practice of which they will be frustrated. Therefore one needs to be rich in the good fortune of possesssing beauty; as the proverb says: "[One] whom God makes beautiful does nothing unsightly." Therefore nature must adapt and sculpt the practitioner of this *métier* from bottom to top. But I say, the virtue of this refined art is not limited to beauty alone.

Note, by God, that in addition to being provided with beauty by nature, you should not ignore your God-given intellect if you wish to learn and analyze the structure of this refined *métier*. [The author] states that its foundation is *mexura*, the same measure by which music determines quickness or slowness. Beside this, one must have a large and deep *memoria* for the safekeeping of all the corporeal motions—natural and incidental—that all performers use according to the form and composition of the dances. And note that beside all these things, one must have an immense, refined *agilitade* and *maniera* of the body. And note that this *agilitade* and *maniera* should in no way be taken to extremes. Rather, maintain the mean in your movement, that is, neither too much nor too little, but with as much suavity as a gondola rowed by two oars through rippling waves when the sea is calm, as its nature permits. The wavelets rise slowly and fall quickly. Always perform the fundamental principle [*causa*], that is, *mexura*, which is slowness answered by quickness.

Also note, and reveal to your intelligence another *mexura* that comprises the grace of *maniera* in the carriage of the whole person and is separate from the musical measure discussed above. This *mexura el tereno* is a light *mexura* requiring that you maintain the mean in your motion from head to foot, which is neither too much nor too little, and that you avoid the extremes, as I have said above.

Beside this, I say to you that one who wishes to gain mastery needs to learn to dance with *fantasmata*. And note that *fantasmata* is a physical swiftness and movement made with the understanding of the *misura* first mentioned above. This necessitates that at each *tempo*, as if you have seen Medusa's head, as the poet says, you move first as if suddenly turned to solid stone, and in the next instant you take wing like a falcon driven by hunger [*paica*]. Do this according to the prescription above, that is, using *mexura, memoria, maniera, mexura de terreno*, and *aire*.

Next, you must perform this action with movement that is good for you and for others, that is, with *concordantia di terreno*. Always place yourself, that is, in relation to your partner, the one with the other, *porzendose aiuto* to the end of the dances, according to where she is.

Now note that wishing to prove that this art form has virtue because of *acidentia*, wise Aristotle says in the tenth [book] that in all things is some natural goodness and in such pleasure there is some good. Therefore, flee extremes and mischief while practicing this virtue. I recall that Aristotle, in the second [book], praised agility as a way of holding to the virtuous mean and fleeing the extremes of the rustic foreigner, the mountebank, and the quack [*ministro*].[22] Using this pleasant [art] to escape sadness and harm is therefore a virtue. Do we not know that *mexura* is a part of prudence and of the liberal arts? Do we not know that *memoria* is the mother of prudence and is acquired through long experience? Do we not know that this virtue is part of harmony and of music? Remember, wise Aristotle stated in the beginning that princes and monarchs are entitled to their pleasures and indulgences. In conclusion, the performance of movement, when done to a good end, is refined, *pelegrino*, and noble when all aspects of it are respected and adopted. And your moderation, Galante, manifests this exceptional virtue.[23]

READING 2.2
Cornazano (trans. Inglehearn and Forsyth)

MEMORIA (MEMORY)

Perfection in dancing is *Misura* (Measure), *Maniera* (Manner), *Aere* (Spirit), *Diversita di cose* (Variety), and *Compartimento di terreno* (Use of space).

You must have Memory so as to remember the steps you are about to per-form when you begin to dance. You must have Measure so that as well as remembering the dance you may move measuredly and in agreement with your musician. While remembering the dance and moving measuredly Manner lies in the grace of the movements you make, balancing [*campeggiando*] and undulating [*ondeggiando*] with the body according to the foot that moves, so that if you move the right foot to make a double you must balance on the left foot which remains firm on the ground, turning the body somewhat towards that side and undulating in the second short step raising yourself smoothly and then very gently lowering yourself on the third which makes the double. Spirit in dancing is that especial grace which you must have above all others and which will make you pleasing to the eyes of those who are watching; and above all everything must be done with a joyousness and gaiety of counte-nance. Variety lies in the art of knowing how to dance the dances differently and not forever repeating the same steps, so that you have *sempi, doppii, riprese, continente, volte tonde,* and *mezo volte* in various guises, and what is done once must not be immediately repeated a second time: but this last point applies more particularly to the man than to the lady. Use of space is understanding how to take into account the appointed area in which you are about to dance, diligently calculating the space and steps which you will perform there, being master in the art of using space, and above all else this must be carried out with a joyousness of spirit.

READING 2.3
Guglielmo Ebreo (trans. Sparti)

BOOK I

Introductory Chapter
Whoever wishes diligently to pursue the science and art of dancing with a joyful spirit and a sincere and well-disposed mind must first understand, with resolute heart, reflecting mind, and with consideration, what dance is in general and its true definition; which is none other than an outward act act which accords with the measured melody of any voice or instrument. This

act is composed of and bound to six rules or principal elements which are the following: Measure, Memory, Partitioning the Ground, Air, Manner, and Body Movement. These six elements must be minutely and perfectly grasped and kept well in mind, for if one of these is lacking in any way, the art [of the dance] would not be truly perfect. Therefore, to gain a fuller knowledge of it, we shall show first what is meant by each one of the aforesaid elements, its nature, and how each is to be used. For they are the foundation, the means, and the true introduction to the complete and perfect art of the dance. We shall, then, first speak of what measure is; therefore, take note.

Chapter on Measure

Measure, in this part, and as it pertains to the art of dancing, means a sweet and measured accord between sound and rhythm, apportioned with judgement and skill, the nature of which can be best be understood through the [playing] of a stringed or other instrument, tuned and tempered in such a way that its weak [beat] equals the strong; that is, the tenor is equal to the contratenor so that one *tempo* measures the same as the next. Therefore, the person who wishes to dance must regulate and gauge himself, and must so perfectly accord his movements with it and in such a way that his steps will be in perfect accord with the aforesaid *tempo* and measure and will be regulated by that measure.

[. . .]

Chapter on Memory

Once measure is understood and firmly imprinted on the mind, as stated above, it is necessary, in second place, to have a perfect memory; that is, constantly trying to recall those elements that need to be remembered, while collecting one's thoughts and paying careful attention to the measured and concordant music so that if it should in any way change, either slowing or quickening, whoever has begun to dance need not be scorned for his lack of forethought or want of memory.

[. . .]

Chapter on Partitioning the Ground

The partitioning of the ground follows in third place. This is supremely necessary to the perfect art of dancing, where there is need of keen discernment and unfaltering judgement in taking account of the place and room for dancing, and carefully apportioning and measuring it in one's mind; . . . Where it [the room] is short or narrow for the aforesaid activity, it is advisable to use one's wits to measure and partition the ground and dancing area in such a way that with every kind of rhythm one is able to dance and keep together with the lady without gaining or losing ground.

[. . .]

Chapter on Air

In the fourth place a further principle and grace called air is necessary to complete and make the aforesaid art more nearly perfect. This is an act of airy presense and a rising movement with one's body which appears, through nimbleness in the dance, as a sweet and most gentle rising up. . . . This action of rising up, then, is called air and should be employed and put into practice at the right place and time with unfailing discretion; and when [done] with moderation, one's steps and gestures will display nimble lightness, so very pleasing and delightful in the dance.

[. . .]

Chapter on Manner

[. . .]

This means that when in the art of the dance someone does a *sempio* or a *doppio* he should accordingly adorn it and shade it in comely manner; that is, he should, for the entire duration of the apportioned time, turn his body completely to the same side as the foot with which he takes the *sempio* or *doppio* step (with the left or right foot, whichever he uses for this action), which is [thus] adorned and shaded by the said rule called manner.

[. . .]

Chapter on Body Movement

In this sixth and last part an essential and final principle called body movement is considered, in which all the perfection of the art and virtue of the dance is clearly demonstrated both in action and appearance. This must itself be perfectly measured, mindful, airy, well-partitioned, and gracious in manner, just as we have shown above. These things are far easier and more amenable for those whose nature and noble make-up have been disposed to it by the heavens above, and whose well-proportioned bodies are pliant, healthy, and agile, with no feebleness of limb; that is, the young, the shapely, the nimble, the lightsome, and those well-endowed with grace, in whom all the aforesaid elements can, through liberal study, be demonstrated with more lasting delight. Thus there is no place for them in persons whose limbs are faulty (like the lame, the hunchbacked, the crippled, and such people), because these particular elements require and have their very essence in exercise and body movement. And there you have what dancing is.

2.4. THOINOT ARBEAU (1520–1595)

Orchesographie, Metode, et Teorie, 3rd ed. (Lengres [sic]: Iehan des Preyz, 1596; facs. ed. Geneva: Editions Minkoff, 1972), fols. 2r–6v.

Like Ebreo/Ambrosio, Thoinot Arbeau is concerned with legitimizing dance within the liberal arts. Arbeau's *Orchesographie*, employing the Platonic dialogue format between the teacher (Arbeau) and a student (Capriol). appeared in three editions: 1588, 1589, and 1596. The title *orchesographie*, essentially synonymous with choreography, emulates Lucian and refers to the practical content of the book, in which dance instructions are written down. The third edition, published posthumously, has an expanded title: *Orchesographie, Metode, et Teorie,* presumably added by the publisher, Iehan des Preyz.[24] There is no internal alteration that explains the late addition of "method" (i.e., practice) and "theory" to the title; one can only venture a hunch that des Preyz perceived dance as an art that, like music, observed this distinction. In any case, we probably owe to Iehan des Preyz the first use of the word "theory," and whatever it implies, with relation to dance.

Arbeau also inaugurates the claim that would become habitual in dance theorists, that no one before him had ever taken the trouble to write about dance, implying that he himself will be the first to preserve knowledge of the dance of his time for posterity. Nevertheless, he offers historical anecdotes from Lucian and other early authors. Like Ebreo/Ambrosio, Arbeau argues that dance is a liberal art, but he offers a double justification: dance not only depends on music; even more important, all learned people agree, it is "a kind of mute rhetoric," thus placing it in both the quadrivium and the trivium (fol. 5rv in orig.; p. 16 in trans.).

Arbeau's title—*Orchesography* in English—is created from the Greek words for dancing and writing.[25] A century after the publication of *Orchesographie*, Antoine Furetière identified Arbeau as the inventor of the first system for recording, or notating, dance instruction through written symbols:

ORCHESOGRAPHY, feminine noun. The art and description of dance, in which the steps are notated beside the notes of music. There is a curious treatise written by Thoinet [sic] Arbeau and printed in Langres in 1588, which he titles *Orchesographie*; he is the first or perhaps the only [person] to have notated and figured the dance steps of his time, in the same way that songs and tunes are notated.[26]

Notation is the interface between theory and practice, combining elements of both. It not only records dance practice; it also codifies and organizes dance movement visually—thus serving as a repository of dance cognition and a quasi-scientific extension of theory. Therefore, in this study the ways in which theory and choreographic systems impinge upon each other must be taken into account.

Claudia Jeschke and Ann Hutchinson Guest, authors of the two major histories of dance notation, recognize five historical notation systems: word abbreviations or letter codes; track drawings; stick-figure; music-note; and abstract symbol.[27] They classify Arbeau's choreographic notation in the words and word-abbreviations category, but this is an oversimplification. Arbeau actually employs two systems. In one, steps are labeled adjacent to the music notated vertically down the left side of the page, and there are woodcut illustrations of dancers in various positions. In the other system, letter codes are used in two ways: as a mnemonic device to memorize the sequence of steps in a *basse-dance* (fols. 38r and 40r in orig.; pp. 76 and 79 in trans.); and to trace, from above, the changing positions of dancers in the course of two dances, the "la haye" bransle (fol. 91r in orig.; p. 171 in trans.) and "Les Bouffons" (fol. 98v–101r in orig.; pp. 185–189 in trans.).[28]

READING 2.4
Arbeau (trans. Evans)

fol. 4v–5v in orig.; pp. 15–17 in trans.

ARBEAU

As regards ancient dances all I can tell you is that the passage of time, the indolence of man or the difficulty of describing them has robbed us of any knowledge thereof. Besides, there is no need to trouble yourself about them, as such manner of dancing is out of date now. Why, even the dances seen in our fathers' time were unlike those of today and it will always be so because men are such lovers of novelty. It is true that we can compare the Emmeleia to our pavans and basse dances, the Kordax to galliards, tordions, lavoltas, gavottes, branles of Champagne and Burgundy, gay branles and mixed branles, the Sikinis to double or single branles, and the Pyrrhic to the dance we call buffens or mattachins.

CAPRIOL

I foresee then that posterity will remain ignorant of all these new dances you have named for the same reason that we have been deprived of the knowledge of those of our ancestors.

ARBEAU

One must assume so.

CAPRIOL

Do not allow this to happen, Monsieur Arbeau, as it is within your power to prevent it. Set these things down in writing to enable me to learn this art, and in so doing you will seem reunited to the companions of your youth and take both mental and bodily exercise, for it will be difficult for you to refrain from using your limbs in order to demonstrate the correct movements. In truth, your method of writing is such that a pupil, by following your theory and precepts, even in your absence, could teach himself in the seclusion of his own chamber. And to begin with, I would ask you to tell me in what esteem dancing is held by the majority of honourable men.

ARBEAU

Dancing, or saltation, is both a pleasant and a profitable art which confers and preserves health; proper to youth, agreeable to the old and suitable to all provided fitness of time and place are observed and it is not abused. I mention time and place because it would bring contempt upon one who became over zealous like the tavern haunters. You know what Ecclesiasticus said.

Cum muliere saltatrice non sis assiduus.[29]

The children of the Roman senators went to learn dancing upon leaving school. Homer bears witness that dancing is an integral part and adjunct to banquets, so much so that none could boast he had given a fine feast unless dancing accompanied it, which, if masquerades are also included, becomes as a sound body joined to a fair intellect. When tragedies, comedies and pastorals were enacted in the ancient theatre, dances and gestures were not forgotten and the part of the theatre reserved for them was called the *orchestra*, which in our French tongue we may call the *dançoir*.

CAPRIOL

Since dancing is an art, it must therefore belong to one of the seven liberal arts.

ARBEAU

As I have already told you, it depends upon music and its modulations. Without this rhythmic quality dancing would be dull and confused inasmuch as the movements of the limbs must follow the rhythm of the music, for the foot must not tell of one thing and the music of another. But, most of the authorities hold that dancing is a kind of mute rhetoric by which the orator, without uttering a word, can make himself understood by his movements and persuade the spectators that he is gallant and worthy to be acclaimed, admired and loved. Are you not of the opinion that this is the dancer's own language, expressed by his feet and in a convincing manner? Does he not plead tacitly with his mistress, who marks the seemliness and grace of his dancing, "Love me. Desire me"? And when miming is added, she has the power to stir his emotions, now to anger, now to pity and commiseration, now to hate, now to love. Even as we read of the daughter of Herodias, who obtained her wish from Herod Antipas by dancing before him at the magnificent banquet he offered to the princes of his realm on his birthday. So it was also with Roscius, who proved to Cicero that, by his employment of gesture and dumb show he could move the spectators, in the judgment of the arbiters, as much or more than Cicero had been able to by his eloquent orations.

2.5. FABRITIO CAROSO (CA. 1530–1605 OR LATER)

Nobiltà di Dame . . . Nuouamente dal proprio Auttore corretto, ampliato di nuoui Balli, di belle Regole, & alla perfetta Theorica ridotto (Venice: il Muschio, 1600); trans. and ed. Julia Sutton, *Courtly Dance of the Renaissance: A New Translation and Edition of the "Nobiltà di Dame" (1600)* (New York: Dover, 1995).

Fabritio Caroso's *Nobiltà di Dame* is presented here not as a reading per se, but as a rare example—perhaps the first—of dance theory iconography.

Caroso published his *Nobiltà di Dame* just a few years after Arbeau's third edition. Its dance repertoire places it, like Arbeau, squarely still in the late Renaissance. The extended subtitle reads, in part: "Newly corrected by its author, with additional new dances, and fine rules, now brought to theoretical perfection."[30] Whether Caroso's reference to "Theorica" was influenced by contact with Arbeau's work is impossible to determine.

Caroso never really clarifies what he means by "theory." The little he wants to say on the subject is encapsulated in the iconography of his title page (see Fig. 2.1). The linkage between perfection and theory harks back to Antonio Cornazano, who begins his treatise by stating that the elements of dance constitute its perfection ("el perfecto dançare"). Julia Sutton, in her translator's introduction to Caroso, explains that his "perfetta Theorica" refers specifically to symmetry, a "fundamental law" of dance practice that Caroso expounds "at length and repetitively." However, the term she translates as "symmetry" is either "Regola Terminata," "Passeggio Terminato," or "Tempo Terminato" in Caroso's original Italian, not *simmetria*, and in context these terms are applied principally to practice—the left-right alternation of feet and the direction of movement at a point where movement momentarily stops—more than to theory.[31]

Figure 2.1. Fabritio Caroso, *Nobiltà di Dame*, title page (Universität Salzburg, Derra de Moroda Archives, DdM 5000).

On the title page are two framed images in the opposite lower corners. That on the left shows a bear licking a small object on the ground, beneath an inscription: "Dall' imperfetto al perfetto"—from the imperfect to the perfect (see Fig. 2.2a). The facing image shows an hourglass and compass, labeled "Tempo e Misura" (see Fig. 2.2b). Caroso provides the key to the riddling icon of the

Figure 2.2a. Caroso, *Nobiltà di Dame*, title page, detail: "Dall' imperfetto al perfetto."

Figure 2.2b. Caroso, *Nobiltà di Dame*, title page, detail: "Tempo e Misura."

bear in his preface: just as the mother bear licks and dries her newborn cub to turn "what was imperfect and monstrous into a perfect [creature]," so too he has corrected the first work, *Il Ballerino*, according to the "rule of termination" and true theory to produce *Nobiltà di Dame*.[32] As emblematized in the two framed images, time and measure are the theoretical principles that Caroso, the theorizing "mother bear," has perfected.

Caroso's treatment of dance theory exemplifies what was referred to in this book's introduction as "flaunting" the term in the title. It is superficial and ornamental compared with the work of the earlier Italians in this chapter, who investigated the field more profoundly, identified many more basic elements, and had much more to say about them. Nevertheless, it stands as a first attempt to produce what seems to have proved an elusive goal in dance history: a visualization of dance theory. Dance notation, we should remember, attempts to visualize dance *practice*, not its basic principles. Beginning in the

Middle Ages, depictions of the hammers of Pythagoras, the *species* or divisions of the monochord, and the Guidonian hand served as pictorial dissertations on the theory of music[33]; in the Renaissance, Leonardo da Vinci's Vitruvian man and Albrecht Dürer's *Unterweisung der Messung* (*Instruction on measurement*) perform the same function with regard to the theory of draftsmanship and painting.[34] It is worth interrogating why, in the course of this book, we will find dance theory so nonconducive to visualization.

NOTES

1. A. William Smith, trans. and ed., *Fifteenth-Century Dance and Music*, Dance and Music Series 4 (Stuyvesant, NY: Pendragon Press, 1995), vol. I, 8–67.

2. Introduction ("Memoria") fols. 3v–4v. Reprint: "Il 'libro dell'arte del danzare' di Antonio Cornazano," ed. C. Mazzi, *La Bibliofilia* XVII/1 (April 1915), 1–30; trans. Madeleine Inglehearn and Peggy Forsyth, *The Book on The Art of Dancing* (London: Dance Books, 1981), 18–19.

3. On theory: 86–99 (fols. 1v–9v).

4. Smith, *Fifteenth-Century Dance and Music*, vol. I, 122–192; theory: 123–134. The additions also appear in Sparti, *De pratica seu arte tripudii*, 229–247.

5. Patrizia Castelli, "Il moto aristotelico e la 'licita scientia.' Guglielmo Ebreo da Pesaro e la speculazione sulla danza nel XV secolo," in Patrizia Castelli, Maurizio Minguardi, and Maurizio Padovan, *Mesura et arte del danzare: Guglielmo Ebreo da Pesaro e la danza nelle corti italiane del XV secolo* (Pesaro: Commune di Pesaro, 1987), 38–39.

6. Smith, *Fifteenth-Century Dance and Music*, vol. I, 193–206. "Guglielmo/Ambrosio" refers to text found in both sources.

7. Sparti, *De pratica seu arte tripudii*, 86–91; see Smith, *Fifteenth-Century Dance and Music*, vol. I, 123–128. Domenico says musical *misura* is the foundation of dance; Smith, *Fifteenth-Century Dance and Music*, vol. I, 13.

8. Sparti, *De pratica seu arte tripudii*, 112–123; Smith, *Fifteenth-Century Dance and Music*, vol. I, 142–148.

9. Cornazano, "Libro dell'arte del danzare," 9.

10. Smith, *Fifteenth-Century Dance and Music*, vol. I, 12–13. Domenico's definition of *misura de terreno* is richer than the other writers' and linked to *maniera* through the dancer's equilibrium.

11. Siena, Biblioteca comunale L.V. 29. Modern (partial) ed.: Smith, *Fifteenth-Century Dance and Music*, vol. I, 200. Domenico also stresses the necessity of physical beauty, free of defects, for refined motion; Smith, *Fifteenth-Century Dance and Music*, vol. I, 10–11. Smith offers a concordance of theoretical terms in all these sources in *Fifteenth-Century Dance and Music*, vol. II, 306–308.

12. Sparti, *De pratica seu arte tripudii,* 9–12. Michael Baxandall, *Painting and Experience in Fifteenth-Century Italy,* 2nd ed. (Oxford: Oxford University Press, 1988) presents an Italian Quattrocento lexicon of the "basic conceptual equipment" (150) that formed the theoretical bedrock of representational painting: color, design, relief, pespective, variety, and so on.

13. Sparti, *De pratica seu arte tripudii,* 90–91: "arte liberale & virtuosa scienza," also 114–115; Smith, *Fifteenth-Century Dance and Music,* vol. I, 128, 145.

14. Sparti, *De pratica seu arte tripudii,* 88–89: "una actione demonstrativa di fuori di movimenti spiritali"; Smith, *Fifteenth-Century Dance and Music,* vol. I, 126.

15. Aristotle, *Nicomachean Ethics,* trans. H. Rackham, rev. ed. Loeb Classical Library 73 (Cambridge, MA: Harvard University Press, 1934), II.2, 74–79, and II.6, 88–97 (on moderation), and X.4, 590–599 (on locomotion).

16. Aristotle, *Physics,* vol. II, trans. Philip H. Wicksteed and Francis M. Cornford, Loeb Classical Library 255 (Cambridge, MA: Harvard University Press, 1934), 216–227 (on three types of motion). Castelli, "Il moto aristotelico," 36, traces Domenico's passage to the *Physics.* Aristotle names three types of motion (local, qualitative, and quantitive) and what causes them. If motion is self-caused, it is natural (e.g., falling water); if caused by something else, it is unnatural (e.g., by pulling, pushing, carrying, twirling).

17. Smith translates *pelegrino* as "elegant." Absent a better alternative, I leave it untranslated, though it possibly connotes a kind of insouciant or wayward wandering.—Ed.

18. Aristotle, *Nicomachean Ethics,* Book II, 2 and 6.—Ed.

19. Aristotle, *Nicomachean Ethics,* Book X, 4. Aristotle states that movement (locomotion, walking) is incomplete because it always involves a whence and a whither. Since pleasure is something whole or complete, movement cannot be a pleasure in itself. However, every activity moves toward and is completed by a pleasure.—Ed.

20. "Note that": There is a blank space following these words ("nota ti"). Smith suggests that the name or title of the reader was meant to be inserted here. The same person would be addressed in the following paragraphs that begin with the same words. Domenico's description of *acidentia* is terse and cryptic: "questo misterio e virtude per acidentia."—Ed.

21. Smith suggests that from this point on, Domenico refers to himself in the third person.—Ed.

22. Domenico is referring to the tenth and second books of Aristotle's *Nicomachean Ethics.* Smith translates Dominico's "in lo 2ª lauda la utropeia"

as: "in the second laude ['verses of praise'] of the *Utopia*." In fact, "utropeia" is *eutropeia* (agility or versatility).—Ed.

23. According to Smith (10), "galante" is a form of polite address, that is, "Gentle Reader."—Ed.

24. Arbeau, *Orchesography* (1589), trans. Mary Stewart Evans (New York: Dover, 1967), 11–18. "Thoinot Arbeau" is an anagram of his true name, Jehan Tabourot. His decision to adopt a pseudonym, albeit thinly disguised, may be related to the fact that he held a church position, as canon of the cathedral of Langres.

25. Orchesography and choreography have parallel etymologies: both are derived from Greek roots meaning dance. They are synonymous in that they both refer to the writing down of dance notation. However, choreography—which has acquired the more widespread usage—has a second meaning, referring to the composition of dances. In this book, it should be assumed that choreography refers to notation, unless otherwise indicated.

26. Antoine Furetière, *Dictionaire universel*, 1690, vol. II, n.p.: "ORCHESOGRAPHIE, subst. fem. Art & description de la danse, dont les pas sont notés avec des notes de Musique. Il y a un Traité curieux fait par Thoinet Arbeau imprimé à Langres en 1588, qu'il a intitulé *Orchesographie*; C'est le premier, ou peut estre le seul qui a noté & figuré les pas de la danse de son temps, de la même maniere qu'on notte le chant & les aires."

27. Claudia Jeschke, *Tanzschriften: Ihre Geschichte und Methode* (Bad Reichenhall: Comes Verlag, 1983); Ann Hutchinson Guest, *Choreo-Graphics: A Comparison of Dance Notation Systems from the Fifteenth Century to the Present* (New York: Gordon and Breach, 1989). A sixth method of dance description, dominant in the nineteenth century, was purely verbal and therefore not a notation system *per se*.

28. Letter coding is used almost a hundred years later by André Lorin, "Livre De Contredance presenté Au Roy" (ms., Paris: F-Pn Mss. Fr. 1697 [ca. 1685]), and later still by Jean-Étienne Despréaux (chap. 7.1).

29. *The Oxford Annotated Apocrypha*, Revised Standard Version, ed. Bruce M. Metzger (New York: Oxford University Press, 1965), 139 (Sirach 9.4: "Do not associate with a dancing [sic] woman.") The original text warns against a *singing* woman.—Ed.

30. "Nuouamente dal proprio Auttore corretto, ampliato di nuoui Balli, de belle Regole, & alla perfetta Theorica ridotto" (trans. Sutton, 70). "Newly corrected" refers to Caroso's *Il Ballarino* (Venice: Francesco Ziletti, 1581), of which he considers *Nobiltà di Dame* the "perfected" second edition.

31. Caroso, *Courtly Dance*, 27 and 339; "Terminata/o": 87–88 (orig. 2), 156 (orig. 98), and 158 (orig. 103–104).

32. Caroso, *Courtly Dance*, title page (70), and 87–88 (orig. 2); the emblem and explanation of the mother bear is based on Pliny the Elder's *Natural History* (77 CE), bk. VIII, chap. 36.

33. See Joseph Smits van Waesberghe, *Musikerziehung*, Musikgeschichte in Bildern III/3 (Leipzig: VEB Deutscher Verlag für Musik, 1969).

34. Leonardo: Venice, Galleria dell'Academia (ca. 1490); Dürer (Nuremberg, 1525).

| 3 |

The Seventeenth Century

Consulting the Appendix: Table of Dance Periodization, we find that up to ca. 1600, the names of the periods have been consistent in historical discourse concerning the arts and Western culture in general. The same consistency obtains from the nineteenth century to the present. Because of the confusing overlapping of terminologies between 1600 and 1800, however, I find it necessary to propose a system of three separate categories over the course of four overlapping time spans. For dance *practice*, I have coined the title "Long Baroque" for the period from 1600 to the 1780s (Chapters 3–5 and most of Chapter 6), followed by the pre-Romantic period in the late eighteenth century (Chapter 6). For dance *theory*, there is the Baroque period in the seventeenth century (Chapter 3), followed by the Enlightenment in the eighteenth century (Chapters 4–6), followed by the pre-Romantic to Romantic periods (Chapters 6–7). For music, the standard periodization is Baroque (seventeenth to mid-eighteenth century), Classical (eighteenth century), and Romantic (nineteenth century). For both dance and music, the most recent two periods are modern or modernist in the twentieth century (Chapter 8), and postmodern or contemporary in the late twentieth to twenty-first century (Chapter 9).

The Baroque period in music and dance offers a fertile example of the problems of periodization in the arts. By general consensus, the musical Baroque began around 1600 with the music of Claudio Monteverdi and his contemporaries, and it lasted until the death of Johann Sebastian Bach in 1750. However, even as Bach and George Frederick Handel (d. 1759) were composing into the mid-eighteenth century, the transitional *galant* and Early Classic styles had already appeared by the 1720s. In fact, the adjective "Baroque" was first applied by Classic-period writers to the previous era, and it was intentionally pejorative. Jean-Jacques Rousseau in 1768 signified the advent of new aesthetic standards by rejecting the obsolete (Baroque) style, which he described as confused, dissonant, difficult, unnatural, and strained—like the misshapen "baroque" pearls it was named after.[1]

There were two major influences on the progress of dance in the seventeenth century: (1) the establishment of the French *académies* of various arts enhanced the status and prestige of dance as an art; and (2) the doctrine of the affections was a vital factor in the evolution of *ballet d'action*.

First, the creation of the Académie royale de danse by Louis XIV in 1661 contributed to the professionalization of the dancing master, the intellectualization of dance, and the promotion of dance from a *métier* to a liberal art.[2] Preceded by the Académie royale de peinture et de sculpture in 1648, and followed by the Académie royale de musique in 1669, dance's inclusion in this company raised it to equality with the other arts. According to the *Lettres patentes* of the Académie, its functions were "to perfect [dance], correct its abuses and defects"; provide professional instruction to dancing masters or those who wished to become dancing masters, and show them old dances as well as new ones invented by the academicians; elect new dancing masters to the *Académie*; and approve all new dances. Academicians and their offspring are permitted to work anywhere in France. The King has the right to call on their services at any time.[3]

The status of dance was of central importance to Louis XIV because he was a dancer himself, and he made dance central to the magnificent entertainments at Versailles through which he consolidated and glorified his reign. His climactic appearance dancing the role of Apollo in the "Ballet de la nuit" (1653) was a transfigurational coup of both stagecraft and statecraft.

Second, from Plato on, dance theorists have talked about how dance expresses the movements of the soul. The French philosopher René Descartes, in *De passionibus animae* (*Passions of the Soul*, 1649), describes many passions, but designates six of them as simple and primitive passions: admiration, love, hatred, desire, joy, and sorrow; and he reasons that they arise physiologically, in the blood and "animal spirits," in response to sensual stimulae.[4] It is easy to understand how this theory of the passions, or emotions, or *Affekte*, as the Germans called them, could be applied to the impressions stimulated by artistic works as well as other phenomena. This in fact is exactly what the music theorist Johann Mattheson (1681–1764) does with regard to musical compositions, in his treatise *Der vollkommene Capellmeister* (*The Complete Music Master*, 1739).[5]

Mattheson bases his explanation of the *Affektenlehre*, or doctrine of the affections, directly on Descarte's theory of the passions.[6] His essential point, with special significance for dance, is that music's expressive power is such that it need not be vocal (set to words) in order to move the passions; instrumental music can do it, too. This idea marks an important first step in the rise of instrumental music over vocal music as an expressive medium; the trend culminates in the Viennese high-Classic symphony, which was perceived as all the more directly and more profoundly moving the soul when unencumbered by words.

Dance music is a species of instrumental music. To exemplify how dance music expresses affects, Mattheson lists all the Baroque social dances—minuet, courante, gavotte, bourrée, gigue, and so forth—each with its typical affect and the corresponding stylistic characteristics of each one.[7] Knowing the affect helps the composer write appropriate music, and it helps the dancers comport themselves in the appropriate spirit. Of course, with ballet and *ballet-pantomime*, the impact of *Affektenlehre* is dramatically multiplied: as the dancers move according to the music's affect, the audience in turn is moved by the passions they see embodied. An emotion is embodied, a story is told, without words. The doctrine of the affections thus becomes increasingly important as the era of *ballet d'action* approaches.

3.1. FRANÇOIS DE LAUZE (B. 1585–1590)
Apologie de la danse by F. De Lauze (1623; facs. ed. Geneva: Minkoff, 1977); trans. Joan Wildeblood (London: Frederick Muller, 1952).

François De Lauze's *Apologie de la danse*, published during the reign of Louis XIII, is a textbook example of dance theory's short memory.[8] De Lauze seems to have known Arbeau personally, though he evinces little familiarity with the *Orchesographie* or any other post-Antiquity work on dance.[9] For example, he laments that, at a time when dance has attained its highest state of perfection, "not one of those who make a profession of it has left to memory the means by which it should be practiced" (23 in orig.; 77–79 in trans.). De Lauze's book is in two principal parts: the first is the "Apologie" proper, which is theoretical; and the second is "Méthode," which is practical. The "Méthode" has a reputation of inscrutability; regardless, the "Apologie" is eminently clear and represents a worthy contribution to dance-theoretical thought.[10]

Acknowledging no predecessor, De Lauze's dance theory is not based on any historical model; nor does any later dance theorist build on his ideas. Philosophy, he says, consists of knowledge in *les arts liberaux & mecaniques* (17 in orig.; 69 in trans.), an early formulation, perhaps, of the extended notion of the "liberal arts and sciences." There are two paths to human perfection: philosophy, acquired through the intellect; and dance, acquired through a well-formed body. He bases his theory on the Stoic philosophy of Seneca (4 BCE?–65 CE), who says that since nature has given us our existence ("l'estre"), we owe it to her to live well ("bien estre").[11] Dance is the only exercise that can eradicate bad behavior while teaching comportment and refinement ("le bel estre"), leading to dance's highest and inseparable goal: "bien-seance" or living wisely and sociably (7 in orig., 53 in trans.; and 17 in orig., 67–69 in trans.).

Barbara Ravelhofer writes of De Lauze: "Throughout the book, de Lauze tries to turn dance into text."[12] Indeed, De Lauze hints that dance can be self-taught through reading. Much about dancing, he says, can be learned by verbal description alone: ". . . I make bold to maintain that whoever has the imagination full of one science or another can make himself understood either through speech or in writing, if not to all, at least to those of his profession." "Figures," furthermore (presumably choreographic), are not needed to teach dancing from a book, and De Lauze includes none (25 in orig.; 83 in trans.).[13] These opinions on the efficacy of written knowledge will find an echo in later works that privilege verbal description over notation and substitute the word "grammar" for "theory." Nevertheless, De Lauze adds that to attain "a certain air, or a bearing sometimes sedate and sometimes negligent, which the pen cannot teach" that "enobles and animates it," it is preferable to model oneself after a good master (24 in orig.; 79–80 in trans.), because "practice and theory should be two inseparable considerations" (26 in orig.; 85). This last statement may be the earliest instance in dance literature in which theory and practice are explicitly paired as the complementary components of a dance education.

READING 3.1
De Lauze (trans. Wildeblood, rev. Russell)

PP. 16–17 IN ORIG.; 67–69 IN TRANS.

I appeal to the judgment of those who are not preoccupied with seeking favors, who would admit, I feel assured, that not only has dance nothing blameworthy about it, but on the contrary, sociability [bien-seance] is an essential part of it; [and] that, if the ancients, having had but the shadow and shape of the perfection that we possess today, honoured it and put it to use, it now appears the more noble, the less it is appreciated [recherchée].

Seneca says that, since nature has given us our being [l'estre], we are obliged to study the virtue of well-being [bien estre], and I dare, without blushing, to elaborate thereto that only the exercise of dance is able, not only to eradicate the bad actions that a negligent upbringing has ingrained, but also to bestow a bearing and a grace which we call conduct, and which I can properly call refinement [*le bel estre*], a thing absolutely necessary to whoever wishes to render agreeable his address and entry into society.

In the order of things there are to be found two means (philosophy and dance) by which a man can raise himself to perfection. Here is their entire difference: the former can be communicated to all those who possess reason, without regard to the condition of the body, which is the principal concern of the latter; to put it plainly, everyone, even the most uncivilized cannibal, can possess what the philosophers offer, and can acquire knowledge with his mind and hands of all the liberal and mechanical arts, provided he applies both labour and tedium; but dance has this particularity, that whoever has an ill-formed body is incapable of acquiring the graces that accompany it. One must have the proper constitution to achieve so worthy a state.

PP. 23–24 IN ORIG.; 77–81 IN TRANS.

. . . Why is it that so many sciences that I would call not only useless but harmful have been popular everywhere, while this one, that attracts the graces to itself, has been in such disrepute that not one of those who make it their profession has recorded the means by which it must be known and practised? Certainly, if one takes into consideration the negligence of past centuries, one will find their failure somehow excusable, but in our century, in which dance can boast its highest degree of perfection, is it not shameful that we should wish to bury the glory it deserves for having come so far, and to deprive posterity of a benefit that gives us so great an advantage over the ancients? For since all things, by dint of chance and historical cycles, almost inevitably return to their beginning, who can doubt that this exercise, changing with the times, will soon return to the abyss from which we have rescued it, unless it finds some charitable pen to sustain it when *ennui* sets in?

But how, someone will ask me, is one to express in writing that which the intelligence wants to see being done? As if things more difficult to understand had never been written! A philosopher told me one day that just as [spoken (*paroles*)] words stand for ideas of our soul, writings are also the images of words. Things engender words in order to be communicated to those present, and from words come writings. But for the sake of those who are not present or who will come hereafter, he [the philosopher] taught me what words cannot express, by examples and such palpable reasoning that a man with common sense could have no doubt that when his intellect has fully understood the knowledge of the things that come to him by way of the senses, he can fortunately clarify it by means of either of the two instruments [i.e., the spoken or written word] of which I have just spoken. This has so strengthened my opinion in that which I had already gained through experience, that I make bold to maintain that whoever has the imagination full of one science or another can make himself understood either through speech or in writing, if not to all, at least to those of his profession. I admit that dance has something particular that ennobles and animates it, such as a certain air, or a bearing sometimes sedate and sometimes negligent, which the pen cannot teach, but [to say] that beyond the steps one is unable further to teach the more necessary actions, which give an easy progress towards this perfection, and that it requires seeing it demonstrated by a good master—these are difficulties which I shall show in this treatise to be imaginary, from which not only many who profess to teach, but scholars themselves, may derive great comfort.

PP. 25–26 IN ORIG.; 83–85 IN TRANS.

The Method for Gentlemen

Those who believe that to teach dancing properly by the book necessitates some figures, in order to describe more simply the movements that should be observed in dancing, are more or less in agreement with that orator of old who, having to harangue before the full senate regarding an atrocious deed, committed the clumsy fault of setting up a picture before the eyes of the judges, trusting the dumb brushstrokes of a lifeless painting rather than the power of living eloquence. To this worthy orator's partisans (who will have some plan to oppose the ruin of this exercise) I leave the practise of such inventions; for myself, it suffices that my pen will make them seem unnecessary to my chosen subject, of which it is now time to speak. But because there is a difference between the steps and actions of a gentleman and those that a lady must make, and instructing both together would entail would some confusion, it has seemed good to me to begin with the gentleman, whom I would readily advise not to wait until too advanced an age. For, being then less receptive or able, he would have more difficulty in acquiring the perfection that he would find easier at a more favourable time; nevertheless, he may gain this satisfaction through determined effort—which a child, lacking wisdom, cannot have—always providing he has a certain grace of movement which is impossible to describe in writing (as I recollect having said elsewhere). Let him take care not to put himself in the hands of an ignoramus, nor, if possible, into the hands of one who, apart from the excellence of his method, is no longer capable of executing what is beyond speech and writing. For it is impossible to appraise a beautiful action of which one is ignorant, and even less to correct it fully if it is botched, and the other person, however gifted, will torment himself in vain to understand a thing that is obtained more by practice than by fakery [*artifice*]. If I should pattern my actions after those of my master, and he knows not how to perform that which he wishes me to do, he might as well make me play the role of a statue. It is a well-proved maxim that in this, practice and theory should be two inseparable considerations [*accidens*].

3.2. CLAUDE-FRANÇOIS MENESTRIER (1631–1705)

Des Ballets anciens et modernes selon les regles du theatre (Paris: René Guignard, 1682; facs. ed. Geneva: Minkoff, 1972).

De Lauze reflects the state of dance theory under Louis XIII (d. 1643), and his "Méthode" deals only with social dance. Claude-François Menestrier's *Des ballets anciens et modernes* reflects an increased complexity and sophistication of theoretical thought, as well as the greatly expanded repertoire, grandeur, and prestige of theatrical dance in the age of Louis XIV (d. 1715); it is the first treatise since antiquity to emphasize this genre. Menestrier was a Jesuit and polymath with wide interests, chief among which were heraldry, emblems, symbols, numismatics, festivals, and spectacles, but he also composed ballets and organized royal festivities under Louis XIV.[14] The Jesuits, in fact, cultivated ballet extensively as a component of their educational mission in their colleges, and as an evangelizing instrument in the Orient.

Stephanie Schroedter calls Menestrier "an early and influential progenitor of the theory of dance," who offered the first historically based taxonomic description of the art of dance.[15] Indeed, Menestrier begins his treatise with the assertion that still, after centuries of perfecting the arts, ballet remains "without rules and precepts"—this, despite his numerous references to Plato, Aristotle, Plutarch, and Lucian (1). His epistemological method is to begin historically at the origin of things; to learn the names of things, and in so doing, arrive at their definition in order to make rules; to survey the plan of the whole "edifice"; and to examine the parts individually, and how they interrelate (Reading 3.2a).

Even though his principal topic is ballet, much of what he says can be interpreted as referring to dance in general, as when he calls ballet the "elder brother" of sister arts music, painting, and poetry.[16] Without these three other arts, ballet is incomplete, but (anticipating Noverre) ballet is superior to painting: "The purpose of painting and ballet is to imitate and represent, but ballet has this advantage over painting: a painting shows only one moment, all its characters remain forever in the same situation, and they are stuck in the same movement that they have been given for all time; ballet, instead, is a continual series of movements following one another" (157). The most basic difference between ballet and social dance is that ballet is imitative and social dance is not: ballet imitates the actions of living creatures, whether humans or animals; other dances are "simply movements of the body adjusted to the *cadence* and the sound of instruments" (153, 158–159) (Reading 3.2b).

Menestrier's comparison of dance to painting is significant because he is the first dance theorist in modern history to refer back to the richly suggestive aphorism of Simonides: painting is unspoken poetry and poetry is a speaking painting. Horace restated this idea concisely and memorably in his *Ars poetica* (ca. 15 BCE): *ut pictura poesis*, literally, poetry should be like a picture; in other words, a poem should, in its own way, be as descriptive of its subject as a picture.[17] Plutarch revised the aphorism by replacing painting with dancing: dance is silent poetry and poetry is spoken dance (see Reading 1.3). Menestrier makes the first connection between Simonides, Horace, and Plutarch: "Ballet is a painting because it is an imitation, and Horace said long ago that poetry, which is a speaking painting, should be modelled on painting, which is a mute poetry: *ut pictura poësis erit*. Therefore, a ballet should be arranged in a way that resembles a *Tableau* . . ." (82). In addition to merely repeating Horace's phrase, Menestrier—connoisseur of mottos—coins one of his own for dance. He bases it on Horace and writes it in Greek, replacing "poetry" with "dance": ". . . according to Plutarch, ballet, though silent, is a speaking painting in that it expresses itself through figures, gestures, and movements: ζωγραφια ὄρχησις σιωπωσα" (*zographia orchesis sioposa*: painting is silent dance)—in other words, dance speaks in ways that painting cannot (138).

Philosophically, Menestrier shares with De Lauze an affinity to Stoicism. His comparison of the dancing body to musical instruments, especially of the string family, seems based on a Stoic mental/corporeal conception of philosophy as a living animal whose bones and sinews are logic, whose flesh is ethics, and whose soul is physics (the latter two pairs being sometimes reversed).[18] Our bodies are "like tuned lutes," Menestrier says, that vibrate sympathetically to music by virtue of the proportional relationship between sounds and the dimensions ("in length, breadth, depth, and position") of various body parts moving diversely but harmoniously—an idiosyncratic allusion, perhaps, to the Vitruvian man. In an instrumental ensemble, violins are universally favored for ballet because their strings, made of organic material (animal gut), vibrate more sympathetically with human body movements than do instruments made only of wood or metal (Reading 3.2c). Citing an image attributed to Clement of Alexandria (ca. 200 CE), Menestrier identifies a violin's four strings with the "tetrachord" of passions: pleasure, sadness, fear, and desire, which are the "movements of the soul" expressed by dance (154–155, 206).[19] The concept of "movements of the soul" is, of course, consonant with the doctrine of the affections (*Affektenlehre*) in Baroque music.[20]

Menestrier taxonomizes ballet as a combination of the Aristotelian categories of *parties de qualité* (relating to content) and *parties de quantité* (relating to extent). Ballet's six *parties de qualité*, which parallel those of poetry, are as follows:

matière, or subject matter (44ff)
invention, or form (55ff);
figures, or characters (138ff);
mouvement, whether of ballroom dance or ballet (153ff);
harmonie, or the relation of musical harmony, rhythm, and meter to dance (196ff); and
décoration, comprising scenery, costume, and machines (212ff).

Each of the *parties de qualité* is followed by numerous examples from specific ballets; these descriptions account for the bulk of the treatise's content (44–257). The *parties de quantité* of ballet have to do with the extent and form of the work: in other words, its *ouverture* or exposition at the beginning; *entrées* or imbroglio in the middle; and *grand ballet* or catastrophe at the end (257–258).

Under *mouvement*, Menestrier translates Plutarch's three basic elements of pantomime (see Reading 1.3) as "les figures [*schemata*], les mouvemens [*phorai*], & les gestes [*deixis*]" (152–153). *Phorai*, meaning movement, is in agreement with Plutarch. The most ambiguous of these terms is *deixis*, which in Plutarch was interpreted as pointing, gesture (especially with the hand), and semiotic sign. Menestrier calls it *démonstration*, elaborating that ballet is "a metaphoric action," and *démonstration* in dance is analogous to the eloquence of rhetorical figures used in oratory (Reading 3.2d).[21]

Figure acquires two definitions in Menestrier. In his chapter "Des Figures" (138–153), Menestrier says that the French word is the equivalent of the Greek word *schemata* used by Aristotle and Aristoxenus (see Reading 1.2). However, in this chapter Menestrier defines *figures* as the characters or roles (symbolic or allegorical) personified by the dancers in a ballet. Elsewhere, though, there are two series of quasi-choreographic diagrams that are also called *figures* (178–195, 231–235).[22] Each series represents an *entrée* in a ballet; each *entrée* contains several *figures* in which each dancer, symbolized by a fleuron, or floral grapheme, is shown as seen from above in various geometric configurations (see Fig. 3.1). There is no indication of how the dancers move from one configuration to the next. The *figures*, therefore, represent only the discrete instants (or *tableaux*)

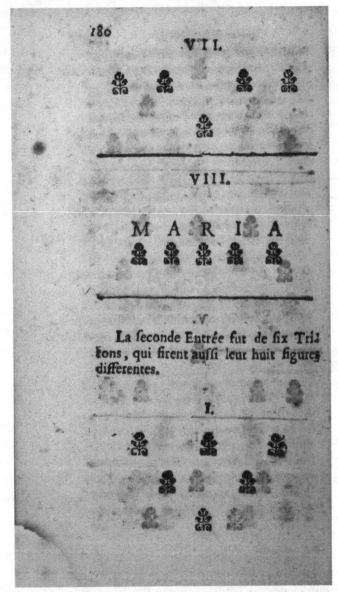

Figure 3.1. Claude-François Menestrier, *Des Ballets anciens et modernes selon les regles du theatre* (Bayerische Staatsbibliothek München, https://reader.digitale-sammlungen.de/de/fs1/object/goToPage/bsb10431517_00240.jpg), 180.

when a particular design is achieved and perhaps briefly held. This visualization of momentarily stopped motion corresponds perfectly with the Aristotelian connotation of *schema*. The floral symbols representing dancers, furthermore, can be seen as "moving emblems which explain themselves in the sequence of images or actions," thereby reconciling Menestrier's two definitions of *figure* by functioning as abstract signifiers of both characters *and* motion.[23]

READING 3.2A
Menestrier (trans. Russell)

PP. 1–2

It is remarkable that so many centuries that have labored constructively to polish and perfect the arts have left us, up to now, without rules and precepts for the conduct of ballets. These spectacles in which the spirit, the ear, and the eyes find delightful diversion, merit no less attention than [ballet's] three admirable sisters: music, painting, and poetry, cultivated by so many. Ballet is their older brother, but although it possesses all their graces and perfections, it has been so neglected that even today some still consider it nothing but an invention of pure caprice into which can be introduced whatever one wants, while some less rash than they but also less informed on the nature of these works are convinced that they must regulate theatrical practice to allow danced comedies, and tragedies without spoken parts, to make proper ballets.

Both these groups are equally in error and at odds with the practice of the Ancients and the few precepts that they occasionally proposed but never took the pains to develop. If this art were so easy, then Lucian's *Apologie de la danse* [i.e., *Peri Orcheseos*], written in response to a dance hater of his time who condemned its use, would have been a futile call for excellence in creators of ballets. If it were nothing but caprice, why would he recommend knowledge of poetry, music, geometry, rhetoric, mythology, history, and even philosophy for its success?[24]

[. . .]

PP. 7–8

My method is to begin by researching the origin of things, because it is good to know how things come down to us. Only the ignorant admire what they see without inquiring into their source. The wise look for these sources, like those of the great rivers whose course they wish to trace. After the origin of things, I usually examine the names people have given them. These names help introduce us to them, and are a means of establishing definitions for use in the rules upon which an art is based. This is the master plan of the edifice, in which the slightest error will lead to irreparable faults. Here in the definition one sees the grand design in a nutshell and at a single glance, yet one must not rest there. The parts must be seen, individually and in relation to the whole; they must be illustrated by examples and authoritative models that are the product of four requisites to validating and communicating the examples: mental acumen, good judgment, knowledge, and experience.

READING 3.2B

PP. 40–41

... But Aristotle, a philosopher who treats all subjects with precision, says in his *Poetics* that ballet consists of actions, customs, and passions expressed in figured dance by harmonious cadences and regulated movements with gestures, actions, and figures. The whole art of ballet is founded on this definition, which must be developed.

Ballet is an imitation like the other arts, and this is what it has in common with them. The difference is that whereas the other arts imitate only certain things, for instance painting which expresses only the figure, colors, and placement of things, ballet expresses the movements that painting and sculpture do not know how to express and that can be apprehended by our senses only through physical movement: the nature of things and the habitudes of the soul. This imitation therefore is produced by bodily movements that interpret the passions and inner sentiments. And just as the body has different parts that make up the whole and form a beautiful harmony, the sound of instruments and their consonances serve to regulate these movements which express the effects of the passions of the soul.

READING 3.2C

PP. 32–33

Let us review the ideas of this philosopher [Plato], and having followed the course of his philosophic reasoning, let us admire their full beauty from another point of view, for we know that this most polished of all philosophers reasoned no less concerning what is beautiful and fine, than what is judicious and solid. He says that man has a sense of order and disorder, a sense uniquely human and absent in animals. It is this sense that regulates our movements and imparts the concepts of number and harmony when they are organized. He recognizes it as a gift and favor of the gods, by which we are moved with a pleasing delicacy in conformity with their designs, and are gently set in motion. Does it not seem as if this philosopher considers us as tuned lutes, on which trained hands play their desired tunes, our body being somehow constructed so that the nerves, fibers, muscles, and tendons work together to make our movements harmonious, and as if the sense man possesses that organizes the operations of the other senses is the god-given sense of order? This sense controlling our motions is the principal agent of reason, and if it is confused, the soul that, jointly with the body, coordinates operations correctly and harmoniously can no longer produce anything correct, and reveals all the disorders that can arise from a troubled imagination. [Plato] adds that dance is born from the union [of body and soul] and serves to maintain their harmony that, committed to memory by reason, animates a dance in which all the movements of man are harmoniously rectified and organized. This reasoning of Plato teaches us that dance is not only an honorable diversion, but is a kind of study and practice that is absolutely necessary for controlling our movements. In effect it is that which imparts a noble and serene air to every action, and a certain grace rarely seen in those who have not learned to dance. [. . .]

PP. 198–199

This four-part harmony [in music] occurs naturally in all the movements of vibrating bodies, their trembling and oscillation naturally resulting from the proportional relationship of the four component parts, which are unequal in length, width, depth, and position. Moving thus together, just as a man's whole body is set in motion when he walks, some [parts] move more slowly and others more quickly. Some vibrate three, four, five, or six times for every one vibration of another. This is what made Aristotle state, in chapter 4 of his *Poetics*, that [in music] harmony is the accord of unequal parts, rhythm is the timing of movement, and meter is the measure, and these are three natural things, and so is the movement of the body.[25] These four things are the essence of ballet, which is a moving body representing certain subjects, in a certain time, to certain meters, and to the sound of instruments or voice; and the whole ensemble, in pleasing concert with the whole moving body, represents something to the spectators and creates intelligible images by imitating, figuratively, natural and moral things.

READING 3.2D

P. 43

These are the things that should be imitated in ballets, that inspired Abbé Tesoro, in his *Canocchiale Aristotelico*, which is a kind of commentary on the *Rhetoric* and *Poetics* of Aristotle regarding the eloquent expression [*élocution*] of inscriptions, mottos, and the art of symbols, to say that ballet is a metaphoric action that expresses the affections of the soul and the external actions by which man expresses them gesturally.[26]

PP. 162–163

There are those movements that the Greeks called *démonstrations*. And ballet movements must produce exactly the same effect as when eloquence brings forth certain [rhetorical] figures that seem to set before one's eyes the very things the orator is speaking about. Plutarch says there are those who dance purely for the sake of dancing, and whose entire performance consists only of following the *cadence* and bearing the body proudly, which amounts to dancing with propriety but without wisdom. For, as when singing, *air* is added to the notes and the rhythm, [so too] ballet has movements and figures or *démonstrations* that distinguish it from simple dancing. This is what today makes for many dances but few ballets, because dancers prefer making fine steps and lovely *cadences* rather than applying themselves to the representation of that which should be represented to make true ballets.

NOTES

1. Jean-Jacques Rousseau, *Dictionnaire de musique* (Paris: Chez la Veuve Duchesne, 1768), 40. See Curtis Price, "Music, Style and Society," *Music and Society: The Early Baroque Era*, ed. Curtis Price (Englewood Cliffs, NJ: Prentice Hall, 1993), 2–3.

2. Marie Glon, "Les lumières chorégraphiques: Les maîtres de danse européens au coeur d'un phénomène éditorial (1700–1760)," unpublished doctoral thesis (Paris, École des Hautes Études en Sciences Sociales, 2014), 389–393, traces the progress of dance's elevation to "academic" status, from Plato's Academy to the learned academies of the Italian Renaissance, to the Académie royale de danse in 1661, to Feuillet's *Chorégraphie* (1st ed., 1700).

3. *Lettres patentes du Roi, pour l'établissement de l'Académie royale de danse en la Ville de Paris. Verifiées en Parlement le 30. Mars 1662* (Paris: Pierre le Petit, 1663).

4. René Descartes, *Observationes de passionibus animae*, new ed. (Hanover: Nicolaus Foerster, 1707 [first ed. 1649]), article 69.

5. Johann Mattheson, *Der vollkommene Capellmeister* (Hamburg: Christian Herold, 1739). See also Weiss and Taruskin, *Music in the Western World*, 212–219.

6. Mattheson, *Der vollkommene Capellmeister*, 15, ¶51.

7. Mattheson, *Der vollkommene Capellmeister*, 223–232, ¶79–129.

8. The place of publication is unknown; London is suggested by Magnus Blomkvist, "François de Lauze und seine 'Apologie de la danse' (1623)," *Tanz und Bewegung in der barocken Oper; Kongressbericht Salzburg 1994*, ed.

Sybille Dahms and Stephanie Schroedter (Innsbruck and Vienna: Studien Verlag, 1996), 31.

9. De Lauze (9–10 in orig.; 57 in trans.) writes that Arbeau has promised to explicate for him various provincial and national dances through his *Orchesographie*—a curious remark in that in his book Arbeau had already published "tabulatures" of almost half the dances that De Lauze mentions. In all, Arbeau provides tabulations of thirty-five dances, as against De Lauze's verbal descriptions of only eight.

10. For negative remarks on De Lauze's description of the courante, see Wendy Hilton, "A dance for kings: The 17th-century French *Courante*," *Early Music* 5, no. 2 (1977), 162: "incomprehensible"; Marliese Glück, "Courante," *Die Musik in Geschichte und Gegenwart*, ed. Ludwig Finscher (Kassel, Basel: Bärenreiter, 1995), Sachteil 2, col. 1031: "undurchsichtiger" (opaque).

11. Stoicism was a philosophical movement of the Hellenistic period (third century BCE–third century CE).

12. Barbara Ravelhofer, ed., *B. de Montagut: Louange de la danse*, Renaissance Texts from Manuscript 3 (Cambridge: RTM Publications, 2000), 51.

13. In the full passage, excerpted here, De Lauze's "plusieurs figures" is translated as "numerous illustrations."

14. As a cleric, Menestrier follows generally in the footsteps of Arbeau.

15. Stephanie Schroedter, "Dance-Music-Theatre in the Shadow of Plato and Aristotle—Claude-François Ménestrier's Reception of Ancient Philosophers in his Dance Poetics," *Images d'action: Claude-François Ménestrier's Theoretical Writings on Festivals and Performing Arts: Translation and Commentary*, ed. Annette Kappeler, Jan Lazardzig, and Nicola Gess (Leiden: Wilhelm Fink, 2018), 448; also *Vom "Affect" zur "Action,"* 45, 47.

16. Dance is more commonly called the offspring or younger sibling of music.

17. Quintus Horatius Flaccus (65–8 BCE).

18. Dirk Baltzly, "Stoicism," *Stanford Encyclopedia of Philosophy* (https://plato.stanford.edu/entries/stoicism/), 2018.

19. Menestrier also refers to the four dangerous passions that are moderated by dance: fear, melancholy, anger, and joy (31). They are mentioned again by early eighteenth-century German dance theorists.

20. See Schroedter, *Vom "Affect" zur "Action,"* 268–269.

21. See Schroedter, *Vom "Affect" zur "Action,"* 128–129.

22. The first series records a ballet that celebrated the marriage of the Duke of Parma and Maria d'Este, Princess of Modena, in 1667. In the first *entrée* (Menestrier, 177–180), the five female dancers represent five basic colors,

and they conclude by somehow "painting" (*peignoient*) the name MARIA, in honor of the bride. The second series contains the *figures* of an equestrian ballet.

23. Kappeler, Lazardzig, and Gess, "Claude-François Ménestrier's Theories on Festivals and Performing Arts Encompassed by an Overarching Image Philosophy: An Introduction," *Images d'action*, 14.

24. See Reading 1.2, par. 35, 36, 74.—Ed.

25. Aristotle writes in section IV of the *Poetics* (39): "Because mimesis comes naturally to us, as do melody and rhythm (that metres are categories of rhythms is obvious), in the earliest times those with special natural talents for these things gradually progressed and brought poetry into being from improvisations."—Ed.

26. Abbé Tesoro [Emanuele Tesauro (1592–1675)], *Il cannocchiale aristotelico* [*The Aristotelian Telescope*] (Turin, 1654). Menestrier's interest in this book is consistent with his interest in heraldry.—Ed.

~~~~~~

| 4 |

The Early Enlightenment

German and English Dance Theory, 1703–1721

Eighteenth-century social dance, called *belle danse* and now called "Baroque dance," was taught and disseminated throughout Europe through the medium of Beauchamps-Feuillet notation, first presented in Raoul Auger Feuillet's *Chorégraphie* (1700), the most significant and influential choreographic development since Arbeau (see Fig. 4.1).[1] The time span of "Baroque dance" practice is exactly contemporaneous with that of Beauchamps-Feuillet notation, from 1700 to the 1780s, and thus roughly equivalent to the Classic period in music, which culminates in the late eighteenth century. In other words, the periodization of dance practice bypasses the Classic era and jumps from the Baroque directly into the early Romantic: from the age of the minuet to the age of the waltz. What we call "classical" ballet is the epitome of Romanticism. This means, in terms of their historical period, that dance practice was "Long Baroque" in style, while dance theory was already early Enlightenment in spirit, and dance music was *galant*—a simple homophonic

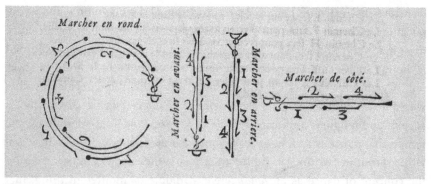

Figure 4.1. Raoul Auger Feuillet, *Chorégraphie ou l'art de décrire la dance*: "Marcher en rond. Marcher en avant. Marcher en arriere. Marcher de côté" (Bibliothéque nationale de France, https://gallica. bnf.fr/ark:/12148/btv1b86232407/f49.item), 35.

style especially well suited to dance because of its clearly and evenly articu-lated melodic and phrase structure. This was, indeed, a time of high creative ferment.

In Germany and England from 1703 to 1721, a coherent theory of dance was postulated that designated itself a theory, comprehended why it is a theory, and clearly, rationally distinguished itself from practice. This theory is based gen-erally on early Enlightenment rationalism, biblical and ethical justifications for dance, and classical wisdom and science. The authors of this theory were Samuel Rudolph Behr, Johann Pasch, and Gottfried Taubert in the Electorate of Saxony; and John Weaver in England. The German treatises differ from most of the works that follow in being purely theoretical, with the exception of Taubert's *Rechtschaffener Tantzmeister,* which contains both theoretical and practical material: along with detailed instructions for the courante and minuet, Taubert provides a complete translated edition of the *Chorégraphie.*[2] These treatises, except for Behr's last publication,[3] also differ from later ones in their lack of interest in theatrical dance. Even though Pasch and Taubert devote sections of their books to theatrical dance, they make it clear that ethics are a product only of social dance. They represent the most lofty and idealistic vision of dance theory ever written.

What is most striking about Enlightenment dance theory is its passion for knowledge for its own sake and from every available source. Even if the *Chorégraphie* was their principal link with French culture at this time, the German theorists and John Weaver were very much a part of the early Enlightenment. They were humanists whose dance knowledge was grounded in the philosophic and scientific literature of Antiquity. Behr and Weaver were also interested in the scientific knowledge of their own time and its application to dance. Taubert in particular realized the encyclopedist impulse to gather everything known about dance in one massive, 1,284-page volume.[4] Although the German theorists' religious, moral, and ethical emphasis was out of step with the high Enlightenment rationalism and secularism that would emanate from France, their defense of dance was based equally on secular and religious authority. From Plato, Pasch and Taubert embrace the notion that dance is a child of reason and therefore conducive to ethics and virtue. From the writings of Lutheran scholars, they depend in particular on the concept of dance as an *adiaphoron*: a middle or indifferent thing, that is, something not expressly prohibited in the Bible, and therefore not only permissible but positively conducive to piety. We stated in the introduction that theory asks the questions "what" and "why." With regard to dance theory, the Enlightenment period is when these issues were most intensively scrutinized.

4.1. SAMUEL RUDOLPH BEHR (B. 1670)

Anleitung zu einer wohlgegründeten Tantz-Kunst (Leipzig: Christoph Heydler, 1703 [1703/I]).
Andere Theil der Tantz-Kunst, oder Ausgesiebete Grillen (Leipzig: Christoph Heydler, 1703 [1703/II]).

Samuel Rudolph Behr never claimed to be a dance theorist and never used the term in his writing. His books are chock-full of disorganized—though no less valuable—gobbets of dance knowledge. His first book, published with slightly different titles in two small, unpaginated volumes (1703/I, 1703/II), introduces his principal contributions to dance theory. He stands out from the other authors in his knowledge of music. While Behr, Pasch, and Taubert all include music in their lists of subjects a dancing master should know something about, only Behr, in 1703, lists it as his highest priority: ". . . a [dancing] master," he says, "is required (1) to be a musician and composer" (1703/I, 8). Not only did he compose his own dance music (though none has survived), but also he is the only one of these authors to name actual composers of music; indeed, in this respect he may be a rarity among all writers on dance. In his next publication, six years later, he names composers of dance music as well as other genres, both historic and contemporary.[5] As he explains elsewhere: ". . . undoubtedly the music must be the vehicle that first excites, heightens, alters, and calms the soul's movement. Indeed, when artistically done, this kindles an utterly magical excitation of the spirit . . ." (1703/II, 67–68).[6]

Behr is the first dance writer to explore the role of anatomy in human movement, his most important contribution to dance theory. Anatomy is directly relevant to the mechanics and physics of dance, as well as to dance medicine and physical culture in general. No one except John Weaver, eighteen years later, approaches the detail of Behr's exposition of this subject in the second volume of his *Tantz-Kunst*. Behr believes a dancing master should know the anatomical names of the muscles and bones involved in dancing. For each of the four basic motions (bending or *flexio;* rising or *extensio;* closing or *adductio;* opening or *abductio*), he names, according to the bone or body part, the muscle group responsible for each kind of motion when initiated at three articulations or joints from the top to the bottom of the leg: at the hipbone, shinbone (tibia), and ankle.[7] He repeats this process with the arms at the shoulder, elbow, and wrist. In the next chapter he goes through the same process with the muscle groups for the four basic motions as they occur in basic steps. In 1709, he lists the leg articulations from ankle to hip, the reverse of his earlier procedure, and reorganizes his data according to basic motion type instead of body part.[8] Behr's reorganization of this data can be interpreted as an exercise in the *ars combinatoria*, or combinatorial art. To consummate this innovatory contribution to the science of dance, Behr maps the muscle groups visually onto four illustrations of a male dancer making the four basic motions, with each plate labeled by numbers keyed directly to the relevant terms in the text (see Figs. 4.2 and 4.3). We need to remember that these plates are primarily anatomical diagrams, not dance depictions.

Behr's anatomic analysis of movement was not received very respectfully by his contemporaries. Louis Bonin humorously discounts the importance of this kind of technical minutia.[9] Taubert actually paraphrases Behr's text quoted here, but only the parts relating to *flexio* and *extensio,* and only for the purpose of ridiculing it.[10] In defense of Behr, he is the first dance writer to apply strictly scientific knowledge to the art of dance. Thus, his interest in anatomy is a milestone in the gradual intellectualization of dance, definitively raising its status from *métier* to liberal art, and concurrently the status of the dancing master from *ménétrier* to *savant*. Marie Glon dates the commencement of this process of intellectualization to the establishment of the Académie royale de la danse in 1662, and she finds it epitomized in the publication of Feuillet's *Chorégraphie* in 1700.[11] In the realm of dance theory, Behr's writing on anatomy plays a parallel role in this process.

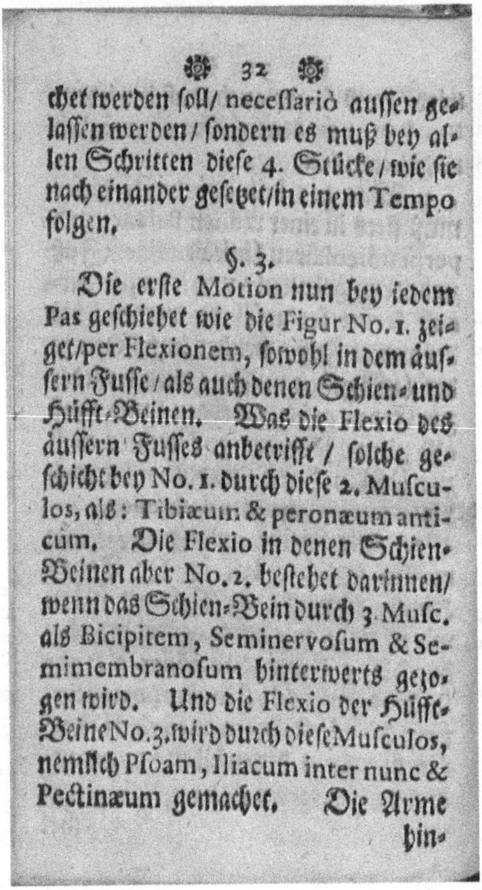
32
chet werden soll/ necessario aussen ge-
lassen werden / sondern es muß bey allen Schritten diese 4. Stücke / wie sie
nach einander gesetzet/in einem Tempo
folgen.

§. 3.

Die erste Motion nun bey iedem
Pas geschiehet wie die Figur No. 1. zei-
get/per Flexionem, sowohl in dem äussern Fusse / als auch denen Schien- und
Hüfft-Beinen. Was die Flexio des
äussern Fusses anbetrifft / solche ge-
schicht bey No. 1. durch diese 2. Musculos, als: Tibiæum & peronæum anti-
cum. Die Flexio in denen Schien-
Beinen aber No. 2. bestehet darinnen/
wenn das Schien-Bein durch 3. Musc.
als Bicipitem, Seminervosum & Se-
mimembranosum hinterwerts gezo-
gen wird. Und die Flexio der Hüffte-
Beine No. 3. wird durch diese Musculos,
nemlich Psoam, Iliacum inter nunc &
Pectinæum gemachet. Die Arme
hin-

Figure 4.2. Samuel Rudolph Behr, *Wohlgegründete Tantz-Kunst*, 3rd expanded and improved ed. (Universitäts- und Landesbibliothek Sachsen-Anhalt, http://digitale.bibliothek.uni-halle.de/vd18/content/pageview/2820455), 32.

READING 4.1
Behr (trans. Russell)

1703/II, PP. 10–18

How Men's Limbs, Which are also Used in the Art Of Dancing, Must First Be Investigated By The [Dancing] Master

Just as a master builder plans his art according to three criteria: (1) adherence to all the architectural principles suited to every structure; (2) construction of a durable, elegant, and well proportioned work; that is (3) built to conform as conveniently as possible to the purpose and use of its inhabitants; so too a

Figure 4.3. Behr, *Wohlgegründete Tantz-Kunst*, facing page [*Flexio*] (http://digitale.bibliothek.uni-halle.de/vd18/content/pageview/2820456).

dancing master must observe the following three basic goals with each of his students: (1) that he has taught them the correct fundamentals; (2) so that in time they will dance with steadiness and grace; and (3) thereby dance adroitly according to the prescribed purpose and use of (i) the feet, (ii) the body, (iii) the arms, (iv) the head and eyes, and (v) every attainable means of agreeable and polite behavior, as have already been fully explained here in *Tantz-Kunst*, Chap. 4.[12]

Like a master builder who must take stock of every detail of the place where he will situate the foundation of a good house, likewise in the art of dance the aptitude of the person who wishes to learn dancing will be evaluated precisely to ascertain whether he is fit and skilled enough to grasp the fundamentals, and in so doing all of his limbs must be considered as to how this and that one articulates and connects with others whenever it moves. Thus can be studied in every respect how the legs, arms, and other separate parts move and work together to make various skilled steps. Yet before I speak further about how the parts of the legs, arms, and other parts of the body must work when dancing, I will remind [the reader] of what, among other things, I said in my *Tantz-Kunst*, Chap. 6[13]: that steps are made not from the upper part of the body, but the lower part, from the hips down; and also I will name the muscles that control movement in this part of the body:

At the hipbone the legs have [four basic motions]: *flexio, extensio, adductio,* and *abductio.*

1. FLEXIO happens through these muscles: the psoas, iliacus internus, and pectinaeus.
2. EXTENSIO, through the glutaeus major, medius, and minor.
3. ADDUCTIO, through the mediante tricipite, when the legs are drawn inward together.
4. ABDUCTIO, through the quadrigemini and obduratores, when the legs are turned outward again.

This is also executed circularly through the same four groups of muscles.

With respect to the shinbone

the same [four basic motions] are made: *flexio, extensio, adductio* and *abductio.*

1. FLEXIO occurs when the shinbone is drawn back by three muscles: the biceps [hamstring], seminervosus, and semimembranosus.
2. EXTENSIO, when the shinbone is straightened by four muscles: the rectus, the vastus internus, externus, and cruralis.
3. ADDUCTIO happens through the sartorius and gracilis, whose function is to lift one leg over the other.
4. ABDUCTIO, through the membranosus and poplitaeus.

The ankle is likewise bent, straightened, opened, and closed.

1. It is bent by two muscles: tibiaeus and peronaeus anticus.
2. It is extended by the gasterocnemius, soleus, and plantaris (these three comprise the calf).

3. It is closed by the tibiaeus posticus.
4. It is opened by the peronaeus posticus.

4.2. JOHANN PASCH (1653[?]–1710)

Beschreibung wahrer Tanz-Kunst (Frankfurt: Wolfgang Michahelles und Johann Adolph, 1707; facs. ed. Leipzig: Zentralantiquariat der DDR; Munich: Heimeran Verlag, 1978).

Both Johann Pasch and Gottfried Taubert after him transmit, via Menestrier, the Platonic idea that the arts are the children of reason.[14] Pasch's idea of dance theory, the most comprehensive and detailed of his time, encompasses two basic, multipartite concepts: prosaic dance and poetic dance.[15] Prosaic dance consists of standing, walking, bowing, and costume, and it is primarily concerned with dance theory. Poetic dance is real dancing to music, and it is primarily concerned with dance practice. Prosaic dance must be taught prior to poetic dance, because only through prosaic dance can *Sitten-Lehre*, or visible ethics, be learned. When Pasch and Taubert define prosaic dance, their headings refer to *Sitten-Lehre* and not to dance.[16] This means that *Sitten-Lehre* is the essence, and the goal, of dance theory and therefore of all dance. There are six parts of visible ethics:

1. *scopus finalis*, or the epitome of physical training;
2. *materia*, or the rationalization and intellectualization of human motion;
3. *inventio*, or the relation of dance to music;
4. *ordinatio*, or social intercourse and the civilising influence of dance;
5. *decoratio*, or the visual elements of decor and dress[17]; and
6. *executio*, which is the theory of the practice of poetic dance. *Executio* is concerned with the practical elements of dancing in general—aptitude, making and connecting steps, *cadence*, figure, and air—in other words, with the theory of dance in the same sense that the theory of music is concerned with melody, harmony, meter, and rhythm. Strange as it may seem, *executio* makes a surprising, and key, reappearance in twenty-first century dance theory.

Invisible but implicitly present beneath this scale of values is practice itself. This does not mean that Pasch and Taubert considered theory based on or derived from practice. On the contrary, theory in its loftiest aspiration rises further and further away from practice. Neither Behr nor Pasch even discusses practice (though Taubert does).

The concept of *Sitten-Lehre* may be compared to De Lauze's "bien séance," and its parts are clearly derived by Pasch from Menestrier's *parties de qualité*. However, whereas Menestrier's *parties de quantité* refer only to theatrical dance, Pasch and Taubert offer an alternative version, based on prosaic dance and the ethical basis of dance theory, and interpreted primarily from the standpoint of social dance. Of crucial importance for Pasch and his German contemporaries is their emphasis on ethics and on dance's relation to movement in a broad spectrum of human activity, not to dance alone. For Pasch and Taubert, *Sitten-Lehre* (visible ethics), prosaic dance, and theory are interchangeable terms, if not essentially synonymous. Taubert not only inherits Pasch's lofty concept of *Sitten-Lehre*; he extends it into higher realms of human aspiration, culminating in piety (see Reading 4.3).

Most dancing masters who wrote treatises, both before and after the early eighteenth century, had no fancy educational background to boast of. In fact, elsewhere in Europe at this time a dancing master could not even be presumed literate. The German theorists, on the other hand, were all university educated, and they took their ideas from a great number and rich variety of learned sources. Pasch's reference to "an inborn natural impulse [to move]" must come from Plato (Reading 1.1). When Pasch explains how *executio* differs from the other parts of *Sitten-Lehre*, he bases his argument on a passage quoted from Aristotle's *Metaphysics*, in which the difference between practical and speculative physics is explained.[18] A reference to the Vitruvian man by Behr seems derived from the Italian humanist tradition.[19] Pasch, Behr, and Taubert present textually overlapping definitions of the elements of dance related to number and measurement: *Zahl* (number); *Masse* or *Mensur* (measure); *Gewicht* or *Pondus* (weight); *Zeit* or *Tempo* (time); *Ziel* (extent); and *Elle* (length).[20] While these terms are comparable to those listed in the Renaissance sources, for the German authors they are derived not from the Italians but from a sentence in the *Apocrypha*: "But thou hast arranged all things by measure and number and weight [*Zahl, Masse, und Gewicht*]."[21] But Pasch also gathered knowledge from the world around him. He recounts a walk with a mathematician: as they observe a farmer spreading manure, the mathematician analyzes the farmer's use of his knee as a fulcrum for the heavy pitchfork, illustrating a principle of movement applicable to dance (432–433).

Pasch had studied with Beauchamps in Paris, and despite the absence of specific choreographic information in his treatise, he does refer to Beauchamps-Feuillet notation in an analogy between the five "universal steps"—*pas droit* (straight), *pas ouvert* (open), *pas rond* (circular), *pas tortillé* (waving), and *pas battu* (beaten)—and the five vowels. As vowels combine with consonants, these five steps "combine with countless consonants or compound steps by means of arithmetic and combinatorial art to produce over two thousand different steps that can be arranged in tables"—a clear reference to Feuillet's step tables.[22] Taubert quotes this analogy to language and expands upon it with additional analogies to colors in painting, the organization of materials for the construction of a house, and, "beginning with single letters, then progressing to syllables, sentences, periods, and paragraphs, as preparation for the composition of an oration."[23] Taubert, furthermore, habitually uses the noun "reading" (*Lection*) in a wide variety of contexts referring to both practice and theory: from the simple step to the combination of steps, to the teaching and learning of dance, to the terminology of dance, to the symbols used in *chorégraphie*.[24]

READING 4.2
Pasch (trans. Russell)

P. 16

Definition of the art of dancing[25]
The true art of dancing, in its theory, is a science that applies rational, philosophical rules of art to rehabilitate the God-given, inborn natural impulse [to move], an instinct buried in the mortal body after the Fall, to a more than highly necessary and also more joyous [kind of] movement, that in practice is executed in a truly natural and rational manner according to mathematical principles, for one or another useful purpose, such as, in particular, visible ethics, physical fitness, and [theatrical] representation of gestures and actions.

PP. 17–25

[. . .]The true art of dance, like other arts, is divided into separate regulated parts, of which there are mainly two, namely:

1. visible ethics and physical agility;
2. theatrical representations, with their gestures, actions, etc.

Each of these has, in turn, six parts, namely:

1. *scopus finalis*
2. subject, or *materia*

3. *inventio*
4. *ordinatio*
5. *decoratio*
6. *executio*

First part of the true art of dance:
namely,
how it improves visible ethics
and agility [also] in the other exercises.[26]

In surveying the above-mentioned six parts, the first is:

1. *SCOPUS FINALIS OF ETHICS*

The primary goal of visible ethics is to make the human body and limbs so skilled and agile, following the good rules of art (which also apply to the spirit and thus even moreso to the body), that they become the outward expression of a disciplined spirit. [. . .] This is what is also known as prose in dancing, in which are contained the skillful and respectable manner of sitting, standing, walking, and bowing on all occasions with the requisite modesty and correct movement of the limbs; how to enter in company, comport oneself there with the proper gestures, take one's leave, etc. For these things there are countless rules based on philosophy and mathematics.

The secondary goal is to prepare the body for further training in the ways of nobility. No other type of exercise trains the whole body, down to the tiniest part, teaches agility, and even conditions the body, as well as dancing. [. . .] And as philosophy is to the three [academic] faculties, so is dance to physical training in equal, but not greater, measure.

2. *MATERIA OF ETHICS*

This refers to the effort of fallen man to regulate and rationalize, through good discipline, the fleeting and formless bodily motions and gestures that result from natural impulses.

We now consider

3. *INVENTIO IN ETHICS*

Inasmuch as man's natural fallibility greatly impedes him in all regular things, and for this reason an unfit body can be made agile only with much difficulty, a way was invented to sweeten his labor and help him attain his goal unawares. For this purpose poetry is used in dance, and steps and gestures laid out metrically just as words are in poetry, which helps in learning long passages by making it much more pleasant and easy thanks to the [rhythmic] connection of words and verse; tones in music have the same effect. Therefore many kinds of dance have developed, like the many types of verse, and the one must be organized in as well regulated a way as the other is. Also all these dances are performed to a [certain] time and accentuation [*à tempo & ad nutum*], and music sets the proper time in which the predetermined steps and gestures are to be executed. And this is especially useful when dancing together, if you lose sight of each other while turning, you can still hear the music and thus keep your steps together and the figures symmetrical. And a dancer who knows all the myriad ways of following music is all the more skilled in performing his prosaic actions nimbly and easily, and at a well regulated ball where ceremony is strictly adhered to, he can acquit himself honorably and well, as doubtless he also can do from habit in other [situations]. We now turn to

4. ORDINATIO OF ETHICS

Society ordains that now and then men and women come together in company for poetic dancing in mixed groups, for example at weddings. And for this [reason] I have written many rules for well regulated dancing.[27]

[. . .]

5. DECORATIO IN ETHICS

This refers to ornament. And since it is neither humane nor rational to hold a civil gathering in a room that resembles a pigsty, a room in which one intends to dance should be, not necessarily magnificent, but sufficiently spacious and level. The dancers should be dressed in keeping with their rank, and in such a manner that they do not incur the displeasure of their betters who might find their dress too splendid, or, on the other hand, provocative, lewd, bizarre, or sluttish. There should be as many lights in the room as necessary to permit the company to recognize one another and observe all the dancing. And even though one can dance to a single violin, an ensemble in four parts is a fine enhancement to the decor, for in this way two senses, hearing and seeing, are gratified at the same time. Also there can be no cause for complaint when step and gesture are coordinated in measure, time, and accentuation. But the decoration is very fine when these things are moderated and, as it were, delicately modulated to avoid the extremes of brightness and dullness, so that they are graceful and pleasant to the eye, and always show a man of moderation and self control in his best light; for it may be assumed that one who displays self control and skill in the tiniest actions will not be behindhand in matters of importance, unless by some aberration whose cause lies elsewhere. And finally we come to

6. EXECUTIO OF ETHICS

This refers to praxis [from the standpoint] of theory, for the two belong together, there being no theory without praxis, and praxis without systematic theory is a very dubious thing from which nothing truly rational can be accomplished. Since all the other parts are involved with this sixth one, it is nothing in itself unless it reflects on the others, just as in practice a step and gesture affect the other parts of the body.

4.3. GOTTFRIED TAUBERT (1670–1746)

Rechtschaffener Tantzmeister (Leipzig: Friedrich Lanckischens Erben, 1717; facs. ed. Leipzig: Zentralantiquariat der DDR, and Munich: Heimeran Verlag, 2 vols., 1976; trans. and ed. Tilden Russell, *The Compleat Dancing Master*, 2 vols. [New York: Peter Lang, 2012]).

Taubert incorporates the word *theory* in his page-long title, which begins in this way:

> GOTTFRIED TAUBERT,
> the Leipzig dancing master's
> Compleat Dancing Master,
> or, basic explication
> of the French art of dancing,
> consisting of three Books,
> the first of which historically investigates
> the origin, development, improvement, different
> uses, acceptance, various benefits, and other particularities of dance;
> the second of which systematically and clearly shows
> the ethical, theoretical, and practical fundamentals
> of the French exercise of ballroom as well as theatrical dance, [. . .]

He considers theory the necessary foundation and, moreover, the precondition of practice. Dancing masters should acquire a strong theoretical foundation in their own training before they start teaching others. They, in turn, must teach prosaic dance prior to poetic dance.[28] In other words, the student cannot properly begin to learn to dance until he has internalized dance theory in the form of *äusserliche Sitten-Lehr*.

Facing the title page is Taubert's frontispiece, titled "The *Compleat Dancing Master*, Learned, and Taught in Theory and Practice" (see Figs. 4.4 and 4.5).[29]

Figure 4.4. Gottfried Taubert, *Rechtschaffener Tantzmeister*, frontispiece (Bereich Sondersammlungen Digitalisierung Universitätsbibliothek Leipzig, aesth_394-1_abb_tanzm_plakat.tif).

The dancing master is shown in three roles. The topmost image may be the only existing picture of a dancing master in his role as theorist. He is shown seated in a book-lined study. A pen and inkwell, pochette, and books are spread out on the table before him, and he seems to be working on a page of dance notation. The wallfull of books represents Taubert's learning, which he shows off copiously throughout the treatise, and it makes the more important point that

Figure 4.5. Taubert, *Rechtschaffener Tantzmeister*, frontispiece, detail: the dancing master as theorist.

his teaching is based solidly on venerable and high authority. Indeed, Taubert cites 450 books—many referenced several times—in eight languages (beside German) and a broad range of subjects and genres. The image of a theorist indicates the importance of theory as the foundation of praxis in his system.

In a recently discovered manuscript, Taubert reveals that he learned the dancing master's profession from Pasch. Indeed, he quotes and borrows from Pasch more than from any other source, and he manifests his admiration and gratitude in all his writing.[30] As stated in the previous reading, Taubert both inherits and expands upon Pasch's description of visible ethics. Of the three internal books comprising the *Rechtschaffener Tantzmeister*, the first and third, surrounding his Book II on practice, require almost as many pages for their full exposition as are needed for practice, and they are bound up in an over-arching agenda for the rehabilitation and ultimate perfection of humanity.[31] The culminating and indeed metaphysical transition is accomplished in the following reading, in which Taubert situates visible ethics, itself a hierarchy, within a larger hierarchy of the justifications of dance that lead beyond ethics. This larger hierarchy is exclusively Taubert's capstone to the theory edifice he and Pasch have constructed. As with *Sitten-Lehre*, the path begins at the bottom and leads upward. There are three mutually reinforcing strands to his argument:

1. Religion. Dance—particularly prosaic dance—is a means for humanity to regain some degree of its prelapsarian perfection, a pathway toward the New Jerusalem. Therefore, the cultivation of dance is a kind of piety.

2. Erudition. Dance—following the idea of Plato, via Menestrier and Pasch—is a child of reason, by virtue of which it belongs to the classical humanistic tradition of the liberal arts and sciences. Thus, dance contributes to erudition, which also is conducive to reverence to God.

3. Ethics. Visible ethics is the specific essence of dance theory that validates its role in humanity's project of regeneration. The study of dance is "a pedagogical stepladder to all the virtues."[32]

Early Enlightenment thought is reflected in Taubert's observation that the nobility is no more generously endowed than other men by God with physical superiority, and the obligation to strive for self-perfection is incumbent upon all equally and beneficial to society as a whole.

Finally, it should be noted that not once in this rationale does Taubert mention or allude to dance practice or poetic dance, that is, to the act of dancing itself.

READING 4.3
Taubert (trans. Russell)

PP. 202–206

Having proved sufficiently in the ten preceding chapters that dancing in and of itself is good and not sinful, we turn now in the following chapters to the profitable and advantageous uses that flow from [dancing], for the principal question one asks of any worldly undertaking is: what good is it? or, how is it useful?

Here, before anything else, we must take a mental leap back into Eden and reflect:

1. that at the Creation man himself was endowed by God with, to put it succinctly, a perfect body, adapted in stature, faculties, and agility to all human activities. (Nor did he lack a beautiful appearance, says Misander in *Delic. evang.*, part 2, p. 927. He was of noble height, eloquent, and physically well proportioned, far surpassing all modern royal and princely personages in manner and skill. For he was a work of God, and God's works are always perfect.) And also

2. that as a result of the grievous Fall, from which all our frailties follow, he woefully lost that high external perfection of stature and skill, together with his internal, spiritual endowments.

But now, even though, due to the latter, the pernicious weed of ruined nature and stature was passed down to all men through original sin, yet still after the Fall there remain left over in us a few tiny particles of our former physical adroitness and beauty, and by the grace of God most men possess an adept and elegantly constructed body with healthy, perfectly matched limbs; nevertheless we are practically all soft, slow, and inept. Do not most people go from youth to grizzled old age crooked and bent, with hanging head and hunched back? Do they not usually stand leaning to one side, with a slack, protuberant belly hanging from a sunken, collapsed ribcage? When they walk their crooked knees knock together, their feet always turn in more than out, their arms swing, and their hands, head, eyes, and mouth make such clownish shapes that one can scarcely refrain from laughing. In short: naturally correct form and adroitness is not to be seen in most men. For even if their body is both healthy and well proportioned, it still falls short of its original perfection.

[...]

But, I say, just because this physical frailty is the result of fallen nature and daily occupation, we commit not the slightest sin when we attempt to root out this innate flaw as much as possible, if not entirely (*potest enim fraenari, sed nunquam vinci natura,* for nature can be weakened but never defeated), and when we attempt to compensate for the lost well proportioned stature and adroitness that, so to speak, are obscured from man's fallen condition, and often are revealed to some extent by dint of reason, art, and tireless effort, but in some more than others, depending on whether or not one "has a natural talent for it," as the well known saying goes. For all arts are the children of reason, because they are themselves the true natural outcome of human aptitude, as the Jesuit Menestrier says, and are improved through rational philosophical rules.[33] This is also why the ancient philosophers, who were not only writers, but also true practitioners and wizards in the natural arts,[34] and came to correct the defects in man's nature through well conceived rules, laws, studies, and arts, were called artful imitators of nature.

And it is to be hoped that no one would say it displeases God when one man comes before another, in the words of the apostle Paul, "with brotherly love" (Romans 12.10), since the Holy Writ expressly commands it when it says to give honor to whom it is due [Romans 13.7]. Thus, too, no one can claim that God would oppose one Christian's well meaning deference when greeting his Christian neighbor [by] trying to please with physical propriety, respectable gestures, and bows.

Indeed, in response to [those who say] that, when God first endowed men with their upright stature and good posture, he was far more generous to all modern kings and princes, who take pains to be superior to other men in physical prowess, I would assert, rather, the opposite: that he who willfully suppresses the aptitude hidden in his limbs, and persists in his innate frailty, is far worse than he who endeavors to restore to some extent his good, inborn physical aptitude; because all our natural defects were inflicted upon us by God as a punishment, and we should [strive] from youth on to acknowledge and improve them, as in walking, talking, and all the arts, with care and discipline, for our own good as well as for the common good.

I freely admit that this is not the highest goal, but rather the third of three principal requirements for a good education of young folk:

1. The first and most important is the good introduction to piety and true religious devotion. For this is the cornerstone of all temporal and eternal welfare.
2. The second is the introduction to the many worthwhile arts and sciences through which man learns how to render homage to God and serve his neighbor, failing which he is of no use to the world. And
3. the third and last is the introduction to visible ethics, by which, specifically, young folk become accustomed from childhood on to morality and true civility, so that they are not only presentable and discreet toward their fellow man, but also prove prompt and apt in all their activities. [. . .]

Now, although this last part is less important than the first two [together], and can in no way be [individually] of equal value to the second, on which the young must spend much more time and trouble, and is even less comparable to the first, which provides a fundamental introduction to piety; nevertheless no intelligent person can deny that it is a beautiful adjunct to piety and a marvelous ornament to erudition and to the other arts, and consequently in our polite times must be conjoined with the other two in the most meticulous manner possible. For when a young man fears God, learns what is right, and conducts himself adroitly and unaffectedly, he imparts a certain elegance to his piety and learnedness that makes him not only amiable and pleasant, but also far more obliging, in the eyes of intelligent people, than those who lack these qualities.

4.4. JOHN WEAVER (1673–1760)
An Essay Towards an History of Dancing (London: J. Tonson, 1712).
Anatomical and Mechanical Lectures upon Dancing (London: J. Brotherton and W. Meadows, 1721).

Of all writers on dance, John Weaver may have been the most multifaceted, and not only of his own era. His writing straddles the two great polarities of eighteenth-century dance theory: between theory and practice; and between social *belle danse* and theatrical pantomime. Weaver's publications can be grouped in four categories:

1. Theory: the three essays in *The Spectator*, nos. 67, 334, and 466 (1711, 1712); *An Essay Towards an History of Dancing* (1712); and *Anatomical and Mechanical Lectures upon Dancing* (1721) treat dance theory in general. *The History of the Mimes and Pantomimes* (1728) has to do with the theory of theatrical dance.
2. Practice of ballroom dance in Beauchamps-Feuillet notation: *Orchesography* (1706); *A Small Treatise of Time and Cadence in Dancing* (1706); *A Collection of Ball-Dances* (1706); and *The Union* (1707).
3. Practice of theatrical dance: *Orpheus and Eurydice* (1718); *Perseus and Andromeda* (1728); and *The Judgment of Paris* (1733).
4. Theory and practice of theatrical dance: *The Loves of Mars and Venus* (1717, 1724) is theoretical in its preface and practical in its scenario, particularly with its concrete descriptions of facial expressions and physical gestures appropriate to various emotions and actions, making it an essential predecessor—and supplement—to Noverre.[35]

Weaver is acutely aware of dance's spotty collective memory, in contrast to that of music. He places the blame on dance's "want of an universal Character" and on its traditional method of oral instruction by an "immediate Master and Scholar" as opposed, presumably, to published methods.[36] He seeks to counteract this insular and insulated condition by reestablishing the Italian Renaissance notion of dance's connection to the liberal arts or, in Weaver's formulation, "the Arts and Sciences." In his second *Spectator* essay, he states that dance should be able to be reduced "into a regular science" just as music was discovered to be when Pythagoras heard hammers of various weights making different sounds when struck.[37] Weaver's interest in the scientific basis of dance, seen especially in the *Lectures*, his most purely theoretical work, epitomizes how he—like the German theorists of his time—regarded the quadrivium as the part of the liberal arts to which dance belongs. Pasch and Taubert both write that "the true art of dancing, in its theory, is a science," and it is worth noting that Taubert's publisher was listing his book in a 1726 catalog under the category of "wissenschaftlichen Büchern," that is, as a learned or scientific work.[38]

The *Orchesography* and *A Small Treatise* are Weaver's English translations of Feuillet's *Chorégraphie* and "Traité de la cadance." While Weaver believes, in the *Essay*, that "common" or ballroom dancing is inferior to pantomime because it is nonrepresentational (158, 162), he nevertheless praises Beauchamps-Feuillet notation as a "great Step toward the Improvement" of dancing that entitles it "to a place among the Arts and Sciences" and brings it "to as great a Perfection as that of Musick" (171). "Perfection" in this context should not be interpreted as implying that *belle danse* is superior to pantomime, but rather that the invention of choreography as a means of codifying human motion is an achievement in the art of dance that puts it on equal footing with the long-established sophistication of music theory.

In the *Lectures*, Weaver states that there is no art without rules, and rules constitute the theory of art (131). In the *Essay*, Weaver says that "Motion, Figure, & Measure" are the basic elements of dance (86). Like Samuel Rudolph Behr (see Chapter 4.2), Weaver makes explicit reference to the Vitruvian man, but his interest in anatomy extends beyond Behr's descriptive treatment to the physics of motion. Certain "first Principles of Mechanicks," he says in the *Lectures*, can be applied to describe human motion. Weaver's discussion of these physical operations, in his chapters "On Standing" and "On Walking," follows a seventeenth-century treatise by Giovanni Borelli, *De motu animalium* (1680–1681), topic by topic.[39] It was Johann Pasch, however, who first introduced the term "mechanics" to the lexicon of dance theory: ". . . the performance of even the smallest physical act depends on the mathematical rules of art, for the body is a machine ("Dann *Corpus est machina*"), and thus is incapable of doing anything regulated that is not subject to mathematical laws."[40]

READING 4.4
Weaver

LECTURES, P. VII

These ensuing Lectures were attempted, in order towards the introducing the *Art of Dancing* among the liberal Arts and Sciences; by laying down Fundamentals, and Rudiments, explaining the Laws of Motion, Mechanical and Natural, so far as they relate to the Regular, or Irregular Position, Motion, and Gesture of the Body, and Parts thereof.

LECTURES, P. 2

So that I flatter my self, this Undertaking will derive to our *Art*, that Esteem so justly due to its Merit, and establish a Reputation equal to its Desert; when the Art of *Dancing* is set in such a Light, as may make it appear to the Ingenious, to be not only useful, and absolutely necessary to all; but also, that it is not unworthy of being introduc'd among the liberal Arts and Sciences, since we shall be able to prove, That the Rules and Institutions of our Profession are built upon the Fundamentals of *Anatomy*; agreeable to the Laws of *Mechanism*;

consonant to the Rules of *harmonical Proportion,* and adorn'd with the Beauty of a natural and cultivated *Gracefulness.*

LECTURES, PP. 130–131

Rules and Institutions for Dancing

Having in the foregoing Lectures endeavoured to inculcate, how requisite some *Anatomical* Knowledge of the Bones, and Muscles, of the Human Body; and how useful a little Skill in *Mechanicks,* would be to the Masters in the Art of *Dancing,* I shall venture to say, That without such a Knowledge, and Skill, *Dancing Masters* will never arrive to any Certainty in their Art, either in the Performance, or Instructive Part; but will always be liable to vary, and change their Manner of Performance, and Method of Teaching, according to Fancy, or Opinion. For 'tis plain, that without Rules there can be no Art; and also, that 'tis impossible to be Master of any Art without the *Theory;* since upon that Foundation 'tis, that the Practice must be built. And I flatter my self I shall be able to evince, That the whole Art of *Dancing* depends upon the foregoing Rules; and, that from an excellent Skill in the practical Part of this Art, and a perfect Acquaintance with the Rules and Institutions of it; great Improvements may be deriv'd to our Profession, which will not only a little add to its Reputation, but be also of universal Benefit to all Lovers of Elegance and Politeness.

ESSAY, PP. 86–87

Dancing therefore consisting of *Motion, Figure* and *Measure,* it is in the Nature of these, we must expect to find what we *seek.* First then as to *Motion.* The Excellence of that is visible to every one, since all things visible owe some, if not their chief Beauty to it. Life is nothing but *Motion,* and when that ceases Death brings on Deformity and Loathsomness. All the charming Variety of the Seasons; the springing Verdure and surprizing Beauty of Plants and Flowers; the murmuring Sound, soft bubling and fluctuating Noise of Waters; the perpetual Rotation of the Celestial Orbs; the Harmonious Dance (as I may say, and as *Lucian* and others term it) of the Planets, are only so many effects of *Motion.* There is so great a Sympathy between *Motion* and the Mind of Man, that we cannot but attend to, and reflect upon an agreeable *Motion,* when strongly presented to the Eye. Thus when in the *Theatre* we see a lazy or unskilful *Actor* on the *Stage,* we grow *supine* and *negligent,* and every one falls into *Discourse* with his next Neighbour; but when an *Actor* that has *Life, Motion* and *Energy* comes on, every one is then *attentive,* and the Pit observes him with a profound and respectful Silence.

LECTURES, pp. 86–87

Mr. Du Fresnoy, in his Observations on the Art of Painting, where he speaks of the Justness of Proportion, and of the Harmony they make with one another, gives us the following Measures of a Human Body.

> "The Antients (says he) have commonly allow'd eight Heads to their Figures, though some of them have but seven. But we ordinarily divide the Figures into ten Faces (that is to say) from the Crown of the Head to the Sole of the Foot, in the following Manner.
> "From the Crown of the Head to the Fore-head, is the third part of a Face.
> "The Face begins at the Root of the lowest Hairs which are upon the Fore-head, and ends at the bottom of the Chin.
> "The Face is divided into three proportionable Parts; the first contains the Fore-head; the second the Nose; and the third the Mouth and the Chin.
> "From the Chin to the Pit betwixt the Collar Bones, are two Lengths of a Nose.
> "From the Pit betwixt the Collar Bones, to the bottom of the Breast, one Face.
> "From the bottom of the Breast to the Navel, one Face.
> "From the Navel to the Genitories, one Face.
> "From the Genitories to the upper Part of the Knee, two Faces.
> "The Knee contains half a Face.
> "From the lower Part of the Knee to the Ankle, two Faces.
> "From the Ankle to the Sole of the Foot, half a Face.
> "A man, when his Arms are stretch'd out, is from the longest Finger of his right Hand, to the longest of his left, as Broad as he is long."
> [. . .]

LECTURES, pp. 89–90

There is a great Difference betwixt Beauty, and Grace; for a Body may be regular, and beautiful in all its Parts, and yet not agreeable to the Eye; for Beauty (as *Galen* says) is nothing else but a just Accord, and mutual Harmony of the Members, animated by a healthful Constitution. How much then ought the Art of Dancing to be valu'd, which, by a just Disposition, and by an harmonious Motion of all the Parts, adds Gracefulness to this just Accord, or Symmetry of the Members; and, at the same Time, by the Exercise arising from it, contributes so much to the preserving of Health?

. . . the *Motions* of the Body and Arms require a Judgment, and Knowledge in several Arts, to qualify them for a just Performance; for it is by the *Motion* of the Body and Arms, that he must express the *Design*, and form the *Imitation*; for this *Address*, and *Motion* of the Body, is not, as some are willing to believe, an Air, or Manner, natural to some; but it is a Perfection acquired with Judgment, and altogether Artificial; and to arrive at this Perfection requires a long Experience gain'd from the Instructions and Observations of good Masters; a constant Practice, and diligent Application join'd with a Genius, and Disposition very particular; and indeed, whoever designs to be excellent in this *Art*, must make it his chief Aim and Application.

NOTES

1. Raoul Auger Feuillet, *Chorégraphie ou l'art de décrire la dance* and *Recueil de dance* (Paris: author, 1700; facs. ed. New York: Broude Brothers, 1968). Beauchamps-Feuillet notation is the correct formal name of the choreographic system believed to have been invented by Pierre Beauchamps, though until Feuillet it remained unpublished. Beauchamps (1631–1705) was a dancer, dancing master, and choreographer under Louis XIV.

2. Taubert translates the second edition: Feuillet, *Chorégraphie ou l'art de décrire la danse*, 2nd ed., augmentée (Paris: author, 1701; facs. ed. Bologna: Arnoldo Forni Editore, 1983).

3. Samuel Rudolph Behr, *L'Art de bien danser, Die Kunst wohl zu Tantzen* (Leipzig: Martin Fulde, 1713; facs. ed. Munich: Heimeran Verlag, 1977).

4. According to the latest and definitive page count, by Gerrit Berenike Heiter, "Tanz in Stich und Typen—Exemplarrecherche zu Gottfried Tauberts *Rechtschaffenem Tantzmeister*," in *Gottfried Tauberts "Rechtschaffener Tantzmeister" (Leipzig 1717): Kontexte—Lektüren—Praktiken*, ed. Hanna Walsdorf, Marie-Thérèse Mourey, and Tilden Russell, *Cadences—Writings on the History of Dance and Music*, Bd. 2 (Berlin: Frank & Timme, 2019), 216.

5. Behr, *Wohlgegründete Tantz-Kunst*, 3rd expanded and improved ed. (Leipzig: Joh. Heinichens Wittwe, 1709), 22–24.

6. Descartes, in the introduction to his *Musicae compendium* (1618), a music theory treatise, writes: ". . . a Complete Musitian . . . lastly . . . must be so far a Magician, as to excite Wonder, with reducing into Practice the Thaumaturgical, or admirable Secrets of Musick . . ."; trans. by Thomas Harper, *Renatus Descartes Excellent Compendium of Musick* (London: Thomas Harper, 1653), n.p. I am grateful to Marie-Thérèse Mourey for alerting me to this connection.

7. Behr, *Andere Theil* (1703/II), 14–18. The four basic motions are subsequently listed by Taubert, 507 (without attribution to Behr).

8. Behr, *Wohlgegründete Tantz-Kunst,* 32–35. The *ars combinatoria* is invoked by Taubert (300, 501, 737, 954) when describing choreographic notation.

9. Louis Bonin, *Die Neueste Art zur Galanten und Theatralischen Tantz-Kunst* (Frankfurt: Joh. Christoff Lochner, 1712; facs. ed. Berlin: Edition Hentrich, 1996), 265.

10. Taubert, 1000–1001. Taubert's paraphrase could have been based either on Behr's 1703 or 1709 version.

11. Glon, "Les lumières chorégraphiques," 389–406.

12. Behr, *Anleitung* (1703/I), [18–22].—Ed.

13. Behr, *Anleitung* (1703/I), [28–45, specifically 35].—Ed.

14. Pasch, 11; Taubert (see Reading 4.3), 204, 292, and 1103.

15. Pasch introduces prosaic dance, 18–19; poetic dance, 29–30.

16. Pasch presents the six parts of *äusserliche Sitten-Lehre* three times: first, with regard to social dance (18–27); second, with regard to representational (i.e., theatrical) dance (47–58); third, with regard to grotesque (i.e., pantomime) dance (59–63). Only the first of these has the title *Sitten-Lehre.* Taubert presents them only with regard to *Sitten-Lehre* (490–493).

17. The inclusion of clothing in *decoratio,* as a part of visible ethics and dance theory, goes back to added chapters in Giovanni Ambrosio; see Sparti, *De pratica seu arte tripudii,* 232–233, and Smith, *Fifteenth-Century Dance and Music,* 150–151.

18. Pasch (27) cites "Arist. Metaph. text. C.I.&c."; the text can be found in Aristotle, *Metaphysics,* Books I–IX, trans. Hugh Tredennick, Loeb Classical Library 271, (Cambridge, MA: Harvard University Press, 1933), VI.I, 294–297.

19. Behr, *L'Art de bien danser, Die Kunst wohl zu Tantzen,* 18–19.

20. Pasch, 8, 12, 41, 82–84, 95, 184, 431; Behr, 52; Taubert, 293, 347, 967–968, 1102.

21. *Apocrypha,* 115 (The Book of the Wisdom of Solomon 11.20).

22. Pasch, 29, 81–82. The five universal steps are presented in Feuillet, 10.

23. Taubert, 500–502, 670–671.

24. *The Compleat Dancing Master,* vol. I, 88–93.

25. Also quoted by Behr, *L'Art de bien danser, Die Kunst wohl zu Tantzen,* p. 111; and Taubert, pp. 290–291 and 490–492.

26. The "other exercises" are fencing and equitation. The three exercises were traditionally *de rigueur* for the nobility and those who aspired to emulate them.—Ed.

27. The ten rules for proper behavior in social dancing (21–24) are omitted here.—Ed.

28. Taubert, *Vorrede*, 22, and 397–398.

29. "Der Rechtschaff'ne Tantzmeister Meditiret, und So wohl in Theoria als Praxis Informiret." See *The Compleat Dancing Master*, vol. I, 80–84.

30. Taubert, "Kurtzer Entwurff Von Der Zuläßigkeit des sowol natürlichen als künstlichen Tantz-*Exercitii*" (ms.: St. Petersburg, National Library of Russia, German. Q. XI. No. 2, n.d. [between ca. 1729 and 1746]). Aside from Domenico da Piacenza teaching Guglielmo Ebreo and perhaps also Antonio Cornazano, this is the only documented connection of a master–student relationship among the theorists in this collection.

31. See *The Compleat Dancing Master*, vol. I, 85–88, and 94.

32. Taubert, *Vorrede* (Foreword), 23.

33. A loose translation from Menestrier, *Des ballets anciens et modernes*, 3: "Tous les Arts à les bien prendre ne sont que le natural, l'esprit & le bon sens mis en preceptes, mais tous ne naissent pas avec un natural heureux, un esprit vif & penetrant, & un jugement assuré, qui ne peut estre que le fruit d'une longue experience, & de plusieurs reflexions." Marie-Thérèse Mourey, "Kultur und Identität, Theologie und Anthropologie: Gottfried Taubert im Kontext des frühen 18. Jahrhunderts," *Gottfried Tauberts "Rechtschaffener Tantzmeister" (Leipzig 1717): Kontexte—Lektüren—Praktiken*, 44, plausibly suggests that Taubert did not read Menestrier in the original, but rather selected passages translated into Latin and published in a learned periodical: *Acta eruditorum anno MDCLXXXIII* (Leipzig: J. Grossius & J. P. Gletitschius, 1683), 238–241.—Ed.

34. The phrase comes from a passage in Pasch that is quoted at length by Taubert, 292–294.—Ed.

35. John Weaver, essays in *The Spectator*, nos. 67, 334, and 466 (1711, 1712); *An Essay Towards an History of Dancing* (hereafter referred to as *Essay*); *Anatomical and Mechanical Lectures upon Dancing* (hereafter referred to as *Lectures*); *The History of the Mimes and Pantomimes* (London: J. Roberts, 1728); *Orchesography. Or, the Art of Dancing* (London: H. Meere, 1706; facs. ed. Westmead, Hants.: Gregg, 1971); *A Small Treatise of Time and Cadence in Dancing* (London: H. Meere, 1706; facs. ed. Westmead, Hants.: Gregg, 1971); *A Collection of Ball-Dances perform'd at Court* (London: author, 1706); *The Union a New Dance Compos'd by Mr. Isaac* (1707); *The Fable of Orpheus and Eurydice* (London: W. Mears, 1718); *Perseus and Andromeda* (London: W. Trott, 1728); *The Judgment of Paris* (London: J. Tonson, 1733); *The Loves of Mars and Venus* (London: J. Mears, 1717, 2nd ed. 1724). All these works are printed in annotated facsimile in Richard Ralph's monumental tome, *The Life and Works of John Weaver* (New York: Dance Horizons, 1985).

36. Weaver, *Orchesography*, dedication, n.p.

37. *The Spectator*, no. 334 (Monday, March 24, 1712); excerpt facs. ed. in Ralph, *The Life and Works of John Weaver*, 381–383. Quoted in the introduction of this book.

38. Pasch, 133–134; Taubert, 295. The publisher's catalogue: *Catalogus derer Bücher, so in Friedrich Lanckischens Erben Buchladen auf dem Kirchhofe unter der Fr. D. Wolfin Hause, oder dem sogennanten Schlößgen, nebst vielen andern, um billigen Preiß zu bekommen. Naumburger Petri-Pauli-Meß*, 1726 [four folio sides with columns]:

Gottfr. Taubert's vollkommener Tantzmeister, Leipzig 1717. 4 [quarto].

Cited by F. Herm. Meyer, "Die geschäftlichen Verhältnisse des deutschen Buchhandels im achtzehnten Jahrhundert," *Archiv für Geschichte des Deutschen Buchhandels* V (1880), 218 and fn. 25.

39. Compare Giovanni Borelli, *De motu animalium*, 2 vols. (Rome: Angelo Bernabò, 1680–1681), vol. I, chap. XVIII ("De statione animalium"), 161–175, with Weaver, *Lectures*, 96–120 (Ralph, 969–994). As Ralph points out (856), Weaver "does acknowledge his dependence" on Borelli in this section (*Lectures*, p. viii [Ralph, 867]). After Weaver, anatomical details are found in Méreau, *Réflexions sur le maintien et sur les moyons d'en corriger les défauts* (Gotha: Mevius & Dieterich, 1760), [31–32], who adds terms from *ostéologie* in footnotes, not for the general reader, but only for those who intend to become dancing masters. Noverre, in his *Lettres sur les arts imitateurs en général, et sur la danse en particulier* (vol. I, letter XIII), recalls having studied *ostéologie* in his youth, which taught him about the body's levers and hinges ("les leviers et les charnières," 128); he describes the four basic motions; and recommends Borelli for further information on "les forces musculaires" (187–188). There is an interesting early twentieth-century echo of this detailed anatomical analysis of movement in Luigi Albertieri, *The Art of Terpsichore: An Elementary, Theoretical, Physical, and Practical Treatise of Dancing* (New York: G. Ricordi & Co., 1923), 138–140. The three pages of detailed anatomical diagrams of the muscles and bones of the leg and foot are keyed to technical instructions throughout the book, but, unlike in Behr, they are of practical and not theoretical relevance.

40. Pasch, 433: ". . . daß sie mit ihrem Leibe auch nicht das Geringste thun können/welches nicht von denen *mathemetis*chen Kunst-Regeln *dependi*ret: Dann *Corpus est machina;* und also kan er *reguli*rter Weise nimmer anders als *per regulas Mathematicas* wohl regieret werden." Also quoted in part by Taubert, 176 (unattributed).

| 5 |

Dance Theory from Feuillet to the *Encyclopédie*

As stated in the introduction, the history of dance theory is disjunct. In the eighteenth century, the first rupture that illustrates this observation involves the collective achievement of the German theorists Behr, Pasch, and Taubert. Although they represent a high point in the development of dance theory in early eighteenth-century Europe, their influence on subsequent thought was eclipsed. The principal reason for this is the hegemony of French culture and the French language.

The unrivalled grandeur and fame of Louis XIV's reign made the French capital—Versailles and Paris—the universally acknowledged central source from which the effulgence of the Sun King radiated. His establishment of the *académies* of the arts set the stage for France's predominance in the arts of the eighteenth century. French became the *lingua franca* of nobility, diplomacy, arts and letters, and cosmopolitan sophistication. According to Marc Fumaroli, "The universality of the French language" created "an eighteenth century that converses and corresponds in French, even when it is not Francophile. [. . .] Paris had managed, without firing a shot, to reduce the rest of Europe to the condition of a province."[1] French dance knowledge spread to Germany, not vice versa. French dancing masters (for example, Louis Bonin, a colleague of Behr, Pasch, and Taubert) found posts in Germany; German dancing masters did not find posts in Paris. Likewise, Taubert received Feuillet from Paris, while his own work—written mostly in Danzig (now Gdansk, Poland) and published in Leipzig—was received to the east and north, and went unnoticed in western Europe.

A concinnity between dance practice, notation, and theory may have approached an ideal realization only in the early eighteenth century. This is due, in large part, to the publication of the *Chorégraphie* at the dawn of the new century. It introduced the consolidated, rationalized system now known as Beauchamps-Feuillet notation, which enabled the spread of ballroom dance— *la belle danse*—to the French provinces and internationally. The first edition sold out quickly and was followed by a second, revised edition the following year. While strictly about practice, the *Chorégraphie* is in effect a fundamental presence in all eighteenth-century writing on French dance, both theoretical and practical. In the new dance treatises that followed in France, England, Italy, Spain, and Portugal, a new format was established. Theoretical content shrank, and what remained lacked the intense focus and rigor of theory in the German sources. With theory treated summarily in the opening section, practice, based on Beauchamps-Feuillet notation, was treated at far greater length in the rest of the book. However, in the second half of the eighteenth century, dance theorists began questioning the efficacy or aptness of Beauchamps-Feuillet notation for theatrical dance or ballet. Their doubts would precipitate a second rupture in the history of dance theory.

With Beauchamps-Feuillet notation and repertoire continuing into the 1780s, the "Long Baroque" period endured in dance practice; dance theory continued to be informed by the Enlightenment; and concert music developed from the *galant* and Early Classic to High Classic.

5.1. GIAMBATISTA DUFORT (CA. 1680–AFTER 1728)
Trattato del ballo nobile (Naples: Felice Mosca, 1728).

Giambatista Dufort covers theoretical material in his "Avviso" to the reader and first chapter. The "Avviso" presents a very brief history of dance. Though Italy, he says, was the first nation to apply rules to dance (Dufort cites Rinaldo Rigoni [1468; presumably lost] and Caroso), the French have brought dance to its highest perfection in both the theatrical and ballroom genres. Along with equitation and fencing, ballroom dance or *ballo nobile* is one of the three *esercizi* taught in all the academies and colleges of Europe. It imparts grace, corrects defects of nature, and promotes health. In chapter I, Dufort describes the seven basic parts of dance: position; equilibrium; movements; *cadence;* steps and their connection; arm motions; and the figure or path (1–4). These seven parts, while nominally reminiscent of those of the Renaissance Italian writers, are described less as theoretical principles than as basic elements of practice; the chapter is less an exposition of theory than a supporting rationale for the succeeding chapters.

Dufort does not use the term "theory," but it is easy to see where his section on theory ends and that on practice begins, in chapter II (4–8), with the foot positions described verbally and in Feuillet notation. The invention of the five positions, attributed to Pierre Beauchamps in the late seventeenth century, can be considered a watershed event in marking the official divide between theory and practice. This moment in dance history is commemorated in Dufort and subsequent treatises at the point where theory ends and practice begins: that is, the abstract principles of symmetry, bearing, equilibrium, and stance on one side; on the other, the physical reality of standing up and setting one's feet in motion.

READING 5.1
Dufort (trans. Russell)

From Notice to the Reader (n.p.)

This dance [*Ballo Nobile*, i.e., ballroom dance, as opposed to theatrical dance] is one of the three noble exercises taught in every academy and college of Europe: equitation, fencing, and dance. What ultimate perfection and grace [it imparts] to all well formed persons, and what defects it conceals in those to whom Nature has been ungenerous in her gifts!

This is the noblest, most graceful diversion of sovereign courts as well as principal towns. And truly nothing is more magnificent than those ceremonial balls at which no one is admired more, and compared more favorably to others, than they who know how to dance to perfection.

This noble exercise, never violent, ever temperate, in addition to being requested and expected of persons of distinction, serves equally those who need physical activity to maintain their health.

PP. I–4
Chapter I

ON DANCE AND ITS COMPONENT PARTS

Dance is an art of organized bodily movement for the purpose of giving pleasure to spectators.

Acquisition of such an art requires knowing the rule for setting the feet on the floor, balancing the body, moving it in time with certain ornaments and lithe steps and coordinated arm movements, and finally knowing how to make a good impression in which all these things find their fulfillment.

And proceeding logically in an exposition of all the parts of noble dance, from the simplest to the most complicated, and in passing, to pause here and there, we will give first place in this treatise to the positions of the feet, so that everyone will know how it is done gracefully, and the right way to set the feet on the floor, and to avoid all the other, false ways that have no place in dancing. Secondly, we will speak of the balance that the body should keep when dancing, and will show how necessary it is to know how to use it. In third place, the feet being placed on the ground and the body balanced, we will show how one must move; and will indicate all the movements that can ever be used in dancing, and the full use to which they can be applied. Then proceeding to steps and the motions of which they are composed, we will speak in the fourth place of *cadence* and meter, ignorance of which makes it impossible to form any step in dancing. In fifth place we will describe all the steps in noble dance, one by one, and treating them analytically we will show their position, balance, movements, and timing [*il valore*]; and these things will be seen not only in words but also in the [choreographic] signs with which each chapter that treats of them will be accompanied and adorned. Next, in sixth place, we will treat of the movements of the arms, another essential part of dance. And in seventh place we will treat of the figure, or path, along which dancers can put into action everything that will be demonstrated in the preceding chapters.

5.2. BARTHOLOME FERRIOL Y BOXERAUS

Reglas utiles para los aficionados a danzar (Capoa: Joseph Testore, 1745).

Dufort and Ferriol y Boxeraus reflect the spread of Feuillet notation to southern Italy. Dufort was written in Italian and published in Naples, Ferriol written in Spanish and published in nearby "Capoa" (Capua), both cities being then part of the Kingdom of Naples and under Spanish rule. Ferriol's book is divided into three "treatises." The first contains twelve chapters, the first ten of which treat theoretical subjects: the origin of dance; its utility; the usefulness of theory; how to choose a dancing master; reasons for disapproval of dance; appraisal of dancers; dress; avoiding errors in dancing; the ceremony of balls; and etiquette. Chapter 11, in which the five foot positions are introduced, marks the commencement of the practical portion of the book, which is more extensive than that in Dufort. Treatise II concerns the arms in dancing; and treatise III contains instructions, with Beauchamps-Feuillet notation, for specific dances.

Unlike Dufort, Ferriol uses the word *theory* prominently and attempts to define it. However, though he refers to precepts, principles, and causes, his remarks apply more to the arts in general than to dance in particular. His ostentatious quotations from classical authorities serve only to advertise his own erudition and to dignify the arts, and therefore dance by association. To prove that dance and music are of equal antiquity, he detects various numerical parallels, mostly based upon the number five, between vaguely understood theoretical concepts from early music and elementary elements of dance practice. While these parallels sound impressively learned, in fact they are purely coincidental and factually unreliable, and even if they did make sense, they would prove nothing about the relative ages of music and dance. The spurious passage concludes, however, with a striking analogy: thanks to their purported parallels, dance and music "speak as if in unison: the man, an animate instrument when performing [dance], creates the most tasteful delectation for the eye, just as all the smooth subtleties [of music] are perceived by the ear."[2] The image of man as an "animate instrument" ("animado instrumento") is similar to (though in no way influenced by) Pasch's corporeal machine and Weaver's mechanical-anatomical analysis of the physics of movement.

READING 5.2
Ferriol y Boxeraus (trans. Russell)

PP. 2–3

To define art in general is quite easy, as Cicero demonstrates with the following words, in my translation: *it is the aggregate of many precepts directed to a single end.* The distinction between the liberal arts and mechanical exercise is common knowledge: the mechanical faculty is that which concerns anything visible; the liberal is that which concerns everything knowable. From this brief comparison, it is evident that our art is of the second species; for what needs to be known is apprehended purely through intellection, since even after it is performed nothing visible remains. The reasons for its usefulness, sociability and decorousness will be briefly recommended in the following chapters; and the signs for the steps and movements will be explained in the [chapters on] teaching and training, bringing them to the level of clarity and correctness that they have and enjoy in the courts of Dresden, Berlin, Vienna, London, Paris, Lisbon, and Naples, and have always held the most distinguished place in this metropolis, the most fecund nurturer of talents.

P. 21–22

Chapter III

ON THE USEFULNESS OF THEORY IN THIS ART.

Authorities affirm that theory is essential to all the arts, although there are some who say that only practice is required; I call this a manifest error, because while practice is very useful, who will not concede that the accompaniment of theory makes it better, because theory teaches us the principles of things, and the causes, which practice alone does not do; as Aristotle says: *Tunc scimus cum causas cognoscimus,* ". . . we only have knowledge of a thing when we know its cause."[3] But follow this statement where it leads and you will find, at the end: *in arte, & doctrina plus esse precidii, quam in natura,* in art and doctrine there is more precision than in nature. What would art be, were it not defined[?].

[. . .]

PP. 24–25

They who have little appreciation of art should listen to how M. T. Cicero praises its grandeur and excellence, saying: Art is a surer captain or leader than nature, though it is clearer to men of understanding. And Quintilian suggests the same in this example: "When the fertile earth brings forth much fruit, it is due more to the laborer who sowed it, than to the earth's bounty." And experience clearly teaches that no one who lacks art attains perfection, because those who lack it are as if walking toward a cliff without a guide, and like those who work at night without a light; for art is the light and the guide; and rightly it can be said that those who act in ignorance know nothing. I do not wish to elaborate any further (although there is much I could say on this subject), and will conclude by saying, with Juan Pontanos: *Cum ars preceptis constet sequiturque rationem nulus artifex bonus esse potest, qui nec facit, nec moderatur, nec artis sua precepta servat*: "Since all art consists entirely of precepts and follows reason, there can be no good artist who neither conforms to, nor is controlled by, nor obeys the precepts of art."

5.3. PIERRE-ALEXANDRE HARDOUIN

[Ms., copied by Jean-Baptiste Médor], "premier Moyen, portrait du Maitre" (Caen, Archives départementales du Calvados, Fonds Médor, Cote 2E697).
[Print] *Phénomène imprévu, ou La Danse en déroute* (Caen: 1748; Rouen Bibliothèque municipale, Mt p 4848-3).

This is the most recently discovered historical source in this book, suggesting that there are still more of them out there.[4]

An extraordinary dancing master's document, existing in both manuscript and printed form (dated 1748), it testifies to a flowering of dance-theoretical sophistication in midcentury France, extending even to the provinces. The author, Pierre-Alexandre Hardouin, of Caen, devised an elaborate, rigorous examination for anyone aspiring to the title of dancing master, to measure professional competence in four areas of expertise, each described or tested by a different method or procedure, which he calls a *moyen*: (1) a "portrait" of the perfect dancing master, to serve as a guide and a standard for evaluation;

(2) dance theory, an extended battery of questions and answers, possibly for oral examination; (3) composition, requiring written assignments in choreographic notation; and (4) execution, requiring various demonstrations of unrehearsed solo performance. The examination would be administered in the Hôtel de Ville of Caen and submitted by mail to the Académie royale de danse in Paris for evaluation.

The first section ("portrait of the [dancing] master") includes the various "scavoirs" or fields of knowledge in which a dancing master must be conversant, including those already named in Weaver and the German theorists (see Chapter 4), along with new ones like *dessein* (i.e., drawing, "la Dance étant un dessein continuel"), *l'obtique* (i.e., optics, "L'art de la vision, et de la perspective"), and *osthéologie*, the branch of human anatomy focusing on the human skeletal system. Hardouin also includes reading and writing—a reminder that literacy itself could not yet be assumed to be part of a typical dancing master's skill set—as well as the ability to read and compose in choreographic notation.[5] Above all, he says, a dancing master should be a great *naturaliste*, with at least a general notion of all the arts and professions, in order that his ballets copy nature and real-life experience.

The section on theory ("the theory of dance reduced to a single point of view") is a veritable, rapid-fire catechism, beginning with the essentials: "What is dance?" There are 118 questions in all, including 41 additional, unanswered questions in the printed version.[6] Much information from Feuillet—that is, terminology, rudiments, and rules—and contemporary ballet practice is covered in verbal form only, with new details and terminology, but without describing technique itself; this is another example of the theory of practice, or *executio* according to Pasch and Taubert. There are also questions on what Pasch and Taubert called prosaic dance (bows, handling of the hat), and on the science of movement as in Weaver's *Anatomical and Mechanical Lectures* (bones, articulations, aplomb, center of gravity). Notably, in answer to the question, "What are character or characteristic passages in all [kinds of] dances?," Hardouin unmistakably anticipates Cahusac and Noverre with regard to the espressive limitations of *belle danse*:

> . . . there are various characters and, one might say, as many different ones as there are different passions; but ordinarily in the gentle character one almost always dances with the legs only, although really the body, head, arms, and eyes ought also to be put to work, but imperceptibly and with much taste and grace, etc. In the furious, violent etc. character, on the other hand, the legs work hard, as do the other parts of the body.[7]

In the print, at the end of his questions—all of which come under the rubric of "Théorie"—Hardouin addresses the reader: "To encompass all the precepts of this art, Monsieur, I would have to extend this chapter infinitely."[8]

READING 5.3
Hardouin (trans. Russell)

[MS., N.P.]

premier Moyen. portrait du Maître.

The good master should have a deep knowledge of language, that is, the language used by distinguished persons, because if he knows nothing but the slang or dialect of his region, he will be able to make himself understood only among lowly artisans and thieves.

The esteemed master should know how to read, in order to study history, lacking knowledge of which he is unable to compose ballets without falling into error: he will make Romans dance like Greeks, and Greeks like Romans; he will dress a hero as a pope, and a pope like a hero; he will arm ancient fighters with modern weapons; will give fire to Bacchus and a jug to Jupiter; a bow to Athena and a shield and spear to Cupid; a garland to Mars and a sword and helmet to Flora; he will make the Furies dance a minuet while the Graces dance to wild tunes; he will give a hammer to Apollo and a lyre to Vulcan, etc.

The good master should know how to write, because dance contains an infinitude of precepts that even the best memory cannot retain without recourse to writing. For isn't an uneducated man one who knows neither how to read nor write, and cannot impart to others what he himself lacks?

The esteemed master should have a perfect knowledge of the *Chorégraphie*, or written dance, because he must be able to compose, and exchange with the best masters of every land, all the dances and ballets, ancient and modern, for the chamber no less than for the theater, and for this purpose he must know how to write serious as well as comic dance perfectly.

[. . .]

The esteemed master should have some knowledge of drawing, for dance is a continuous drawing and therefore a written work [*par consequent la dance ecritte*].

The good master should have an idea of geometry, dance being a species of land survey using straight, curved, parallel, and perpendicular lines, also describing angles, triangles, squares, and even composite figures; circles can be reduced to squares and squares to circles.

He also should have knowledge of optics, which is the art of vision, and of perspective, in order to plan the actions and movements of his dancers [who are] at some distance from the spectators. He should know arithmetic, because dance goes entirely by number and measure, and in addition because he may be in charge of the expenses of some grand public ceremony.

Military exercise and saluting with the long and short pike are also within his competence.

The esteemed master should know music, to have an ear attuned to all *cadences* so as not to confuse them as do certain inept Terpsichoreans lacking the slightest knowledge of dance, who have the nerve to dance chaconnes in tragic ballets as if they were gigues, sarabandes like rigaudons, musettes like tambourins, passacaglias like rustic bransles, serious dances like comic and comic like serious—which is all the more comic for having no relation to the subject announced in the program. [. . .]

The good master must have some knowledge of poetry, because dance often has a rapport with verse, especially in tragedies and comedies.

The good master should be somewhat of a connoisseur of painting, which furnishes many subjects proper to ballet; he should not ignore osteology, so as not to demand of the body something it is incapable of doing.

He should, above all, be a great naturalist, in order to copy in his ballets the characters, costumes, customs, and manners of all nations and different states, and for this reason he should have at least some notion of all the arts and professions, without which all his compositions will be bereft of the *beau naturel* that audiences find so charming.

2ᴱ·MOIЁN

The theory of dance reduced to a single point of view.

 1. What is dance?

It is an art that perfects the capabilities with which nature has endowed man, allowing him to move and walk gracefully: that which comprises the noblest parts of his education.

 [. . .]

16. How many essential qualities are in dance?

Three: measure, grace, and lightness.

17. Of what is grace composed, or, how many attractions does it require?

Five: the head held at ease; the shoulders relaxed and held back; the waist neither too high nor too low; the legs behind; and a grand sense of ease or liberty through the whole body.

18. How many waists [*cintures*; i.e., body-halves] does the body have?

Two: namely, the upper and the lower. The former extends from the hips to the head, and the latter from the hips to the feet.

[...]

98. What is the name of the point at which the dancer is in aplomb?

The center of gravity.

99. What is equilibrium?

It is a body at rest, the two sides of which, at the center of gravity, are equal.

100. How many kinds of equilibrium are there?

Two. Natural equilibrium, in which neither side changes place; artificial equilibrium, in which a change in place of one part of the body obliges the other parts to move in order to transfer weight and provide support.

101. How many meters does one dance to?

No more than two: duple and triple.

102. What makes the body jump when dancing those dances that require more gentleness?

The misconduct of the knees.

103. How is this remedied?

Soften the movements of the knees, which are formed by the lower part of the femur, the upper part of the tibia and fibula (which are the leg-bones), and the kneecap. The knee moves by a hinge-like action; this is why making the heads of these bones gently rotate out of their socket when bending makes it impossible for the body to jump, etc.

[PRINT, P. 28]

To encompass all the precepts of this art, Monsieur, I would have to extend this chapter infinitely; but, for fear of boring you, it is enough for me to report in abridged form the first elements of dance, which may still seem too long only to those who are ignorant of them. In conclusion, Monsieur, here are 118 questions on dance, and as assurance that I do not offer [only] problems, it will be my privilege to deliver the answers to you in person whenever it will please you to convene my colleagues and me in order to effectuate my proposed methods.

5.4. LOUIS DE CAHUSAC (1706–1759)

"Danse," *Encyclopédie, ou, dictionnaire raisonné des sciences, des arts et des métiers*, Denis Diderot and Jean le Rond D'Alembert, eds. (Paris: Briasson, Le Breton, Faulche), vol. IV (1751), 623–629.

La danse ancienne et moderne ou traité historique de la danse (The Hague: Jean Neaulme, 1754), 3 vols.

The Enlightenment was an era of encyclopedism, that is, the collaborative project of collecting and consolidating the world's knowledge in rationally organized, multivolume reference works. The *Encyclopédie* (including its later *Suppléments, Encyclopédies méthodiques,* etc.), emblematic of this vast undertaking, was only one of several such projects begun in England, France, and Switzerland.[9] Specialized encyclopedias and dictionaries also proliferated.

The number and range of articles on dance in the *Encyclopédie* (1751), by Louis de Cahusac and others, in itself marks a milestone in the history of dance epistemology. Cahusac contributed articles as the *Encyclopédie* was being produced—alphabetically and one volume at a time. Of the approximately 142 dance articles in the entire *Encyclopédie*, Cahusac wrote over a quarter, more than any other author, despite the fact that he died before he could get past the letter G ("Geste" is his last entry).[10] The major articles "Danse," Danseur, danseuse," and "Ballet" are his work. That there is no article titled "Théorie de la danse" in the *Encyclopédie* indicates that among the *Lumières*, unlike the Germans, theory—at least by this name—was not yet recognized as an official division of dance. Nevertheless, they used the word "theory" and other words, such as *poétique*, to express the idea of an intellectual counterpart to practice, and Cahusac's writing, in which everything *but* dance practice is discussed, qualifies as theory, albeit narrower in scope than that of the Germans. The first several paragraphs of his article "Danse" parallel the "Avant-propos" and first six chapters of his book, *La danse ancienne et moderne ou traité historique de la danse*, in which his general idea of dance theory is more fully explained. Both the book and the *Encyclopédie* articles would have been in preparation during the same period.

Cahusac repeats the now traditional definition of dance as the art of gestures that express the affections of the soul with grace and measure (vol. I, 17). He differentiates between practice and theory: whereas, he says, Arbeau, Beauchamps, and Feuillet offer only the rudiments of dance, he claims to "treat a subject new to the [French] language": "a kind of poetics of this art"—not *préceptes,* but simply *réflexions* (see Reading 5.4a). Gesture is the instrument of dance, and nature its principle (vol. I, 15). Poetics has to do with the nature, facture, and rules of making or doing something like writing, painting, or dancing. One sees the concept of a poetics of dance embodied earliest—and to perfection—in the lists of dance attributes of the Italian Renaissance writers. *Poétique,* incidentally, is not the only quasi-synonym for theory used by the *Lumières*. Taubert connects theory with "Scientia speculativa"[11]; Weaver speaks of "either the speculative or practick part of the *Art*"[12]; and Denis Diderot, in his article on "art" in the *Encyclopédie*, defines "Spéculation & pratique d'un Art": ". . . it is evident that every art has its speculative and its practical aspect: the former consists in knowing the principles of an art, without their being applied, the latter in their habitual and unthinking application."[13] This definition is reinforced in the more concise *Encyclopédie* entries on *pratique*, *spéculation*, and *théoretique: spéculation* is defined as the opposite of practice and a synonym of theory.[14] As Noverre would say, in 1807: "The wise, according to Quintilian, understand the principles of the arts; the ignorant only experience their effects."[15]

Cahusac's conception of dance theory is based on dance history. The basic elements of dance ("formed of measured steps, gestures, attitudes in rhythm that are executed to the sound of instruments or voices"), he says, have remained the same since Antiquity.[16] Therefore, one who would understand the art of dance (or any art) must seek its first causes, a notion that originated with Menestrier. "Theory will forever be the compass of the arts," he continues, and the compass points backward through time: "The organized history of the arts is thus their true, effective, and perhaps their unique theory" (see Reading 5.4b).[17] Yet as his statement on Arbeau, Beauchamps, and Feuillet implies, Cahusac's view of *la belle danse* points forward (see Reading 5.4c). Nine years prior to Noverre's *Lettres sur la danse*, in fact, Cahusac uses and defines the term *danse en action* in his article "Ballet": "In our times, ballet has ventured forth into the marvelous and inserted the *danse en action*: an episode intrinsic to the principal subject."[18] The book's conclusion, a stirring exhortation to a young dancer to transcend "soulless *copies*" and to dance expressively in "imitation of beautiful nature," indicates his conviction that, despite theory's dependence on its historical roots, a luminous future beckons.

READING 5.4A
Cahusac (trans. Russell)

VOL. I, AVANT-PROPOS, PP. XIX–XXI

I seek the truth, I hope to find it, I aspire even to have the honor of disseminating it, but I make no claim to legislating it; precepts are not what I want to write here. It is simply reflections that I write, views I point out, means that I propose. If a conclusive word escapes me, if a trenchant expression slips into my style, I want to assure my readers that my only desire is to be precise.

The subject I am dealing with is new in our language, even though we already have a *Histoire de la danse* and a *Traité des ballets*.[19] The first of these works did not touch on the subject that I have in view. The second is an excellent book, but it revolves solely around a genre that no longer exists and has only one very farfetched connection with what I believe theatrical dance should be.

The choreographies of Thoinot Arbeau, Feuillet, and that of which Beauchamps was declared the author by an act of Parliament, are only the rudiments of dance. My goal is a kind of poetics of this art.

A writer, finally, who wishes to write a philosophical treatise on rhetoric, need not fritter away his time in grammatical research. Aristotle and Quintilian presumed letters, words, language, to be, basically, understood and agreed-upon elements. I, in writing about dance, presume the same of steps and figures, which are nothing other than the letters and words of this art.

READING 5.4B

VOL. I, PP. I–8

Chapter I

ON THE UTILITY OF THEORY IN THE ARTS.

There is a fixed point from which all the arts set forth and a single goal towards which they are ceaselessly impelled to strive. Talent is indispensable to practicing [the arts] with success; to write about them fruitfully, they must be more deeply understood.

Sometimes an artist, led by that species of instinct that comes from nature and nowhere else, painlessly attains a career whose difficulty he could never calculate; whereas a philosopher who, compass in hand, describes it in an organized way, discovers its principles, and follows all its byways, would surely be out of breath at the very first step if he dared to start out at a run.

To conclude from this that practice is enough, and theory is useless, would be a gross error. Theory will always be the compass of the arts; pointing out the cardinal directions of the route, it shortens it and makes it trustworthy.

[. . .]

To excel in an art, therefore, requires not only certain necessary predispositions, but also profound knowledge of the means by which to develop it with confidence. It is the rare man who unites theory and talent, raising himself up on eagle wings toward the sublime. The common person who confuses or splits them apart loses vision, strength, and confidence: he creeps through life with the masses.

Chapter II

ON THE MEANS THAT LEAD TO KNOWLEDGE IN THE ARTS

There is a real affinity among all the arts, a kind of chain that attracts and unites them. If sometimes we fail to perceive the connections between their various mainfestations, if their linkage seems to get lost in the multiplicity of their operations, it is only because the eyes are distracted by the objects immediately before them; yet the link remains unbroken: they who search it out always find it.

When that happens it is as if one is seeing some children, siblings, fortunate by birth, raised with care, and assigned different tasks. Each of them has distinguishing features but also traits in common with the others. It is the family resemblance that is striking and cannot help but remind one of their father and brothers.

This is true, moreover, of all the arts, as of all human societies. To understand it one must go back to first causes.

Do you want to know the dominant customs of a flourishing monarchy, a sagely governed republic, an intimately close family? Just consider the character of the reigning king, the spirit of the laws governing the mass of citizens, the favorite maxims of the head of a family: you have found the key. People instinctively model themselves on their masters; citizens in a republic are voluntarily slaves to their laws; children habitually imitate their fathers.[20]

This is likewise the key to the arts when one knows how to trace their primitive sources, because these are their first causes. The artist who ignores them is nothing but a clumsy machine that blindly obeys its power source, and anyone in general who busies or amuses himself in the arts, who looks for, expects, perceives only their effects, will experience only a flawed joy that constantly risks misjudgment and negation.

On the contrary, the moment one has recognized the primitive sources of the arts, it seems as if the doors to their temple open and the veil over the sanctuary is rent; one sees [the arts'] birth, growth, and embellishment; one traces them through the ages, has the pleasure of untangling the different revolutions that at certain times have interrupted their progress, or under more favorable circumstances have aided it. One soon has a sense of the combination of effects and causes; one possesses the experience of all eras, including his own. The trained artist perceives perfection and grasps it; the amateur discovers the secrets of craft, borrows selectively from them and gains assurance. Meanwhile the masses derive enjoyment and the state flourishes more every day from the redoubled efforts of artists, which theory clarifies and at the same time augments in prestige, delight, and glory.

The systematized history of the arts is therefore their true, functional, and perhaps their unique theory. Only long after [the arts'] earliest successes did philosophers write about them. They had to wait for time to resolve differing opinions on what was pleasurable to men before they were able to teach the true means of acquiring it.

READING 5.4C

VOL. III, CHAP. XII, PP. 166–168 (ITALICS ORIGINAL)

Here is a sure and simple rule: *Nature must be the sole guide of art*, and art should strive *to imitate nature in every way*.

In addition, it is always up to talent alone to realize through practice that which the precepts of theory can but foreshadow.

[You] monotonous *copies* of cold preexisting *copies*, banal subjects that consist only of mechanical and soulless motions of the feet, legs, and arms: it is not for you I have written. You can do everything you have done and can do, without even knowing how to read. Continue to define yourself according to the models and you will achieve nothing. Your existence is as imaginative as that of a Turkish dervish whose masterwork is one continuous pirouette. You have realized your vocation; I congratulate you.

But you upon whom nature has lavished her riches, lively and shining youth, ornament of the stage, darling of the public, and the hope of art: open your eyes and read. [. . .]

Up to now they have shown you nothing but ancient rubrics, the tired old routines unworthy of you. A wider and more fertile field presents itself to your view. Dare to follow the path that taste marks for you. Harken to the voice of glory that calls you. The course is set: hasten to the goal art sets for you. Think of the inestimable reward awaiting you.

Ennoble your labors. Study the passions, recognize their effects, the way character transforms them, the impressions they make on facial features, the external movements they provoke.

Accustom your soul to feelings, and your gestures will soon express them accordingly. Therefore inhabit, to the point of enthusiasm, the subject that you must represent. Your heated imagination will retrace the varied situations for you in flaming images. Draw yourself, draw them: one can tell you in advance that they will produce an imitation of beautiful nature.[21]

THE END.

NOTES

1. Marc Fumaroli, *When the World Spoke French*, trans. Richard Howard (New York: New York Review of Books, 2011), xxv and 179.

2. Ferriol y Boxeraus, 8–9: ". . . la antiguedad de la Musica, està averiguada, y confirmada la de la Danza; como que hablando de una vez, es el hombre executandola, animado instrumento, que hace participe para la mas gustosa delectacion à la vista, de todas las suavidades que percibe el oido."

3. Ferriol's Latin translation of Aristotle, *Posterior Analytics*, trans. Hugh Tredennick, Loeb Classical Library 391 (Cambridge, MA: Harvard University Press, 1960), I.II, 30–31.—Ed.

4. Hardouin's dates are unknown. His print is dated "A Caen ce 25 Avril 1748," 34. Marie Glon is the first dance historian to describe and insightfully discuss this source; see her "Les lumières chorégraphiques," 394–400. I am grateful to her for sharing her photographs of both the ms. and print with me.

5. Glon, "Les lumières chorégraphiques," 404–405.

6. Hardouin, *Phénomène imprévu*, "Second moyen," 21–28.

7. Hardouin, "la Théorie de la danse," n.p.: "Quest-ce que Caractere ou passages caracterisés dans toutes les danses? . . . il ya differens caracteres et pour dire tant il y en a autant de differents qu'il y a de passions differentes; mais dordinaire dans le Caractere tendre on ne danse presque pas des jambes; mais en revanche le corps, la tête, les Bras, et les yeux doivent beau travailler; mais tres imperceptiblement et avec bien du goût et de la grace. &c. au contraire, dans le Caractere furieux, violant &c les jambes travaillent beaucoup et les autres parties du Corps de même." Hardouin's use of the word *caractère* is equivalent to *passion* in Descartes or *Affekt* in German; see the introduction to chap. 3.

8. Hardouin, *Phénomène imprévu*, 28: "Ce chapitre, Monsieur, me conduiroit à l'infini, si je parcourois tous les préceptes de l'Art."

9. The *Encyclopédie* numbers 17 vols. and was published between 1751 and 1765.

10. I am grateful to Dominique Bourassa for the number of dance articles, which is approximate because there is no uniform reference system linking every article within a given subject.

11. Taubert, *Rechtschaffener Tantzmeister*, 983–984.

12. Weaver, *Orchesography*, dedication, n.p.

13. Denis Diderot, "Art," *Encyclopédie*, vol. I, 714: "Il est évident . . . que tout Art a sa spéculation & sa pratique: sa spéculation, qui n'est autre chose que la connoissance inopérative des regles de l'Art: sa pratique, qui n'est que l'usage habituel & non réfléchi des mêmes regles." Translation by Nellie S. Hoyt and Thomas Cassirer, *Encyclopedia Selections*, The Library of Liberal Arts (Indianapolis: Bobbs-Merrill, 1965), 4. Charles Pauli, *Elemens de la danse* (Leipzig: Ulr. Chret. Saalbach, 1756), introduction, echos Diderot: ". . . la danse a sa téorie & sa pratique; la première est la connoissance de ses premiers principes; la seconde en montre l'application; affinité indissoluble . . ." (n.p.). André Levinson's remark quoted in the introduction, on the nonempirical nature of theory in comparison to practice, makes the same point.

14. *Encyclopédie*, vol. XIII, 264; vol. XV, 448 (attributed to Diderot); and vol. XVI, 252.

15. Jean-Georges Noverre, *Lettres sur les arts imitateurs en général, et sur la danse en particulier* (Paris: Léopold Collin; La Haie: Immerzeel, 1807), vol. I, 126: "Les savans, dit Quintilien, connoissent les principes des arts; les ignorans en éprouvent les effets."

16. Cahusac, vol. I, Avant-propos, xiii–xiv: ". . . formée de pas mésurés, de gestes, d'attitudes en cadence qui s'exécutoient au son des Instruments ou de la voix. . . . les nôtres leur sont en tout parfaitement semblables." The earlier version in the *Encyclopédie*, 623, is slightly different: "mouvemens réglés du corps, sauts, & pas mesurés, faits au son des instrumens ou de la voix."

17. Cahusac, vol. I, 8: "L'Histoire raisonnée des Arts, est donc leur vraie, leur utile, & peut-être leur unique théorie." Here Cahusac echoes Menestrier, 7–8 (see Reading 3.2).

18. Cahusac, "Ballet," *Encyclopédie*, vol. II, 45: "De nos jours on a hasardé le merveilleux dans le *ballet*, & on y a mis la danse en action: elle y est une partie nécessaire du sujet principal"; also Cahusac, vol. III, 158. See Marie-Joelle Louison-Lassablière, "Une discipline en gestation: L'Orchestique," *L'Encyclopédie ou la création des disciplines*, ed. Martine Groult (Paris: CNRS Éditions, 2003), 158–159.

19. Jacques Bonnet, *Histoire générale de la danse sacrée et profane* (Paris: Chez d'Houry fils, 1723); and Menestrier, *Des ballets anciens et modernes* (see Reading 3.2).—Ed.

20. " . . . les Républicains sont esclaves volontaires de leurs Loix": an uncanny foreshadowing of Jean-Jacques Rousseau's *Du contract social* (Amsterdam: Chez Marc Michel Rey, 1762), book I, ch. 7, 36: ". . . qu'on le forcera à être libre."—Ed.

21. "Dessinez-vous; dessinez-les, d'après elle: on peut vous répondre d'avance, qu'ils feront une imitation de la belle nature." For *dessein* as a *Leitmotiv* in French dance writing, see Hardouin (Reading 5.3: "la danse étant un dessein continuel et par consequent la danse ecritte") and, later, Noverre (Reading 6.1), Despréaux (Reading 7.1), Blasis (Reading 7.2b), and Adice (Reading 7.4). *Se dessiner* does not appear in a French dictionary in connection with dance until the sixth edition of Institut de France, *Le Dictionnaire de l'Académie française* (Paris: Firmin Didot Frères, 1835), vol. I, 532: "Il signifie encore, Prendre des attitudes, des positions propres à faire ressortir les avantages extérieurs. *Cette danseuse se dessine bien.*" This means that the dictionary definition was based on an expression minted by dance theorists.—Ed.

| 6 |

Divergent Paths: Noverre

Even as Beauchamps-Feuillet notation was being perfected and disseminated, its raison d'être was being questioned and undermined. One reason for this is that Beauchamps-Feuillet notation concentrates on the lower body, whereas theatrical dance was increasingly seen as demanding the expressive capabilities of upper-body movement and gesture.[1] Another reason is that Beauchamps-Feuillet notation is oriented around social dance instruction and ballroom dancing. Even though many of its choreographies and their tunes are derived from theatrical productions, they offer no hint as to their original scenic context or dramaturgic role of the dancer.[2] While practical manuals were still teaching Beauchamps-Feuillet notation into the 1780s, theorists, basing their arguments largely on what was known or inferred of dance in classical Antiquity, began finding ballroom dance meaningless, soulless, and mechanical, and insisting that only mimetic theatrical dance can adequately express the affections of the soul. Their criticism extended to theatrical dance choreographed in the Beauchamps-Feuillet step vocabulary.

The literature of dance theory, from Menestrier through Weaver and Jean-Georges Noverre and beyond, follows a bifurcated tendency. While the spirit and practice of Beauchamps-Feuillet notation continued its reign in the ballroom, theatrical dance practice was reconceived and relaunched in a new, progressive direction, with *ballet en action* supplanting *la belle danse*. The new direction, spearheaded by Noverre, marks the second critical schism that typifies the disjunct history of dance theory. The "Long Baroque" period of dance practice ended as *ballet en action* inaugurated pre-Romanticism in theatrical dance and dance theory. In concert music, this was the High Classic era of Joseph Haydn, Wolfgang Amadé Mozart, and early Ludwig van Beethoven.

6.1. JEAN-GEORGES NOVERRE (1727–1810)

Lettres sur la danse et sur les ballets (Lyon: Aimé Delaroche, 1760).
Lettres sur les arts imitateurs en général, et sur la danse en particulier (Paris: Léopold Collin; La Haie: Immerzeel, 1807), 2 vols.[3]

In Noverre's *Lettres sur la danse et sur les ballets* (1760), the word *théorie* does not appear in the title and in fact appears precisely once in the text, where Noverre criticizes the composer of dance music who looks for inspiration in the wrong place: ". . . so far from taking the pains to acquire the first elements of this art and to learn the theory of it, he avoids the *maître de ballet*, he imagines that it is his art which elevates and gives him superiority over dancing."[4] Unfortunately, this sentence provides no clue as to what the word *theory* signifies to Noverre. Nevertheless, the *Lettres* is purely theoretical in that it does not also instruct in practical matters such as how to make steps or dance dances, as Carlo Blasis later would point out.[5] It is, however, totally unlike the other theory books in this survey and its uniqueness requires explanation.

By 1760, a theory book would conventionally be expected to express pride in the current state of dance and to recommend its benefits to those who don't yet know them. Contrariwise, easily fifty percent of Noverre's *Lettres* is about what is wrong with most of the dance of his time. His argument is couched along generic and aesthetic lines. Generically, he focuses almost exclusively on theatrical dance at the expense of *la belle danse*, the predominant style of social dance through the 1780s, but also used in ballet. On aesthetic grounds, he rejects those basic elements of *belle danse*—its symmetry, restraint, sublimated emotion, and courtly formality—that are encoded to perfection in Beauchamps-Feuillet notation (Reading 6.1a). In theatrical dance, Noverre wants to replace *belle danse* with what he calls "ballet en action," a kind of dance that doesn't yet exist except, he says, in his own work (Reading 6.1b).

The *Chorégraphie* is useless to Noverre (1760, 365): once the "rudiment" of dance, it is now its "grimoire" or book of runes (1760, 386).[6] Its ten (five true and five false) foot positions are "good to know and better yet to forget"; they are components like alphabet letters that, connected, can produce only mechanical or marionette-like dancing (1760, 277–278, 288). *Danse figurée* "says nothing . . . it lacks a soul" (1760, 127–128). As antidotes, Noverre proposes: less symmetrical, more diagonal figures (1760, 8, 183); no masks, more attention to facial expression (1760, 198–209); less attention to legs, more to arms; fewer fancy or difficult steps, more gesture; less *exécution*, more *esprit*; fewer strict rules, more soul, action, and impressions of nature (1760, 261–262).

Even if the word *theory* hardly ever occurs in Noverre's writing, there are nevertheless certain terms and passages that might suggest at least the traits of an inchoate theory. Noverre accepts, with reservations, certain traditional elements: "The steps, the ease and brilliance in their connection, equipoise, firmness, swiftness, lightness, precision, the opposition between arms and legs: these are what I call the mechanism of dance" (1760, 27). His advocacy of pantomime is based on historical precedents; also, like his predecessors, he follows Lucian in recommending that a *maître de ballet* study geometry, painting, anatomy, drawing, and music, and a bit ("une teinture") of each of the sciences (1760, 63–76). Noverre's post-1760 *lettres* include an excellent one on the anatomical knowledge that a ballet master must possess, carrying forth ideas earlier seen in Samuel Rudolph Behr and John Weaver.[7] He transmits Menestrier's *parties de qualité* (consisting of *sujet, forme,* and *figure*) and *parties de quantité* (extent), but classicizes them in ascribing them, correctly, to Aristotle (1760, 123–124). He extends Menestrier's simile of dancers' bodies to "tuned lutes" into an extended metaphor comparing the dancer to a singer whose body is like a stringed instrument that vibrates to "the language of the passions" (Reading 6.1b). Noverre's protestation "This is no metaphor," at the conclusion of this metaphor, is a purely rhetorical device (aporia) testifying to the immediacy, literalness, and passion of his convictions.

Like many writers before him, and after, Noverre declares himself the first to write a poetics of dance: "I should not be judged by the same laws that condemn a dramatic author; no man of art has written one word on the poetics of dance; it does not exist. I am the first who dares to write and who has the courage to throw out the [rustic] clogs, guitars, rakes and vielles, in order to shoe my dancers in the cothurnus of tragedy and let them represent noble and heroic actions" (1807, vol. II, 340).[8]

Noverre may come closest to articulating his own theory of dance when he compares ballet-pantomime to the other arts and finds that it most closely resembles painting (Reading 6.1c). The two arts, he says, share the same rules: proportion, contrast, position, opposition, distribution, and harmony. He is not concerned with the fact that these rules have more to do with the way dance looks to the choreographer or scenographer—or, for that matter, the audience—than with how it is manifested kinetically by the dancer. Nor is he bothered by the crucial difference between the two arts—that dance moves but painting is "fixed"—though he does observe the paradox that a painting can capture only an instant of its story, while dance links sequentially a vast gallery-full of *tableaux*; conversely, a painting lasts for centuries, but dance is instantly erased by time (1807, vol. II, 168–169).

Why all this emphasis on poetics and painting? Why did Cahusac tell the young dancer to "draw himself"? The answer is humanism: the rediscovery, translation, and emulation of the literature and arts of ancient Greece and Rome, which began in the Renaissance and still dominated Western culture in the Enlightenment. To review briefly: we begin with the aphorism of Simonides; which Horace concisely summarized in the lapidary phrase *ut pictura poesis*; and Plutarch modified further by replacing painting with dancing (see Reading 1.3); and then Menestrier was the first to link Simonides, Horace, and Plutarch with a new motto in the Horatian mold (see Reading 3.2). This cyclic process of theorization, from *ut pictura poesis* to *ut saltatio poesis* to *ut saltatio pictura,* is revived by and culminates in Noverre, who sets out to establish dance as an art fully capable of expressing ideas and images with its own communicative language (movement and gesture) and its own theory (poetics).[9]

The Greek word *schema*, used by both Aristotle and Plutarch and convincingly defined as momentarily arrested movement, provides additional support for the analogy between dance and painting.[10] "A ballet is a picture, or rather a series of pictures connected one with the other by the plot which provides the theme of the ballet; the stage is, as it were, the canvas on which the composer expresses his ideas; the choice of the music, scenery and costumes are his colours; the composer," Noverre says, self-referentially, "is the painter" (1760, 2–3; Beaumont, 9).

We have seen that beginning in the Italian Renaissance, some theorists (Guglielmo Ebreo; Arbeau; Weaver; Ferriol y Boxeraus) claimed that dance is a liberal art, though the assertion was based on their own authority and predisposition, without reference to classical sources. Though Noverre found Simonides's aphorism in Plutarch, what matters is that he traces it to a source in classical Antiquity.[11] The *Poetics* of Aristotle and the *Ars poetica* of Horace are the only treatises from that era that treat a single art form at length and in detail, and poetry is that art form.[12] Demonstrating the parallels between poetry and an art form originally considered a *métier* or mechanical art, like painting or dance, and basing that demonstration on a classical source, were crucial in raising the art to the status of a liberal art.[13] Since *belle danse*, to Noverre, was irredeemably mechanical, only a dance genre that "speaks" like a wordless painting could be worthy of that status. *Ballet-pantomime*, or *ballet en action*, was that genre.

READING 6.1A
Noverre (trans. Beaumont [1760 (1803 edition)], Russell [1807])

1760, PP. 261–262 (BEAUMONT, PP. 99–100)

Letter X

I have said, Sir, that dancing was too complicated, and the symmetrical movements of the arms too uniform, for the pictures to have variety, expression and simplicity; therefore, if we desire to approach our art in the light of truth, let us give less attention to the legs and more to the arms; let us forsake *cabrioles* for the benefit of our gestures; perform less difficult steps and put more expression into our faces; not put so much energy into the execution, but invest it with more expression; let us gracefully set aside the narrow laws of a school to follow the impressions of nature and accord to dancing the soul and action which it must possess in order to interest. By the word *action*, I do not mean anything which only makes for bustle and scurry, and a forcing of oneself to labour like a galley-slave to jump, or to depict a soul which one does not possess.

Action, in relation to dancing, is the art of transferring our sentiments and passions to the souls of the spectators by means of the true expression of our movements, gestures and features. Action is simply pantomime. In the dancer everything must depict, everything must speak; each gesture, each attitude, each *port de bras* must possess a different expression. True pantomime follows nature in all her manifold shades. If it deviate from her for an instant, the pantomime becomes fatiguing and revolting. Students of dancing should not confuse the noble pantomime of which I speak with that low and trivial form of expression which Italian players have introduced into France, and which bad taste would appear to have accepted.[14]

I believe, Sir, that the art of gesture is confined within too restricted limits to produce great effects. The single action of the right arm which is carried forward to describe a quarter circle, while the left, which was in this position, moves contrariwise in the same manner to be again extended, and form opposition with the leg, is not sufficient to express the passions; so long as the movements of the arms are so little varied, they will never have the power to move or affect. In this respect the ancients were our masters, they understood the art of gesture far better than we, and it was only in this part of dancing that they went further than the moderns. I grant with pleasure that they possessed what we lack, and what we shall possess when it pleases dancers to break away from the rules opposed to the beauty and spirit of their art.

The *port de bras* must be as varied as the different sentiments which dancing can express; set rules become almost useless; they must be broken and set aside at each moment, or, by following them exactly, the *port de bras* will be opposed to the movements of the soul, which cannot be limited to a fixed number of gestures.

The passions can be varied and sub-divided ad infinitum, and hence would require as many rules as there are modifications of them. Where is the *maître de ballet* who would undertake such a task?

1760, P. 288 (BEAUMONT, P. 108)

In order that our art may arrive at that degree of the sublime which I demand and hope for it, it is imperative for dancers to divide their time and studies between the mind and the body, and that both become the object of their application; but, unfortunately, all is given to the latter and nothing to the former. The legs are rarely guided by the brain, and, since intelligence and taste do not reside in the feet, one often goes astray. The man of intelligence disappears, there remains nothing but an ill-ordered machine given up to the sterile admiration of fools and the just contempt of connoisseurs.

Let us study then, Sir, let us cease to resemble marionettes, the movements of which are directed by clumsy strings which only amuse and deceive the common herd. If our souls determine the play and movement of our muscles and tendons, then the feet, body, features and eyes will be stirred in the right manner, and the effects resulting from this harmony and intelligence will interest equally the heart and the mind.

1807, vol. II

"Réflexions Justificatives Sur le Choix et l'Ordinnance du Sujet" (1807, vol. II, 333–343) (commentary on *La Mort d'Agamemnon*, also titled *Agamemnon vengé* [1771])

PP. 342–343

In effect, I have been forced to renounce the mechanical part of dance in order to allow pantomime to shine; dancers must speak, expressing their thoughts by means of gestures and facial signals; all their movements, their acting, even their silence must be significant, eloquent, and adapted precisely to the characteristic style of the music and the varied measure of the tunes.

READING 6.1B

1807, VOL. I, P. 135
Letter X.
DIVISION OF DANCE.

To avoid confusion, Sir, I divide dance into two classes: the first, mechanical dance or *danse d'exécution;* the second pantomime dance or *danse en action.*

The first speaks only to the eyes, and charms them by the symmetry of its movements, the brilliance of its steps, and the variety of its rhythms; by the elevation of the body, its aplomb and steadiness, the elegance of its attitudes, the nobility of its positions, and the grace of the dancer. This is only the material part of dance.

The second, called *danse en action,* is, if I may put it this way, the soul of the first, giving it life and expression, and, in seducing the eye, captivates the heart and evokes in it the most vivid emotions; here: this is what art is.

[...]

1807, VOL. I, PP. 138–142

Couldn't one regard that which constitutes perfect intonation [in singing], the effect of vocal control, as an instrument with an infinite number of strings that, in order to be in tune and sonorous, must be attached to our emotions and tuned, according to their sentiment, to all the tones and modes that properly express the various accents of the passions? These strings, no matter how well placed, will produce among themselves nothing but false and dissonant sounds if only art wills them to speak; but they will obey and resonate, on the contrary, with all the tones belonging to the language of the passions if they are touched by the soul, and if the heart determines all their vibrations.

This is no metaphor; it is an observation based on how the organ that controls different vocal sounds operates. No doubt someone will tell me that this comparison bears no relation to the pantomime actor, whose speech is not vocal. I would reply that his gestures, the animated play of his face, the lively expression of his eyes, are equivalent to tongues he has at his command; to all these instruments I would add the expression offered by music, which is the organ that furnishes pantomime with all the accents it could need.

The dancer who is concerned only with the mechanical part of his profession has far less study and research to do than he who would reunite art with the combined movements of the feet and arms. If this dancer is favored by nature, his progress will be rapid: he would have to be, so to speak, cast in the mold of the graces and constructed as the elder Vestris and le Picq were. Both these dancers brought their art to such perfection that they are irreplaceable, there being no way to imitate them and follow in their footsteps.

The physical beauty that results from the combination of stature, proportion, and elegance, set off moreover by charm, will not assure success if the person possessing these qualities lacks the taste and inclination to practice his art with the hard daily work that it imperiously demands. Those who are not so disposed will get nowhere; their professional training is grueling, their effort feeble. Others, unmotivated, tasteless, dull and shapeless, languish in obscurity; they are relegated to the rearmost rank in ballets and are called breakwaters because of their resemblance to rocks at the sea's edge often depicted in scenic backdrops.

I think it can be stated as incontrovertible fact that man is born bearing a precious seed capable of germinating to produce an affinity to some art or science; this miraculous seed, sown by providence in all creatures, does not develop in all creatures equally. There are barren soils that bring forth nothing but thorns and thistles; but there are excellent soils that guarantee abundant harvests to attentive, assiduous cultivators.

Behold the image of man in general: his diverse tastes, his inclinations, must be assimilated with diverse environmental influences and the particular conditions of every patch of soil.

The physical faculties of man, such as they are, require constant movement to develop; the muscles, levers, and hinges that are the components of our mechanism must be exercised in every way so as not to lose their mobility, their functionality, their flexibility.

Likewise the moral and intellectual faculties require instruction and cannot be perfected without persistent application and tenacious labor.

The man who is employed from birth with working the land becomes habituated to heavy labor and forced positions: his infinitely repeated motions in the same direction become a routine that he follows mechanically; the stronger he gets, the more his muscles stiffen and lose the capability and suppleness needed for a range of arm movements. Behold the man-machine, the creature of routine.

The moral faculty, in turn, cannot grow if it stays mired in ignorance: its ideas are vague and incoherent; the intellect contracts and becomes incapable of grand conceptions. In this state, man is eclipsed; he does not think, he ruminates.

But in the midst of so many inept creatures, as I have said, can be discerned men who are naturally privileged and favored, for whom study is but pleasure, and who carry the sciences and the arts incrementally toward the ultimate degree of perfection.

READING 6.1C

1807, vol. II
"Réflexions Justificatives Sur le Choix et l'Ordinnance du Sujet"

PP. 336–337

Having proved that a ballet-pantomime neither is nor can be a drama, I dare to believe that, if it could be compared to some type of poem, it is [still] only to a poem; but it is much more perfectly analogous to painting: a painting is a fixed and peaceful pantomime, while this is a living pantomime; a painting speaks, inspires, and touches by imitating nature to perfection, while this seduces and involves by being a true expression of nature herself. Painting has rules of proportion, contrast, position, opposition, distribution, and harmony; dance has the same principles. That which makes a scene [*tableau*] in painting, makes one in dance: the effect of these two arts is the same; having the same goal to achieve, they both speak to the heart through the eyes; both are deprived of speech; the expression of the head, the action of the arms, the manly and bold positions: these are what speak in dance as in painting; everything that is adopted by dance can be used as a scene, and everything that constitutes a scene in painting can serve as a model for dance; likewise whatever is rejected by the painter should be treated the same way by a ballet master.

6.2. GIOVANNI-ANDREA GALLINI (1728–1805)
A Treatise on the Art of Dancing (London: author, 1772).

Giovanni-Andrea Gallini is more egalitarian than Noverre in his praise of both ballroom and theatrical dance, though his preference seems to be for the latter. Dance has the moral value of "adorning and making Virtue amiable" (xii). His claim for the utility of dance—grace, urbanity, health, beauty, diversion, entertainment—is presented mostly in the context of ballroom dance and especially with regard to the minuet, though he also speaks well of dances that were by then long outmoded: the sarabande, passepied, forlane, rigaudon, and others; indeed, his praise of the "Louvre" (loure) would suggest he was fairly out of touch with the contemporary dance scene (177–178). Nevertheless, the principles he expounds are consistent with those of Noverre: technical skill and brilliance by themselves are meaningless; steps must signify something (53–54); and "merely mechanical" dancing is "a body without a soul" (93–97). It seems that as much as Gallini appreciates ballroom dance, he would like to see it improved by an infusion of theatrical expressivity: "A dance should be a kind of regular dramatic poem" (119).[15]

READING 6.2
Gallini

PP. XII–XIII

I shall not, for example, presume to recommend dancing as a virtue; but I may, without presumption, represent it as one of the principal graces, and, in the just light, of being employed in adorning and making Virtue amiable, who is far from rejecting such assistence [sic]. In the view of a genteel exercise, it strengthens the body; in the view of a liberal accomplishment, it visibly diffuses a graceful agility through it; in the view of a private or public entertainment, it is not only a general instinct of nature, expressing health and joy by nothing so strongly as dancing; but is susceptible withall of the most elegant collateral embellishments of taste, from poetry, music, painting, and machinery.

P. 51

In Dancing, the attitudes, gestures, and motions derive also their principle from nature, whether they caracterise [sic] joy, rage, or affection, in the bodily expression respectively appropriated to the different affections of the soul. A consideration this, which clearly proves the mistake of those, who imagine the art of dancing solely confined to the legs, or even arms; whereas the expression of it should be pantomimically diffused through the whole body, the face especially included.

PP. 99–100

Certainly the best season of life, for the study of this art, is, as for that of most others, for obvious reasons, the time of one's youth. It is the best time of laying the foundation both of theory and practice.

But the theory should especially be attended to, without however neglecting the practice. For though a dancer, by an assiduous practice, may, at the first unexamining glance, appear as well in the eyes of the public, as he who possesses the rules; the illusion will not be lasting; it will soon be dissipated, especially where there is present an object of comparison. He whose motions are directed only by rote and custom, will soon be discovered essentially inferior to him whose practice is governed by a knowledge of the principles of his art.

A master does not do his duty by his pupil, in this art, if he fails of strongly inculcating to him the necessity of studying those principles; and of kindling in him that ardor for attaining to excellence, which if it is not itself genius, it is certain that no genius will do much without it.

6.3. JOHANN GEORGE SULZER (1720–1779)
Allgemeine Theorie der Schönen Künste (Leipzig: M. G. Weidmanns Erben und Reich, 1775), vol. II.

Johann George Sulzer is better known among music historians than dance historians, for the simple reason that his general (*allgemeine*) theory privileges music above the other arts, which are treated more as adjuncts and for the purpose of analogy and comparison. Several of Sulzer's articles, notably "Ballet," were used in the *Supplément* to the *Encyclopédie*.[16] The *Theorie* is really a dictionary of terms used in the arts, showing, whenever possible, how a term used primarily in music can be applied with different signification to other arts. For example, "tone" is defined first in its musical sense, and subsequently as it applies to oratory and painting. There is no article on theory—even music theory—*per se*, the components of theory all being treated in individual articles. The article quoted here, on the rules of art (513–519), comes closest to a definition of the term *theory* in its most general sense. In it, Sulzer fortuitously uses dance theory to demonstrate by example.

Since Sulzer comes from outside the world of dance, it may stand to reason that his concept of dance theory diverges from the mainstream. It is common-sense in style, based on history and empiricism, though its historical orientation differs from Cahusac's. While Cahusac bases his idea of theory on "the systematized history of the arts" grounded in classical Antiquity, Sulzer proposes a simple anthropological evolution that skips historical details: dance practice was originally primitive and uncouth; theory began as an attempt to improve it; thanks to theory, rules have been established; good practice is the outcome. Theory, therefore, can be defined as the sum total of everything needed to transform primitive dance into modern, civilized dance.

The fundamental idea in Sulzer's concept of theory—and the most novel—is that practice precedes theory. Consequently, his rules of theory have more to do with performance and composition than with the principles of poetics, and his theory in general is primarily a theory of practice. Above all, the dancer-artist must thoroughly understand and express how movement embodies the affect and style of any dance. At the same time, theory should be concise and flexible, and not bogged down by contingencies. Ultimately, whether derived from a practice-based or a theory-based premise, the basic principles should be essentially identical.

READING 6.3
Sulzer (trans. Russell)

Rules; Rules of Art (Beaux Arts)

PP. 514–515

True theory is none other than the process [*Entwicklung*] through which a work is perfected with respect to its medium and its intention [*Endzweck*]. As long as one does not know what he wants something to be, it is impossible to judge whether it is complete or incomplete, good or bad. If we see an artist working on a certain project without forethought of what he plans to make, it is impossible to decide whether he is doing well or badly; as when we see a man walking in the street but we cannot say whether he is going the right way if we don't know where he wants to go. But if one knows the purpose and the nature of a work, he can also decide what must be done in order to see it realized as desired. Such knowledge of the necessary constitution of a thing will be called the theory of that thing. Once this necessary constitution of a thing is ascertained, the maker will draw from its theory the practical consequences; he will say: As my work must be—thus must I proceed. These practical consequences are then the rules of art.

. . . I shall now turn to the art of walking, and apply it more correctly to our case. We are both of one mind, that it would be foolish to elevate the theory of everyday walking to the same status as a general art.[17] But because our investigation has nothing to do with arts that all men learn, as it were, instinctively, but rather with the fine arts, which are bestowed to only a few men's genius, and not necessarily inborn in everyone's fine taste; therefore it seems to me that the art of dance is a better choice for comparison. Men of a certain genius, but lacking theory and rules, invented dance. Still-primitive folk helped themselves to it without troubling themselves about theory: feeling and taste are sufficient. But also there were those here and there who, being somewhat more clever than others, made certain rules that they communicated to any group of simple instinctive dancers [Naturalistentänzer] they met who were willing to accept them.

Thus was laid the first stone, the cornerstone of the theory of the art of dance. One began to reflect on the character of dances derived from nature; it was discovered that they were joyful or gentle or courtly [galant], and so forth; further it was gradually noticed that certain turns, steps, leaps, and gestures are better suited, and others less well, while others not at all, to the particular character of certain dances. Upon further investigation, it was also found that those steps, turns, and gestures that corresponded best with [a dance's] special character were those that had lightness, elegance, and a certain charm. Special attention was paid to how this happened, and this was explained and demonstrated to others as clearly as possible. Thus gradually the theory of dance developed, and thus rules were made.[18]

Now when a theorist comes along and tells a dancer that he must distinguish the different styles [Charaktere] of dance well; that one dance is serious and dignified, another merry and joyful, and a third amorous and sweet, etc.; that each style has its own identity and its own proper speed, such that, e.g., the merry dance must move more swiftly than the serious one; that every movement and every gesture, in addition to its own expression, must also be light and elegant; and whatever other observations there are of this kind: if, now, all of this is said as clearly and thoroughly as the nature of the thing allows, and is presented as an organized and intelligible system, then, I believe, we have a theory of dancing.

"Certainly."

And this theory and these rules are, I think, neither useless nor detrimental to anyone who wants someday to be a dancer.

"That may be good for dancing. But from the point of view of poetry, painting, and other arts, it may not be the case."

My friend, I have no time now to show you that the case is identical in all the fine arts. If you haven't the desire to prove it to yourself, which could be accomplished without excessive mental labor, then think what you will and fare thee well.

It is easy to conclude from this conversation that the author does not consider himself obliged to know the whole pack of rules that are to be found in all the rhetorical, poetical, and other books on art. Reckless art critics have overloaded theory with an abundance of rules that are either simply arbitrary, or only incidentally related to form and substance; without distinguishing what is essential from what is contingent in an artwork, they accept whatever strikes them as necessary and enshrine it as a rule. Where there are many paths to a goal, they compel the artist to follow only the one rule that appeals to them. Even Aristotle himself is not free of such rules.

True rules that are of service to the artist are those that teach him to judge what is essential, and what is simply useful, to the completion of his work. But more force must not be attributed to the best rules than one has in his own nature. Rules give only the direction to genius, not the strength to work; like signposts erected along roads, they are of use only to those who have the strength to walk, but to the tired and lame they impart not the least bit of energy.

Any rule that the artist, in the heat of inspiration, unconsciously discovers, selects, organizes, and arranges, he must thereafter, through the help of rules, examine and improve in every way. Some rules have to do with the mechanics of art, others with its spirit and good taste. If they are observed, the work will be free of error. For the artist who obeys them, it will go well.

6.4. GENNARO MAGRI (CA. 1730–?)

Trattato teorico-prattico di Ballo (Naples: Vincenzo Orsino, 1779; repr. ed. *Theoretical and practical treatise on dancing*, trans. Mary Skeaping with Anna Ivanova and Irmgard E. Berry, ed. Irmgard E. Berry and Annalisa Fox [London: Dance Books, 1988]).

Gennaro Magri's prefatory material indicates that the word *Teorico* in his title had aroused some negative prepublication comment; in his scathing "Warning to the Courteous Reader," Magri derides this attack for being based on trivial and irrelevant quibbles about peripheral details that had little or nothing to do with theory *per se*.[19] In his first six chapters, Magri praises theory as the prerequisite of practice: "In all arts, practice is necessarily the daughter of theory, and if the latter is ignored, the former cannot be exercised. Some may be good theorists but bad practitioners; however, it is impossible for one to be a good practitioner if one is not a perfect theorist" (46). Theory consists of "principles," "rules," and "precepts"; these include equilibrium, simple and compound body movements (specifically only the bend and rise are named), *cadence*, and utility (51–62). Citing Lucian, Magri says dancers must learn other disciplines, including anatomy (54–55). He also quotes the famous saying of Simonides as applied to dance: "As poetry is a speaking picture, so the dance is moving poetry" (48). Magri follows Dufort's format at the end of this introductory section with his chapter 7 on the positions of the feet.

Although Magri's path apparently never crossed Noverre's, he definitely read Noverre.[20] Thanks to his own professional experience as a grotesque, or comic, dancer, he reflects the reform influence of what came to be known as *ballet d'action* in his observation that certain steps in the grotesque and *mezzo carattere* genres are produced by a lack of equilibrium (57), and his inclusion, in the practice portion of his book, of noncanonic steps used in *ballet-pantomime*.

Magri also reflects Noverre's influence with regard to the waning presence of Beauchamps-Feuillet notation. His choreographic tables and notated dances use only "Contraddanze" [sic] notation, a highly simplified version of Beauchamps-Feuillet notation that shows only the tracks of male and female dancers without indicating their steps, gestures, style, or the rhythmic relationship between steps and music; these dances are generically distinct from the courtly *belle danse* repertoire. The last known source of Feuillet notation, Guillemin's *Chorégraphie, ou l'art de décrire la danse* (1784), dates from only a few years after Magri, and not only shows the debased quality of Feuillet notation writing by this time, but also marks the beginning of an approximately thirty-year period in which no systematic choreographic writing was used at all.[21] In terms of longevity and legibility, Beauchamps-Feuillet may have been the most successful notation system ever devised. Through it, Ann Hutchinson Guest writes, "The number of publications in different countries and the system's level of popularity reached a height not since enjoyed by any method of notation."[22]

READING 6.4
Magri (trans. Skeaping, with Ivanova and Berry)

PP. 52–53
[Part I, chap.] 2

HOW TO LEARN TO DANCE PERFECTLY
Those things in the world which are only practised, and denuded of theory, are only half learned. He who wishes to delve immediately into the heart of a subject, without first having applied himself to the rudiments, learns little or nothing and that little imperfectly. To learn the general rules, and to be

instructed in their particular exceptions, is the only method by which man may reach perfection in whatever he wishes to learn. To some, it seems that Practice is master of everything. I say that the Practice is an edifice which needs a foundation to support it, and this foundation is the Theory. Some wish to reach the peak of perfection through experience alone. Experience convinces, but does not persuade; it demonstrates, but does not conclude; it is an art, and not reason.

[...]

Now let us speak about the Dance. Those who have the will to learn it perfectly, if they do not diligently apply themselves to study thoroughly the principles, the rules, the precepts of our fine Art, will never know anything about the Dance but it is only through these that they will be able to dance all the possible dances existing in the world, and those that might exist; but those who, without knowing the principles, suddenly want to learn through practice this or that Dance to show that in a short space of time, thanks to their ability, they have been taught a great number of dances, these will not have learned anything and will not know how to form a step or a dance as it should be; and thus they are miserably deceived, and all that time has been wasted that they believed to have been doubly gained. Therefore there is no other means of succeeding in dancing than a long patient study of the first rudiments and then, little by little, bringing them together, adjusting them with precise symmetry and, in order to make great headway, taking them slowly. Therefore the foolish idea must be banished that one is going to be able to teach oneself a miscellany of Dances, of *caprioles*, of sequences of steps, as soon as the positions are barely known; from this it follows that, having only a light smattering of something, they suddenly wish to begin something else. Whoever wishes to learn to read, first has to know the letters, then how to form the syllables and thus gradually will achieve perfect reading: dancing is no more and no less; and whoever derides these my warnings, and executes the contrary, will find himself unhappily derided and deceived. I do not pretend other than to set forth the truth and to manifest not only what I think myself, because it is my understanding, but because through long experience, and in training the dilettante, I have found similar talents necessary.

6.5. CHARLES COMPAN (B. CA. 1740)

Dictionnaire de danse (Paris: Chez Cailleau, 1787; facs. ed. Geneva: Minkoff, 1979).

The *Encyclopédie*, according to Marie-Joelle Louison-Lassablière, was the first "dictionnaire de la danse"—that is, the earliest alphabetical organization of dance knowledge in a reference work.[23] This remark can be accepted only with certain reservations. The dance entries in the *Encyclopédie* are alphabetized but scattered among thousands of articles on a world of subjects. The first true dictionary of dance is incorporated within the *Encyclopédie méthodique par ordre des matières*, edited initially by Charles-Joseph Panckoucke. The general aim of the *Méthodique*, as we will refer to it, was to extract all the articles in the *Encyclopédie* on specific subjects, and to unite and republish them—updated as needed—as discrete dictionaries in separate volumes. With regard to dance, however, of its approximately 142 articles in the *Encyclopédie*, only 44 were selected for inclusion in the *Méthodique*. Too few to fill an entire volume, they are squeezed ignomiously—with equitation, fencing, and swimming—as a section of a volume devoted to the "academic arts," that is, exercises tradition-ally taught privately and in academies to young nobles and gentlemen.[24]

The articles on dance in the *Méthodique* are in general well chosen for their contemporary relevance, though there are many irregularities, including the egregious absence of any article labeled "Dance," and the new insertion of a large number of Noverre's *Letters*, apparently a measure "to quickly update the *Encyclopédie* by documenting reforms in theatrical dance."[25] The *Dictionnaire de danse*, by Charles Compan, with 265 articles, is, in fact, the first true dic-tionary devoted exclusively and comprehensively to dance.[26]

There seems to be no published scholarship on Compan, and precious little biographical data. While clearly connected with the dance intelligentsia of his time, he is the only writer in this collection with no direct professional con-nection to the dance world. He is reported to have been the author of several *romans* (novels), the *Dictionnaire*, signed "Compan" after the dedication but not on the title page, being his only known work on dance.[27] The dedicatee, a "Mademoiselle G******," has been identified as the celebrated dancer Marie-Madeleine Guimard, who, incidentally, was the wife of Jean-Étienne Despréaux (see Chapter 7).[28] Compan concludes his article "Opéra," following descriptions of several of the greatest female dancers of the day, with an extended tribute to Guimard as the unique paragon among them all (263).

To trace the sources of any dance theory treatise would contribute greatly to dance historiography, and to carry out such a project with Compan's *Dictionnaire* would be particularly rewarding. His title page advertises that the entries are "taken entirely from the best authors who have written about this art."[29] Some articles are attributed to their original author, some not. The article "danse" is mostly copied from Cahusac's book rather than the *Encyclopédie* article. Compan repeats Cahusac's equation of theory and history (though at variance with his own concept of dance theory), and the familiar definition of dance as an expres-sion of the movements of the soul.[30] His definition of "maître des ballets" is al-most entirely quoted from Lucian, in Cahusac's translation.[31] "Le grand bal du roi" and "règles du bal" substantially follow Pierre Rameau's two chapters on these subjects in his *Le Maître à danser*.[32] "Menuet" begins with the definition by Jean-Jacques Rousseau in his *Dictionnaire de Musique* and continues with Rameau's practical instructions.[33] "Chorégraphie" is copied from the article by Louis-Jacques Goussier in the *Encyclopédie*, based mostly on Feuillet but also on the earlier, unpublished work of Jean Favier.[34] In his reasoned consideration of the pros and cons of *Chorégraphie* in his preface, Compan alludes to the influence of Cahusac and Noverre (Reading 6.5a). Compan's definition of "grace" as the addition of movement to beauty (Reading 6.5b) seems indebted somehow to English sources—primarily, Weaver (see Reading 4.4).[35]

Compan repeats the boast that "until now no one has come forward to provide the terminology and principles of this art" (viii–ix). The irony of this by-now clichéd and evidently false claim is that Compan quotes or cites numerous writers on dance, including, in addition to those just named, Plato, Plutarch, Lucian, Arbeau, Menestrier, and Noverre, as well as major nondance-specialist authors of Antiquity such as Homer, Aristotle, Xenophon, Ovid, and even Confucius. Under "saltation" he mentions Plutarch's description of the three principal parts of ancient Greek dance (Reading 1.2; and here 6.5c), a reference he could have found in Noverre.[36]

The last paragraph of Reading 6.5c reflects a momentous transformation in late eighteenth-century musical aesthetics: the ascendance of purely instrumental music over vocal music, a process that originated with the *Affektenlehre* of the Baroque era. It was this transformation that brought us the great symphonic and chamber masterpieces of Joseph Haydn, Wolfgang Amadé Mozart, and Ludwig van Beethoven.[37] Instrumental music (sometimes called "pure" music), lacking the explanatory lyrics and libretti that vocal music had always supplied, was at first perplexingly nonspecific or ambiguous in meaning, especially to the French. Rousseau's article "Sonate" (sonata) in his *Dictionnaire de Musique* deplores the growing trend toward abstraction in music and concludes by quoting a famous, exasperated question posed by Bernard de Fontenelle: "Sonate, que me veux-tu?" (Sonata, what do you want of me?, meaning: what are you trying to tell me?).[38] Meanwhile, dance aesthetics were moving precisely in the opposite direction, from abstraction to representational clarity. What Compan disapprovingly calls "dance, today restricted to imitating the movements of a kind of music that usually expresses nothing on its own," is *belle danse*, which was increasingly perceived as being devoid of expression and meaning, in contrast to the ballet of the ancients and the principles of *ballet d'action* espoused by Cahusac and Noverre, in which sentiments and narrative were explicitly enacted. It is interesting to observe that, at the same time that dance was moving toward greater literalism (that is, word dependence), music was moving away from it—both, however, in quest of heightened significative effect.

Though the *Dictionnaire* is no theory book, a lot of dance theory can be gleaned from its pages in articles such as "astronomique," "cadence," "chironomie," "effé" [sic], "équilibre," "expression," "goût," "grace," "gymnastique," "maître à danser" and "maître des ballets," "mesure," "mouvements," "oreilles," "passion," "physionomie," "reins" (related to *à-plomb*), "révérences," "rythmique," "sensibilité," "situation," "Terpsichore," and so forth. There is no article on the theory of dance per se. However, in Reading 6.5a, from Compan's preface, *chorégraphie*, "la partie Poétique," and "la partie Historique" are named as the three parts of dance. Choreography deals with "la méchanique" of dance and therefore, presumably, corresponds to practice. "Poetics" is the term introduced by Cahusac (see Reading 5.4a). As elaborated by Compan, it includes "reflections, views, means, principles and precepts that are recommended for the perfection of an art," and it is based on nonpractical dance writings such as Cahusac's; poetics, therefore, is theory. History's status as a separate category follows Cahusac's privileging it as the cornerstone of his idea of theory.

But there is a more significant—indeed more philosophical—rationale behind Compan's three-part definition of dance. Though he does not make the connection explicitly, it appears to follow the "Système figuré des connaissances humaines," a large, complicated schematic diagram or "tree" of human knowledge, inserted as a foldout page after the front matter of the *Encyclopédie*. It is divided into three columns devoted to the three *entendements,* or faculties, of the mind: Memory, which is the basis of history; Reason, which is the basis of philosophy; and Imagination, which is the basis of poetry. It is easy, then, to see where Compan has found his *"partie Historique"* and *"poétique."*

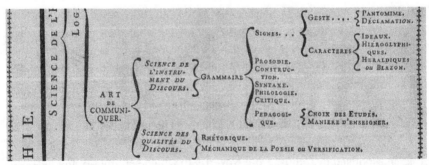

Figure 6.1. *Encyclopédie, ou, dictionnaire raisonné des sciences, des arts et des métiers:* "Système figuré des connaissances humaines," detail (Bibliothèque nationale de France, Tolbiac, Cote: Z-342, Vol. I; Text, t.1).

As for *chorégraphie*, the word does not appear in the "Système figuré," but its source can be traced to the Reason column, which is divided into three main categories: the science of God (theology); of nature; and of man. The science of man is further subdivided, seven more times: (1) logic; (2) communication; (3) discourse; (4) grammar; (5) signs; (6) characters; (7) ideograms [*Idéaux*], hieroglyphs, and heraldry (see Fig. 6.1).[39] As a system of symbols or ideograms, *chorégraphie* belongs here. Compan's three parts of dance correspond to the three basic sources of knowledge on which the *Encyclopédie* is founded.

READING 6.5A
Compan (trans. Russell)

PP. VII–X

Preface

Dance, which the philosophers have defined as the art of gestures, is indisputedly the most ancient of the beaux-arts. Ever since there were humans, there were dances. This exercise existed in every time and place; the Chinese, the Egyptians, the Persians, the Indians, etc., all the peoples of the earth have made it the object of their culture and their pleasures.

But man did not regard dance as an exercise invented only for pleasure; he sought ways to make it useful, and one can say that it justifies all these efforts, as long as he avails himself of this usefulness in the earliest stage of youth. It is dance that adds grace to the advantages bestowed on us by nature, by regulating all movements of the body and strengthening it in the correct positions. If we are born with a few imperfections, it is dance that conceals or at least minimizes them, and sometimes erases them entirely; in sum, dance characterizes only a fine education.

It was not the allure of dictionary-making that persuaded me to write this one, but since until now no one has come forward to provide the terminology and principles of this art, I have ventured to undertake the task, based on the skill, experience, and teaching of the grand masters who have written about it.

Dance is considered to have three parts: that which concerns the mechanics of dance and is called *chorégraphie;* followed by the poetics of dance, which includes reflections, views, means, principles, and precepts that are recommended for the perfection of an art; and finally the historical part, through which an artist takes possession of his own experience and that of all eras.

Most dancers and composers of ballets are contemptuous of choreography. I agree that, for them, it is of no real use, but in a work entirely devoted to dance, is it permissible to neglect mentioning the elements of an art, useless to the man of genius, but quite necessary to those who wish to be instructed and who search out the means? Upon thinking this over, I have included the article *"Chorégraphie"* in this work; as it is the most concise and clear of all the methods that have appeared, it will prove not useless to those young persons who, using it, will be more easily able to understand and execute that which the master will have taught them.

PP. XII–XIII

The *Traité* on dance, by Cahusac, and the *Lettres* of M. Noverre, have provided me with the precepts that I follow in this *Dictionnaire*. These two excellent works constitute a perfect *poétique* of dance, in which these skilled masters demonstrate that theory by itself is not enough unless it includes knowledge of the rules and the means by which it is developed. The common person, who separates theory from talent, crawls along with the masses; the man of genius reunites them and ascends toward the sublime.

READING 6.5B

FROM "GRACE, (DE LA)," PP. 168–169

Beauty is a product of the proportion and symmetry of parts, and *Grace* arises from the unity [*l'uniformité*] of internal movements caused by the affects and sentiments of the soul; this is the harmony of which it consists.

There are three *Graces*, whom the poets identify as the companions of Venus. They are named Aglaïa, Thalia, and Euphrosine; daughters of Jupiter and Diana, they always hold hands and are never separated. If they are always depicted nude, it is to show that the *Graces* borrow nothing from art because their charms are derived solely from nature. One holds a rose, another a thimble, and the third some myrtle. The poets always say they are petite and slender of form. This is to show that charm is found in small things, sometimes a gesture, or a careless manner, a smile, etc.

There are *Graces* associated with every part of the body and its attitudes; to recognize at what point the arms and legs are susceptible to *Graces*, one must watch how an adorable person dances; he will certainly discover their presence as much in the parts of the body as in the head, the neck, etc. That which is most attractive in the arms, the legs, etc., is manifest in dancing.

[. . .]

However difficult it may be to recognize *Grace*, one can say with certainty that there is no *Grace* without movement, that is, without any slight agitation of the body or of any of its parts; this is what allows Horace to define *Grace* as movement that is honorable and decent. Virgil, to express the majesty of Juno and the gracefulness of Apollo, has merely to describe the way they walk and move.[40]

READING 6.5C

FROM "SALTATION," PP. 343–344

Dance, according to Plutarch, was composed of three parts. The first was *movement*, whether by step or by leap. The second was the *figure*. And the third was the demonstration or representation of a subject [*la démonstration, ou la représentation de l'objet*]. Dance was either simple or compound [*composée*]. That which was called simple was composed only of single movements of the limbs, as in the leap, hop from one foot to the other, the crossing and the beating of feet, the forward, backward, and turning path, the flexing and extension of the legs, the clapping of hands, the lowering and raising of the arms, and the various figures that involve not only moving, but also staying still when one wished to imitate someone who sleeps, thinks, shows admiration or fear, who gazes, cries, laughs, etc.

What was called compound dance was that in which the actor added different feats of skill [*tours d'adresse*] to the movements of his limbs, which he executed while holding baskets, plates, thyrses, spears, swords, etc. The masters of true dance were the poets; they themselves taught the actors their assigned figured movements, and we read that Thespis, Pratinus, Cratinus, and Phrynichus[41] danced in the theater in performances of their own dramas.

For us it suffices to comprehend how many of the signs and, so to speak, the hieroglyphics of this art have lost their nobility and importance. Dance, today restricted to imitating the movements of a kind of music that usually expresses nothing on its own, in that earlier time expressed not only actions but also tendencies, habits, customs; it enacted the most grand events; it taught the body strength, skill, and grace; in a word, the art that nowadays is so arbitrary, unclear, and limited, in that era embraced and ruled the entire art of gesture.

NOTES

1. See Schroedter, *Vom "Affect" zur "Action,"* 443.
2. Glon, "Les lumières chorégraphiques," 508–509. The "Menuet de la Cour," for example, is a couple's ballroom dance that, in its first Beauchamps-Feuillet score (Malpied, ca. 1780) or in any other version, preserves no vestige (other than its music) of its origin as the "Ballet des Nymphes de Diane" (for three principals and a corps of sixteen) from a *ballet-héroique* by André-Ernest-Modeste Grétry, *Céphale et Procris* (1773); see Tilden Russell and

Dominique Bourassa, *The Menuet de la Cour,* Terpsichore Tanzhistorische Studien 4 (Hildesheim: Georg Olms Verlag, 2007), 5–6.

3. There are fifteen letters in Noverre's *Lettres* of 1760. These and additional letters, fifty-four in all, were collected in several subsequent editions and rearranged in varying sequences. The most complete edition is *Lettres sur les arts imitateurs en général, et sur la danse en particulier* (1807). Noverre's "Théorie et pratique de la danse simple et composée," 11 vols. (ms. [Louisbourg, 1766], Warsaw: Bibliotecka Uniwerzytercka), contains a condensed version of the *Lettres,* along with much additional nontheoretical material. For a summary of Noverre's publications of his *Lettres,* see Flavia Pappacena's introduction to *Lettres sur la danse et sur les ballets et les arts (1803)* (Lucca: Lim Editrice, 2012), 7–9, 16–18, and Appendix B (69–73).

4. Noverre, *Lettres,* 163: " . . . mais loin de s'attacher aux premiers éléments de cet Art & d'en apprendre la théorie, il fuit le Maître de Ballets; il s'imagine que son Art l'éleve & lui donne le pas sur la Danse," trans. Cyril W. Beaumont, *Letters on Dancing and Ballets* [1803 ed.] (London: author, 1930), 66–67. The first English translation of Noverre, by Joseph Parkyns MacMahon (1782), renders the passage similarly; see *The Works of Monsieur Noverre Translated from the French: Noverre, His Circle, and the English* Lettres sur la Danse, ed. Michael Burden and Jennifer Thorp, The Wendy Hilton Dance & Music Series 19 (Hillsdale, NY: Pendragon Press, 2014), 303.

5. Carlo Blasis, *An Elementary Treatise upon the Theory and Practice of the Art of Dancing,* trans. Mary Stewart Evans (New York: Dover, 1968; orig. pub. 1820), 5.

6. Diderot agrees, saying of *la belle Danse:* "This is like knowing how to solfege a song instead of how to sing it" ("Ce n'est pas là savoir chanter, c'est savoir solfier"): "Entretiens sur *Le fils naturel*" (1757), *Oeuvres Complètes de Diderot,* ed. J. Assézat (Paris: Garnier Frères, 1875; repr. ed. Nendeln: Kraus, 1966), vol. VII, third *entretien,* 158.

7. The chapter on anatomy is in *Lettres sur les arts imitateurs en général,* vol. I, letter XIII, 169–188. Having studied *ostéologie* in his youth, Noverre knows about the body's levers and hinges ("les leviers et les charnières," vol. I, letter 9, 128); he describes the four basic motions; and recommends Borelli for further information on "les forces musculaires" (187–188).

8. The cothurnus is the shoe worn by actors in Greek tragedy.

9. This paragraph is based on Arianna Beatrice Fabbricatore, *La Querelle des Pantomimes: Danse, culture et société dans l'Europe des Lumières* (Rennes: Presses universitaires de Rennes, 2017), 34–42, 61; Fabbricatore, however, bypasses the critical role of Menestrier.

10. Peponi, "Aristotle's Definition of Dance," 226–227.

11. Noverre, *Lettres* (1760), 120.

12. It should be emphasized that these treatises interpret "poetry" in its broadest sense: epic, lyric; tragic, comic, and (most significantly for dance) dramatic; style; technique; form; function; content; presentation.

13. Fabbricatore, *La Querelle des Pantomimes*, 34–35, 57.

14. A reference to the commedia dell'arte.—Ed.

15. Diderot, in "Entretiens sur *Le fils naturel*," 158, had said: "La danse . . . c'est une pantomime mesurée."

16. Jean Baptiste Robinet, ed., *Supplément à l'Encyclopédie, ou Dictionnaire raisonné des sciences, des arts et des métiers*, vol. I (Amsterdam: M. M. Rey, 1776). Most of the articles on music, as Sulzer acknowledges in his "Vorrede" (n.p.), were actually written by J. A. P. Schulz and J. P. Kirnberger. Indeed, Joel Lester, *Compositional Theory in the Eighteenth Century* (Cambridge, MA: Harvard University Press, 1992), 255, calls Sulzer merely the "organizer" of this book.

17. The entire essay is couched as a (very unequal) pedagogic conversation.—Ed.

18. It is interesting to note that Edwin Denby (1903–1983) hypothesized a similar primeval evolution of dance principles: "electing a base from which to move"; following "a formal path"; "stepping to a manmade beat"; "grace of movement"; and "a formal limitation of movement." Denby, "Forms in Motion and in Thought (1965)," *Dance Writings and Poetry*, ed. Robert Cornfield (New Haven, CT: Yale University Press, 1998), 290–292.—Ed.

19. Magri, 46–49. See also Salvatore Bongiovanni, "Magri in Naples: Defending the Italian Dance Tradition," trans. Bruce Alan Brown, *The Grotesque Dancer on the Eighteenth-Century Stage: Gennaro Magri and His World*, ed. Rebecca Harris-Warrick and Bruce Alan Brown (Madison: University of Wisconsin Press, 2005), 101–104.

20. See, e.g., Magri, 55; also *The Grotesque Dancer on the Eighteenth-Century Stage*.

21. Guillemin, *Chorégraphie, ou l'art de décrire la danse* (Paris: L'auteur, Petit, 1784).

22. Guest, *Choreo-Graphics*, 21.

23. Louison-Lassablière, "Une discipline en gestation,"165; she considers the *Dictionnaire* of Charles Compan the second.

24. Charles-Joseph Panckoucke, ed., [*Encyclopédie méthodique par ordre des matières*] *Encyclopédie méthodique. Arts académiques. Équitation, escrime, danse, et art de nager* (Paris: Chez Panckoucke, and Liège: Chez Plomteux, 1786), 312–424.

25. Dominique Bourassa, "Terpsichore in the Spotlight of the *Lumières*: Dance in the Classification of Knowledge During the Age of Reason" (unpublished

paper, read at the 20th Annual Oxford Dance Symposium, New College, Oxford, April 2018). I am grateful to the author for permission to use material from her presentation.

26. By way of comparison, the long tradition of dictionaries of musical terms begins, in Europe, in the early Renaissance (Johannes Tinctoris, ca. 1494).

27. Pierre Larousse, "Compan, Charles," *Grand dictionnaire universel du XIXe siècle* (Paris: Administration du Grand Dictionnaire universel, 1869), vol. IV, 770.

28. Antoine-Alexander Barbier, *Dictionnaire des ouvrages anonymes et pseudonymes*, 2nd ed. (Paris: Barrois L'ainé, 1822), vol. I, 286. I am grateful to Dominique Bourassa for this reference.

29. "Le tout tiré des meilleurs Auteurs qui ont écrit sur cet Art."

30. Compan, *Dictionnaire*, vii–xvi (preface), and 111–123 (copied chiefly from Cahusac, bk. I, 13–21, 59–64, 130–141, 165–167); unattributed. See Louison-Lassablière, "Une discipline en gestation," 165.

31. Compan, *Dictionnaire*, 205–214; attributed, within quotation marks.

32. Compare Compan, *Dictionnaire*, 20–25, with Pierre Rameau, *Le Maître à danser* (Paris: Chez Jean Villette, 1725; facs. ed. New York: Broude Brothers, 1967), 49–59.

33. Compan, *Dictionnaire*, 231–239; Rameau, *Le Maître à danser*, 76–103; Rousseau, *Dictionnaire de musique*, 279–280.

34. Compan, *Dictionnaire*, 83–99; *Encyclopédie*, vol. III, 367–373. Goussier's two accompanying plates present a hybrid of Feuillet and Favier notation without any delineation of which details belong to which system. Compan presents Feuillet's text only, which, lacking the figures, is essentially nonfunctional. As in the *Encyclopédie* article, Compan makes no distinction between *chorégraphie* as dance notation and the *Chorégraphie* of Feuillet.

35. Compan, *Dictionnaire*, 168; Weaver, *Lectures*, 89–90. The idea reappears midcentury in Edmund Burke, *A Philosophical Enquiry into the Origin of our Ideas of the Sublime and Beautiful* [1st ed. 1757], ed. James T. Boulton (Notre Dame, IN: University of Notre Dame Press, 1958), 119; and, especially with reference to dance, William Hogarth, *The Analysis of Beauty* [1753], ed. Ronald Paulson (New Haven, CT: Yale University Press, 1997), 50–51, 109–110.

36. Noverre (1760), Letter VII, 120; (1807), Letter XXI, 267.

37. Haydn (1732–1809) was an almost exact contemporary of Noverre, and both Haydn and Noverre lived long enough to have heard Beethoven's Fifth and Sixth Symphonies.

38. Rousseau, *Dictionnaire de Musique*, 459–460. For a translation of the entire passage, see Piero Weiss and Richard Taruskin, *Music in the Western World: A History in Documents* (New York: Schirmer Books, 1984), 287–288.

39. *Idéaux* is also the category in which Menestrier's *fleurons* belong. It should be further noted that signs also branch off to another category: gestures, which is subdivided into pantomime and declamation.

40. The last two paragraphs of this excerpt can be traced to "Criton, ou de la grace et de la beauté," in an anthology: *Les Graces* (Paris: Laurent Prault, and Bailly, 1759), 218–224; also in an anonymous translation of Sir Harry Beaumont (*nom de plume* of Joseph Spence), *Crito: or, A dialogue on beauty* (Dublin: George Faulkner, 1752).—Ed.

41. Ancient Greek poets, dramatists, and actors.—Ed.

〜〜〜〜〜〜〜〜〜〜〜〜〜〜〜〜〜〜〜〜〜〜〜〜〜〜〜

|7|

The Nineteenth Century and Fin de siècle: Practice Ascendent

At the beginning of the nineteenth century, according to Stephanie Schroedter, Paris became the "focal point" of a "new impetus" in dance theory writing, the "common denominator" of which was to "have all been developed against the backdrop of practical experiences, thus turning practice and theory into an inseparable unit."[1] Moreover, within this unit, dance theory abruptly weakened and ceded priority to dance practice. Most works that purport to deal with theory, and may even use the word in their title, are really concerned with practice, that is, positions, steps, notation, and how to perform specific dances. Even works that do present some notion of what inheres in theory tend to jump quickly from the abstract to the physical, from the ideal to the real: "walking," a paradigm of equipoise and adroitness and the physics of human locomotion in Weaver's *Anatomical and Mechanical Lectures upon Dancing*, is reduced to the *pas marché*.

As definitions of theory and practice increasingly blurred, "theory" became by default whatever content—no matter how trivial or tangential—precedes the five positions.[2] The traditional line of demarcation between theory and practice, established by Dufort and located precisely where the five foot positions are introduced, was obliterated in 1797 by J. J. Martinet: "The entire theory of the art of dance, having been founded upon the five natural positions, from which one should never diverge . . . I shall place at the reader's disposal for perfect self-instruction."[3] The status of dance notation also was affected by the blurring of theory and practice. Theory and various notation systems had been developing side by side, though in a nonparallel and unsynchronized relation. By the early nineteenth century, notation was incorporated into—indeed, considered synonymous with—dance theory and eventually would be seen as theory's defining feature.[4]

Noverre's influential animadversion to Beauchamps-Feuillet notation led to a critical period in which the very idea of dance notation was interrogated. For a long period after the 1780s, on the one hand, a few new systems, based on principles of visualization quite different from that of Beauchamps-Feuillet notation, were invented but not widely adopted; on the other, numerous published dance instructions eschewed notation entirely in favor of purely verbal instructions—a method better suited to social dance than ballet. As a result, Friedrich Albert Zorn, who invented his own notation system, lamented at the end of the nineteenth century that dance was not being adequately preserved for posterity: ". . . what is left us of the works of old—of the last century—even of the last few decades?"[5]

7.1. JEAN-ÉTIENNE DESPRÉAUX (1748–1820)

Mes passe-temps: Chansons suivies de L'art de la danse, Poëme en quatre chants, Calqué sur l'Art Poétique de Boileau Despréaux, 2 vols. (Paris: author, 1806).

"Danse-Ecrite, ou Terpsi=Coro=Graphie, ou nouvel Essai de Théorie de la Danse, par J. E. Despréaux." Ms. (Paris, Bibliothèque-Musée de l'Opéra, Fonds Deshayes F-Des P 4, 1815[?]).

The first new choreographic system after Feuillet's *Chorégraphie* in 1700 was invented by Jean-Étienne Despréaux (1748–1820), the husband, it will be recalled, of the dancer Marie-Madeleine Guimard. Despréaux was active in many roles in the Paris dance world of the Opéra and the Napoleonic court— dancer, dancing master, *répétiteur, maître de ballets*—and in arts officialdom. He was also a choreographer in both senses: a composer of dances and the inventor of a new notation system. His best-known published work is *Mes passe-temps*, which contains a poem in four cantos, "L'art de la danse."[6] This poem is modeled after a famous work by Nicolas Boileau-Despréaux, *L'art poétique* (1674), which in turn was modeled after Horace's *Ars poetica*. The two Despréaux names are sheer coincidence, but by printing their poems on facing pages, our J.-É. Despréaux makes explicit the parallelism in word and spirit between poetry on the left and dance on the right.[7]

Because of the necessity to parallel Boileau-Despréaux's text, the subjects covered in Despréaux's poem seem somewhat jumbled categorically. The first canto covers the requisites of a good dancer, and a short history of dance; the second, the characteristics and rules of French and foreign dance, exemplary dance personnages from Antiquity, comportment at a ball, and the faults of contemporary dancers; the third, theatrical dance in general; and the fourth, pantomime, *ballet d'action*, and the fields of knowledge required of a dancing master (quoting from Lucian).[8] The poem introduces no new theoretical ideas. It reflects Noverre's influence in its epigraph quoting the Simonides *dictum* in alexandrine verse:

Des Ballets d'actions, la sensible peinture,
Est pour aller au coeur la marche la plus sûre.[9]

He also paraphrases Cahusac: "Occupez-vous sans cesse à vous bien dessiner" ("Ceaselessly endeavor to draw yourself well").[10]

After his death, Despréaux's collection of books and other belongings was offered for sale in a seven-day auction. The book sale catalogue reveals the extensive and well-balanced library of a learned and intellectually curious bibliophile, with a particularly noteworthy collection of books on music and dance, including the works of Plutarch, Menestrier, Bonnet, Cahusac, Noverre, Compan, and Berchoux.[11] His interest in the history of choreography is reflected in his rare copy of Arbeau's *Orchesographie* (1589 ed.), annotated by himself, and other treatises from the Renaissance to his own day.[12] While he did not possess an original copy of Feuillet's *Chorégraphie*, he did possess two later eighteenth-century sources that present condensed expositions of Beauchamps-Feuillet notation. Among his other "objets de curiosité" was the *pochette* purportedly presented to Beauchamps himself by Louis XIV.

Despréaux's most important original work is his own choreographic system, which survives in manuscript: "Danse-Ecrite, ou Terpsi=Coro=Graphie, ou nouvel Essai de Théorie de la Danse, par J. E. Despréaux." Quoted as an epigraph beneath the title is a sentence from Plutarch: "Dancing consists of movements and positions, as melody does of its notes and intervals. In the case of dancing the rests are the terminating points of the movements" (see Reading 1.3). This quotation establishes a spiritual connection to Antiquity rather than any direct association with the elements of written dance (*danse-écrite*). In the following paragraph, Despréaux explains the derivation of his title:

Orchesographie is the authentic name for this work: but since the Greek word *orchestra* refers to dance or a room for dancing, and since for more than a hundred years it has come to designate the place [in a theater] occupied by the musicians, I have decided not to use this word for the title of a work on dance. The *Corégraphie* of <u>Beau-Chant</u> [*sic*] has been copied uselessly [illegible], therefore I would prefer a totally different name. The title of a charming ballet by Gardel (*La Dansomanie*) encourages me to foresake the rules of grammar, and I have given this work the name of <u>Terpsi coro graphie</u>, and I dedicate it to my Terpsichore. ([4r])

Despréaux knew about the term and the book *Orchesographie*, of course, from the exemplar in his own collection (as well as from his copy of Compan).[13] He wishes to dissociate his new system from Beauchamps-Feuillet notation, by then utterly *passé*. He justifies the novelty of his own title by citing *La Dansomanie* (1801; "dance-fever"), a neologism of the previous decade. And we can easily surmise that his Terpsichore is none other than his wife, *la* Guimard.

Despréaux's notation system is the first significant new system to be invented since Beauchamps-Feuillet, and it is innovatory in two significant ways. First, it introduces what appear to be stick figures viewed vertically, as opposed to Feuillet's track figures that show not the dancer, but his or her horizontal foot positions and path on the floor as viewed from overhead. Despite the fact that Despréaux indicates the body only from the waist down, the verticalized viewpoint is the earliest choreographic attempt to incorporate Noverre's emphasis on the whole body's engagement in dance movement. This can be seen as the first stage of a "body-building" process, so to speak, in which choreography rises from the flat floor and the dancer's image is increasingly fleshed out with human detail—a viewpoint, in other words, more attuned to anatomy and figure painting than to cartography and plane geometry.[14]

Despréaux's second innovation is his introduction of new symbols for positions and movements based on letters of the alphabet, which may well have been inspired by his study of Arbeau. In fact, Despréaux's manuscript "Théorie de la danse" is entirely based on this new choreographic system and contains several lists of the positions and their symbols. Despréaux's letter-code system allows the dance instructions to be fitted concisely below a musical staff like the words of a song, a format possibly inspired by Arbeau, and later incorporated in the choreographic systems of E. A. Théleur, Arthur Saint-Léon, and Friedrich Albert Zorn. In Despréaux's letter-code, vowels stand for foot positions, and what look like pictographs of the legs are also letters, as Despréaux interprets them: "X" indicates *croisé*; a capital "L" signifies the right leg seen in profile, and a backward capital "L" signifies the left leg; "J" is an *élevé*; and a slightly unbent "Z" is a *plié* on the flat of the foot. Additional consonants are used to signify conventional dance steps in the style of choreography called "Wortkürzel" by Claudia Jeschke, and "Words and Word Abbreviations" by Ann Hutchinson Guest.[15]

Note how Despréaux effectively leapfrogs from the title "Theory" to the first lesson of practice, the foot positions ([44v]).

THEORY OF DANCE
Introduction

> It is necessary to teach students the positions of the feet and the movements originating from the hips, knees, and ankles, which will give them the basic principles of dance and the essential knowledge that precedes walking, dancing, and jumping.

Article 1

Question: How many positions of the feet are there?

Answer: Seven, counting the fourth behind and the fourth *croisé*.

Q.: What are their names?

A.: A, E, I, O, U, X.

[A = first position; E = second position; I = third position; O = fourth position, right foot forward; U = fourth position, right foot behind; X = fifth position, feet crossed heel to toe; OX = fifth position with one foot forward as in fourth position. Of these letter-symbols, only X can be considered a pictograph.]

Flavia Pappacena, who has been instrumental in drawing dance scholars' attention to Despréaux, believes that his letter-codes, notation, dance theory, and pedagogy were based in some sense upon a linguistic framework, leading him, she writes, "to interpret the term 'Théorie' as 'grammar'. . . As in school, Despréaux conceives of 'theory-grammar' as a support for practical study, based on a methodology of analysis and breaking down movement, which assumes familiarity with the etymology of the terms, understood as structural definitions."[16] The word *grammar* or *grammaire* appears precisely once in Despréaux's work, in the title-page paragraph quoted earlier, and his usage of it indicates clearly that his understanding of its meaning is vague and inaccurate: grammar has nothing to do with the creation of neologisms; moreover, he rejects *grammaire* to create an imaginative new title of his own. *Grammar* did, later on (beginning perhaps with G. Léopold Adice), become the most popular of several terms loosely associated with, or substituting for, theory. Conceptually, however, this usage of the word *grammar* is as inappropriate as it would be to assign a linguistic basis to music just because pitches are designated by the names of letters (A, B, C . . .) or of syllables (do, re, mi . . .).

The term *grammar* seems to have entered the lexicon of dance by way of Compan's conjectural interpretation of the "Système figuré des connaissances humaines" in the *Encyclopédie* (see Reading 6.5) and its explanatory text in the "Discours préliminaire des editeurs," by Jean Le Rond d'Alembert: "Grammar includes the science of characters, pronunciation, structure, and syntax." Choreography fits within the subgroup *Caracteres*: "Characters are either ideograms, hieroglyphs, or heraldry."[17] Therefore, it corresponds to a part of grammar, not the whole, which includes elements both mechanical (the parts of speech, subject-verb agreement) and rhetorical (syntax, coherence, meaning).[18] Grammar, therefore, shows how the layered elements of language cooperate organically to produce meaning. By analogy, grammar in the world of dance should be concerned with dance composition and the analysis of actual dances, precisely the generative processes Gottfried Taubert describes when he compares the art of dance to oratory:

> . . . just as a worthy professor instructs his student in the art of speaking by beginning with single letters, then progressing to syllables, sentences, periods, and paragraphs, as preparation for the composition of an oration; so too will a compleat dancing master consider first of all how he should present information to his student in an orderly sequence, one bit at a time, that is, from the smallest and most rudimentary step and motion to the biggest and most imposing, so that subsequently he will be able to dance by connecting such details confidently and coherently.[19]

In comparison, the new notation systems of the nineteenth century are rather like illustrated dictionaries or *catalogues raisonnés* of their respective symbol systems. They provide no indication of any discrete element's function in connection with other elements in a dance composition, and thus—apart from differences in style, technique, aesthetics, and so forth—provide no more or less grammatical information than is contained, say, in the Feuillet step-tables.[20]

In my opinion, there was no reorientation of dance-theoretical thinking, circa 1800, to a new paradigm based on deep-structure grammatical principles. Rather, the post-Noverre crisis in notation was a collateral effect of the growing emergence of ballet which, as a dramatic, storytelling medium, with character development intensified through pantomime, presented seemingly insurmountable complexities for notation, while its plot narration was provided by printed programs and libretti. The ultimate significance of the new emphasis on a written language and so-called grammar of dance is that dance theory, which originally justified dance on the basis of its kinship with the quadrivium, now does so on the basis of its relationship to the trivium—an incipient paradigm shift from science and mathematics to grammar and rhetoric.

7.2. CARLO BLASIS (1797[?]–1878)

Traité élémentaire, théorique et pratique de l'art de la danse (Milan: Joseph Beati et Antoine Tenenti, 1820; facs. ed. Bologna: Arnaldo Forni Editore, 2002; tr. by Mary Stewart Evans, *An Elementary Treatise Upon the Theory and Practice of the Art of Dancing* [New York: Dover, 1968]).

Nouveau manuel complet de la danse ou traité théorique et pratique de cet art, new ed. (Paris: Librairie Encyclopédique de Roret, 1866).

In the readings gathered here, the last theorist to state unambiguously that theory precedes practice is Gennaro Magri in 1779. Excluding the anomalous contribution of Sulzer, the first professional dancer to clearly rank practice before theory is Carlo Blasis in 1820 (though the notion is already implicit in the work of Despréaux).

Blasis's several publications concerning dance theory and practice can be reduced to two basic texts: the *Traité élémentaire* and *The Code of Terpsichore.*[21] The latter work was translated into French as the *Manuel complet de la danse* in 1830, the same year as its publication in English; and republished in a condensed version as the *Nouveau manuel complet de la danse* in 1866.[22] There is considerable repetition of material from one book to the other. Two versions of the plates can be distinguished, in which the dancer's garment is either more fitted (1820) or more flowing, with additional, fully clothed figures (1830). (There are no plates in the *Nouveau manuel complet.*)

Blasis exemplifies the break with the past observed by Schroedter. In the preface to his *Elementary Treatise,* he quotes a poem by J. Berchoux, in which Plato, Aristotle, Lucian, Arbeau, Cahusac, and others are described as "persons worthy of respect and known for their science, who say much about dancing without being dancers."[23] From this baseless allegation, Blasis draws his own corollary:

The absence of any really valuable literature upon the subject of dancing has led me to publish this treatise. Most of the existing works are by writers who, though able men of letters, have no practical experience of dancing.... It would be of far greater value if such lyrical fantasies were replaced by a sound treatise on theoretical technique by a Dauberval, a Gardel, a Vestris

or some other great master"—in other words, by a distinguished professional dancer.[24]

Blasis again shows his distrust of theorists and theoretical abstraction
in the *Code de Terpsichore* (1831) and later in his *Nouveau manuel complet*
(1866): "Neither follow the precepts of simple unpractised theorists, utterly incapable of demonstrating clearly the true principles of the art: nor be guided by
the imaginary schemes of innovating speculators, who, whilst they think themselves contributing to ameliorate the elementary rules of dancing, are gradually
working its destruction."[25]

Blasis begins the *Nouveau manuel complet* with three quasi-theoretical
chapters, on the *histoire, utilité*, and *principes de la danse*. The "principes"
are *positions, salut* (bows), *pas*, and *maintien*—that is, aspects of both theory
(*maintien*) and practice (*positions, pas*), or both (*salut*), but preeminently
practice.[26] His section "Théorie de la Danse Théatrale," in both the *Code de
Terpsichore* and the *Nouveau manuel complet*, retains some of the traditional
elements of theory: the teacher-student relationship; carriage, equilibrium,
lightness and elasticity (*ballon*); relation of dance to music; and pantomime.[27]
However, in Reading 7.1a, the first item listed under "the theory and execution"
of dance is the five foot positions, clearly exhibiting the same conceptual framework as in Despréaux.

Blasis also follows Despréaux in his focus on the upright human figure to
illustrate positions and movements, as opposed to abstract symbols disposed
along a horizontal dance track, and in describing his system of visualization in quasi-alphabetic terms. The fifty-nine figures in the *Traité élémentaire*
are engraved after his own designs, in the chaste, planar neoclassical style
epitomized by John Flaxman (1755–1826) (see Fig. 7.1).[28] He declares that he
has no intention of illustrating every possible position, even those among the
most elementary: "In order to avoid a multiplication of plates, the positions
on point in third and fourth, as well as the pliés in the four other basic dance
positions, are omitted; these positions are very easy, and one can visualize
and reproduce them without figures" (50). In adddition to these figures, he
has devised a system of highly simplified, headless stick-figure drawings that
can be used as an instructional shortcut in teaching huge dance classes ("100
students at a time"; see Reading 7.1b) (see Fig. 7.2). Whereas *belle danse* choreography projected regular geometric patterns onto the dance floor, Blasis
projects lines and angles onto the dancer's body. In the act of copying these
easily readable images and attempting to "reproduce" or embody them, the
student internalizes an "alphabet" of dance movement. Blasis's approach to

Figure 7.1. Carlo Blasis, *Traité élémentaire, théorique et pratique de l'art de la danse*, Plate VI, Fig. 1 ("Danseur à la seconde en l'air et sur la pointe") and Fig. 3 ("Attitudes diverses; dérivés de la quatrième et de la seconde position"), n.p. (descriptions from "Explanation des Planches," 105–106) (Bibliothèque nationale de France, https://gallica.bnf.fr/ark:/12148/bpt6k6546277m/f145. item).

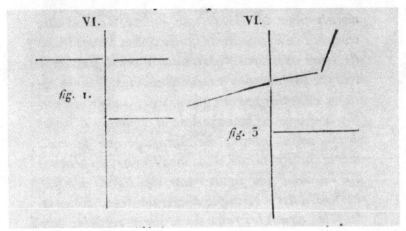

Figure 7.2. Blasis, *Traité élémentaire, théorique et pratique de l'art de la danse* (Bibliothèque nationale de France, https://gallica.bnf.fr/ark:/12148/bpt6k6546277m/f26.item), 16.

the analysis and visualization of dance movement will be shown soon to be in marked contrast to that of G. Léopold Adice (Reading 7.3).

READING 7.2A
Blasis (trans. Russell)

Nouveau manuel complet de la danse

PP. II–16
Chapter III
PRINCIPLES OF DANCE

Positions, Bowing, Steps, Bearing

Several persons have described various systems for teaching social dance; but their works contain a fault common to everything that has been written about dance in general, namely the absence of principles that are clear and solidly established. Such works, though read, are hardly instructive.

In establishing the rules of theory for any art, and the methods of perfecting this art, not only must the rules be clear, but the methods must be easy to execute. We can never demonstrate something well to others unless we ourselves have already seen and experienced that of which we speak.

With this in mind, we hope that our work will not merit the severe critiques often directed at works that are not validated by the author's own practice.

We cannot insist too highly on the grace and elegance that students must bring to their *attitudes*. These perfections of our art are both lovely to look at and essential in their execution; but at the same time, they are quite difficult to acquire. We will attempt to guide our readers towards this goal.

Every dancer is capable of taking part in any kind of quadrille; but that amiable air, those gracious manners and that attractive motion that one expects in those who have learned the art of dance cannot be acquired by every sort of professor, most of whom have neither the will nor the talent to study their art deeply enough to produce these important effects in their students. Although social dance demands neither extraordinary ability nor intense effort for its devotees to attain perfection, nevertheless certain physical qualities and aptitude are required for successful study. Without these qualities, one will always be embarrassed and ridiculed when dancing, and will much prefer passive spectating to maladroit performance. It should also be noted that, while knowledge of dance adds to the attractions of a naturally comely and agile person, it can only serve to accentuate the physical defects of those who are misshapen, overweight, and unfit for any graceful movement.

We have already explained the utility and advantages that can accrue to those who consider this attractive art only a simple amusement or a complement to any good education. We will now describe in more detail the theory and execution of the kind of dancing that is done in good company and studied by every respectably born and stylish person.

Positions [The five positions are described.]

Bowing The art of stopping gracefully, bowing, presenting and comporting oneself in company: these are essentials, and the student must perform them as naturally as possible.

[Technical instructions for bowing follow.]
After these preliminary lessons and exercises, which are the basis of dance and set [the student] on the path to perfection in all their applications, the master should instruct his student about steps, measure, quadrilles, the waltz, and all the other dances used in good company.

The master should not allow his student to learn dances before having first spent some time practicing the principles, for good or bad results depend entirely upon the first lessons and assiduous attention to fundamental rules. It is necessary constantly to take care not to forget the line of demarcation existing between theatrical and social dance. It would be inappropriate at a ball to perform intricate steps and high *entrechats* because they would be out of place, their pretentiousness would be emphasized by their incongruity, and their effect would consequently be utterly ridiculous.

Steps As soon as the professor is confident of his student's natural qualities, aptitude, and ability, he will teach him dance steps. The principal steps are: the *grands* and *petits battements*, the *battements sur le coude-pied*, the *assemblé*, the *jeté,* the *échappé,* the *glissade,* the *coupé-dessus* and the *coupé-dessous.* We are not going to describe them here. The reader will find their description either under each dance in which they are used, or in chapter V which is specially reserved for the choreography of theatrical dance.

The student should practice them, first being held by the hand, later without support, in order to acquire equilibrium. The professor should position the student's body and arms in a straight position, in order to make all his *attitudes* firm, supple, and graceful.

Bearing Social dance calls for steps along the ground and the simplest and most natural *attitudes* possible. Ladies should dance with an amiable and gracious bearing. Gentlemen should constantly show consideration for their partners, and everyone in the group should move with perfection of steps and *attitude.* It is necessary to pay the closest attention to the music, as well as to demonstrate an understanding of its every mood and harmony.

One should hold the arms slightly bent and allow them to fall naturally next to the body.

As to the position of the joints and articulations of the body, the student must submit to the same exercises as the theatrical dancer, in order to impart a pleasing affect to his dancing.

[Technical instructions on bearing follow.]

READING 7.2B
Traité élémentaire, théorique et pratique de l'art de la danse

PP. 15–17

If I were to establish a school of dance, I would immediately put into practice a method I have imagined and believe to be of essential use, and which any professor can employ without needing to know how to draw, that is: I would create for students a kind of abecedarium composed of straight lines for every position of the limbs, giving these lines and their respective combinations the terms used by geometers—namely, *perpendicular, horizontal, and oblique lines, and right, acute, and obtuse angles, etc.*—language I believe to be indispensable to our lessons, and I would draw these straight-line figures on the blackboard, [so that] 100 students at a time, keeping their eyes trained on the model, will quickly and very easily comprehend their positions and their attitudes without the master having to *strain his lungs* in long explanations to each one individually. The more diligent students, furthermore, will be able to copy the same figures on their own personal slates, to take home and study in the same way a child just beginning to learn how to spell studies his ABCs, without the presence of a teacher . . . and his hickory stick nearby.

Here are the plates:

I have preferred this new method, definitely the surest and most efficient, to that of a long and tiring description of dance movements that often accomplishes nothing but embarrassing the student and confusing his spirit. The figures are drawn by Mr. Casartelli, and engraved by Mr. Rados.

One can recommend nothing more highly to young people who aspire to this imitative art than to look at masterpieces of painting and sculpture—especially those of classical Antiquity: these immortal children of the genius of the beaux-arts, these models of ideal beauty, will inform their taste. A dancer who does not know how to draw himself, and consequently lacking in this seductive, charming grace, will never be regarded as an artist, and *will never be able to inspire either interest or pleasure.*[29]

7.3. ARTHUR SAINT-LÉON (1821–1870)

La Sténochorégraphie (Paris: author and Brandus & Cie., 1852; facs. ed. by Flavia Pappacena [Lucca: Libreria Musicale Italiana, 2006]).

The first notation system based on abstract symbols, that is, lacking any systematic resemblance to letters, numbers, or the human form, was invented by E. A. Théleur (fl. ca. 1817–ca. 1844). In fact, Théleur created two versions of this system, one more compact and abstract than the other. Both he called "Chirography," a misnomer unless he was referring specifically to hand movements and pantomime, which does not appear to be the case.[30] The notation systems devised by Arthur Saint-Léon and Friedrich Albert Zorn further refined the stick-figure method.[31] In stark contrast to the reception of Beauchamps-Feuillet notation through most of the eighteenth century, it seems none of these new systems except Zorn's was adopted by fellow dance pedagogues. The same lack of a sustained following holds true for most of the new systems that would proliferate in the twentieth century.

Saint-Léon's notation system, called "sténochorégraphie," uses the same vertical orientation as Despréaux, but now showing the figure's full height, albeit with the upper and lower parts of the body shown on separate lines. In contrast to Despréaux's system, the figure is seen from the front, or from the notator's point of view, instead of from the dancer's. This means that the leg depicted on the left represents the dancer's right leg, and so forth.

Without a written system of choreography, St.-Léon says, there can be no theory. Indeed, *sténochorégraphie* in this Reading *is* theory. St. Léon may be the first to state this, bluntly and unequivocally; it will be seen again, soon, in purely verbal choreographies with "Theory of . . ." at the beginning of their title.

READING 7.3
Saint-Léon (trans. Russell)

Preface

P. 13

However worthy of respect the authority of this author [Noverre], I cannot concede to him such a proposition [as the uselessness of the *Chorégraphie*]. Principles must be indestructible, immutable, respected like laws: therefore they must be written in a language. And while I agree with Noverre that the style of choreography to which he refers is worthless, I cannot agree with him that the art itself of writing dance is useless, since he should grant the author the *correctness of his works*, with the proviso that his *method* facilitates writing them. And with regard to method, I will never cease to reiterate that I believe it indispensable to teach a dance student all the elements of this art, just as one teaches a music student the notes, their character, their value, etc., prior to teaching him how to solfège or play an instrument; in a word, to join *theory* to *practice* in dance classes by introducing simultaneous instruction in *sténochorégraphie* and *exécution*.

Thus the difficulties pointed out by Noverre will vanish, especially when the professors require their students of dance to gain an elementary, if not extensive, knowledge of the principles of music.

7.4. G. LÉOPOLD ADICE
Théorie de la gymnastique de la danse théatrale (Paris: Imprimerie centrale de Napoléon Chaix et Cie., 1859).[32]

"Grammaire et Théorie de la gymnastique de la danse théatrale" (ms.: Paris, Bibliothèque nationale de France, Bibliothèque-musée de l'opéra, B-61(1), gallica.bnf.fr/ark:/12148/bpt6k311742d).

G. Léopold Adice had a grand plan for a major, multipartite work on the theory of theatrical dance, of which only one part, the *Théorie de la gymnastique de la danse théatrale*, was published. The other parts survive in manuscripts dated 1859–1871. Some of them were originally intended for inclusion in the published book, others for subsequent volumes (see Reading 7.4a, no. VII). His unpublished manuscripts are gathered in five volumes in the Bibliothèque-musée de l'opéra, Paris (BnF). The first contains his "Grammaire et Théorie de la gymnastique de la danse théatrale," with its important "Avertissement" and the first thirteen leçons; it also contains a randomly inserted disbound copy of the Théorie.[33] The second volume contains the fourteenth through nineteenth leçons.[34] The third volume is entirely devoted to a detailed descriptive analysis of the arabesque.[35] The fourth contains mostly first drafts and outlines of material that appears in more complete form in the preceding three volumes, in addition to an essay near the end, the "Partie Esthéthique," which Adice had promised, in the preface of the Théorie, to publish in his unrealized "second volume."[36] A fifth volume consists of a single essay: "Notes sur la direction E. Perrin."[37]

Adice was an embittered and quarrelsome soul. His writings are full of repeated grievances and complaints about the shortcomings of his predecessors and contemporaries. Adice considered himself unfairly demoted by Emil Perrin, director of the Paris Opéra from 1862 to 1870.[38] His main objection to Noverre addresses Noverre's remark that the positions are "good to know and better yet to forget"—a blasphemous claim to Adice. Noverre speaks of gestures of the body and head without categorizing and describing them as positions: this, Adice says, shows "ignorance of theory." Further, Noverre's emphasis on gesture, dramatic expression, and physiognomy—things of which Adice never speaks—confuses "the lesson [i.e., pedagogy] and the composition" [i.e., "refined and ideal expression"].[39] Just as Blasis denigrated Cahusac and others, Adice denigrates Blasis for spending too much time talking about the "more or less dubious" Arabian origin of the arabesque, while, "as always in his book, failing to provide a basis, a principle, a precept, a theoretical demonstration for educational use either by artists or students."[40] In general, he blames Noverre, Cahusac, Blasis, and others for bringing about the ruin of French dance by overemphasizing dance history (see Reading 7.4a). He has special contempt for Saint-Léon, whose sténochorégraphie has already fallen into "deep oblivion" ("l'ubli [sic] profond")—poetic justice for this "habitual charlatan" who claimed authorship of the sténochorégraphie when it was really the creation of Adice's own, revered teacher, Albert.[41]

Adice's criticism of Noverre is not as momentous as it might seem, because the reception and consequent influence of the two authors were so unequal. Noverre was widely read, translated, republished in new editions, and quoted, whereas Adice's one published work made few ripples. How could it, when its subject matter was limited to two topics of scant appeal to those enthused and inspired by Noverre: the "decadence" of theatrical dance in France and the occupational maladies of dancers?[42] Moreover, the most valuable fruit of Adice's thought is contained in his unpublished writing.

Adice makes it perfectly clear in his preface to the *Théorie* that, for him, "theory" is about practice: "Our book is a method, nothing more. . . . This book is directed at students, parents, and teachers, but students above all; it is all practice."[43] The instantaneous leap from the title "theory" to practical content, already seen in Despréaux, is also seen in the title of the "Grammaire" manuscript:

Grammar

and

choreographic Theory

Composition of the physical exercise [*gymnastique*]

of theatrical dance.

The physical exercise of theatrical dance is composed of movements on the ground; and of movements in the air.

These movements on the ground, and movements in the air, are designated also by the words **Temps posés**, and **Temps sautés**.

These *temps posés* and *temps sautés*, or movements on the ground and in the air, are distributed among the following four parts:

movements of the legs
movements of the torso [*corps*]
movements of the arms
movements of the head

In gymnastic performance, these four parts operate simultaneously, but by different motions pertaining specifically to each of the four parts.[44]

Atypically, and unlike Despréaux, Adice begins his "theory" with two basic types of movement instead of the five foot positions. Both authors, nonetheless, move directly from the title "Grammar" to an elementary concept in practice, and the five positions in Adice are introduced soon enough to assume a decidedly central role.

The "Partie Demonstrative" commences with the five positions established in Feuillet's *Chorégraphie*: "Première Leçon/Mouvement des jambes . . . Formation des cinq positions élémentaires des jambes sur les talons/Tableau d'Ensemble," with five line-drawings of uniform male figures (called *manequins*) in the five positions with feet flat on the floor (see Fig.

7.3).[45] This lineup of five figures is followed by individual images of the same *manequins*, usually two or four to a page, with a verbal description and often alternative views—for example, either from the right or left side, front or back. Adice follows this procedure systematically, introducing in turn the remaining *temps posés* of the feet, then all the movements of the body, head, and arms.

Adice presents a highly systematic and detailed analysis of dance movement, entirely derived from the five foot positions. He expands the quintuple principle in two directions:

I.   He introduces four variations of *temps posés* in the five foot positions:
   1. five *positions élémentaire* or *sur les talons* (both feet flat on floor)
   2. five *positions derivée* (weight on one foot, other foot pointed)
   3. five *positions demi-* (one foot *en l'air*)
   4. five *positions grande* (one leg bent and *en l'air*)[46]

II. He assigns five positions to the other moving parts or zones of the body (head, arms, and torso). Each of the four zones has its own version of five positions, analogous to those of the foot positions. Along with the foot positions and variations, "these four parts operate simultaneously, but by different motions pertaining specifically to each of the four parts." This means that any given *pose* can require different combinations of positions in any or all the four body zones, yielding a total of 625 possible permutations (not counting the *temps sautés* [never completed] and arabesque positions).[47]

In nineteen lessons and over a thousand pages, Adice systematically delves deeper and deeper into the permutational labyrinth of possible combinations of *temps posés* and body positions, with the intention of listing and describing, verbally and pictorially, every one of them. As he works through the nineteen lessons, he adds the positions of body zones one at a time to the foot positions: first the arms, then the head, then the torso. By lesson 13, all four parts of the body are involved with the feet in first position; and by lesson 19, all the parts are involved in all positions. For example, here is the label for one of the later figures in lesson 19, showing two *manequins*, each of whose four body zones is executing a different position (see Fig. 7.4).

Pose No. 829
Bras, en 3eme pos^on élémentaire
Tête, en 1re pos^on en face
corps, en 2eme pos^on penché à droite
jambes, en Cinquième [5th position] avec la droite croisée devant V
Grande position

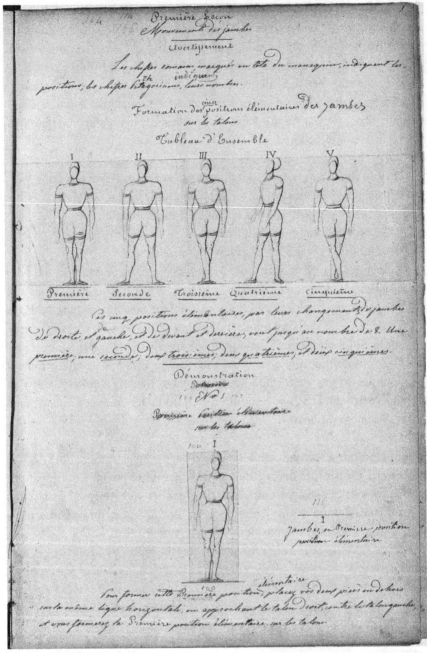

Figure 7.3. G. Léopold Adice, "Partie Demonstrative" (Bibliothèque nationale de France, B-61(1): gallica.bnf.fr/ark:/12148/bpt6k311742d "1r—View 423/934," https://gallica.bnf.fr/ark:/12148/bpt6k311742d/f423).

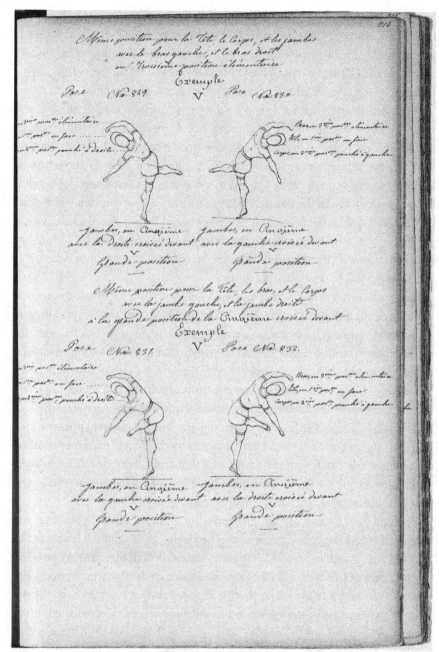

Figure 7.4. Adice, "Pose No. 829" (Bibliothèque nationale de France, B-61(2): https://gallica.bnf.fr/ark:/12148/bpt6k312027q?rk=107296;4 "713r—View 725/790").

(The left arm is bent over the head; the right arm straight out to the side. The head faces forward. The torso is bent at the waist to the right. The right leg is raised and bent horizontally in front. The supporting left foot rests on its ball, with the heel raised, in demi-point.) "Pose No. 830," following, is the mirror image of "Pose 1," with all the right and left directions reversed.[48]

While Adice clearly acknowledges Feuillet's five positions as the spiritual and symbolic source of his theory (a glowing ember from the past that irradiates his entire vast system), unlike Feuillet he does not apply his admiration toward further refinement or innovation of a notation system to show how to dance dances or even to dance specific steps. Instead of paths and steps, Adice focuses exclusively on the dancer's body (a culmination of the "body-building" process initiated by Despréaux). If his thought can be construed as a theory, it is a theory of practice analogous to the concept of *executio* of Pasch and Taubert. For them, however, the theory of practice was based on ethics; for Adice, it is based on *gymnastique* or physical culture.

Adice presents a rare—perhaps unique—instance of an explicit connection between dance and gymnastics. The connection is not fortuitous. According to *Il Gimnasta in pratica, ed in teorica*, a treatise republished in several Italian cities in the 1750s, the traditional elements of gymnastic theory—time, measure, order, and movement—are consonant with those of the Italian dance theorists of the Renaissance.[49] In early eighteenth-century printed catalogues of private libraries, *gimnastica* is found grouped with *saltatio* under the general rubric of *mathesis* (learning).[50] Furthermore, gymnastics (but not dance) appears in the "Système figuré des connaissances humaines" in the *Encyclopédie* (see Reading 6.5), under the *entendement* of Reason, as a terminal subdivision of the natural science zoology (zoology—medicine—hygiene—athletics—gymnastics), and thus a legitimate subject of human knowledge.

Through Adice's use of the *manequins* to illustrate all the positions and *poses* of the feet, legs, body, arms, and head, the "Grammaire" becomes, effectively, an obsessive exercise in permutational description and analysis: an extravaganza of combinatorial art expressed through the draftsman's art. Adice estimates there are "nearly four thousand" *manequins*, produced over "fifteen years of patience and determination"; many more were left unfinished or not even begun.[51] It is hard to imagine how, with its thousands of illustrations, it would have been publishable even if Adice had been able to complete it. Adice's *Théorie*, the only work he succeeded in publishing, contains no illustrations. The *manequins*, all of which would have had to be redrawn and engraved to Adice's detailed specifications, were no doubt the major obstacle to publication.[52] Furthermore, it is hard to imagine how Adice's meticulous but unwieldy labels would find any practical application in the dance studio. Since every *manequin* represents a split-second snapshot of movement, imagine how long it would take to teach and learn even a fleeting dance phrase at the level of detail in "Pose No. 829."

Sandra Noll Hammond says, "[Adice] produced the most extensive visual 'alphabet' of mid-nineteenth century ballet technique and style—at least for the *temps posés*."[53] Indeed, linguistically based terms are liberally deployed in Adice's "Avertissement" preceding the "Grammaire": alphabet, dictionary, grammar, stenography—even *"téllégraphie"*—epitomizing the vogue for allusion to written language in mid-nineteenth-century dance writing (see Reading 7.4b).[54] Adice says: "What we are writing is, in a word, a grammar, a counterpart to the treatises on music and drawing."[55] However, Adice's "alphabet" of thousands of letters/*poses*, despite its title, does not fulfill the grammatical functions of syntax and meaningful continuity—even Feuillet's *Chorégraphie*, in this sense, is more "grammatical" than Adice's system. The "Grammaire" does mention successive levels of growth through "the combination and composition" of movements on the ground: (1) a *temps* is a simple or compound leg movement and (2) a *pose* is a single position (*posture*); two or more *temps* produce (3) an *enchaînement,* and two or more simple or compound *poses* produce (4) an *adage;* and a combination of *adages* for two or more persons is (5) a *groupe*.[56] In general, though, the *manequins* are detached, stationary, and illustrative of the eighteenth-century concept of *tempo* as the ephemeral, in-the-moment nature of how dance is experienced.[57] There is hardly any indication of how one *pose* is connected to another, and none at all of how sequences of *groupes* can be joined to produce a complete dance. In fact, names of dance types and titles of specific dances are absent from Adice's writing.

Nevertheless, there are exceptional instances in which movement is suggested graphically, especially in the sequences of images toward the end of the "Note sur l'Arabesque." Hammond describes their effect: "Here the poses fairly dance off the pages. If the manuscript pages could be rapidly flipped, the reader would surely see an animated ballet dictionary" (see Fig. 7.5).[58] Adice himself seems to have anticipated Hammond's observation: "Choreography, in its composition as well as its instruction, is simply a painted image set in motion; this requires no explanation."[59]

It is obvious that Adice values *dessein* (or *dessin*), the art of drawing, above all as an anatomically precise medium for dance study. His *manequins* are in fact quite ingeniously adaptable and informative.[60] He praises his teacher, Albert, as a master of the art of *dessein* as well as of dance who, he implies, originated the idea of a teaching system based on the *manequin* drawings. Only

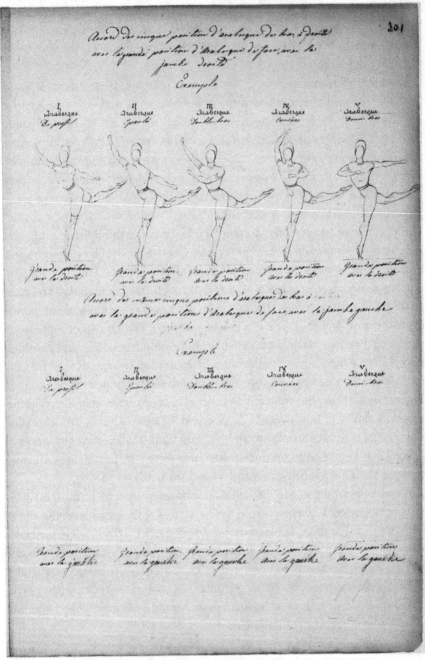

Figure 7.5. Adice, "Accord des [*sic*] cinque position d'arabesque des bras, à droite avec la grande position d'arabesque de face, avec la jambe droite" (Bibliothèque nationale de France, B-61(3), https://gallica.bnf.fr/ark:/12148/bpt6k311971p "301r—View 605/650").

the knowledge of anatomy, he writes, or else a sufficiently advanced notion of linear drawing, can be of use to both teacher and student.[61]

READING 7.4A
Adice (trans. Russell)[62]

Théorie de la gymnastique de la danse théâtrale
   Preface

PP. 5–7

I.

Our purpose in writing this work is in no way to pretend to evoke the history of theatrical dance and plumb the obscure depths of its past; rather, we intend neither to extol its presumed significance, nor to boast of its usefulness which, though real, is perhaps somewhat exaggerated by our predecessors.

Those who wish to learn these matters will do well to consult Cahusac, Menestrier, Baron, Noverre, Blasis, and others. As for us, our tastes and labors have always deferred from such investigations that, while certainly of some interest, seem mired in futility to the extent that they have failed to give a rational theory of dance of based on physical exercise [*gymnastique*].

   [...]

Music, architecture, poetry, sculpture, and painting have their own theory, their own method. Dance does not yet have a firm basis of established principles, of theoretical documents. To guide their students, teachers have only words and tradition as inspiration; not only all students, but also a great number of trained artists and, even worse, the teachers themselves are ignorant of the mechanism of dance.

It is this lacuna that we aim to fill. The fundamental theory of the mechanism of theatrical dance, the fulfillment of tradition consolidated in a regular method: these constitute the subject contained in our book.

II.

To undertake such a task demanded great devotion and immense faith in the art of theatrical dance, which today is in such a disgraceful state; it meant having to ignore the willful and vain ignorance of all those who ought to care the most about this subject; it demanded that we, too, resolve to ignore documents and materials that absolutely lack any content that could aid us in our labors; and it compelled us, alone and unaided, in a subject as yet unexcavated, a métier difficult to organise, to be the first to study, observe, organize, untangle, sort, classify, and taxonomize, and finally to dispel confusion, bring order to chaos, and shed light therein.

P. 10

[III.]

Our book is a method, nothing more; our desire is not to write a novel: we wish to be useful to students, and our book is addressed to students rather than to the public, and the more methodical and precise it is, the more ease the student will derive from it in learning and progressing; this is the success we are aiming for, and if Noverre, Baron, Cahusac, and Blasis, instead of describing dance history—charmless and boring fantasies—had thought only of elucidating the principles and theories of our art, and of educating our students, one would have no reason to regret the harsh condition in which the French school now finds itself forced to cede its former rightful supremacy to the foreign school that previously was by far its inferior.

PP. 18–20

VII.

Now, prior to entering into the subject matter, we will establish the divisions into which our book is separated.

In the first part, we will examine the causes of the decadence of French theatrical dance.

In the second part, we will study the various injuries that are unavoidable consequences of theatrical dance, such as cramps, stiffness, chest pains, etc.

The nomenclature of movements on the ground [*temps posés*] will comprise the third part.

The fourth and last part will contain the theory of the mechanism of theatrical dance.

It is subdivided into:

1° Movements on the ground [*Temps posés*];
2° Movements in the air [*Temps sautés*].

The study of movements on the ground is subdivided thus:

1° The technical part;
2° The aesthetic part.

The technical part, which is the subject of the present volume [*sic*], includes developmental progression of all the positions that form the basis of the mechanism of all the movements on the ground.

The aesthetic part repeats each of the positions described in the technical part and develops them, one by one, into their most refined and ideal expression.

This aesthetic part will be the subject of the second volume.[63]

The movements in the air, including all their names, will be the subject of succeeding volumes.

READING 7.4B
"Grammaire/et/Théorie chorégraphique" (ms.)

GALLICA 311742, PP. 259–267

Avertissement

It is impossible either to write dance rapidly, or to show how to dance using an open book in the way writers of choreography have claimed to teach.

Stenographic dancing is not yet practicable for the reason that this art still possesses neither an alphabet nor a vocabulary for its movements.

For a language is written only when its dictionary is established, and it is stenographed only by means of its alphabet.

The day will surely come when stenography can be applied to dance; but even then, this system will be useful only to performers who are quite advanced and are perfectly conversant with the choreographic dictionary: the reason for this being that it will indicate the composition of a step, an *enchaînement*, a variation, an *entrée*, a *forté*, but not the manner in which to execute it.[64]

Only pictures in such a book can aid in rendering my explanations palpable as I desire, through visual demonstration.

Also, I have added infinite detail to the drawings because it is proven that the more illustrations in such a method, the more useful it is to the student by providing the visual representation that facilitates mental labor and saves time.

Thanks to these precautions, the student will comprehend at a single glance the movement he has to execute, and besides that, he will find it explained with the full detail pertaining to it, and thanks to the care I have taken to fill in all the gaps, he will the more quickly and easily come to know, not mechanically, but rationally, the entire internal working of theatrical dance.

With regard to precision of the series of positions on the ground, as I have already said, thanks to the signs and simple explanations, the student will be able to perceive the line, level, elevation, and inclination, be it of the body, the head, the arms, the wrists, the legs, the ankles, the toes, and thus too the turnout of the feet and the calves, in order to observe precisely all the movements in the position that he will want to execute.

For the same reason, I have marked all the leg positions with the roman numerals I, II, III, IV, and V; and with pythagorian numerals 1, 2, 3, 4, 5, . . . 10 . . . 20 . . . 30 . . . etc., [and I have marked] all the poses that form part of the development of these same positions of the legs, and that constitute the ensemble of each *manequin* by the simultaneous interaction of other positions of the body, arms, and head.

By this very practical method, and when I will have entirely finished the two first parts, [namely] the part **on the ground** and the part **in the air**, I will show with the greatest simplicity, if not correctly then at least systematically, using the attached numbers and other simple signs similar to those used in music, the sole more or less rational way known up to now for indicating an adagio, a *forté*, a variation, just as well as when the words are placed beneath the notes of a song or other piece of music.

As to the art of writing dance rapidly, published recently by M. St. Lion [*sic*], I think it unnecessary to undertake even the most superficial analysis to prove its insufficiency—absurdity is the word that says it best. The deep oblivion into which this book has sunk almost since its release, due to its total lack of exact and theoretical principles for facilitating its application, justifies my ignoring it entirely. But I will only say that this idea of a telegraphic system applied to theatrical dance is absolutely not his property, even if the inventor himself of this system likes to call it a child's plaything [*guiéserie d'enfant*], but is the rightful property of the celebrated artist, ballet master, and professor Albert, with whom I am closely connected; together he and I often spoke of this plaything. This is not, furthermore, the only appropriation by M. St. Lion [*sic*], and if his book contained them, I could cite the titles of ballets, entire scenes of which belong to someone quite other than him; but as we are born to render unto Caesar that which is Caesar's, we reserve the right to render likewise unto the most abused Per[r]ot.[65]

M. St. Leon [sic] is one of Albert's best students. Yet, truly, he has not shown himself to be very appreciative. But isn't it said that ingratitude is the heart's independence? . . . For without it, what could we claim as our own? . . . As for ingratitude, I know a thing or two about that.

I now begin the elements of choreographic grammar.

7.5. FRIEDRICH ALBERT ZORN (1816–AFTER 1895)

Grammar of the Art of Dancing: Theoretical and Practical, trans. Benjamin P. Coates, ed. Alfonso Josephs Sheaff (Boston: International Publishers, 1920).

In Friedrich Albert Zorn's title, *Grammar of the Art of Dancing*, the term "grammar" encompasses material related to both traditional theory (a term he avoids) and notation. "Grammar" is a term loaded with significance for Zorn. It refers to the way language is systematically taught, and thus serves as a model of the way he would like to see dance taught (xiv). Since writing is an integral part of literacy, "grammar" also refers to "script" as a medium of teaching and preservation, making Zorn's notation, as presented in his book, a kind of linguistic instrument (11). Finally, since the word "grammar" also refers to a schoolbook that teaches the structural functions and rules of grammar, Zorn's title is fully justified.

Zorn's stick-figure notation system is the first to show a connected, full-length body, viewed frontally as in St. Léon's system. Zorn's was the only system that was adopted and used by other teachers (his influence spread through his own promotional activity and the English translation of his treatise, published in Boston). The original German edition (Leipzig, 1887) was divided into three parts: grammar (an instructional textbook on his choreographic system); "Atlas" (illustrations and choreography with dance melodies); and "Notenheft" (dance music arranged for violin and piano) (vii); in the translation, the text and images are helpfully integrated.

Like Dufort and Magri, Zorn directly follows his discussion of theory (chapter I) with the introduction of the five foot positions (chapter II), the traditional sequence that puts theory before practice. Nevertheless, Zorn is ambivalent with regard to the priority of theory *versus* practice. Whereas the grammar (or "principles of the dance") is presented first, the principles are to be learned through reading notation: "a system analagous to those employed in teaching language or drawing," implying that notation (based on practice) must come before theory.

The principals of dance are familiar from traditional dance theory: a definition of dance; the four "factors" of dance (position, movement, figure, and measure); and a description of carriage (which is the same as *maintien*). The four "factors" and carriage are nearly parallel to Blasis's four *principes*; "movement" for Zorn is how transition between positions is accomplished, and therefore is equivalent to *pas* in Blasis.

READING 7.5
Zorn (trans. Sheafe)

PP. 15–16
Chapter I
METHOD

The first condition of success or of accomplishment in science or in art is a method based upon the natural principles of the subject and so adjusted to the capabilities of the student as to lead from the base to the acme of perfection, without unnecessary waste of time.

Without such a method or system, and without the necessary specific names for even the most minute details and objects, progress in the Art of Dancing will be rendered well nigh impossible, on account of the numberless difficulties and apparent contradictions that must naturally arise.

Such a system should be devised as will lead the student easily and gradually from the simpler to the more complicated portions in such a manner as to enable him not only to comprehend but to demonstrate as he goes. A competent teacher is not often at a loss to thoroughly communicate his ideas.

The first necessity is, therefore, what we may term a Grammar of the Art of Dancing which shall contain a system analagous to those employed in teaching language or drawing, and which shall so clearly define the principles of the dance, that, while it does not exceed the comprehension of a child, it shall be none the less valuable and useful to teachers and to professional dancers.

A grammar of this sort will quickly be appreciated by educators and by dancers, and, indeed, by the general public, as a means of promoting correct principles, and at the same time of leading to an understanding of the true objects of conscientious dancing-masters and of overcoming the present degradation of dancing in society and upon the stage. May it not also, perhaps, induce careless and indifferent teachers to work more diligently for their own improvement, by raising the standard of professional requirement through the enlightenment of the public?

From the foregoing one may plainly discern the object of the author and his ideal of the nature of a Grammar of Dancing. Time and experience alone can determine the degree of success with which he has performed his task.

Grammar

1. Dancing is the expression of pleasure or of other sentiments by means of prescribed movements, which are regulated by music, either imagined or expressed.
2. Its factors are Position, Movement, Figure, and Measure.
3. Before or after a movement, a Position may be either correct or incorrect.
4. Transition from one position to another is accomplished by means of Movements which are either simple or compound.
5. The lines described upon the floor by the dancers constitute the Figure.
6. The division of the movements into periods of equal duration to correspond with the music is called Measure.

7. To compare dancing to language, the positions correspond to vowels; simple movements to consonants; compound movements to syllables; steps to words; enchainments to phrases or sentences; and the combinations of enchainments to paragraphs.

Simple figures correspond to verses, compound figures to stanzas, and the connection of compound figures or strophes, as in a Quadrille, to an entire poem.

7.6. EUGÈNE GIRAUDET (1861–AFTER 1921)

Traité de la danse; Tome II: Grammaire de la danse et du bon ton à travers le monde et les siècles depuis le singe jusqu'à nos jours (Paris: author, 1900).

The crisis in dance notation in the early nineteenth century resulted in a development even more radical than the invention of new notation systems: the elimination of notation altogether. For G. Desrat, Eugène Giraudet, Charles d'Albert, and others in the second half of the nineteenth century, the term *théorie* refers only to a list of the steps used in a dance, or to an entire verbal choreography; "theory," in other words, connotes practice.[66] Verbal choreography needs to be distinguished from the "Wortkürzel" or "Words and Word Abbreviations" types of dance notation that used single letters and abbreviations to indicate step names and floor positions. The new type, on the contrary, uses only full text without any collateral symbols or other nonverbal elements. Perhaps the total absence of symbols persuaded Jeschke and Hutchinson Guest to disregard this type as a valid category; it cannot be thought of as "notation" in any normal sense. Yet from 1801 until the 1930s, it was the dominant form of choreographic description.[67]

The prolific Giraudet published nine books prior to this one, three of which are titled *Traité de la danse* . . . , making it impossible to determine which of them is to be considered the volume preceding the *Grammaire de la danse et du bon ton; Tome II*.[68] Its delightful frontispiece depicts a winding procession of dancing couples dressed in the costumes of their eras, beginning with a droll simian forbear in a tree and ending with an elegant couple of circa 1900. Giraudet does not explain the significance of the term *grammaire*, and it may refer simply to the alphabetical organization of the bulk of material (over five hundred pages) in this tome, although Giraudet's other books are organized in the same way and not named "grammaire." In his article on theatrical dance, Giraudet paraphrases, without attribution, Compan's division of dance into three parts: choreography, poetics, and history, calling them "the primordial foundations of [the ballet master's] experience, based on immovable principles."[69] Whereas Giraudet uses the term *théorie* hundreds of times in this book to designate a verbal choreography, theory in the traditional sense is mentioned in only one article: "How one learns to dance," in which theory—whatever that word means to Giraudet—is put in its place subordinate to practice (Reading 7.6a).

For an example of verbal choreography, see Giraudet's "theory" of the "Menuet de la cour" for four couples (Reading 7.6b).

READING 7.6A
Giraudet (trans. Russell)

PP. 72–73

HOW ONE LEARNS TO DANCE.—**Practice precedes theory.**—In general, theory should precede practice, but in studying dance, the lesson should proceed in parallel fashion, with practice in first place and theory completing the course. This principle is applicable in the waltz and the classic dances. To commence the study of dance with theory is to read without comprehension. On the contrary, just as it is best to strike while the iron is hot, it is while the student is being trained in good practice that theory arrives as needed to help inculcate the lessons.

This will become more comprehensible when I make this comparison: try reading the theory of cycling for one month and you will not, for all that, be able to pedal correctly. On the other hand, take practical lessons and you will make progress daily.

To become a good waltzer, first make the legs supple, accustom yourself to overcoming dizziness, learn how to lead your partner, and after that we will provide the theory to define what we are doing. I repeat, in choreography, just as in the creation of the world, the act comes first; the commentary will follow later. This way, I can successfully instil confidence in you; in the old days, the way theory was then taught, it would have taken me a year to train a good waltzer, while today, thanks to my new method, fifteen days of training suffice to produce a quite capable dancer.

The boredom of the old way of teaching annoyed and discouraged students. Now, the first class in choreographic study is enjoyable and interesting, and instils a taste for dance. The polka, the mazurka, the waltz, the quadrille and the "Lancers" are learned beginning from the very first lesson. The student dances with the professor who leads, advises, inspires him. After that, the students dance with each other; then they are partnered with an experienced lady who knows how to lead, and teaches them that skill. This is the only practical way to acquire ease, grace, and suppleness, and to become familiarised with the leading [*conduite*] of ladies at court or at a ball.

You will agree with me that the beginner is always a bit clumsy, and the first stages of training can only be extremely beneficial to him. It will not take long for him to be light as a feather, and knowledgeable to perfection in the correct way to lead his partner. Some of my students have justly observed that a female, because of the weakness of her sex, cannot be well suited to be a professor and teacher. In fact, a lady is no more likely than a weak and feeble [male] to be an effective teacher, for the professor who desires genuine and quick results must give his all, and be supported by devoted assistants.[70] This is how he succeeds in forming good students, even among those who are least favored by nature. In conclusion, I repeat that which cannot be too often affirmed, namely that dance is an inoffensive pleasure, a hygienic diversion for the spirit, and the most healthful of medicines.

READING 7.6B

PP. 230–232: "MENUET (LE) DE LA COUR, SOUS LOUIS XV, RÉGLÉ PAR E. G."

Theory of the minuet, *for four couples beginning together and on the same foot.*—

4 measures.—2 minuet steps forward, one with the right foot, one with the left foot, bow and curtsy face-to-face while releasing hands.

4 measures.—Gentleman and lady of each couple, with two steps back, face each other and bow.

4 measures.—Gentleman and lady give hands, turning their back to the center, then returning to place with two minuet steps, bow to the lady, etc., face-to-face.

4 measures.—The gentlemen and ladies take 3 minuet steps back, bow, etc.

4 measures.—The gentlemen only go to the center with walking steps, bow, etc., gentleman to his lady, the ladies being returned to their respective places with walking steps.

4 measures.—Gentleman and lady, 2 minuet steps in place, face-to-face, with the *jeu de robe* for the lady and the *jeu de bras*[71] for the gentleman, bow.

4 measures.—Repeat the 4 previous measures.

8 measures.—Gentleman and lady give right hands, make 6 minuet steps in place as they change hands (they begin on the left foot when giving the right hand, and *vice versa*), bow, etc.

4 measures.—One circle holding right hands with 6 walking steps, bow, etc. (in returning to place).

4 measures.—One circle holding left hands with 6 walking steps, bow, etc.

4 measures.—The gentleman turns his lady under his right arm with the right hand, bow, curtsy (pirouette).

4 measures.—The lady turns her gentleman with the right hand, bow, etc. (pirouette).

4 measures.—Idem. 2 pirouettes, the gentleman to his lady.

8 measures.—The *faux-pas* 6 times, in two circles holding right hands, bow. (Gentleman and lady give right hands and, both beginning with the left foot, take three walking steps, as follows): Advance the left foot, the right, the left, lightly raising the right as it brushes along the floor, extended and lifted off the ground; repeat 5 more times, bow, etc.

4 measures.—Gentleman and lady give hands, and 2 minuet steps forward, bow, etc.

4 measures.—They give hands and return to place, walking, bow.

6 measures.—Finale. Each gentleman faces his lady. He gives his right hand to her left hand. He makes one minuet step left with his left foot; id. the lady with the right (1 measure), holding the arms in front.—Repeat this measure on the other foot, without releasing hands (raising them behind).—Repeat these 2 measures; they release hands, pirouette only once in place, bow.

7.7. EDMOND BOURGEOIS

Traité pratique et théorique de la danse (Paris: Garnier Frères, 1909?).

The introductory chapter of the *Traité* of Edmond Bourgeois, titled "Aperçu général sur la danse," is remarkably long and presents theoretical content (1–45). According to Bourgeois, the four principal genres of dance, described from a nontraditional, predominantly ethnographic perspective (leading to a defense of the cancan), are martial, hunting, *pantomime amoureuse,* and religious. *Danse d'amour,* referring to any dance in which a woman takes part, is the most widely used type. The chapter proceeds with more traditional theoretical subject matter, including classical and biblical dance history, a history of mimetic dance culminating in modern ballet, and discussions of dance and religion and dance's utility.

But the most interesting moment comes at the beginning of the following chapter, "Principes généraux," in which Bourgeois turns from theory to practice. In an *apologia* in all but name, he makes it clear that mainly a sense of duty compels him to discuss all the dry, traditional theory topics that to him seem relevant to professional, theatrical dancers, but irrelevant to the modern tastes and needs of his intended audience. Bourgeois uses the adjectives "theoretical" and "general" synonymously with regard to other terms referring only to practice: "steps, tempos, movements, gestures, attitudes." To refer to theory, as he does, as a "more literary, more scientific than technical issue" is to consign it to mere book learning and dismiss it as an essential part of dance as an art, whereas, ironically, for John Weaver the *Chorégraphie* was a triumph of scientific thinking applied to dance practice.

READING 7.7
Bourgeois (trans. Russell)

PP. 47–49
General Principles

Dance that is truly, purely artistic—that is, theatrical dance—obviously requires, of those who embrace it as a career, a great many special aptitudes: for dedication, work, care, and perseverance. It requires that those men and women who consecrate themselves, who swear allegiance, to the dancer's profession feel within themselves, in a word, the sacred flame of this art.

But it is not such initiates whom we claim to serve. Our aim is far more modest. It is a simple matter of exposing our readers to the spectacle—the lessons, if you will—of dance in its most everyday existence; to show its usage, its theoretical, practical, and mechanical execution, so to speak. This is why we have decided to commence our arduous work with a brief, general survey of dance, and after having disposed of this more literary, more scientific than technical issue, to arrive directly at the general principles, which include the steps, tempos, movements, gestures, attitudes, etc., etc., and to treat them strictly from the point of view of those who do not cherish the hope of becoming distinguished ballet-masters, but who desire only to know how dancing is done, and how they themselves may dance without cutting a poor figure in a salon or public ball; to be, in a word, a cavalier, as elegant in the famed dances of our fathers—the minuet, pavane, passepied, or gavotte—as in our contemporary dances—the waltz, polka, quadrille, and mazurka.

Having said that, it is quite evident that social dance or public balls do not require either extraordinary ability or persistent, tiresome application in order for one to attain—without needing to gain, or even feign, perfection—a satisfactory bearing, a comportment that will not tempt spectators to smile. Yet it is essential to possess certain physical qualities and some natural, instinctive aptitude. Without that, one will be forever awkward, embarrassed, and it will serve him better, at a ball or salon, to remain a passive spectator of those who know better than to act maladroitly. It is necessary also to observe that whereas dance knowledge adds to the attraction of one who is comely, agile, gracious, and in possession of whatever conduces all the more to the seduction of dance, it cannot flatter those who are unattractive, overweight, and sloppy in every elegant motion, which only renders them more ridiculous than they are innately. No need to explain any further the utility and advantages of dance to those who practice this seductive art as merely a simple diversion or complement to a good education. Let it suffice us to treat more particularly the theory and execution of dance for those who can appreciate it properly and dance without shame and awkwardness.

Let us speak first of the positions. [. . .][72]

NOTES

1. Stephanie Schroedter, "The Practice of Dance at the Crossroad Between Pragmatic Documentation, Artistic Creativity and Political Reflection: Sources of the Theatrical Dance of the Early 19th Century," *Society of Dance History Scholars Proceedings*, 508.

2. Not all nineteenth-century dance books follow this "new impetus." In Francis Peacock, *Sketches Relative to the History and Theory, but More Especially to the Practice of Dancing* (Aberdeen: J. Chalmers & Co., 1805), ix–71, and James P. Cassidy, *A Treatise on the Theory and Practice of Dancing* (Dublin: William Folds, 1810), 1–31, the introductory material is traditional (though Cassidy adds the "effects of music on animate and inanimate bodies," and "curious anecdotes").

3. J. J. Martinet, *Essai ou principes élémentaires de l'art de la danse* (Lausanne: Monnier- et Jacquerod, 1797), 25: "Toute la théorie de l'art de la danse, ayant été établie sur cinq positions naturelles, dont on doit point s'écarter . . . je vais mettre le lecteur à portée de s'en instruire parfaitement."

4. See, for example, Marie-Joëlle Louison-Lassablière, *Études sur la danse: De la Renaissance au siècle des Lumières* (Paris: L'Harmattan, 2003), 57(re Arbeau): "His course is theoretical in that it specifies the steps, figures, the dances" ("Son cours est théorique puisqu'il définit les pas, les figures, les danses").

5. Friedrich Albert Zorn, *Grammar of the Art of Dancing: Theoretical and Practical*, trans. Benjamin P. Coates, ed. Alfonso Josephs Sheaff (Boston: International Publishers, 1920; first pub. in German [Leipzig, 1887]), 4.

6. Jean- Étienne Despréaux, *Mes passe-temps*; "L'art de la danse" is in vol. II, 171–306.

7. Several passages from Boileau-Despréaux are either omitted or expanded upon by Despréaux, necessitating blank spaces on the facing page.

8. "L'art de la danse," 300–301.

9. "L'art de la danse," 235: "*Ballet d'action,* a painting brought to life, is the surest way to the heart."

10. "L'art de la dance," 199.

11. *Notice des livres de la bibliothèque de feu M. J.-E. Despréaux* (Paris: Olivier, Royer, and Brunet, 1820). I am grateful to Dominique Bourassa for tracking down this fascinating document. A *pochette* is a dancing master's violin, compact enough to fit into his coat pocket.

12. The volume is now in the collection of the Nederlands Muziek Instituut, request number NMI Kluis B 16.

13. Compan, *Dictionnaire,* 275–277.

14. I owe this insight and term to Dominique Bourassa.

15. Jeschke, *Tanzschriften,* 168–175; Hutchinson Guest, *Choreo-Graphics,* esp. 1–6. Both cite Arbeau; see his fols. 38r and 40r (abbreviated step names) and 91r and 100r–103v (changing floor positions).

16. Flavia Pappacena, "*Danse écrite ou La Terpsi-choro-graphie ou Nouvel Essay de Theorie de la danse:* manuscript dated 1813 by Jean-Étienne Despréaux kept at the Bibliothèque of the Paris Opéra," *Society of Dance History Scholars Proceedings,* 498–499; see also Pappacena, "La 'Terpsi-choro-graphie' di J.-E. Despréaux (1813): la trasformazione della notazione coreutica fra il XVIII e il XIX secolo," *Chorégraphie: Studi e richerche sulla danza* 4, no. 7 (1996): 26–30.

17. *Encyclopédie,* vol. I, xlviii: "*La Grammaire* se distribue en Science des *Signes,* de la *Prononciation,* de la *Construction,* & de la *Syntaxe.* . . . Les *Caracteres* sont ou *idéaux,* ou *hiéroglyphiques,* ou *héraldiques.*"

18. This definition is consistent with those in contemporary dictionaries; see Nicolas Beauzée and Jacques-Philippe-Augustin Douchet, "Grammaire" [signed "E.R.M."], *Encyclopédie,* vol. 7, 841–847, especially the "Système figuré des parties de la grammaire," 846; also, Émile Littré, *Dictionnaire de la langue française,* vol. 2 (Paris: Librairie Hachette et Cie., 1874), 1913–1914.

19. Taubert, *Rechtschaffener Tantzmeister,* 500–501.

20. Noverre, it should be recalled, disparagingly called the *Chorégraphie* a mere alphabet.

21. Blasis, *The Code of Terpsichore: The Art of Dancing. Comprising Its Theory and Practice, And A History of Its Rise and Progress, from the Earliest Times,* trans. R. Barton, 2nd ed. (London: Edward Bull, 1831 [1st ed. 1830]).

22. Blasis, *Manuel complet de la danse,* trans. M. Barton (Paris: Librairie Encyclopédique de Roret, 1830). See Cyril W. Beaumont, *A Bibliography of Dancing* (New York: Benjamin Blom, 1963), 14–18.

23. J. Berchoux, *La danse, ou les dieux de l'opéra* (Paris: Giguet et Michaud, 1806), 53: "Tous gens dignes de foi, connus par leur science,/Qui, sans être danseurs, parlent beaucoup de danse." Though not as worthy of respect, the amateur John Lecointe, *An Apology for Dancing*, trans. J. Peyton (London: J. Kippax, 1752), would be eminently qualified to join this group: "That I understand the Theory of Dancing, which is sufficient to make a Man a complete Judge of it without the Help of Practice, I can confidently affirm" (xiii).

24. Blasis, *Traité élémentaire*, 7–8 and 4. Note, by the way, the translator's fancy minting of a new hybrid field: "theoretical technique" in place of Blasis's "mécanisme."

25. Blasis, *The Code of Terpsichore*, 50; *Nouveau manuel complet*, 59–60.

26. Blasis, *Nouveau manuel*, 1–18 ("Principes," 11–18).

27. Blasis, *Code de Terpsichore*, 49–58; *Nouveau manuel*, 59–70 (chap. V).

28. The plates are located on unpaginated *recto* pages at the end of the book. Blasis identifies himself as the artist in the *Traité élémentaire*, 14. On Blasis's background in the graphic arts, see Lillian Moore, *Images of the Dance: Historical Treasures of the Dance Collection 1581–1861* (New York: The New York Public Library, 1965), 37–38.

29. The phrase "se dessiner" comes from Cahusac (Reading 5.4c), the final sentence of his book.—Ed.

30. Théleur, *Letters on Dancing*, 61–80. Théleur's "Chirographies" have no symbols for arm or hand positions. Théleur may have been thinking of Lucian: "Indeed, Lesbonax of Mytilene, a man of excellent parts, called dancers 'handiwise'" (see Reading 1.4, ¶69).

31. For an excellent overview of choreographic developments during the nineteenth century, from Despréaux to Zorn, see Flavia Pappacena, "The Sténochorégraphie in the context of the experimentations of the 18th and 19th centuries," *Arthur Saint-Léon, Sténochorégraphie*, ed. Flavia Pappacena, *Chorégraphie* 4 (Rome: LIM, 2006), 61–71.

32. Adice does not normally add a circumflex accent over the first "a" in "théatrale."

33. BnF, Bibliothèque-musée de l'opéra, B-61(1), Gallica 311742d. The disbound *Théorie* appears in this volume on view nos. 55–255 (view numbers, except for within the published *Théorie* itself, refer to Gallica images, not to the inconsistent pagination systems of the unpublished ms. texts). On the first three volumes and their author, see Sandra Noll Hammond's invaluable introduction, "Ballet's Technical Heritage: The Grammaire of Léopold Adice," *Dance Research: The Journal of the Society for Dance Research* 13, no. 1 (Summer 1995): 33–58.

34. BnF, Bibliothèque-musée de l'opéra, B-61(2), Gallica 312027q.

35. BnF, Bibliothèque-musée de l'opéra, B-61(3), Gallica 311971p.

36. BnF, Bibliothèque-musée de l'opéra, B-61(4), Gallica 3119722. See Adice, *Théorie*, 20.

37. BnF, Bibliothèque-musée de l'opéra, B-61(5), Gallica 311973.

38. For a more detailed biography, see Hammond, "Ballet's Technical Heritage," 34.

39. Adice, *Théorie*, 98–105 ("ignorance de la théorie" . . . "le leçon et la composition"); also p. 20 ("tout leur fini et leur idéal"), the goal of Adice's "aesthetic part."

40. Adice, "Note sur l'Arabesque," Gallica 311971p, view 9. See also Gallica 311742d, views 551 and 565.

41. Adice, "Avertissement," Gallica 311742d, views 263–265; and "Note sur l'Arabesque," Gallica 311971p, view 15. Albert (*nom de métier* of François Decombe, 1787–1865), dancer and ballet master, was also a teacher of Saint-Léon.

42. In the second part of the *Théorie,* dealing with dancers' injuries, Adice identifies the affected bones, muscles, and nerves by their anatomic name. A footnote (*Théorie*, 146) states that relevant anatomical drawings are to be found at the end of the volume. They were not present in the two copies I have seen, nor are they present in the manuscript sources.

43. Adice, *Théorie*, 10, 16.

44. Adice, Gallica 311742d, view 267.

45. Adice, Gallica 311742d, view 423.

46. Although Adice uses the words *mouvement, position*, and *pose* somewhat interchangeably, as best I can tell, a position refers to a specific part of the body, while a *pose* refers to the whole body, each of whose four parts can be in a different position.

47. $625 = 5 \times 5 \times 5 \times 5$ (i.e., 5^4), testifying to the almost talismanic significance of the number 5 in Adice's system. I am indebted to Prof. William Lepowsky for this mathematical solution.

48. Adice, Gallica 312027q, view 725.

49. Giustiniano Borassatti, *Il Gimnasta in pratica, ed in teorica* (Venice, 1753), 36: "tempo, misura, regola, e moto"; the frontispiece adds *vis* and *robur* (force and strength); Gallica: Il_gimnasta_in_pratica_ed_[...]Borassatti_Giustiniano_bpt6k882579g.pdf. The treatise was republished in the cities the troupe visited on tour. Gerrit Berenike Heiter presented a fascinating introduction to it: "*Il Gimnasta* (1751–1756): Acrobatic Performances in Connnection with Other Theatrical Performances" (unpublished paper: 20th Annual Oxford Dance Symposium, New College, Oxford, 2018).

50. For example, Gabriele Martin, *Bibliotheca Bultelliana: seu Catalogus librorum Bibliothecae V. Cl. D. Caroli Bulteau* (Paris: Petrus Giffart and author, 1711), 329–330.

51. Adice, "Remarque Sur l'Esthétique," Gallica 3119722, view 707: "près de quatre mille en quinze années de patience et d'assiduité." Adice's high count, far exceeding the total of 625 possible permutations, includes additional *manequins* in alternative views, unfinished sketches, or blank reserved spaces, especially toward the end of the "Partie Arabesque."

52. Adice, "Remarque Sur l'Esthétique," Gallica 3119722, view 705, states that each *pose* must be fifteen "centimètre sur sa verticale" (ca. six inches tall).

53. Hammond, "Ballet's Technical Heritage," 38.

54. Stenography is shorthand writing, also called "the art of writing dance rapidly" ("l'art d'écrire la danse prontement [sic]") by Adice in the reading that follows, in direct reference to Arthur Saint-Léon's "sténochorégraphie" (see Reading 7.3). Telegraphy (distance writing) may refer to the communication of information over a distance by means of signs and pictures, according to Hammond (private correspondence, August 5, 2016).

55. Adice, *Théorie*, 102.

56. Adice, "Grammaire/et/Théorie chorégraphique," Gallica 311742d, views 269–271.

57. A similar notion of *Tempo* is suggested earliest by Pasch, Behr, and Taubert: Pasch, *Beschreibung wahrer Tantzkunst*, 84: "*Tempo* is in general a quantity of duration; time present is the moment that comes after all the moments of time past and before all the moments of time future." Behr, *L'art de bien danser* (1713), 52: "As to *Tempo*, it is the duration of time during which many small motions combine to produce action." Taubert, *Rechtschaffener Tantzmeister*, 968: "*Tempo* is in general a quantity of duration during which one out of many small connected motions is executed; time present is the moment that comes after all the moments of time past and before all the moments of time future, and it encompasses within itself the time required for every infinitesimal motion." Similarly, Noverre, *Lettres sur les arts imitateurs en général* (1807), vol. II, 140, writes: "I perceived that the language of gesture is nothing but that of grand passions, that the only time available to it is the present moment, without reference to either the past or the future" ("Je m'aperçus que la langue du geste n'est que celle des grandes passions, que l'instant présent est seul à sa disposition, qu'elle ne peut rendre ni le *passé* ni le *futur*").

58. Hammond, "Ballet's Technical Heritage," 38. See especially the sequences in the "Théorie descriptive, et demonstrative de la grande position de L'Arabesque," Adice, Gallica 311971p, view 573–605. As Hammond suggests,

Adice's illustrated motion sequences may be said to anticipate Eadweard Muybridge's innovative stop-action photography around two decades later.

59. Adice, "Remarque Sur l'Esthétique," Gallica 3119722, view 711: "La chorégraphie, dans sa composition, aussi bien que, dans son instruction, n'est que l'image mouvementée de la peinture; ceci n'a point besoin de commentaire." Cf. Hardouin (Reading 5.3): "Dance is a continuous drawing."

60. It is unfortunate, as Hammond points out ("Ballet's Technical Heritage," 55n3), that Sarah Jeanne Cohen's excerpt of Adice's *Théorie* (in *Dance as a Theatre Art*, 71–77) is illustrated by figures from Blasis's *Traité élémentaire* (inaccurately cited as the *Code of Terpsichore* by Cohen). Adice's functional *manequins* are a far cry from Blasis's elegant engraving.

61. Adice, "Grammaire/et/Théorie chorégraphique," Gallica 311742d, "Des Bras; Avant propos," views 585–587, 595–597. For earlier references to *dessein* and *se dessiner*, see Hardouin (Reading 5.3), Cahusac (Reading 5.4), Noverre (Reading 6.1), Despréaux (Reading 7.1), and Blasis (Reading 7.2b).

62. All ellipses are original.—Ed.

63. The aesthetic part refers to the *manequins*. Adice seems to have envisioned a first volume of text and a second of illustrations.—Ed.

64. Adice, *Théorie*, 109, defines *forté* as a style used by "dancers in the noble genre . . . [characterized by] vehement gestures typical of Arabs" ("danseurs du genre noble . . . les tours de force dignes des Arabes").—Ed.

65. "Most abused" Jules Perrot (1810–1892), dancer and choreographer, was denied official credit for choreographing Carlotta Grisi's role in *Giselle* (Paris, 1841).—Ed.

66. G. Desrat, *Traité de la danse*, new ed. (Paris: H. Delarue et Cie., n.d. [190?]); Eugène Giraudet, *Traité de la danse*, 7th ed. (Paris: Imprimerie A. Ventin, [1894 or later]); Giraudet, *La danse, la tenue, le maintien l'hygiène & l'éducation*, 55th ed. (Paris: author, [1897 or later]); Charles d'Albert, *Dancing. Technical Encyclopaedia of the Theory and Practice of The Art of Dancing* (London: author, 1913–1914); d'Albert, *The Encyclopedia of Dancing*, revised ed. (London: T. M. Middleton & Co., [1920]). Much earlier, Taubert speaks of "the theory of any one dance" (380).

67. Sophie Jacotot, "Les 'théories' de danses nouvelles en France dans l'entre-deux-guerres: quelles sources ces documents constituent-ils pour la connaissance des pratiques dansées?," *Society of Dance History Scholars Proceedings*, 502. Also, see Russell and Bourassa, *The Menuet de la cour*, 158–159 (Table 6).

68. Giraudet, *Traité* (1900), list of publications, 534–536.

69. Giraudet, *Traité* (1900), 450: "Les bases primordiales de son expérience, s'appuient sur ces immuables principes."

70. It is interesting to note that elsewhere Giraudet lists the names, addresses, and credentials of female as well as male *professeurs* of dance, *Traité* (1900), 642–644.—Ed.

71. Giraudet does not define these terms.—Ed.

72. The remainder of the chapter, following this paragraph, is paraphrased from Blasis and Giraudet, as Bourgeois admits on p. 54; for example, compare the paragraph in this reading that begins: "Having said that . . . ," with Reading 7.2a: "Every dancer is capable . . . ."—Ed.

~~~~~~

| 8 |

The Twentieth Century: Modernist Theory

The contemporary art of any era is forever "modern," with the impatient "avant-garde" continually forging ahead to the future. Periodization—the naming, dating, and generalized description of historical eras—has until recently been retrospective, our way of sloughing off the past. Also, because of infinite historical perspectives and parameters, periodization is extremely subjective and perpetually subject to disputation. In the early twentieth century, periodization ceased being retrospective; nomenclature finally caught up with the present tense. "Modern" stuck as the default name of the period, and it was accepted so pervasively that the period that grew out of modernism, but with significant differences, almost inevitably had to define itself by merely tacking on the prefix "post."

To avoid the endless and fruitless quest for exactitude in naming, dating, and description, the two eras in dance theory and practice that began around 1900—modernism, then postmodernism—will be characterized here by analogy to the concurrent, dominant movements or "isms" in concert music and the visual arts. This method seems preferable to abstract generalizations full of specialist terminology. Readers may make their own analogies between their sensory and intellectual experiences of art, music, and modern and contemporary dance. Parallels or divergences are implicit but not necessarily evident in the following readings. Readers should judge for themselves in what manner, and to what extent, meaningful connections can be drawn among these "isms" in different fields, and thereby formulate their own conception of what the theory of modern and postmodern dance is all about.

Modernism in music began with the breakdown of tonality and the introduction of serialism, *musique concrète*, electronic music, and aleatoric music, as well as a compensatory "neo"-tonalism and a lively interest in historically informed performance practice.[1] Modern art begins with expressionism, ends with abstract expressionism, and includes everything in between: cubism, surrealism, dada, deco, futurism, and so forth. The dominant philosophical "ism" is structuralism.

Postmodernism in music begins with expanded applications of serialism leading to "total" or "integral" serialism, and diversifies to minimalism, intense interest in world musics, and continued interest in historically informed performance. It is often semi-improvisational in both conception and performance, and increasingly interested in multimedia and experimental "fusions" of styles, genres, and cultures. Postmodern art begins with pop art and continues with op art, conceptual art, photorealism, and earth art. The dominant philosophical "ism" is poststructuralism.

The difference between structuralism and poststructuralism will be discussed in Chapter 9.

8.1. RUDOLF VON LABAN (1879–1958)
Die Welt des Tänzers (Stuttgart: Walter Seifert, 1920).
Modern Educational Dance, 2nd, rev. ed., trans. Lisa Ullmann (London: Macdonald & Evans, 1963; 1st ed. 1948).

Rudolf von Laban considered himself, justifiably, "the First among today's dancers to speak of a world for which our language has no words"; nevertheless, in spite of the pioneering nature of his work, his ideas can be traced back to Feuillet and the Renaissance.[2] He is a rare if not unique figure among writers on dance, epoch-making in theory, practice, and notation. His works on theory and choreography are of equal weight and influence, and each informs the other. From the standpoint of his legacy, his theoretical writing is a foundational document of modern dance, while the choreographic notation he invented has lasted to this day as the sole universally recognized system for the written preservation of dances. His major contributions in both areas were first set forth in a series of books published in the 1920s.

Among all other notation systems proposed and published in the nineteenth and twentieth centuries, Laban's stands out as the only one that attracted a sufficiently large following to survive beyond its first or second edition. Hutchinson Guest writes: "In the publication of books the Laban system has the greatest number and widest range, textbooks alone being available in eleven languages."[3] It is one of the dominant three systems in dance history: Beauchamps-Feuillet in the eighteenth century; purely verbal description in the nineteenth; and Laban in the twentieth and beyond.

Walter Paul Misslitz called it a track system because its information is laid out along a single vertical line that is read from the bottom to the top of the page.[4] It resembles Beauchamps-Feuillet notation both as a track system and in being legible from the dancer's point of view as opposed to the observer's (as in, e.g., Zorn notation). However, its symbols are as abstract as can be, lacking any anthropomorphic reference or evocation; therefore, both Jeschke and Hutchinson Guest classify it as an abstract-symbol system. Jeschke sees it as Laban's constructive response to the highly personal vision of dance embodied, for example, by Isadora Duncan, a vision that existing choreographic systems were inadequate to translate.[5]

Laban's first attempts at devising a new system, published in his *Choreographie* (Jena, 1926), present a variety of approaches, from the impressionistic squiggles of "swallow-tail writing" (*Schwalbenschwantzenschrift*) to more systematic symbol-systems such as letter-abbreviations, the "body-cross" (*Körperkreuz*), and abstract symbols corresponding to various parameters of body position and movement analysis. His *Kinetographie Laban,* also known as Labanotation, published first in *Schrifttanz* (Vienna, 1928; English translation 1930), coordinates all these variables—and more—in the single abstract system still in wide use today.[6]

Laban's choreographic thinking was based in large part on a historical source: Feuillet. In fact, in his preface to *Principles of Dance and Movement Notation,* he acknowledges his debt to Beauchamp and Feuillet, who "opened much wider horizons than Noverre suspected," and he enumerates the principles of their system that he has "kept intact" in his own.[7] The five foot positions codified by Feuillet, in Laban's view, implied potential directional movement: first and fifth imply vertical movement; second, motion to the side; third, oblique; fourth, forward and backward, making six directions altogether. Laban extends this concept to analogous positions and directions of the arms, resulting in a total of twelve axial planes passing through the center of the dancer's body.[8] The axial planes are divided into three groups that intersect along a central axis: vertical, horizontal, and forward-backward (or sagittal).

Laban's ideas on step shape also are derived from Feuillet. He noticed that four of Feuillet's five fundamental steps (*droit, ouvert, rond, tortillé,* and *battu*) are similar in shape to numbers and letters of the alphabet: *droit* is like a "1" or an "I"; *tortillé,* like a "2" or an "S"; *rond,* like a "3" or an "E"; and *ouvert,* like a forward or backward "C." These observations led him to hypothesize a primal linguistic connection between words and dance:

> Dancing is thus the expression of one of the many movement-impulses that slumber in our volition. To jump around joyfully is only a primitive form of dancing, a kind of happy extension and torsion (sinuosity) of the self. The art-dance or performed dance is an end-product in which the initiatory

impulse of primitive dance is clarified, elaborated, and organized for expression (communication) through dance movements.

Every movement, every part of a movement, becomes a dance-letter, a dance-word, a dance-feeling. And the sum total has artistic purpose and artistic form. Dance becomes a work of art.[9]

Laban's theoretical ideas developed in tandem with his choreography. Although he kept modifying and refining his ideas and terminology in successive books, his first, *Die Welt des Tänzers* (*The Dancer's World*, 1920) already contains *in nuce* his core theoretical principles, which he formulated under a new title: *Tanzwissenschaft*.

While Aristides Quintilianus (see the introduction) was the first to state that music theory has a scientific component, the term *Musikwissenschaft* or music science was not used until the late nineteenth century; in English it is translated as musicology. At first it encompassed all branches of musical knowledge, including history, theory, and notation; now, however, musicology is concerned primarily with music history. In 1707, Johann Pasch defined dance as a science (*Wissenschaft*) with respect to its theory.[10] Laban may have coined the word *Tanzwissenschaft*, in emulation of *Musikwissenschaft*, as the equivalent German term for dance science.[11] In *Die Welt des Tänzers* he divides the world of dance knowledge into three branches that differ from those of music: *Tanzkunst* (dance-art) is practice; *Tanzschrift* (dance-writing) is notation; and *Tanzwissenschaft* (dance-science) is theory—a selection of traditional topics and one innovatory concept of great importance to Laban: crystallography (Reading 8.1a).

Laban strove throughout his career to express his ideas visually, either through symbols in several choreographic notation systems, or through drawings of the moving human figure, often interacting with geometrical designs. He observed that a walking man with arms outstretched to the side forms a tetrahedron (a four-sided three-dimensional figure, each side of which is a triangle) when the fingertips and toes are connected by straight lines (see Fig. 8.1).[12] Laban drew many variations on the theme of a dancer within a tetrahedron, and of abstract concatenations of tetrahedrons that can be construed either as sculpture or movement in an expressionistic modern dance.[13] This notion of a human figure inscribed within a geometric form is similar to the Vitruvian man, whose body is inscribed within a circle or a square, with the key difference being that the Vitruvian man is motionless and two-dimensional, whereas Laban's figures move in three dimensions.

Tetrahedrons exist in nature as the crystalline forms of certain minerals. Just as crystals are formed from the geometry of their molecular structure, Laban derives a twenty-sided polyhedron, the icosahedron (from the Greek εἴκοσι, twenty), composed of twenty tetrahedrons, each of its twenty sides being an equilateral triangle. The vertices at which the corners of the triangles touch coincide with the endpoints of the vertical, horizontal, and sagittal planes (see Fig. 8.2).[14] The icosahedron thus served as a three-dimensional grid within which dancers could conceptualize moving along the diagonal axes drawn through its center point. Laban students actually constructed life-size isocahedrons for demonstration and practice.

The most traditional aspect of Laban's theory is the four components (or factors) of motion, the first three of which are described, again, in *Die Welt des Tänzers:* time (*Zeit*), force (*Kraft*), and space (*Raum*).[15] The fourth, added in *Gymnastic und Tanz* six years later, is flow (*Flucht*):

We mentioned, and it is the generally held and commonly understood opinion, that there are three principal characteristics of movement that give

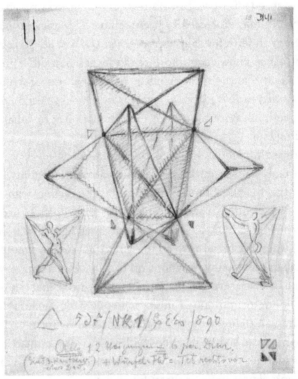

Figure 8.1. Rudolf Laban, pencil drawing by Rudolf Laban of two figures in tetrahedrons, and a shape made by interlocking tetrahedrons (Ref No: L/C/S/77). From the Rudolf Laban Archive, University of Surrey © University of Surrey.

- The intersection of the three planes creates the Icosahedron Crystalline Figure:

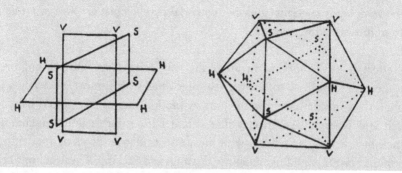

Figure 8.2. [Laban] Ciane Fernandes, *The Moving Researcher.* "The intersection of the three planes creates the Icosahedron Crystalline Figure" (license granted by Publishers' Licensing Services Limited [PLS Clear]), 224.

it a certain quantitative proportionality. And we measure these basic characteristics under the names of force, time, and space. Now, however, we perceive another, fourth, characteristic, transitoriness/volatility [*Flüchtigkeit*], which here we will call flow, for short. Whereas in force, time, and space we observe the contrasts of strong and weak, slow and fast, far and near, in flow we have the contrast of tight and loose.[16]

These characteristics or factors correspond, respectively, to the rhythmic, dynamic, metric, and kinetic dimensions of movement.[17] They also—all except force—hark back to the earliest lists of dance elements in the Italian Renaissance sources: time corresponds to *misura;* space to *compartimento di terreno;* and flow to any combination or all of *agilitade, aere, maniera,* and *passeggiare misurato con arte.* Laban's definition of force was later nuanced to include weight and tension, bringing it more in line with traditional concepts such as equilibrium, symmetry, and "movements of the soul." Flow was variously referred to as lability and flux.[18]

Later still, the four factors of motion were incorporated within the broader concept of "effort theory" (Reading 8.1b). In *Effort: Economy in Human Movement* and *Modern Educational Dance* (both 1947), Laban applied his ideas about dance movement to a wide range of nondance activity, including work, play, education, and social or civic functions:

The contemporary inclusion of industrial psychology as a part of work study arose from the recognition of the immense importance of the human factor and the unaccountable behaviour of individuals and groups within industrial concerns. Mechanical planning has been spoiled by the uncoordinated efforts of people who have had to perform the various tasks. Both the work study specialist and the industrial psychologist are able to profit from modern effort research.[19]

In "effort theory," workers in an industrial society are "human engines" who need to learn how to operate real machines with utmost efficiency and economy—a mechanistic view of human motion that can be traced back to Pasch and Weaver.[20] Laban classified "eight basic effort actions," including some not primarily associated with the world of dance: pressing, punching, wringing, slashing, gliding, dabbing, floating, and flicking. These actions can be controlled in terms of being free or bound, sustained or sudden. Laban invented a symbolic shorthand system, separate from his choreographic notation, to read these effort patterns at a glance.[21] "Effort theory" has wide-ranging applications and implications, by extending dance's movement repertoire to encompass the innovations of modern dance, and also, when applied to nondanced spheres of contemporary life, by broadening the ethical function in society of dance theory—a clear if not intentional reminder of the primary function of Pasch's and Taubert's "prosaic dance," as well as Plato's belief in dance as an instiller of civic virtue.

READING 8.1A
Laban

From *Die Welt des Tänzers* (trans. Russell)

PP. 64–66

Dance science (*Tanzwissenschaft*). In the most passionate dance, in the wild tarantella and the awe-inspiring gestures of wise men, the dancer perceives the effect of the same laws of form in motion as in the autonomous growth of crystals. It will be the duty of newly created dance science to point out the dominance of harmonic laws of dynamic stress in all of nature.

These are the sources of dance science:

1. The cognitive, psychological, physiological, and physical certainties of the movements of living things.
2. Geometric and crystallographic spacial knowledge.

3. The monuments of visual arts in sculpture, painting, lesser arts [*Kleinkunst*], including the hieroglyphic and abstract signs for counting and concepts, and ornamentation.
4. Musical and cognitive research on harmony.
5. The written, disregarded theories on historic dance as well as on mystical [*mantisch*], religious, ceremonial, and ritualistic forms of movement.
6. The theories behind movement in acrobatics, fencing, and sports.
7. The mimetic tradition of theater.
8. The traditional practice of European art dance and the folk dances and national dances of all peoples.

The art of dance (*Tanzkunst*). In music the physical and physiological laws of rhythmic and harmonic organization were instinctively known by artists for centuries, and long practiced. It is the same in the art of dance. Dance science must now establish what a dancer-like bearing is, and how harmony in a sequence of gestures depends on the internal relationship of its parts. In this way it will be revivified and blossom anew in festivities in general and the art of dance in particular.

Dance writing (*Tanzschrift*). It is important that the present written language of movement be improved. It is essential that written dance symbols be established, for only from comparison and inquiry, repetition and imitation, will come the kind of tradition that makes possible a deeper appreciation of dance's artistic worth. Where would poetry and music be if their works came down to us only by way of oral transmission?

The universal dance experience and its benefit to humanity. Dance is not only of artistic and scientific value. Latent within it are important educational powers, because it manifests experience in three dimensions. It is hoped that the understanding of the dance experience will spread to the broadest social contexts. Through it the general conduct of life can only be benefited. The role of rhythm in every type of work and organisation is known. The necessary reawakening of ceremonial culture, which gives men, besides recreation and diversion, also uplift and edification, will be encouraged everywhere. The dancer anticipates its origin in the art of dancing in the round, which is a synthesis of all human impression and expression. Its most potent and pure manifestation is, above all, the human body's intellectual, mystical, and willful predisposition to purified dance.

READING 8.1B
From *Modern Educational Dance*

PP. 8–10

A new conception of the elements of movement based on modern work research has been introduced into dance tuition. The basic idea of the new dance training is that actions in all kinds of human activities, and therefore also in dance, consist of movement sequences in which a definite effort of the moving person underlies each movement.

The distinction of a specific effort becomes possible because each action consists of a combination of effort elements. The effort elements derive from attitudes of the moving person towards the motion factors Weight, Space, Time, and Flow. The new dance training fosters the development of a clear and precise awareness of the various efforts in movement, thus guaranteeing the appreciation and enjoyment of any, even the simplest, action movements.

Knowledge of human effort, and especially the efforts used by industrial man, is the basis of the dance tuition applied by many pupils of the author who, when they become teachers or artists, have played a prominent rôle in the development of this contemporary art of movement.

It becomes necessary at this point to clear up a few fundamental conceptions concerning the art of movement, which comprises more than dance in its narrower sense.

The art of movement is used on the stage in ballet, pantomime, drama, and in any other kind of performance, including films. All forms of social dancing, country or ballroom dancing and so on, constitute part of the art of movement, as well as a great number of party games, masquerades and many other social plays and entertainments.

The art of movement is implicated in all ceremonies and rituals and forms part of the speaker's outfit in all kinds of oratory and meetings. Our everyday behaviour is ruled by certain aspects of the art of movement, and so is a great part of the behaviour and activity of children in schools. Games imply the knowledge and experience of the movements used in them, which require a technique of moving. This technique, like that used in the skilled performance of industrial operations, is a part of the art of movement.

The technique of moving has several aspects, one of which is that cultivated in dance tuition.

Traditional dance technique deals with the mastery of individual movements required in particular styles of dancing. The performance of dances is not restricted to the stage. Apart from the theatrical dance compositions of the ballet, each of the social forms of the art of dance, such as national, folk, and ballroom dances, has its own forms of movement and technique.

The new dance technique promoting the mastery of movement in all its bodily and mental aspects is applied in modern dance as a new form of stage dancing and of social dancing. The educational value of this new dance technique can be ascribed to a great extent to the universality of the movement forms which are studied and mastered in the contemporary aspect of this art.

8.2. MARGARET N. H'DOUBLER (1889–1984)
Dance: A Creative Art Experience (New York: F. S. Crofts and Company, 1940).

"Miss H'Doubler ranks among America's great dance educators and pioneers. She was the first to introduce dance into the college curriculum, and the University of Wisconsin, where she has taught for 23 years, was the first to offer major courses in the dance."[22] Margaret N. H'Doubler's dance program was offered through the department of physical education at Wisconsin: "Dance studies entered the academy, if not through the back door, then through a side door—a gym door, to be precise."[23] The *entrée* of dance studies in academe initiated a "quest for a theoretical base and productive research methods" in order to legitimate the new discipline as a degree-granting course of study.[24] H'Doubler's books pioneered in pursuing these goals in American higher education.

H'Doubler published two books prior to *Dance: A Creative Experience*.[25] Both are chiefly pedagogical manuals, "addressed primarily to the teacher," but also of use to students, mainly college women.[26] Large sections of both books are in outline form, like lecture notes. *The Dance and Its Place in Education* is embellished with photographs clearly influenced by Isadora Duncan, of young girls in flimsy Grecian costumes, dancing either in a studio or an Arcadian landscape. At the end of the book there are simple patterns for constructing one's own costumes and sandals, followed by nude drawings of girls in various class exercises.

Dance: A Creative Art Experience is more ambitious than the earlier two books. It is artistically produced, with each chapter preceded by its own frontispiece with a "dance sketch" by Wayne Lm. Claxton, facing a full-page title; the sketches show dancers in various states of swirling motion, and they may have been expressly produced for this book. The Editor's Introduction, by C. H. McCloy, suggests the book was intended for "those teachers of dance for whom the part continues to obscure the whole but also to integrate *all* dance forms into their proper places as seen in the perspective of a complete and unified philosophy of that art" (viii). The concepts therein would surely have informed H'Doubler's classroom lessons.

The review calls this book "A Study in Dance Theory," and the Preface states: "Its main purpose is to set forth a theory and a philosophy that will help us to see dance scientifically as well as artistically" (xi). H'Doubler says that the three parts of dance knowledge are theory; "the psychology of the emotions and the part they play in the urge to expression in movement"; and technique. Theory must be built "on a knowledge of the stucture of the body and the laws of bodily movement" (59–60). It should be pointed out, however, that the word "theory" itself occurs no more than three times in the entire book.

The most theoretically significant chapter in the book is Chapter 7, "Form and Structure" (134–151), in which many terms and definitions of the elements of dance are presented. At the end of the chapter, two fascinating and—to say the least—unusual diagrams graphically delineate the interaction of these elements. In general, there is no clear-cut relation between the text and the diagrams: not every element described in the text appears in the diagrams; and some terms and categories that appear on the second diagram are not tied to any particular part of the text. Both diagrams are based on spinning and weaving, a craft traditionally associated with women's work and therefore intrinsically relatable to H'Doubler's students.

The first diagram (144) is an eight-pointed spiderweb (see Fig. 8.3). The points are labeled, in clockwise order, Transition, Balance, Sequence, Repetition, Harmony, Variety, Contrast, and Climax. These eight terms will be found again in the second diagram as comprising the "Form Factors" category. H'Doubler explains the web diagram in a caption:

> The composing of a dance may be compared to the spinning of a spider web. The pattern is woven from that which is within. In the process, structure is made possible by the medium's being fastened to supporting units (principles of composition). The pattern grows and takes its shape in accordance with inner necessity and the capacity, power, and excellence of execution.

Unity, mentioned previously with the chosen eight terms (141–142), is absent here for no apparent reason other than the web having eight instead of nine points, and there are many other terms mentioned throughout the book that are not included here but could have been: form, proportion, visual design, technique, expression, and so forth. The terms are arranged around the web in no apparent sequential or functional order.

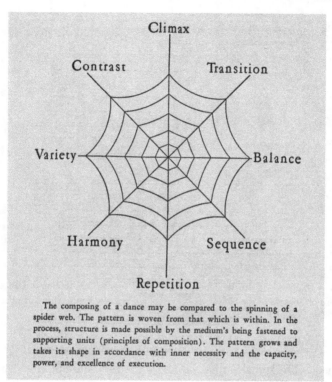

The composing of a dance may be compared to the spinning of a spider web. The pattern is woven from that which is within. In the process, structure is made possible by the medium's being fastened to supporting units (principles of composition). The pattern grows and takes its shape in accordance with inner necessity and the capacity, power, and excellence of execution.

Figure 8.3. Margaret N. H'Doubler, *Dance: A Creative Art Experience*: "The composing of a dance. . ." (© 1957 by the Board of Regents of the University of Wisconsin System. Reprinted by permission of The University of Wisconsin Press), 144.

The second diagram, "Schematic Representation of Elements Contributing to Dance" (150–151), presents the most complete and coherent version of H'Doubler's theory (see Fig. 8.4). The central image is a loom on which strands are woven longitudinally (i.e., the warp) and latitudinally (i.e., the weft, also known as the woof). The warp, labeled "TECHNIQUES" along the top, represents "movement studies" (strength, flexibility, quality, coordination, specific skills); the woof, labeled down the right side, represents the three "FACTORS" of dance: RHYTHMIC, SPACE, and FORM (the elements of FORM having already been depicted as the points of the spiderweb).

On the left side, H'Doubler further interprets the woven fabric as representing the (A) anatomical, (B) physiological, and (C) psychic "determinants" of dance (see Reading 8.2a), which are symbolized, respectively, by the heavy outline, and the tiny dots and x's that fill the interstices between the interwoven threads (as explained in the interpretive note on the facing page; see Reading 8.2b). The image as a whole, which somewhat resembles a musical score in its

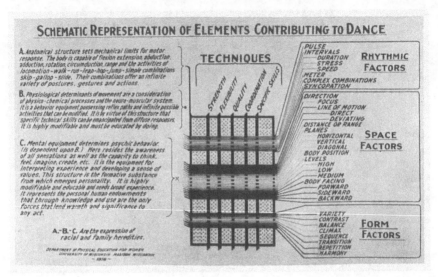

Figure 8.4. H'Doubler: "Schematic Representation of Elements Contributing to Dance" (© 1957 by the Board of Regents of the University of Wisconsin System. Reprinted by permission of The University of Wisconsin Press), 150.

simultaneous horizontal-vertical layout, is the first attempt at a visualization of dance theory since Fabritio Caroso in 1600 (see Reading 2.5). It should be noted, in addition, that H'Doubler lists flexion, extension, abduction, and adduction among the anatomically determined species of "motor response." We have seen these four basic motions (in Latin: *flexio, extensio, abductio, adductio*) repeated by theorists ever since Behr in 1703 (Reading 4.1).

READING 8.2A

H'DOUBLER

P. 150

A. Anatomical structure sets mechanical limits for motor response. The body is capable of flexion, extension, abduction, adduction, rotation, circumduction, range and the activities of locomotion—walk—run—leap—hop—jump—simple combinations skip—gallop—slide. Their combinations offer an infinite variety of postures, gestures and actions.

B. Physiological determinants of movement are a consideration of physico-chemical processes and the neuro-muscular system. It is a behavior equipment possessing reflex paths and infinite possible activities that can be modified. It is by virtue of this structure that specific technical skills can be emancipated from diffuse responses. It is highly modifiable and must be educated by doing.

C. Mental equipment determines psychic behavior. (Is dependent upon B.) Here resides the awareness of all sensations as well as the capacity to think feel, imagine, create, etc. It is the equipment for interpreting experience and developing a sense of values. This structure is the formative substance from which emerges personality. It is highly modifiable and educable and needs broad experience. It represents the personal human endowments that through knowledge and use are the only forces that lend warmth and significance to any act.

A.—B.—C. Are the expression of
racial and family heredities.[27]

READING 8.2B

P. 151

The chart above is a visible representation of the integration of all the elements that enter into the study of dance.

It is conceived in the form of a loom.

>   A. The confining outline represents the limitations of movement determined by anatomical structure.
>   B. The dotted area represents the physiological determinants of movement.
>   C. The crosses represent the psychical equipment.

B and C form the matrix—that substance of our make-up that furnishes the background which receives impressions and out of which arise, in high relief, personality and patterns of behavior. They form the plastic material that is sensitive and educable.

A, B, and C represent the native equipment which every student brings to the study of dance. The strands of the warp represent movement studies that are entered into for the specific purposes of flexibility, strength, co-ordination, and specific skills; but inherent in them are the elements represented by the woof strands. Each strand is a particular interest that is "pulled out" for special study, so that the student may not only master it as technique but discover what contributions it makes to a larger organization, and how it is in turn affected by the whole of which it is a part.

8.3. African American Dance Theory I

8.3A. ZORA NEALE HURSTON (1891–1960)

Zora Neale Hurston: Folklore, Memoirs, and Other Writings, ed. Cheryl A. Wall (New York: The Library of America, 1995).

Lucy Anne Hurston and the Estate of Zora Neale Hurston, *Speak, So You Can Speak Again: The Life of Zora Neale Hurston* (New York: Doubleday, 2004).

The Complete Stories (New York: Harper Perennial Modern Classics, 2009).

8.3B. KATHERINE DUNHAM (1909–2006)

"The Negro Dance," *Negro Caravan: Writings by American Negroes*, ed. Sterling A. Brown, Arthur P. Davis, and Ulysses Lee (New York: Dryden Press, 1941), 990–1000; reprinted in: *Kaiso! Writings by and about Katherine Dunham*, ed. VèVè A. Clark and Sara E. Johnson (Madison: University of Wisconsin Press, 2005), 217–226.

The work of Zora Neale Hurston and Katharine Dunham represents the earliest research-based writing on African American dance. These women would probably not have known what to make of a concept such as African American dance theory, much less to call their work by that name. What they were writing conformed to no existing tradition. It was created from raw empirical data—predominantly anthropological, sociological, and ethnological in nature—that would guarantee the construction of a totally new kind of dance theory, one that has proved a harbinger and model of twenty-first-century approaches to dance theory in general. Susan Manning, in her chronology of African American dance, 1897–2012, writes: "Taken together, Hurston's 1934 essays and Dunham's 1941 essay suggest both 'roots and routes' for black dance."[28]

Zora Neale Hurston, a leading figure in the Harlem Renaissance, was herself, in the breadth of her curiosity and her literary and scholarly legacy, a "Renaissance" soul: poet, playwright, ethnographer, folklorist, essayist, novelist. She was in no sense a dance insider, nor did she write extensively about dance, but what she did write can be said to constitute an initiatory document in the theorization of African American dance by African Americans. It was instrumental in drawing attention to African American dance not only as a venerable and genuine art form, but also one that exhibited striking stylistic, spiritual, and ethical affinities with the contemporaneous (and predominantly white) modern dance movement.

Hurston describes dances as she saw them, without scholarly terminology or analysis. Nevertheless, contemporary scholars of African American dance regard her as "an originary theorist concerned with aesthetic composition of black performance." Her essay, "Characteristics of Negro Expression" (Reading 8.3a) is "a taxonomy of African American performativity . . . that referenced sites, modes, and practices of performance. . . . Hurston theorizes Negro performance of the American South in the early twentieth century in provocative, unabashed style. . . . Perhaps this is her grand achievement: she allows black performance to be in dialogue simultaneously with itself, the world around it, and the lives of black people."[29]

Katherine Dunham was an "iconic" professional dance soloist, choreographer, and scholar.[30] After earning her doctorate in anthropology at the University of Chicago, she received a grant to continue her research in Trinidad, Martinique, Jamaica, and Haiti; later she made Haiti her second home. Her life's work epitomizes a "research-to-performance" process, a kind of cross-germination in which her ongoing research in the West Indies not only led to published ethnological scholarship, but also was crucial in forming her artistic repertoire, performance, and philosophy. Dunham's approach to theory was based more on her identity as an anthropologist than as a dancer. Halifu Osumare observes: "Dunham adapted this functionalist construct and developed her theory of Form and Function in dance. In the Dunham dance technique, the student learns that the actual movements and body orientation of a particular dance directly relates to the function of that dance in the social sphere."[31] This means that her "dance theory" has more to do with dance in its sociological context than with dance as an art form, and thus is interdisciplinary—and well before its time.

The aspects of Dunham's technique that Joanna Dee Das lists: "isolations of the head, shoulders, torso, and hips, an increased freedom of movement of the pelvis and spine, an emphasis on percussion, and the concept of polyrhythm in the body," are the same as those Dunham reports observing in Haiti and elsewhere in the Caribbean, in her essay, "The Negro Dance" (Reading 8.3b). According to Dee Das: "Though other African American choreographers had come before her, Dunham was the most successful in bringing African diasporic aesthetics to the concert dance stage and developing her own technique. Thus she is widely considered the founder of black concert dance in the United States and also a major influence on the idioms of both modern and jazz dance."[32]

READING 8.3A

HURSTON

From "The Eatonville Anthology," *The Messenger* **(1926), 64–65. Reprinted in** *The Complete Stories,* **59–72.**

XI
Double-Shuffle

Back in the good old days before the World War, things were very simple in Eatonville.[33] People didn't fox-trot. When the town wanted to put on its Sunday clothes and wash behind the ears, it put on a "breakdown." The darling younger set would two-step and waltz, but the good church members and the elders stuck to the grand march.[34] By rural canons dancing is wicked, but one is not held to have danced until the feet have been crossed. Feet don't get crossed when one grand marches.

At elaborate affairs the organ from the Methodist church was moved up to the hall and Lizzimore, the blind man, presided. When informal gatherings were held, he merely played his guitar assisted by any volunteer with mouth organs or accordions.

Among white people the march is as mild as if it had been passed on by Volstead.[35] But it still has a kick in Eatonville. Everybody happy, shining eyes, gleaming teeth. Feet dragged 'shhlap, shhlap! to beat out the time. No orchestra needed. Round and round! Back again, parse-me-la! shlap! shlap! Strut! Strut! Seaboard! Shlap! Shlap! Tiddy bumm! Mr. Clarke in the lead with Mrs. Mosely.

It's too much for some of the young folks. Double shuffling commences. Buck and wing.[36] Lizzimore about to break his guitar. Accordion doing contortions. People fall back against the walls, and let the soloist have it, shouting as they clap the old, old double shuffle songs.

> Me an' mah honey got two mo' days,
> Two mo' days tuh do de buck.

From "Characteristics of Negro Expression," *Negro: An Anthology*, ed. Nancy Cunard (London: Wishart & Company, 1934). Reprinted in *Zora Neale Hurston: Folklore, Memoirs, and Other Writings*, 834–836.

Asymmetry

[. . .]

It is the lack of symmetry which makes Negro dancing so difficult for white dancers to learn. The abrupt and unexpected changes. The frequent change of key and time are evidences of this quality in music. (Note the St. Louis Blues.)

The dancing of the justly famous Bo-Jangles and Snake Hips are [*sic*] excellent examples.

The presence of rhythm and lack of symmetry are paradoxical, but there they are. Both are present to a marked degree. There is always rhythm, but it is the rhythm of segments. Each unit has a rhythm of its own, but when the whole is assembled it is lacking in symmetry. But easily workable to a Negro who is accustomed to the break in going from one part to another, so that he adjusts himself to the new tempo.

Dancing

Negro dancing is dynamic suggestion. No matter how violent it may appear to the beholder, every posture gives the impression that the dancer will do much more. For example, the performer flexes one knee sharply, assumes a ferocious face mask, thrusts the upper part of the body forward with clenched fists, elbows taut as in hard running or grasping a thrusting blade. That is all. But the spectator himself adds the picture of ferocious assault, hears the drums and finds himself keeping time with the music and tensing himself for the struggle. It is compelling insinuation. That is the very reason the spectator is held so rapt. He is participating in the performance himself—carrying out the suggestions of the performer.

The difference in the two arts is: the white dancer attempts to express fully; the Negro is restrained, but succeeds in gripping the beholder by forcing him to finish the action the performer suggests. Since no art ever can express all the variations conceivable, the Negro must be considered the greater artist, his dancing is realistic suggestion, and that is about all a great artist can do.

From *Mules and Men* (Philadelphia: J. B. Lippincott, 1935). Reprinted in *Zora Neale Hurston: Folklore, Memoirs, and Other Writings*, 224.

We were to dance three hours, and the time was divided equally, so that the more participants the less time each was called upon to dance. Plenty of liquor was provided . . . But the fury of the rhythm more than the stimulant kept the dancers going. The heel-patting was a perfect drum rhythm, and the hand clapping had various stimulating breaks.

From *Tell My Horse* (Philadelphia: J. B. Lipincott, 1938). Reprinted in *Zora Neale Hurston: Folklore, Memoirs, and Other Writings*, 323.

The dancing begins in earnest now. The Governess is like an intoxicating spirit that whips up the crowd. Those rackling men become fiends from hell. The shuckers do a magnificent muscle dance which they tell me is African. The drums and the movements of the dancers draw so close together that the drums become people and the people become drums. The pulse of the drum is their shoulders and belly. Truly the drum is inside their bodies. More rum, more fire.

From "Harlem Slanguage," first published in the *American Mercury* 54 (July 1942). Facsimile of original typescript page inserted in *Speak, So You Can Speak Again*, 16.

35. BOOGIE WOOGIE, type of dancing and rhythm. For years in the South it meant secondary syphillis [*sic*].

50. JOOK, a pleasure house in the class of gut-bucket. The houses originated in the lumber, turpentine and railroad camps of Florida. Now common all over the south, even in the towns. They are the cradle of the Blues, and most of the dance steps that finally migrate north.

51. JOOKING, playing the piano, guitar, or any musical instrument in the manner of the Jooks. (Pronounced like 'took') 2. Dancing and "scronching" in the manner. A player may be "getting low-down" at the piano and his listeners may yell out in admiration, "Jook it, papa! Jook!"

120. TRUCKING, strolling, (2) dance step from the strolling motif.

142. STOMP, low dance, but hot man!

READING 8.3B

DUNHAM

PP. 220–222

In North America, however, there is less compromise and more real assimilation of African religious forms into European religious ideology. In 1938–1939 I had occasion to direct a group in the Federal Writers' Project in an investigation of religious and magic cults in the city. Here, while the ideology was clearly and definitely Christian (with added flourishes), the entire pattern of religious behavior associated with it was almost as purely African. The rhythmic percussion-type hand-clapping and foot-stamping, the jumping and leaping, the "conversion" or "confession" in unknown tongues which is a form of possession or ecstasy (induced, in some cases, by a circle of "saints" or "angels" closing in upon the person in rhythmic motion of a dance), the frequent self-hypnosis by motor-activity of the shoulders—all these African forms were present. This last type of movement, for example, is called *zépaules* in Haiti and is formally recognized there as a basic dance movement of great ritualistic importance in practice. In general form, even in function, the motor activity connected with the religious expression of "store-front" churches in this country is strikingly similar to that of the Haitian peasant.

More often, however, the disintegration of African religious ideology under the impact of European influences led to the incorporation of the forms of its dance into secular dance. The West Indies, representing that stage of folk culture in which such transitions are apparent, provides, once more, some excellent examples.

In the more formalized of secular dances, in the dance-halls at carnival time, the young people of Haiti perform what they refer to as *do-ba* dances, whose characteristic feature is a wavelike motion of the spine performed in a squatting position, back forward, body bent double. The *do-ba* begins in an erect position, but gradually, by a simultaneous forward movement of shoulders and back, is lowered until the dancer is in an almost squatting position. Anyone who has seen the dance to Damballa, snake-god of the Rada-Dahomey cult, will certainly recognize the secular *do-ba* as a derivative of the ritual in imitation of the undulations of the snake-god. In the ritual, the low squatting position is the climax of the dance and usually indicates a state of supreme religious ecstasy, bordering on or participating in a state of possession by the snake-god to whom the dance is sacred. In the secular dance, the climax of intensity is also reached at the same point, although, of course, the ecstasy is not, in these cases, of the religious impetus.

[...]

Thus we see that in the history of the Negro, the transition from tribal to folk culture expressed itself in three ways as far as the dance is concerned: (1) the use of African ritual patterns for the expression of Christian ideology; (2) the degeneration of religious ritual patterns, by virtue of the disintegration of the ideology which sustained them, into secular use; and (3) the combination of secular African patterns with the secular patterns of whatever European nation happened to dominate the territory.

By the time we come to analyze the transition from folk to urban culture, as the next stage in the acculturation of the Negro, the problem becomes more difficult; for by now the patterns are so intermixed, and so dissipated and broken, that tracing them from one complex to another is at times almost impossible. Sometimes the transition is implicit in the difference in the organization, the social procedures which are involved, in the dance as we proceed from country community to urban center.

8.3C. **ROBERT FARRIS THOMPSON** (B. 1932)
"An Aesthetic of the Cool: West African Dance," *African Forum* 2, no. 2 (Fall 1966), 85–102.

African American dance has existed ever since slavery made landfall in the Western Hemisphere, but it did not begin to be theorized until the second half of the twentieth century when, thanks to the civil rights movement, African studies programs began to percolate into college-level curricula. It should come, then, as no surprise, that at a time when there were still few blacks in the professoriate, the first major work on African American dance theory was published by Robert Farris Thompson, a white professor (now emeritus) in the History of Art and African American Studies at Yale University. Before Thompson, knowledge about African dance was largely limited to reportage, like Hurston's, based on traditional practice, legend, and superstition. Thompson's is the first scholarly study to show solid connections between African and African American dance. His work is still regarded by scholars as an indispensable and authoritative reference point in the field.

READING 8.3C
Thompson

PP. 88–96

Four shared traits of West African music and dance are suggested here, together with a fifth, which, although nonmusical, seems very relevant. These shared characteristics appear to be the following: the dominance of a percussive concept of performance; multiple meter; apart playing and dancing; call-and-response; and, finally, the songs and dances of derision.

The first phrase, which is Alan Merriam's—the dominance of a percussive concept of performance—describes a core element. In the Western classic symphony, two tympani are outnumbered by some forty-three melodic instruments, which is symptomatic of an ascendancy of harmonic and melodic concepts and the relative unimportance of percussive traditions. But in tropical Africa even instruments outside the membranophone and idiophone classes will be played with percussive bias instead of in ways soft and legato. Africans do not traditionally bow fiddles legato, but pluck them energetically, with vigorous attack. So striking is this emphasis upon percussive musical diction (which has to do with aesthetic choices and not the inevitable use of a drum or even hardwood sticks) that I am tempted to designate West Africa as a percussive culture. In fact, heaven itself has been portrayed by a West African poet in terms of percussive display and onomatopoeia:

Let the calabash[37]
Entwined with beads
With blue Aggrey beads

Resound
Let the calabash resound
In tune with the drums
Mingle with these sounds
The clang of wood on tin:
Kentensekenken
Ken—tse ken ken ken

In the West African world, it is one of the dancer's aims to make every rhythmic subtlety of the music visible. When the master drummer of the Ijebu Yoruba rises in level of pitch, during a ceremony for the waterspirit named Igodo, the master dancer is said to rise, correspondingly, upon his toes. When a Thundergod drum choir of the Egbado Yoruba plays music expressive of the hot-tempered God of Iron, the master dancer immediately becomes explosive in her gestures to maintain an appropriate balance with the emotional coloring of the percussive patterns being rendered.

Surface appreciation of such procedures may mask the fact that it is West African *dancing* that is percussive, regardless of whether or not it is expressed with a striking of one part of the body against another (the chest whacking with the hands of Dahomean *Kpe*) or with stamping patterns and rattles. Percussive flavoring governs the motion of those parts of the body that carry no weight—the gestures—as well as the steps that do. Unsurprisingly, a good drummer in West Africa is a good dancer, and vice versa, although the degree of specialty and professionalism varies with each individual.

The mnemonic retention of dance steps shares the same verbal basis of drummers who are attempting to impart the memory of a given drum pattern to an apprentice drummer. This verbal basis often consists of drum syllables: They are used when a dancer wishes to speak out the drum or bodily rhythms of a particular dance in order to make clear the duration of the gestures and steps and the contrasts with which a particular movement is built. To return to the master dancer of Ajilete, Nigeria, we note that she pays close attention to the syllables enunciated by the drums, and when she hears the pattern *gere gere gere gekan*, she swings her hands across her body during the first six syllables. Each time the last two syllables sound, she draws her hands up to her breasts with a simultaneous inhalation of breath.

Thus, West African dances are *talking dances*, and the point of the conversation is the expression of percussive concepts. This gift reappears in the Negro New World: Marshall and Jean Stearns have informed me that tap dancers sometimes spell out their ideas with syllables, in the West African manner, and I have observed similar instances among New York's Afro-Cuban dancers. Perhaps the absorption of this tradition has sharpened the exceptional mambos of James Evans, one of the finest Negro dancers of New York:

> Over the years Evans has worked out a "semaphoric" mambo that is his own, a means of metrically conversing with his hands. Unlike the hand-work in certain Polynesian dances, Evans' is only occasionally pictorial; it is his aim to capture and describe percussion, not specific images, and the extent to which he succeeds is perhaps best summarized by [Hoyt Warner] who once shouted to him "You *caught* that riff."

Warner, a young white mathematician and amateur of mambo, meant that the music indicated a sudden repeated phrase and that Evans had convincingly translated the iteration into motion.

Instead of emphasizing the expression of West African dance (and its derivatives) in terms of taps and rattles, clapping and stamping, it would seem far more penetrating to say that it is West African dancing itself that is percussive. The vigor and the attack of the idiom can be so subtly elaborated as when Ohọri Yoruba open and close their shoulder blades in time to a mental gong.

Multiple meter, the second trait, is a well-documented element of West African music. The phrase means the simultaneous execution of several time signatures, not unlike the sounding of the 3/4 of waltz and the 4/4 of jazz at the same time, survivals of which enliven the Negro barrios of the Americas. Polymeter in the West African manner turns up in the urban music of the Spanish-speaking segments of the United States. A pleasing example has been recorded by Mongo Santamaria, wherein two types of drum establish parallel lines of 4/4 time with machine-gun celerity while another type of drum lays down a 6/8 at a slow tempo.

Multiple meter qualifies much West African dancing as a mirror image. A useful theoretical introduction to the problem was established in 1948 by Richard Alan Waterman:

> The dance of the West African is an essay on the appreciation of musical rhythms. For the performance of a good dancer the drums furnish the inspiration, in response to which the thread of each rhythmic element contributing to the thunderous whole of the percussion *gestalt* is followed in movement without separation from its polyrhythmic context.

Waterman describes a maximum instance. The dancer picks up each rhythm of the polymetric whole with different parts of his body; when he does so, he directly mirrors the metric mosaic. But it is important to note that in many instances West Africans find it convenient to dance to only one rhythm, or to shift from two basic pulsations in their footwork to three (as in a kind of Ewe virtuoso dancing), or to follow three mental pulsations while the gong player actually strikes four. In other words, there are minimum instances of multimetric dancing to oppose against the full expression described by Waterman.

In this context, the notion of balance is not only a canon of West African dancing but an aesthetic acid test: The weak dancer soon loses his metric bearings in the welter of competing countermeters and is, so to speak, knocked off balance, as if a loser in a bout of Indian wrestling. Multiple meter is, in brief, a communal examination of percussive individuality.

Bertonoff defines multimetric dancing as bodily orchestration:

> The Ewe dances are the most fervent among all the Ghanaian tribes, for in them the body moves as though it were orchestrated. The various limbs and members, head, shoulders, and legs are all moving simultaneously but each in a rhythm of its own. The main movement is carried out at dizzying speed by the elbows. The motion resembles that of the wings of an injured bird, yet it is as light and easy as the swaying of a fish's fins.

I suspect dancers from different African societies choose different parts of the body for emphasis within the polymetric whole. We know that the rhythmic emphasis of West African music shifts back and forth from meter to meter, and the parts of the dancer's body that reflect these shifts may also constitute major determinants of local styles.

On the northwest "verge" of Ghana, at Lawra, Bertonoff documented a second manifestation of multiple meter. The movement was actually the seated "dance" of the musician playing a xylophone:

> He held a stick in each hand, and the rhythm of the left hand was opposed to that of the right. His head was moving in a third rhythm between the strokes. It seemed to me that the soles of his feet were also on the move and giving the rhythm and counter-rhythm an interpretation of their own. During the dance the feet interpret the rhythm according to which the other parts of the body are moving.

The last observation is interesting. Implied is a notion of the dancer monitoring the rhythmic *donnée* of the music with his feet while with other parts of his body he duplicates or comments upon the polymeters of the music. The metric "given" of the music in West Africa is normally the accents of a gong.

Significantly, A. M. Jones, who has also briefly studied Ewe dancing, finds that in the *Adzida* club dance ("very popular in Eweland") the foot and hand movements are staggered, though the feet are in phase with the gong. It should be noted, however, that Jones's careful notation shows the bell pattern in 12/8 time, the feet in 3/4; thus, even though the dancer follows the organizing meter of the music with his feet, he has executed a statement at metrical variance from it.

The notion of the feet interpreting the foundation beat of gongs finds an interesting corroboration among the Tiv of central Nigeria. Laura Bohannan reports a confrontation with informants who insisted that she dance at a wedding to prove her solidarity with the relevant family: " 'Teach me then,' I retorted. Duly, she and the other senior women began my instruction: my hands and my feet were to keep time with the gongs, my hips with the first drum, my back and shoulders with the second." Whenever Mrs. Bohannan subsided into an "absent-minded shuffle," indignant old women promptly poked her in the ribs and commanded "Dance." Thus, in at least one Tiv society, the articulation of multiple meter seems to amount to protocol.

Cult and secular dancing among the Negroes of Cuba evinces some multimetric dancing. Rumbaists, for example, sometimes introduce a passage of 6/8 elbow-work at a fast tempo in opposition to the basic 2/4 or 4/4 pulsations marked by their footwork. Señor Julito Collazo, an excellent dancer of an entire range of Cuban cult dances, told me that "there have been many times when I was dancing rumba with or against the 2/4 of the music when I varied my steps by adding passages of Cuban-Ibibio style in 6/8 time." Whenever this happened, his steps were immediately at variance with the basic beat.

The third trait is apart playing and dancing. And perhaps the best way to gain an insight into the dissection of experience that affects Western life may be to study the physical movements of the musicians of a classic symphony orchestra. The violin section is seated in ordered rows; and when the violinists are observed in profile, their silhouettes, a repeated pattern of human figures seated stiffly erect, form a kind of step-fret series. At the sign of the conductor's baton, more than a score of violinists take up their instruments and, holding them against their chins, bow-and-finger them in unison; as they do so, their restricted action hovers like a nimbus over the more-or-less motionless body. Action has been restricted, essentially, to the right arm and to the fingers and wrist of the left hand, although the body may sway somewhat.

In dramatic contrast to this remarkable compression of motion, West African musicians move the whole trunk and head, whether seated or standing, in response to the music. West African musicians dance their own music. They play "apart" in the sense that each is often intent upon the production of his own contribution to a polymetric whole. The members of a drum choir of three do not strike the skins of their instruments in unison. At least one—normally the master drummer—creates pleasing clashes with the rhythmic structure of his helpers; he departs from their text, as it were, and improvises illuminations. "Apart playing" defines much of the production of music in West Africa whereas "synchronous" playing defines much of the music of the West. (But certainly not all: "Classic" compositions come to mind wherein the clarinets may do something different from the violins.) Africans unite music and dance but play apart; Europeans separate dance and music but play together. As A. M. Jones notes: "With Western music deliberate synchrony is the norm from which our music develops; that is why it is possible for one man with a baton to conduct a whole orchestra." Playing apart, on the other hand, grants the West African space in which to maintain his own private or traditional meter and to express his own full corporeal involvement in what he is doing.

A close inspection of dance modes in West Africa will reveal that "apart dancing" is as important a part of choreographic custom as "apart playing." It is one of the more striking traits of sub-Saharan dance, and it is one of the few dance constituents that European outsiders consistently identified in verbal descriptions. F. de Kersaint-Gilly noted in 1922: "In Negro Africa—I have spent time among Bakota and among various societies of West Africa—man and woman never put their arms around each other while dancing, as we generally do in France."

Apart dancing is not correlated with the apart playing of instruments in the sense of absence of body contact. The unity which the musicians and dancers share seems, rather, to constitute a constellation of solo and chorus performances. The master drummer (or drummers) plays alone, intent upon improvisation; the master dancer (or dancers), intent upon following or challenging these improvisations, also dances alone. And the drum chorus and the dancing chorus interact by repetitive patterns, which means that a certain amount of performing together balances the apartness. But the critical fact seems to be this: West Africans perform music and dance apart the better to ensure a dialog between movement and sound.

Dancers of the classic ballet do not touch either, as a rule, but these dancers are governed by a single metrical reference and, moreover, dance together in the sense that all their actions are governed by identical demands of pictorial legibility—which is to say that their *pliés* and *tours en l'air* must project crisply across row upon row of seated spectators. Considering the literary bias of the West, this tendency was inevitable. (Modern dance, in which apart playing and dancing are not uncommon, might be described as a dramatic break with this tendency, comparable with Cézanne's shift from representation to expression; but to what extent African influence and/or independent inventions shaped this revolution cannot be estimated in this article.) Africans seem to dance with full muscular actions so palpably syllabic that one can scarcely fail to comprehend the sense of linguistic community that pervades the whole. To dance with arms enlaced around the partner, in the manner of pre-jazz Western ballrooms, lessens the opportunity to converse. Even when Africans dance together, as in certain performing pairs of Abomey, they are actually operating apart to achieve a playing of hand movements against hips, something not possible were their hands locked in an embrace. Nor could their hands find individual metric inspiration were the members of the percussive choir similarly locked into a single metrical scheme. To recapitulate, West Africans and Afro-Americans dance apart and play apart to liberate their attention, as it were, for continuous conversation between motion and music, instead of specializing in purely musical or choreographic activity.

The fourth trait of West African music and dance is a special form of antiphony, wherein a caller alternates his lines with the regularly timed responses of a chorus; it is the formal structure of indigenous singing, and it is known as call-and-response. The important fact is that the caller frequently overlaps or interrupts the chorus. Antiphony exists the world over, but nowhere else in the world does the overlapping of the phrases of leader and followers so consistently occur. Are there similar patterns in the dance? Yes. J. Van Wing summarized the dances of the important Bakongo peoples of what is now the Democratic Republic of Congo (Kinshasa): "There are always two bodies or two groups of bodies in movement: a solo dancer in front of a group, or an individual before another in a group, or an individual before another in a couple, or two groups placed in front of the other. They perform periodic movements that are like questions and responses."

Similar patterns appear in the world of Spanish Harlem ballrooms, where Puerto Ricans improvise constantly varying steps—dancing apart while their partners maintain a recurrent movement. These men "interrupt" the movement of their women in a call-and-response manner, for they begin a new step or flourish considerably before their partners have finished the execution of their basic movements. In Ushi, an especially musical Ekiti Yoruba village, my wife and I observed a lead dancer improvise patterns that consistently began before a "chorus" had finished its "refrain," which consisted of swinging the ends of their head-ties in concerted rhythm, first to the right, then to the left, over their wrists.

The fifth trait, a nonmusical element, is the moral function of the songs of social allusion and the dances of derision. "In West Africa," Laura Boulton writes, "songs are frequently used as an important moral agent in the community. Songs of satire are very powerful because there is no punishment an African dreads more than being held up to the ridicule of his fellow men." (A wealth of similar examples may be found in Alan P. Merriam's *Anthropology of Music*.) Although we are, of course, referring to *content* rather than to form or style—a different analytic level—we intend to illustrate briefly, in the conclusion, that a relationship between content and style is best displayed by singers' deliberately distorting their voices when singing in traditions noted for moral allusion and inquisition.

The dance of derision, the choreographic correlate of the song of allusion, is a striking trait of much West African dancing. Even in Zululand, outside the purview of West Africa, derision dances are found and have been described by Kaigh as "dances of domestic oddities":

They dance after any event, white or black, which takes their fancy. I have seen danced imitations of myself and party too veracious to be flattering, or even comfortable. After I had lost a steeplechase by being thrown from the horse my boys danced the accident so faithfully that I came away a sadder, if not a wiser clown. The boy who took the part of me was most embarassingly accurate as to detail.

Pride and pretension are as much a target of the African dancer as they are of the singer of allusion. Surprisingly, the connection between the arts in this regard has not, to my knowledge, been pointed out. The former colonial authorities of what is now the Republic of Zambia were aware of the potentialities of African derision dancing, or so Chapter 120. Section 7, of the former laws of that area implies: "No person may organize or take part in any dance which is calculated to hold up to ridicule or to bring into contempt any person, religion, or duly constituted authority." This apparent characteristic was noted in 1825 by Captain Hugh Clapperton, who witnessed a dance, evidently danced at his expense, at Old Ọyọ, the ancient imperial capital of the Yoruba Peoples.

Dances of derision in the Negro world are legion. Camille Poupeye mentions them in the Bamako area of Mali and calls them "satires in action," and S. F. Nadel has described one instance at Bida in northern Nigeria. I have observed over the last ten years Puerto Rican dancers mock fatuous or eccentric dancing with cruelly accurate movements in New York City. The dance of derision brings home the fact that Africans and Afro-Americans are interested not only in force and the affirmation of fertility in their controlled energetic dancing, but also with ethics and right living. The man who misbehaves may not only have to "face the music," as in the "signifying songs" of the old-time New Orleans Negroes, but he may also have to face the movement.

8.3D. BRENDA DIXON GOTTSCHILD
Digging the Africanist Presence in American Performance: Dance and Other Contexts, Contributions in Afro-American and African Studies 179 (Westport, CT: Greenwood Press, 1996).

Robert Farris Thompson's "constellations of essential attributes in West African aesthetics" have been substantively embraced by later writers on African American dance, though their individual responses have varied somewhat with regard to the five traits presented in his essay, "An Aesthetic of the Cool."

Dolores Kirton Cayou adds some important basic elements, but she fails to credit Thompson's leading role, although her list is clearly indebted to him:

1. bent knees, with the body close to the earth;
2. tendency toward use of the whole foot and immediate transfer of weight;
3. isolation of body parts in movement;
4. rhythmically complex and syncopated movement;
5. carrying as many as two or three rhythms in the body at once—polyrhythm;
6. music and dance as a single expression;
7. individualism of style within a group style;
8. functionalism—becoming what you dance—the art of real life.[38]

Brenda Dixon Gottschild (Reading 8.3d) hews more closely than Cayou to Thompson's five traits. She offers five "Africanist elements" of her own, based loosely on Thompson but with this essential difference: whereas Thompson traces the African origins, Gottschild emphasizes the hybridized "Africa*nist*" (my emphasis) consequences of the diasporic trauma: conflict, discord, irregularity, contrariety, and alienation. She juxtaposes the distinctively Africanist characteristic of each element (theory) with a detail from a dance routine (practice) of Earl "Snake Hips" Tucker, dated 1923 (12–18). Hurston, it will be recalled, praised Tucker as an "excellent" example of asymmetry and "abrupt and unexpected changes."[39]:

1. Embracing the Conflict. "The conflict inherent in and implied by difference, discord, and irregularity is encompassed, rather than erased or necessarily resolved."

"[Tucker] came slipping on with a sliding, forward step and just a hint of hip movement. . . . Using shock tactics, he then went directly into the basic Snake Hips movements, which he paced superbly, starting out innocently enough, with one knee crossing over behind the other, while the toe of one foot touched the arch of the other. At first, it looked simultaneously pigeon-toed and knock-kneed."[40]

2. Polycentrism/Polyrhythm. Movement may be centered in any part of the body, and different parts of the body may respond simultaneously to different meters.

   "As he progressed, Tucker's footwork became flatter, rooted more firmly to the floor, while his hips described wider and wider circles, until he seemed to be throwing his hips alternately out of joint to the melodic accents of the music."

3. High-Affect Juxtaposition. Shifts between contrasting moods are managed abruptly, without transitional passages, to produce surprise, irony, and humor.

   "The next movement was known among dancers as the Belly Roll, and consisted of a series of waves rolling from pelvis to chest—a standard part of a Shake dancer's routine, which Tucker varied by coming to a stop, transfixing the audience with a baleful, hypnotic stare, and twirling his long tassel in time with the music."

4. Ephebism (from Greek ἔφηβος, a youth), refers to the kinaesthetic vitality and percussive force associated with youthfulness; ephebism can be expressed by the contrast of old people dancing as if they were young (or, perhaps, the young dancing as if old).[41]

   "Tucker raised his right arm to his eyes, at first as if embarrassed (a feeling that many in the audience shared), and then, as if racked with sobs, he went into the Tremble, which shook him savagely and rapidly from head to foot."

5. The Aesthetic of the Cool. Again, Gottschild defines this concept, taken directly from Thompson's article by the same title, in terms of a contrast: "the juxtaposition of detachment with intensity." Here Gottschild notes the "sexual heat" of Tucker's pelvic movements contrasting with his "disengaged" facial expression; his balance between "the sinister and the seductive"; and his manipulation of "the interface between character and self . . . the watcher as well as the watched."

Contrast is clearly an *idée fixe* running through all five of Gottschild's elements, and she employs it further in her comparison of Africanist dance and its "quintessential European referent"—ballet. The "idioms" she finds in Africanist dance, on the other hand, reveal affinities between African American dance and modern dance style: specifically, the role of gravity and pelvic impulse embodied both in Doris Humphrey's "fall and recovery" and Martha Graham's angularity and "contraction and release."[42] The passage in the reading is validated by two contemporary African dance theorists who quote it, with this introduction: "Now, here's where we enter the realm of the politics of dance and culture: Europeanist body languages and Africanist body languages have been speaking with each other ever since they first met and clashed over four centuries ago. But they are different languages."[43]

READING 8.3D
Gottschild

PP. 8–9

In traditional European dance aesthetics, the torso must be held upright for correct, classic form; the erect spine is the center—the hierarchical ruler— from which all movement is generated. It functions as a single unit. The straight, uninflected torso indicates elegance or royalty and acts as the absolute monarch, dominating the dancing body. This vertically aligned spine is the first principle of Europeanist dance, with arm and leg movements emanating from it and returning to it. The ballet canon is organized around this center. In fact, this structural principle is a microcosm of the post-Renaissance, colonialist world view. Like the straight, centered spine of its dancing body, Europe posited itself as the center of the world, with everything else controlled and defined by it.

Africanist dance idioms show a democratic equality of body parts. The spine is just one of many possible movement centers; it rarely remains static. The Africanist dancing body is polycentric: One part of the body is played against another, and movements may simultaneously originate from more than one focal point (the head and the pelvis, for example). It is also polyrhythmic (different body parts moving to two or more rhythms simultaneously), and privileges flexible, bent-legged postures that reaffirm contact with the earth (sometimes called a "get-down" stance). The component and auxiliary parts of the torso—shoulders, chest, rib cage, waist, pelvis—can be independently moved or articulated in different directions (forward, backward, sideward, or in circles) and in different rhythms. From an Africanist perspective, a pulled-up, aligned stance and static carriage indicate sterility and inflexibility, and the performer is encouraged to "dance with bended knees, lest you be taken for a corpse."[44]

8.4. MARTHA GRAHAM (1894–1991)

"A Modern Dancer's Primer for Action," in *Dance: A Basic Educational Technique,* ed. Frederick Rand Rogers (New York: The Macmillan Company, 1941), 178–187.[45]

Though the literature on Martha Graham, the towering figurehead of American modern dance, is voluminous, her own written legacy, consisting of her autobiography and notebooks, is quite small in comparison to her monumental legacy of performance and choreography.[46] "A Modern Dancer's Primer for Action" seems to be her only official published comment on theory. Presumably, it was written expressly for inclusion in Frederick Rand Rogers's anthology.

Graham herself states forthrightly: "It has not been my aim to evolve or discover a new method of dance training." Indeed, this essay, though personalized in its style, is essentially traditional in its content. Considering the sheer originality of her creative work, it might come as a surprise that her "Primer" is organized according to four basic principles that would be recognizable to Pasch and Taubert and their contemporaries (see Reading 4.2):

1. "Certain Basic Principles" ("through the medium of discipline and by means of a sensitive, strong instrument, to bring into focus unhackneyed movement: a human being"; parallel to *scopus finalis*).
2. "Posture, Movement, Balance" (the physics of posture and movement, as in Behr [1703/II and 1709], and Weaver's *Lectures*; parallel to *materia*).
3. "The Aim of Method" ("an exposition of the theory behind the practice of the technical training I employ"; parallel to *executio*).
4. "Primer for Action" (pedagogy and practice).

Consistent with dance theory writing since Blasis, practice begets theory in Graham's system: "My theory, if it can be called such, had its origin and has its justification in practical experience." Yet in spite of its traditional orientation, Graham's theory in no way contradicts her own highly innovative practice (which obviously looms much larger than theory in her *oeuvre*).

Graham's signature principle of "contraction and release" is included in section 4.F.1 (Exercises on the floor) of the "Primer for Action":

The first principle taught is body center. The first movement is based upon the body in two acts of breathing—inhaling and exhaling—developing it from actual breathing experience to the muscular activity independent of the actual act of breathing. These two acts, when performed muscularly only, are called "release," which corresponds to the body in inhalation, and "contraction" which corresponds to exhalation.

READING 8.4
Graham

A Modern Dancer's Primer for Action

I. CERTAIN BASIC PRINCIPLES

I am a dancer. My experience has been with dance as an art.

Each art has an instrument and a medium. The instrument of the dance is the human body; the medium is movement. The body has always been to me a thrilling wonder, a dynamo of energy, exciting, courageous, powerful; a delicately balanced logic and proportion. It has not been my aim to evolve or discover a new method of dance training, but rather to dance significantly. To dance significantly means "through the medium of discipline and by means of a sensitive, strong instrument, to bring into focus unhackneyed movement: a human being."[47]

[...]

2. POSTURE, MOVEMENT, BALANCE

One of the first indications of change, because it is the total of being—physical, emotional, mental, and nervous—is posture.

Posture is dynamic, not static. It is a self-portrait of being. It is psychological as well as physiological.

I use the word "posture" to mean *that instant of seeming stillness when the body is poised for most intense, most subtle action, the body at its moment of greatest potential efficiency.*

People often say that the posture of this dancer or that dancer or of all dancers is not natural. I ask, "Not natural to what?—natural to joy, sorrow, pain, relaxation, exaltation, elevation, fall?"

Each condition of sensitivity has a corresponding condition of posture. Posture is correct when it is relative to the need of the instant.

There is only one law of posture I have been able to discover—the perpendicular line connecting heaven and earth. But the problem is how to relate the various parts of the body. The nearest to the norm, as it has been observed and practiced over centuries, has been the ear in line perpendicularly with the shoulder, the shoulder with the pelvic bone, the pelvic bone in line with the arch of the foot.

The criticism that the posture of some dancers is bad because they appear to have a "sway back" is usually not justified, for a "sway back" is a weak back. Often the development of the muscles for jumping, leaping, and elevation, all of which concentrate in the hips and buttocks, is so pronounced as to give the appearance, to the uninformed critic, of "sway back."

Through all times the acquiring of technique in dance has been for one purpose—so to train the body as to make possible any demand made upon it by that inner self which has the vision of what needs to be said.

No one invents movement; movement is discovered. What is possible and necessary to the body under the impulse of the emotional self is the result of this discovery; and the formalization of it into a progressive series of exercises is technique.

It is possible and wise to teach these exercises even to the person who has no desire to dance professionally. It must, however, be emphasized that performance of these exercises is not a mere matter of "having a good time," but of achieving a center of body and mind which will eventually, but not immediately, result in a singing freedom. Throughout the performance of these technical exercises, a woman remains a woman, and a man a man, because power means to become what one *is*, to the highest degree of realization.

As in any other architectural edifice, the body is kept erect by balance. Balance is a nicety of relationship preserved throughout the various sections of the body. There are points of tension which preserve us in the air, hold us erect when standing, and hold us safely when we seem to drop to the floor at incredible speed. We would possess these naturally if they had not been destroyed in us by wrong training, either physical, intellectual, or emotional.

Contrary to opinion, the dancer's body is nearer to the norm of what the body should be than any other. It has been brought to this possible norm by discipline, for the dancer is, of necessity, a realist. Pavlova, Argentina, and Ruth St. Denis all practiced their art past the age of fifty.

3. THE AIM OF METHOD

There is no common terminology for describing the technique of modern dance. Furthermore, to describe two or three exercises would give an accent to these few beyond their importance. Therefore, rather than being a description here of actual specific practice of exercises, this is intended as an exposition of the theory behind the practice of the technical training I employ.

The aim of the method is coordination. In dance, that means unity of body produced by emotional physical balance. In technique, it means so to train all elements of body—legs, arms, torso, etc.—as to make them all equally important and equally efficient. It means a state of relativity of members in use that results in flow of movement. I have discovered whatever it is that I have discovered through practice and out of need. My theory, if it can be called such, had its origin and has its justification in practical experience.

What I say is based on one premise—dance is an art, one of the arts of the theater. True theatricality is not a vain or egotistic or unpleasant attribute. Neither does it depend on cheap tricks either of movement, costume, or audience appeal. Primarily, it is a means employed to bring the idea of one person into focus for the many. First there is the concept; then there is a dramatization of that concept which makes it apparent to others. This process is what is known as theatricality.

I believe dancing can bring liberation to many because it brings organized activity. I believe that the exercises I use are as right for a lay person as for a professional dancer, because they do no violence anatomically or emotionally. The difference in their use for the lay person and for the professional dancer is not in their basic approach but in the degree and intensity of their application. I have always thought first of the dancer as a human being. These exercises, though their original intention was the training of professionals, have been taught to children and adolescents as well.

What follows might be termed a "Primer for Action."

4. PRIMER FOR ACTION

A. *An Attitude Toward Dance*

1. There must be something that needs to be danced. Dance demands a dedication, but it is not a substitute for living. It is the expression of a fully aware person dancing that which can be expressed only by means of dance. It is not an emotional catharsis for the hysterical, frustrated, fearful, or morbid. It is an act of affirmation, not of escape. The affirmation may take many forms—tragedy, comedy, satire, lyric or dramatic.
2. There must be a disciplined way of dancing. This means learning a craft, not by intellection, but by hard physical work.

B. *A Dancer's Attitude Toward the Body*

The body must be sustained, honored, understood, disciplined. There should be no violation of the body. All exercises are but the extensions of physical capabilities. This is the reason it takes years of daily work to develop a dancer's body. It can only be done just so fast. It is subject to the natural timing of physical growth.

C. An Attitude Toward Technique

Technique is a means to an end. It is the means to becoming a dancer.

1. All exercises should be based on bodily structure. They should be written for the instrument, a body, male *or* female.
2. As the province of dance is motion, all exercises should be based upon the body in motion as its natural state. This is true even of exercises on the floor.

D. Technique Has a Three-Fold Purpose

1. Strength of body.
2. Freedom of body and spirit.
3. Spontaneity of action.

[The remaining sections are abridged to only their main titles.]

E. Specific Procedure in Technique

F. Four Main Classes into Which Technique Is Divided

1. Exercises on the floor.
2. Exercises standing in one place.
3. Exercises for elevation.
4. Exercise for falls.

8.5A. ALWIN NIKOLAIS (1910–1993)
nik: a documentary, ed. Marcia B. Siegel, *Dance Perspectives* 48 (Winter 1971).

8.5B. MURRAY LOUIS (1926–2016)
"Forward Is Not Always Going Ahead," *Dance Perspectives* 38 (Summer 1969), 28–33.

It is refreshing to read the theory of Alwin Nikolais: his style is down-to-earth and his work is proof that there is life still in the body of traditional theory, which can be modernized to underpin avant-garde dance. Theory fosters creativity.

In *The Nikolais/Louis Dance Technique*, a textbook by Nikolais and his younger collaborator Murray Louis, who published it after Nikolais's death, "The Major Principles of Dance (The Big Four)" are shape, time, space, and motion: traditional dance theory in a nutshell. Space, in turn, is broken down into Space and Direction, Space and Volume, Focus through Space, Space as Illusion Planes, and Peripheral Action (158).[48]

Nikolais is very much in tune with the spirit of his own era. The photo-essay "nik" abounds in images of expansion, extension, exploration, and discovery (Reading 8.5a). His "time-space canvas" channels the "uncharted areas of science and space" of John F. Kennedy's famous "New Frontier" speech (1960), as well as Einstein's Theory of Relativity. The "masks and props" and costumes are influenced by science fiction and the cubist costumes of Oskar Schlemmer's "Triadisches Ballett" (1922).[49] The Beat ethos is channeled in "bare-assed or dressed." The emphasis on expansion—of space, time, consciousness, imagination—speaks the language of psychedelic experience. "Consonant members of the environment" suggests an awareness of the nascent ecology movement. All these influences contribute to Nikolais's dance theory.

Louis's excerpt, furthermore, takes us inside the dance theorist's workshop to show how he applied Nikolais's concept of "vertical exploration," to broaden his own "sentient awareness" of the fluidity of time. "The Big Four" itself is expanded to include textural and spatial behaviorism, mathematics, dynamics, and dispersion, and by Louis's concept of different concurrent time systems, "inner molecular activity," and "physical earth forces" (Reading 8.5b).

Nikolais's dances (but not always Louis's) were nonnarrative, reflecting the influence of abstract painting and especially abstract expressionism, as attested by Louis's reference to Jackson Pollock. The dances also incorporated Nikolais's own electronic or electronically mediated ("choreosonic") music, not necessarily metrically congruent with the dance, and light-show ("chrome-key") effects that included abstract slides projected onto or behind the dancers.[50] One might say that the high-Romantic concept of the complete artwork or *Gesamtkunstwerk* (a term associated with the music dramas of Richard Wagner) survives and plays a central role in Nikolais's creative process and "total theater concept."

READING 8.5A
Nikolais

PP. II–I2

My total theater concept consciously started about 1950, although the seeds of it began much earlier I'm sure. First was expansion. I used masks and props— the masks, to have the dancer become something else; and props, to extend his physical size in space. (These latter were not instruments to be used as shovels or swords—but rather as extra bones and flesh.) I began to see the potentials of this new creature and in 1952 produced a program called Masks Props & Mobiles. I began to establish my philosophy of man being a fellow traveler within the total universal mechanism rather than the god from which all things flowed. The idea was both humiliating and grandizing. He lost his domination but instead became kinsman to the universe.

With the breakdown of story-line, choreographic structure necessarily changed. With the further breakdown of physical centralization—the lid was off. Logic of metronome & sun time was no longer necessary. Time no longer had to support logical realistic events. It too could be decentralized but more importantly, breaking the barrier of literal time throws the creator into visions and possible motional itineraries way beyond the literal visions (particularly if physical emphasis is subdued). The time-space canvas was now free. The ecology of the space canvas now could be balanced—no dominant Aunt Minnie—no non-returnable bottles grinning out of the landscape. Now we are permitted visions into the world in which we live and perhaps into the universe. We might even, then, return to the vision of self but placed more humbly into the living landscape, adding grandeur to vision of self—not in proud pigeon arabesques but as consonant members of the environment—enriched by the resonance of that which surrounds us, a shared energy interplaying with vital discussions rather than domineering argument.

P. 25

Now when the dancer by his action creates other linear boundaries or volumes of space these also are made visible & alive by the textural behaviorism of his body—all of this taking intense realization & concentration of the dancer upon the spatial involvements. If he cannot do this—the involvements will be dead— without audibility—they remain unspoken—in reality—unperformed. The relationships exist only as symbols—unexplained.

Let's take the space environment as I outlined above & qualify it further by the presence of another dancer or several dancers—all alive & responsive to the spatial behaviorism as it is activated by their orchestral involvement with it & each other. Suppose we think of time & shape in the same terms—not involved in the drama of boy meets girl—nor even in humanistic presence—but rather as dynamic musicalities of action of fabulously sensitive instruments, reminding one of things beyond the physicalities of the instruments—yet seen through them. Abstract expressionism? Perhaps—but basic dance—relieved of the romantic fallacy of the inviolability of a dull fat arse (or a puny skinny one—for that matter). Here our identification is with the rumblings & utterings

& songs of generative primal stuffs—the stuffs which disclose & qualify not only the dimension of nature—to which man belongs—but of man as well. Dehumanization?

From the point of view of mathematics, dynamics, dispersion of visual & auditory events & energies I caused the whole upset to dance dynamics. Whatever anyone else might have done or still is doing within that or this period of so-called avant garde dance theater, this particular creative vision seems to be peculiarly my own—and is still often misinterpreted & mostly unexamined in terms of its basic social and esthetic germination. Most interpretations still evolve around the Nureyev principle and the brother-in-spirit identifications with humanistic events on stage no matter how abstractly whacky [sic] the dance gesture might be. It's still Nureyev or Fonteyn doing it. Bare-assed or dressed—frontal or back-all—jeans or tutus—whiskers or wigs. Of course the specialists are bewildered. Reminds me of a shoe store man in Hartford. He often stood outside his shop. When I passed he never said "Hello" to me—it was always to my shoes.

READING 8.5B
Louis

PP. 31–33

Fifteen years later [ca. 1967] when I began teaching concentrated summer sessions I happened into a presentation of material which gave me a clear vision of the direction and nature of my work. Part of Nikolais' thinking and teaching dealt with what he called "vertical exploration"—an in-depth penetration into the layers of any area of motion, which released its vertical "essential" nature, as opposed to the horizontal "narrative" nature of motion. This eventually led to all the sentient emphasis made in our technique, improvisation, and composition classes.

Nik used, in his definition of dance, motion, time, space, shape, and, motivating and underlying all these—as it does all of life—energy.

For the first twenty years of my life I had been taught "Time" in terms of pulse, rhythms, and speed. These were all musically sound, and that a dancer functioned with a metabolic rate that differed from a tuba didn't seem to matter. It seemed that when you said "time" you were now talking a musician's private language, and very precious it was too. But with the concept of vertical exploration as part of my working habit, it occurred to me that I had been using this thinking solely in my devising of new movement, and not with the principles of the art itself. The sentient awareness so stressed in classes seemed reserved solely for motion. Wider application lay dormant until that kid asked me after a concert, "was I going forward or was I going backward in my search?" Then my own personal wide range of movement, my eclectic nature and curiosity, my compatibility with nature, my voracious appetite for books, all these things pulled together, and I discovered that forward often was not going ahead. Sometimes it meant going backward toward principles.

[. . .]

Speed—not in terms of fast or slow, but in terms of the juxtaposition of movement. In and out of time—which had nothing to do with being off the pulse, but instead had to do with the conscious facility to play both life and art experiences against each other. Since both these worlds were so closely housed in the same body it seemed a shame not to use the additional vocabulary which the pedestrian functions offered. The object here was to deliberately go from time consciousness to pedestrian gesture and then finally to pulse, which is the musician's starting point.

[. . .]

I've done this reverse forward-going with space, which I no longer deal with as an outward architectural definition, but instead investigate as an inner molecular activity, density, grain, focus, projection. All this is space, and the energy which vitalizes this space originates within the body.

I've made this investigation with motion, shape, the physical earth forces, and emotion. The results of these many years of work have been staggering to me, particularly in grasping the wonder of the mechanisms of dance and the dancer, and make it even more painful to read the naïve level of criticism that exists today. It is as if they (critics) tasted a candy bar by reading the wrapper.

Going back towards the principles of the art rather than to where historically an art began was a freedom which only the last 20 years allowed. Although Cézanne had a vision and insight 100 years ago, Jackson Pollock cracked the scene 20 years ago.

8.6A. FLAVIA PAPPACENA
"Accademia Nazionale di Danza, Elenco dei Nuovi Codici, Ambiti Disciplinari, Settore Disciplinari, Declaratorie e Campi Disciplinari di Competenza" (n.d.).

8.6B. SUSANNE FRANCO
"Re-thinking 'practice' and 'theory' from an Italian perspective," *Society of Dance History Scholars Proceedings: Thirtieth Annual Conference Co-sponsored with CORD, Centre national de la danse, Paris, France 21–24 June 2007* (Society of Dance History Scholars, 2007), 122–125.

Flavia Pappacena's comprehensive and detailed curriculum "della teoria della danza classica," instituted at the Accademia Nazionale di Danza in 1974 and still in use, is a pragmatic and inclusive approach to teaching dance theory at the college level that respects dance's heritage while embracing contemporary perspectives (Reading 8.6a).[51] The inclusion of notation and choreography is consistent with dance theory since the early nineteenth century. New related disciplines, most of them consistent with traditional norms and parameters, include the following: music theory, history, and technique; languages; sociological, ethnological, and anthropological studies; historical theories, methods, styles, and reconstruction; and incorporation of new technologies and media.

In 2007, a joint international conference of the Society of Dance History Scholars and the Congress on Research in Dance was held at the Centre national de la danse in Paris-Pantin, on the theme: "Repenser pratique et théorie/ Re-Thinking Theory and Practice." The Call for Papers posed prospective topics entirely as questions:

How might we historicize practice and theory and practice now, at the beginning of the 21st century?

In this moment of intensified circulation of dance forms worldwide, and with the advent of new digital technologies for representing the body in motion, what kinds of activities are categorized as "theorizing" and what others as "practicing"?

What are the various histories of these terms? How do their genealogies inflect or determine their current usage?

Do earlier notions of practice or theory continue to be utilized in different dance communities?

What are the culturally distinctive meanings and understandings of the terms? How have these meanings been translated and interpreted in moments of cross-cultural contact?

What do dancers do when they practice? What do they do when they theorize?

Do dances put forward a theory of the body or of identity? Do they promote or inspire specific corporeal practices?

How might the methodologies utilized in phenomenology, semiotics, and cultural studies assist in understanding these terms?

How might the perspectives afforded by studies of gender, colonization, and globalization help to elucidate their meanings?

What ideological work is accomplished when they are deployed as a dichotomy?

Is theorizing a form of labor? Is practice mental or physical or both?[52]

Noteworthy in all these questions is a sense of uncertainty as to the current status of theory, and its relation to practice; a sense of flux in research methods and directions, and in the definition of basic terms; and a sense of anxiety concerning the incursion of cultural theory.

Susanne Franco offers a "mainstream" definition of dance theory that many dance scholars could still embrace at that point (Reading 8.6b):[53]

> Dance theory, whose aim is giving cultural substance to the practice of the dancer, is then meant to comprehend a wide array of approaches, ranging from the structural and anatomical analysis of movement, to the dynamic, rhythmic and stylistical analysis of dance, the comparative analysis of the historical methods and styles, and the analysis of the system of notation and choreography.

This definition accords hand-in-glove with Pappacena's theory curriculum at the Accademia Nazionale. However, the interrogatory spirit of the Call for Papers, as well as Franco's own opening questions, suggests that even as she wrote it, her definition was under threat of obsolescence. Her paper is an extended response to a related question of her own: "How might the content of the form of delivering a paper be re-envisioned so as to provoke new understandings of theory and practice?" Her response, in turn, raises new questions, to which her answers, again, reflect ambivalence toward cultural theory, and concern about what it portends for the definition—indeed, the very identity—of "theory" and "practice."

READING 8.6A
Pappacena (trans. Russell)

p. 6

Dance program outline

ADTI   Technical-interpretative
ADES   Educational and technical-scientific
ADTC   Technical-compositional
ADTS   Theoretical-critical-historical-reconstructive
ADTS/01   Music theory
ADTS/02   Dance theory
ADTS/03   Music history
ADTS/04   Dance history
ADTS/05   History of the visual arts

ADTS/06 Scenic space
ADTM   Technical-musical
ADEA   Sociological-ethnological-anthropological
ADPP   Psychological-pedagogical
ADGE   Juridical-economic
ADDC   Communication in foreign languages

course number: ADTS/02

area: Theoretical-critical-historical-reconstructive
section: Dance Theory
course description: This section concerns the theoretical-critical and philological studies related to dance as a science and as an art, and provides the analytical and methodological-critical tools for a correct reading of documents
   and works of art. Cultural context, interconnections between dance and the
   visual and musical arts, aspects of preservation, notation, and communication and transmission, in an educative and formative sphere, constitute
   particular perspectives for investigation and specific levels of intensity.

ADTS/02: fields of disciplinary competence

1. Theory of dance
2. Theory of classical dance
3. Fundamentals of the theory of classical dance
4. Theory and structural analysis of movement in classical ballet
5. Comparative analysis of the historical methods and styles of classical ballet
6. Choreographic analysis of classical ballet
7. Aesthetics of classical dance
8. Analysis and reconstruction of dances of the 18th and 19th centuries
9. Historical theories of dance in education
10. Terminology of classical dance
11. Dance notation
12. Theory of *Orchestica*[54]
13. *Orchesticografia*[55]
14. Theory and structural analysis of contemporary dance
15. Structural analysis of contemporary choreography with new technological
    elements (theoretical part)
16. Laban theory and Kinetography
17. Laboratory of structural analysis (theoretical part)

18. Terminology, bibliography, and videography of contemporary dance
19. Composition, reading, and writing for dance

READING 8.6B
Franco

PP. 122–123

How might the content of the form of delivering a paper be re-envisioned so as to provoke new understandings of theory and practice?

I now respond to two related questions:

What are the various histories of these terms?

How might we historicize practice and theory now, at the beginning of the 21st century?

The Italian history of the term "theory" in relation to dance and in an educational context is very much a 20th century history. "Dance theory" is the name of the subject introduced and taught at the Accademia Nazionale di Danza (National Academy of Dance) by Jia Ruskaia in 1948.[56] Ruskaia, whose real name was Eugenia Borissenko, was a Russian artist and performer of Futurist shows and of a personal version of the free dance inspired by Duncan and Dalcroze in the Twenties and Thirties. The generating core of this subject was "orchesticografia," namely the system of analysis and movement notation that she created in the 1930s, inspired by central European models and quite revolutionary for Italy, where modern dance was still a marginal phenomenon. Dance theory has been understood in close connection with Ruskaia's pedagogical conceptions, that were themselves oriented towards a full cultural legitimation and institutionalization of dance, and a rationalization of its teaching. [. . .] Ruskaja taught dance theory almost until her death in 1970, the year that also saw the publication of her book significantly titled *Teoria e scrittura della danza* (*Theory and Writing of Dance*). In the 1970s the dance scholar Flavia Pappacena, who took over from Ruskaja the teaching of dance theory and the curriculum planning of the Accademia, integrated and modified some key concepts underscoring the link with other disciplines taught there and led to a revision of its contents. As it was for Ruskaja, her approach to dance theory is closely connected to the participation in practical interdisciplinary workshops. In her textbooks, dance theory is defined as a historical and critical overview of the figures, steps and postures, and an aesthetic analysis of the language of (classical) dance, as a structural-anatomical analysis and a framing of the general theoretical terms, and, last but not least, as a historico-critical perspective on the construction of figures in the relationship between dancer and space. Dance theory, whose aim is giving cultural substance to the practice of the dancer, is then meant to comprehend a wide array of approaches, ranging from the structural and anatomical analysis of movement, to the dynamic, rhythmic and stylistical analysis of dance, the comparative analysis of the historical methods and styles, and the analysis of the system of notation and choreography.

Since this is still the mainstream definition of dance theory, any other use of the term theory, in the Accademia as much as in other contexts, requires a preliminary qualification, precisely for its being alien to the Italian cultural tradition in dance studies. I'm referring in particular to the use of the term "theory" as directly connected with "cultural theory." Only in recent years and to a very partial extent have dance studies (and performance studies in general) responded to cultural theory in Italy. This distance is due to cultural, linguistic and generational obstacles, and the resistance to its critical instruments on the part of the Italian scientific community. Critical theory also introduced a drastic terminological shift often seen in many fields of research as self-referential and overriding its subject matter. In this light, the development of concepts like "theory" and "practice" in Italy has not yet been submitted to a full historical analysis, let alone with the critical agenda suggested by the Call for Papers.

Following a traditional historical and philological approach, the most widely accepted among Italian dance scholars, to explain how the terms "theory" and "practice" of dance have rooted themselves in Italy, it is necessary to retrieve a substantial body of archival documents and to place it in a broad framework of historical and sociological references to cast light on their thick web of relations.

On the other hand, following a postmodern approach to the study of history informed by cultural theory, it is necessary to raise issues regarding the mechanisms of productions of these documents and the archives that hold them, their reception in history, [and] the subjective implications that guide us in the way we select, examine and situate them in a temporal and hermeneutical framework.

NOTES

1. The historically informed performance practice movement in music coincided with a parallel such movement in historical dance studies.
2. Laban, *Die Welt des Tänzers*, 7: "als Erster unter den heutigen Tänzern von einer Welt zu sprechen, für die unserer Sprache Worte mangeln."

3. Guest, *Choreo-Graphics*, 157. This observation can be verified by the paucity of new editions (*Neuauflagen*) recorded by Jeschke for twenty-six new choreographic systems published during the nineteenth and twentieth centuries.

4. Jeschke, *Tanzschriften*, 34.

5. Jeschke, *Tanzschriften*, 116.

6. Jeschke, *Tanzschriften*, 376–387; Guest, *Choreo-Graphics*, 106–110.

7. Laban, *Principles of Dance and Movement Notation* (New York: Dance Horizons, 1956), 7–9.

8. Vera Maletic, *Body-Space-Expression: The Development of Rudolf Laban's Movement and Dance Concepts* (Berlin: Mouton de Gruyter, 1987), 59.

9. Laban, *Gymnastic und Tanz*, 6th ed. (Oldenburg: Gerhard Stalling Verlag, 1926), 78–79. See Feuillet, *Chorégraphie*, 10; also Maletic, *Body-Space-Expression*, 63.

10. Pasch, *Beschreibung*, 16: "Wahre Tantz-Kunst ist in *Theoria* eine Wissenschafft"; also Taubert, *Rechtschaffener Tantzmeister*, 290–291. See Reading 4.2.

11. Laban, *Die Welt des Tänzers*, 64–65.

12. Laban, *Die Welt des Tänzers*, 24–25; Maletic, *Body-Space-Expression*, 58–59. Figure 8.1 is reproduced in Lisa Ullman, *A Vision of Dynamic Space* (London: Laban Archives and The Falmer Press, 1984), 18.

13. See Ullman, *A Vision of Dynamic Space*, 17, 18, 30–31, and 33.

14. Ciane Fernandes, *The Moving Researcher: Laban/Bartenieff Movement Analysis in Performing Arts Education and Creative Arts Therapies* (London: Jessica Kingsley, 2015), 222–226; also Maletic, *Body-Space-Expression*, 60–62.

15. Laban, *Die Welt des Tänzers*, 54.

16. Laban, *Gymnastic und Tanz*, 67–68 (translation—Ed.). Cf. Maletic, *Body-Space-Expression*, 93–94. The four factors also appeared in Laban's *Choreographie* in the same year as *Gymnastic und Tanz* (1926); see Maletic, *Body-Space-Expression*, 109.

17. Maletic, *Body-Space-Expression*, 54.

18. Maletic, *Body-Space-Expression*, 54, 110.

19. Laban, and F. C. Lawrence, *Effort: Economy in Body Movement*, 2nd ed. (Boston: Macdonald and Evans Limited, 1974), 62. The slightly changed title appeared in the second edition. The factory scene in Charlie Chaplin's film *Modern Times* (1936) can be viewed as a comedic prequel to "effort theory."

20. Laban and Lawrence, *Effort: Economy in Body Movement*, 8–13. Daniel Black, *Embodiment and Mechanisation: Reciprocal Understandings of Body and*

Machine from the Renaissance to the Present (Farnham, Surrey: Ashgate, 2014), 70, ties this concept to the Renaissance study of anatomy through dissection: ". . . the unified, individualised body becomes a subsystem within a larger mechanism—the machine of society—just as the individualised body itself is understood as a collection of subsystems, continuing the idea that the body is microcosm for larger systems of organisation."

21. Laban, *Modern Educational Dance*, 52–84; Maletic, *Body-Space-Expression*, 93–112.

22. Margaret Lloyd, Review: "A Study in Dance Theory," *The Christian Science Monitor* (September 28, 1940), 5. The name H'Doubler is a contraction of Hougendoubler, the original family name of H'Doubler's ancestors who emigrated from Switzerland in the early eighteenth century. See Janice L. Ross, "Margaret Newell H'Doubler (1889–1982)," *100 Dance Treasures* (Dance Heritage Coalition), http://www.danceheritage.org/treasures/ hdoubler_essay_ross.pdf.

23. Ellen W. Goellner and Jacqueline Shea Murphy, "Introduction: Movement Movements," *Bodies of the Text: Dance as Theory, Literature as Dance*, ed. Ellen W. Goellner and Jacqueline Shea Murphy (New Brunswick, NJ: Rutgers University Press, 1995), 3. This introduction is an excellent, concise history of academic and critical dance writing in the United States, from H'Doubler to the 1990s. On the historical relation between dance and gymnastics, see Reading 7.4.

24. Judith B. Alter, *Dance-Based Dance Theory*, New Studies in Aesthetics 7 (New York: Peter Lang, 1991), 2; her chapter on H'Doubler, 83–103.

25. *A Manual of Dancing: Suggestions and Bibliography for the Teacher of Dancing* (Madison, WI, 1921); *The Dance and Its Place in Education* (New York: Harcourt, Brace and Company, 1925), with drawings by Bernice Oehler.

26. *The Dance and Its Place in Education*, viii.

27. The gratuitous two-line note at the end of the "A.-B.-C." is regrettably off-putting. It is offset, however, by quite different comments in *The Dance and Its Place in Education*: "First of all, the dance is not to be considered peculiar to any one race or nationality. It is inborn, a heritage common to all mankind. . . . The United States has no dances of its own, no dances which are expressive of the race which is an amalgamation of all races, no dances which are truly American. Each race has its dance, but there has been no dance to express the spirit of the race to which all these others have together given birth" (18 and 26).—Ed.

28. Susan Manning, "Key Works, Artists, Events, Venues, Texts: Black Dance on U.S. Stages in the 20th Century," Black Arts Initiative, bai.northwestern. edu/wp-content/uploads/2012/08/Black-Dance-Timeline.docx.

29. Thomas F. DeFrantz and Anita Gonzalez (eds.), *Black Performance Theory* (Durham, NC: Duke University Press, 2014), 2–3.

30. Halifu Osumare, "Dancing the Black Atlantic: Katherine Dunham's Research-to-Performance Method," *AmeriQuests* 7, no. 2 (September 2010), 5.

31. Osumare, "Dancing the Black Atlantic," 4.

32. Joanna Dee Das, "Katherine Dunham (1909–2006)," Dance Heritage Coalition (2012), http://www.danceheritage.org/treasures/dunham_essay_deedas.pdf.

33. Eatonville, Florida, was Hurston's hometown. It was and apparently still is an all-black town. See Alice Walker, "In Search of Zora Neale Hurston," *Ms. Magazine* (March 1975), 74–89.—Ed.

34. The grand march was originally a "white people's" dance in which couples paraded down the middle of the room, separated, and turned back to meet again at the top.—Ed.

35. The Volstead Act was passed by Congress in 1919 to implement the Eighteenth Amendment, establishing Prohibition.—Ed.

36. An African American dance style: "buck" involves heavy stomping; "wing" involves flapping the bent arms and legs. For a video demonstration by Thomas F. DeFrantz, see https://www.youtube.com/watch?v=A34OD4eA170.—Ed.

37. A calabash is a gourd used as a percussion instrument.—Ed.

38. Dolores Kirton Cayou, *Modern Jazz Dance* (Palo Alto, CA: Mayfield, 1971), 6.

39. For a video of Tucker, see www.youtube.com/watch?v=7U4ww-MmAY4.

40. Gottschild quotes the descriptions of his dance from Marshall and Joan Stearns, *Jazz Dance: The Story of American Vernacular Dance* (New York: Schirmer, 1979), 236–237.

41. Ephebism does not appear in Thompson's 1966 article but was introduced in a subsequent publication of his: Robert Farris Thompson, *African Art in Motion* (Berkeley: University of California Press, 1974), 5–7.

42. See Gottschild, *Digging the Africanist Presence*, 49, on Martha Graham and Africanist dance.

43. Charles Uji and Tijime Justin Awuawuer, "Towards the Theories and Practice of the Dance Art," *International Journal of Humanities and Social Science* 4, no. 4 (Special Issue on Contemporary Issues in Social Science, February 2014), 255–256.

44. Quotation from Thompson, *African Art in Motion*, 9–10.—Ed.

45. Reprinted unabridged in Selma Jeanne Cohen, *Dance as a Theatre Art: Source Readings in Dance History from 1581 to the Present* (New York: Harper & Row, 1974), 135–143.

46. Martha Graham, *Blood Memory* (New York: Doubleday, 1991); *The Notebooks of Martha Graham* (New York: Harcourt Brace Jovanovich, 1973).

47. The source of this quotation is not noted.—Ed.

48. Alwin Nikolais and Murray Louis, *The Nikolais/Louis Dance Technique: A Philosophy and Method of Modern Dance* (New York: Routledge, 2005), 158.

49. See Lincoln Kirstein, *Four Centuries of Ballet: Fifty Masterworks* (New York: Dover, 1984), 214–217.

50. For "chrome –key": see *nik*, 49, 51; for "choreosonic": see Nikolais, "Choreosonic Music of the New Dance Theatre of Alwin Nikolais" LP recording (cacophonic 10ACKLP, 1959).

51. Undated document attached to personal correspondence, October 21, 2015.

52. Call for Papers: "Re-Thinking Practice and Theory: International Symposium on Dance Research" (dp-colloquerpt-juin07.pdf), 20.

53. Susanne Franco is professor of dance history at Università IUAV in Venice.

54. *Orchestica*: a style of modern dance created by Jia Ruskaja. Ruskaja (1902–1970) founded the Regia Scuola di Danza in 1940, which became the Accademia Nazionale di Danza in 1948; she established the dance theory program in 1948 and taught in it until 1968.—Ed.

55. *Orchesticografia*: Ruskaja's dance notation.—Ed.

56. Franco uses both spellings of her name: Ruskaia/Ruskaja.—Ed.

| 9 |

Postmodern Dance Theory and Anti-Theory

The introduction to Chapter 8 sketched the major traits in postmodern music and visual arts. We need to keep in mind, however, that we are living in the middle of this era, our own, and therefore in the midst of a maelstrom of trends and fads. Like the denizens of any previous era, we lack the historical hindsight to identify the signature traits that will survive and someday characterize our "now." But our situation is even more complicated than theirs, because we have so much more history behind us, and the most enduring styles of the accumulated past are still very much with us, while the global reach and instantaneity of communications exposes us to infinitely more stimuli, all the time. Therefore, the readings in this final chapter are more heterogeneous than we have seen in the previous chapters: misgivings and skepticism (as we have just seen in Reading 8.6b) are rife, as are rebellion and rejection of the past, giddy excitement over new playthings, brave-new-world triumphalism, pioneering spirit and pride, and even a hint of déjà vu. Indeed, within the next decade or two, this chapter may well prove to be the soonest outdated in the entire book.

An overt hostility toward theory can be seen in dance writing of the early twentieth century. The general idea is adumbrated in Gertrude Stein's pithy dictum on the "continuous present": ". . . no one formulates until what is to be formulated has been made."[1] This vein of distrust and outright rejection of intellectual, nonempirical, noninstinctual discourse—that is, theory—is also seen in a "well-known" statement of the dancer Mary Wigman: "Talking about dance has nothing to do with dance."[2] More recently, Suzanne Farrell, when asked if she reads to prepare for a role, echoed Wigman's distrust of words: "What does reading have to do with dancing? . . . Dancing is not a translation of words to movement. . . . I got all twitchy and neurotic in my performance because I knew about facts and theories which had no counterpart or realization in movement. I should have known better."[3] Anna Sokolow has written:

> I hate academies. I hate fixed ideas of what a thing should be, of how it should be done. I don't like imposing rules, because the person, the artist, must do what he feels is right, what he—as an individual—feels he must do. If we establish an academy, there can be no future for the modern dance. An art should be constantly changing; it cannot have fixed rules.[4]

And Pina Bausch has said: "I reject systems."[5] Such statements seem to have been almost *de rigeur* among modernist artists as a declaration of independence from all dogma and ideology. Their pronouncements may reflect an ill-informed or imprecise understanding of what was being rejected, but in a period of rebellion there is little concern with fine points of distinction.

9.IA. MERCE CUNNINGHAM (1919–2009)
"Two Questions and Five Dances," *Dance Perspectives* 34 (Summer 1968): 46–53.

9.IB, C. YVONNE RAINER (B. 1934)
"Some Retrospective Notes on a Dance for 10 People and 12 Mattresses Called 'Parts of Some Sextets,' Performed at the Wadsworth Atheneum, Hartford, Connecticut, and Judson Memorial Church, New York, in March, 1965," *The Tulane Drama Review* 10, no. 2 (Winter 1965): 168–178.

Merce Cunningham, who (like Sokolow) began his professional career in the Martha Graham Company, addresses theory with contempt:

If a dancer dances—which is not the same as having theories about dancing or wishing to dance or trying to dance or remembering in his body someone else's dance—but if the dancer *dances*, everything is there. The meaning is there, if that's what you want. It's like this apartment where I live—I look around in the morning and ask myself what does it all mean? It means: this is where I live. When I dance, it means: this is what I am doing" (1955).[6]

Later (1968), Cunningham disposes of all the theoretical preliminaries in five blunt monosyllables: "I start with a step" (Reading 9.1a).[7] These statements seem a direct throwback, in substance if not style, to Despréaux's and Adice's fusion of "theory" with the pedagogy of steps and movements, except it is performative, not pedagogical, in nature. (Doris Humphrey states a similar, minimal idea in less brutal terms: "In the human animal, the walk is the key pattern of fall and recovery, my theory of motion—that is, the giving in to and rebound from gravity. This is the very core of all movement, in my opinion."[8]) For Cunningham, the traditional theoretical elements of movement, space, and time are still present, but only as the outcome of that spontaneous, first step: the emblematic *in principio* of practice.

Cunningham was one of the midcentury dancers associated with the Judson Dance Theater at the Judson Memorial Church on Washington Square in New York City's Greenwich Village. This freewheeling program, having lasted, officially, only around two years (1962–1964), was a brief but legendary and seminal confluence of dancers, artists, and composers. Even after it disbanded, its members and their followers have continued to spread its avant-garde ethos in every corner of the dance world.

In an era of anti-establishment "underground" movements in art and politics, Jill Johnston, dance columnist at the now defunct *The Village Voice*, called the Judson Dance Theater "the dance underground of the sixties" and fondly summed up the Judson scene with this seal of approval: "Within a positive assertion of old creative values was the negative idea of the annihilation of all preconceived notions about dance. In retrospect, it was a beautiful mess."[9] The general principles of postmodern dance developed by the Judson Dance Theater include the subversion of, and liberation from, outmoded or "classic" styles and traditional procedures; permissibility of any movement, by any body, using any method; privileging of conceptualization over realization, or "process over product," resulting in the impermanence and "instant obsolescence" of the product; a preference for improvisation and chance (the latter based on the compositional procedures of the composer John Cage, 1912–1992); incorporation of mixed media, through collaboration with contemporary artists (Robert Rauschenberg in particular) and composers, but distaste for the verbal or literary, in the spirit of anathematizing dance's historic overdependence on literary sources of inspiration; and, finally, a refusal to please or coddle the audience.[10]

It will be noticed that all these principles have to do with practice. Yet they also carry implications for theory: conceptualization either proceeds from, or leads to, theory, but if theory can't be preserved because of the aversion to writing and the disincentive of "instant obsolescence," the time and effort spent in conceptualizing can only lead to a discursive vacuum. Nancy Reynolds and Malcolm McCormick write: "Ideas that flourished were too open-ended and slippery to become the basis for systematic development, and it was impossible for anything resembling an academy to emerge from the embers of this initial ferment."[11] In the following readings, we will see how and where this vacuum was eventually filled. ("Academy" is the key word.)

From the 1940s until Cage's death, Cunningham and Cage were life partners, and their artistic relationship is indicative of the contrarian Judson ethos. The intimate relationship between an illustrious dancer and an equally illustrious composer is probably unique in the history of the arts. One might think that two such luminaries, cohabiting (after 1970) and creatively collaborating, would inform and enrich each other's art. Ironically, the outcome was quite the opposite. The products of their teamwork exhibit, in fact, minimal choreomusicality, that is, minimal correspondence, or none at all, between dance and music. Since the Middle Ages, the general modus operandi of dance composition and performance was to ensure that choreography and music fit together in every respect: duration, rhythm, phrasing, tempo, dramaturgic or mimetic content, affect or emotion, and so forth. To put it as simply as possible, it would look "wrong" if the dancing and music were "out of synch" in any way. Yet, except for certain exceptional instances, this was the very essence of Cunningham and Cage's most typical—and most admired—works, which eschewed all but the crudest, most elemental operation: starting and stopping at the same time. Both constructed their compositions independently by chance or aleatoric procedures (the term aleatoric comes from the Latin *alea*, a dice game), using dice, coins, or sticks, and consulting a popular text in 1960s counterculture: the *I Ching*, as an interpretive guide. The inevitable result has been called the "divorce of music and dance."[12]

Yvonne Rainer, like Cunningham, was an original Judson group member. Her style, fully consistent with the group's general principles described earlier, is epitomized in her dance *Trio A*, first performed at Judson in 1966. Originally for three dancers, it has been performed by fewer or more than three but, refusing to emulate a corps de ballet or the Rockettes, the movements are casually and intentionally individualized, and no two performances can be the same. In one performance, available on YouTube, a live dancer performs in front of a video projection of Rainer, while her shadow is superimposed on the screen between her and Rainer's image, creating the impression of a trio. The live dancer and her shadow are perfectly synchronized, but always slightly "off" with respect to Rainer behind them.[13] The movements themselves, seemingly arbitrary and unmotivated, are purposely affectless, everyday, banal—a style Rainer referred to as "found" movement, which also exemplifies "pedestrianism," an attitude, or demotic nonstyle, that evokes what Jane Jacobs esteemed as the "intricate sidewalk ballet" of a New York street.[14] The dance was originally performed in silence.

In contrast to Cunningham's writing, Rainer's comes of its own volition and quite eloquently sets forth her aesthetic stance and creative purpose. In her mischievously titled article "A Quasi Survey of Some 'Minimalist' Tendencies in the Quantitatively Minimal Dance Activity Midst the Plethora, or an Analysis of *Trio A*," she explains seven basic principles embodied in that dance:

1. Energy equality and "found" movement: all movements should be "of equal weight and are equally emphasized."

2. Equality of parts, repetition: "no one part of the series is made any more important that any other."

3. Repetition or discrete events: "My *Trio A* dealt with the 'seeing' difficulty by dint of its continual and unremitting revelation of gestural detail that did *not* repeat itself, thereby focusing on the fact that the material could not easily be encompassed."

4. Neutral performance: ". . . never permitting the performers to confront the audience. Either the gaze was averted or the head was engaged in movement."

5. Task or tasklike activity: "The desired effect was a worklike rather than exhibitionlike presention."

6. Singular action, event, or tone: ". . . there are no pauses between phrases. . . . the end of each phrase merges immediately into the beginning of the next with no observable accent. . . . The execution of each movement conveys a sense of unhurried control."

7. Human scale: "The display of technical virtuosity and the display of the dancer's specialized body no longer make any sense. Dancers have been driven to search for an alternative context that allows for a more matter-of-fact, more concrete, more banal quality of physical being in performance, a context wherein people are engaged in actions and movements making a less spectacular demand on the body and in which skill is hard to locate."

An eighth principle meshes neatly with the procedure developed by Cunningham and Cage: indeterminacy "used with respect to timing. . . . Such is the case with the trio I have been speaking about, in which small discrepancies in the tempo of individually executed phrases result in the three simultaneous performances constantly moving in and out of phase and in and out of synchronization."[15] "By 1965," Reynolds and McCormick say, "Rainer was looking for 'undynamic movement,' attempting to eliminate rhythm, emphasis, and extremes of either tension or relaxation. . . . *Trio A* became a model for a whole genre exemplifying the aesthetic goals of postmodern dance."[16]

An earlier article, published in 1965, concludes with a stark stream-of-consciousness statement in which the general principles of postmodern dance are restated as prohibitions (Reading 9.1b). Subsequently, the "NO"-text was extracted as a stand-alone and widely republished list of thou-shalt-nots, titled "Manifesto" (Reading 9.1c). In it, Rainer is an exterminating angel, purging dance of all the impurities and excrescences from the past that stifle pure movement. The contrast between Martha Graham's and Yvonne Rainer's ideas on theory is striking. They span the gamut from the traditional (Graham: "It has not been my aim to evolve or discover a new method of dance training")[17] to the iconoclastic. Rainer's "Manifesto" is, in fact, an anti-theory, in that it is not prescriptive, but proscriptive.

READING 9.1A
Cunningham

P. 47

How do you go about composing a particular dance?
In a direct way. I start with a step. Using the word "step" is a hangover from my adolescent vaudeville days. I "step" with my feet, legs, hands, body, head— that is what prompts me, and out of that other movements grow, and different elements (theatre) may be involved.

This is not beginning with an idea that concerns character or story, a fait accompli around which the actions are grouped for reference purposes. I start with the movement, even something moving rather than someone (*pillows in the air*).[18] And I ordinarily start with myself; not always, it may be with one or two of the dancers. But then out of this the action begins to assume its own proportions, and other possibilities appear as the dance proceeds. New situations present themselves—between the dancers, the dancers and the space, the space and the time. It is not subject to a prearranged idea as to how it should go any more than a conversation you might have with a friend while out walking. It can take a momentum of its own, that is. That leaves open the possibility of surprise (chance), and that is essential.

[. . .]

P. 53

The variables in the structure, which are changed at each performance, are: the length of the whole, and the length of the separate sections, and the placement of the sections in the continuity. The relationship of the sound is constantly varied, as the only agreement between the dance and the music is the length decided upon for that performance. Although the dancers listen to the sounds and are sometimes engaged by them, this is not a support and certainly cannot be counted upon to happen again.

The title does not refer to any implicit or explicit narrative, but to the fact that each spectator may interpret the events in his own way.[19]

READING 9.1B
Rainer

P. 170

2. The work. . . . Since there was nothing else to do, I worked. Worked mechanically and at times despairingly on movement. It was necessary to find a different way to move. I felt I could no longer call on the energy and hard-attack impulses that had characterized my work previously, nor did I want to explore any further the "imitations-from-life" kind of eccentric movement that someone once described as "goofy glamour." So I started at another place—wiggled my elbows, shifted from one foot to the other, looked at the ceiling, shifted eye focus within a tiny radius, watched a flattened, raised hand moving and stopping, moving and stopping. Slowly the things I made began to go together, along with sudden sharp, hard changes in dynamics. But basically I wanted it to remain undynamic movement, no rhythm, no emphasis, no tension, no relaxation. You just *do* it, with the coordination of a pro and the non-definition of an amateur. It's an ideal, still to be worked on.

PP. 177–178

3. Postscript. All I am inclined to indicate here are various feelings about "Parts of Some Sextets" and its effort in a certain direction—an area of concern as yet not fully clarified for me in relation to dance, but as existing as a very large NO to many facts in the theatre today. (This is not to say that I personally do not enjoy many forms of theatre. It is only to define more stringently the rules and boundaries of my own artistic game of the moment.)

NO to spectacle no to virtuosity no to transformations and magic and make-believe no to the glamour and transcendency of the star image no to the heroic no to the anti-heroic no to trash imagery no to involvement of performer or spectator no to style no to camp no to seduction of spectator by the wiles of the performer no to eccentricity no to moving or being moved.

The challenge might be defined as how to move in the spaces between theatrical bloat with its burden of dramatic psychological "meaning"—and—the imagery and atmospheric effects of the non-dramatic, non-verbal theatre (i.e. dancing and some "happenings")—and—theatre of spectator participation and/or assault. [. . .]

READING 9.1C
Rainer, "Manifesto"

No to spectacle.

No to virtuosity.

No to transformations and magic and make-believe.

No to the glamour and transcendency of the star image.

No to the heroic.

No to the anti-heroic.

No to trash imagery.

No to involvement of performer or spectator.

No to style.

No to camp.

No to seduction of spectator by the wiles of the performer.

No to eccentricity.

No to moving or being moved.

9.2. SUSAN LEIGH FOSTER (B. 1949)
"New Areas of Inquiry," *International Encyclopedia of Dance*, ed. Selma Jeanne Cohen (New York: Oxford University Press, 1998), vol. 4, 376–379.

The *International Encyclopedia of Dance* (*IED*) is the most recent, direct descendant of the late eighteenth-century *Encyclopédie méthodique*'s dictionary of dance, though far more extensive and comprehensive (see Reading 6.5). Its six volumes contain nearly 2,000 articles by more than 650 authors. Twenty-four years elapsed between its initial conception and publication, but this prolonged "genesis story" has the unintended benefit of allowing us to trace "the powerful influence of the modernist movement over twentieth-century dance and its historiography up to the end of that century."[20] The *IED*'s treatment of dance theory as a topic offers an excellent case in point.

As noted in the introduction, the *IED* contains no article titled "dance theory." This statement requires some qualification. An article titled "Technical Manuals" offers a historical survey of many of the same treatises discussed in this survey. The article is divided into three essays by different authors on three historical periods: Ingrid Brainard on 1445–1725; Sandra Noll Hammond on 1765–1859; and Kennetha R. McArthur on "Publications Since 1887" (ending in the 1980s).[21] According to Brainard:

> A technical manual instructs the reader in the technique of dancing. In nearly all instances the technical portion of a manual contains sections on style, gesture, manners, the proper handling of accessories (swords, hats, fans, cloaks, gloves, kerchiefs, and so on) and on musical performance practice, meter, rhythm, and instrumentation. With few exceptions the technical manuals from the early Renaissance to the middle of the seventeenth century contain choreographic descriptions of dances, with or without musical accompaniment, in addition to their theoretical-technical introductions.[22]

While recognizing that technique occupies only a "portion of a manual," Brainard does not address the content of the other portion: the "theoretical-technical introductions." It is obvious from Brainard's criteria how peripherally dance theory is treated in the entire article, further proof of the marginalization of theory that took place in the post-1800 dance world. In comparison with the present book, the three "Technical Manuals" authors mention many more works (if only by author and publication date) because they are listing manuals in general, without discriminating between purely theoretical and purely practical content: the article's title itself militates against any serious consideration of theory.

With hostility or contempt toward traditional theory being the prevailing sentiment among the artists themselves, it will come as no surprise that the prognosis for traditional dance theory was bleak indeed by the 1990s. Randy Martin writes in 1998:

> Nor has a secondary literature emerged that has articulated a grammar of dance criticism specific to its object or a more general meditation on this predicament for the representation of dance in writing. The other side of

the resistance of the dance object to representation, therefore, has been the challenge (that only recently has begun to be addressed) to generate a theoretical language of its own or a sustained dialogue with theory from other sources.[23]

Noël Carroll sounds the death knell in 2003: "The achievements of postmodern dance have rendered past theorizing about the nature of dance obsolete."[24] And *Wikipedia* proclaims the new reality: "Dance theory is the philosophy underpinning contemporary dance . . . It is a fairly new field of study, developing largely in the 20th Century."[25]

As it approached publication in 1998, the *IED* brought its coverage of dance research more in line with contemporary intellectual currents. The multiessay article "Methodologies in the Study of Dance" reflects the allure for dance studies of the dominant theoretical model of its time, poststructuralism, with "articles focusing on sociology, cultural context, linguistics, anthropology, ethnology, and new areas of inquiry."[26] Susan Leigh Foster has written the final "Methodologies" essay: "New Areas of Inquiry."[27] As a pair, the Brainard and Foster articles represent two generations of scholars and two faces of late twentieth-century dance scholarship: the first looked at historical sources and saw only practice; the second looks beyond the sources and adopts new paradigms of epistemology.

Foster begins her second paragraph with a sentence that seems so self-evident it hardly needs saying: ". . . the body and its movement are typically construed as natural phenomena." Why is this premise so prominent and consequential? Contemporary dance theory is informed by "cultural theory," an "umbrella term" under which various disciplines are gathered. It is based on semiology, "the examination of language initiated by Ferdinand de Saussure [1857–1913] in the early twentieth century." Behind this statement lies a lot of basic postmodern theory and philosophy, with which Foster appears to assume the reader's prior familiarity. For the benefit of those who lack this background, here is an attempt to sketch a brief introduction.

Saussure introduced the concept of the *sign*, a unitary and arbitrary conveyance of meaning. A sign—conventionally speaking, a word—consists of two parts: the *signifier*, which is the word itself; and the *signified*, which is whatever thing or idea the word refers to. Signs combine to form aggregates that, semiologically, constitute speech. Saussure theorized two kinds of speech, giving them French names: *langue* and *parole*, both of which translate generally as "speech," but with different connotations. In *langue* (language), words are abstract and arbitrary symbols for *signifieds* with which they have no intrinsic or essential connection; this explains why different languages have different words for the same thing. In *parole* ([spoken] word), speech is examined in terms of its everyday usage, subject to all sorts of extralinguistic contexts and contingencies. *Langue* is impersonal and normative; *parole* is individualistic and vernacular.

Recognizing that signs are not exclusively linguistic and can signify things that are not speech, Saussure's "single most daring theoretical move" was to conceive of semiology as "a general science of signs ... applicable to all meaningful human actions or productions."[28] Just as verbal signs in a written composition come together as a *text*, movements and gestures are the "signs" made by dancing bodies to communicate the "text" in the form of a dance work or performance. Texts relate to each other on an open and equal basis; the old apples-and-oranges standard of categorization no longer applies. Hence the concept of *intertextuality*, by means of which dance and its theory can be studied interdisciplinarily through signs and texts, whether verbal or nonverbal.

One can plausibly deduce that Saussure's *parole* interests Foster more than *langue*. Traditional dance theory, which considers dance principally in terms of its constituent elements—its internal structure, so to speak—corresponds semiologically to *langue*. It relates to dance in a systematic, arbitrary, artificial, and prescriptive way, and is therefore untrue to what is natural in dance. The poststructural approach to "speech" about dance is therefore more in line with Saussure's concept of *parole*. It is natural because it is interdisciplinary, borrowing methodologies from the other disciplines that affect the subjects of its research.

Roland Barthes (1915–1980) radically deepened the concept of the sign. "The sign," he says (loosely translated), "is a crack through which one can perceive nothing other than the face of another sign."[29] His understanding of texts—that is, sign-aggregates—is geometrically expansive in proportion to his concept of the sign. In his encyclopedia article "Texte (Théorie de)," he writes:

> If the theory of the text tends to abolish the separation between genres and arts, it is because it no longer considers works as simple "messages" or even "statements" (that is, as finished products whose purpose is fulfilled at the moment of emission), but as perpetual *utterances* by means of which the subject is continually discussed; the subject belongs, undoubtedly, to the author, but also *to the reader*. The theory of the text leads, therefore, to the promotion of a new epistemological object: the *act of reading*. . . . The theory of the text expands the liberties of reading to infinity [. . .].[30]

Poststructuralism, which came to prominence in the 1960s and 1970s, involves the necessity of studying objects of research contextually rather than in isolation. It regards dance as a product of the many contingencies that influence and affect its existence: race and class; production, funding, and marketing; the global exchange of styles and influences; and the politics of gender, especially as interrogated through feminist theory. Inevitably, the distinction between theory and practice will be erased, as Michel Foucault (1926–1984) observes:

> A new mode of the "connection between theory and practice" has been established. Intellectuals have got used to working, not in the modality of the "universal," the "exemplary," the "just-and-true-for-all," but within specific sectors, at the precise points where their own conditions of life or work situate them.[31]

Given this new paradigm, plus Barthes's concept of the infinitely expansive capability of texts, one can sense how far afield dance studies are now licensed to roam.

Foucault's phrase ". . . the precise points where their own conditions of life or work situate them," implies that the production and reception of texts are further problematized through the inevitable subjectivity and individuality of textual interpretation between any author-source and any reader-receiver in any field. Barthes recognizes two types of writing. The first type he calls *littérature*, which represents "a finite world" that is immediately and unambiguously intelligible; the second is *texte*, which represents "the infinity of language." Dance is an excellent example of *texte*, ripe for speculative journeying in the realms of knowledge (*mathésis*, in Barthes's word).[32] Subjectivity complicates interpretation at every stage of the reception chain—dance creator, dance composition, dancer, audience, critic, theorist, and scholar—each of whom will experience and interpret the text differently and, to some extent, validly. Since every "reader" confronts the text from a unique standpoint—biographical, intellectual, psychological, sociocultural, political, and so on—her or his interpretive process must integrate interdisciplinary, pluralistic knowledge and methodologies from every applicable discipline. Given these premises, dance "theorization" can be a product of only two things—choreography and the dancer's own experience of dancing—both of which are parts of what traditionally was called dance practice. Here Foster explicitly conflates theory and practice. The dancer is the researcher, and to dance is to theorize. Theory can only come from the dancer's own empirical, solipsistic meditation on what it means, personally, to exist as a dancer. Thus, every dancer is her or his own theorist. This state of affairs is called *reflexivity* (or *reflectivity*)—a term that will crop up frequently in subsequent readings.

The concluding paragraph of Foster's article situates contemporary dance theory with regard to the historical legacy. From her perspective, "dance theory" as discussed so far in the present survey has ceased to exist except as a historical phenomenon, and it has been replaced by an extensive menu of interdisciplinary theories and strategies whose collective historical memory dates back no further than Karl Marx (1818–1883). In this final paragraph, Foster not only proclaims traditional dance theory dead, but stands upon its ruins and exults. Would it not have been seemly, first of all, for an academic dance historian to give the redoubtable Louis de Cahusac his due as author of the words quoted from the *Encyclopédie*?[33] But more to the point, what makes Cahusac's eminently obvious and reasonable statement a mere *assertion* or *claim* that demands destabilization? When did dance cease to consist of "movements of the body, jumps, and measured steps"? You don't have to be an incorrigible traditionalist to sense Foster's condescension toward those simple and naïve *Lumières*.

READING 9.2
Foster

PP. 376–379

The theoretical and methodological perspectives articulated in cultural theory had a substantial impact on dance research in the 1980s and continue to open up significant lines of inquiry. *Cultural theory* as used here is an umbrella term that encompasses developments within post-structuralist textual criticism, cultural studies, contemporary Marxist and postcolonial discourse analysis, feminist and gender studies, and interpretive and reflexive research strategies. These areas of inquiry share a common orientation toward the natural as a historical and cultural category deserving critical investigation. Inquiries into what has been construed as natural in a given cultural and historical context have influenced methods in all disciplines of the humanities.

The immediate relevance of this orientation for dance research lies in the fact that the body and its movement are typically construed as natural phenomena.

[...]

The critical investigation of the natural, relevant to both cultural theory and dance research, can be traced to the examination of language initiated by Ferdinand de Saussure in the early twentieth century. De Saussure characterized the basic unit of meaning in language as the *sign*, a unit composed of a sound or acoustic element known as the *signifier* and a conceptual element (lexical meaning) known as the *signified*. De Saussure proposed that the relationship between these two elements is arbitrary in that it is based on cultural agreement rather than on any natural order. This theory of language was subsequently applied by researchers to a wide variety of cultural phenomena. This work, loosely referred to as the practice of *semiotics*, undertook to study all cultural objects and events as signs whose decipherment depended on the interpretation of the vast number of cultural codes and conventions through which the signs operate.

To see dance movement as sign is to assume that a non-natural relationship obtains between movement, the signifier, and the concept to which it refers, the signified; therefore, one assumes that such a relationship can be constituted in varying ways. Dance's meaning becomes the product of cultural agreement, the result of a systematic use of various choreographic codes and conventions. Such an approach not only permits one to detect different kinds of meanings in dance, but it also focuses attention on how a dance means what it does.

Semiotic analysis of dance divides choreographic codes and conventions into two kinds: those that order the dance by giving it an internal coherence and structure; and those that organize the dance with respect to the world that surrounds it. Conventions that give dance its internal order include the vocabulary of movements that make up the dance, and the syntactical principles—such as repetition, reiteration, theme and variation, or algorithmic and aleatory techniques—that govern the selection and combination of these movements. Conventions through which the dance makes reference to the world include its frame, the aspects such as publicity and venue that set the dance apart from all other events; its style, including the specific use of space, body parts, and movement qualities that give the dance a signature; and its modes of representation, indexical, iconic, or symbolic, through which the dance summons up its subject matter.

[...]

This kind of semiotic analysis forms the basis for each of the various interpretive strategies that constitute cultural theory. For example, poststructuralist textual criticism uses a semiotic analysis to map resonances between specific texts or traditions of text-making and the larger cultural context in which they occur. These inquiries have expanded the notion of the text to encompass cultural phenomena as diverse as film, television, advertisements, comics, computer-aided communication, and all forms of printed matter. As kinds of texts, each of these cultural events manifests a syntactic coherence, ways of referring to the world, and a theoretical orientation through which it comments on its position as a text among other texts. By extension, any given dance or dance practice embodies a theorizing of relationships between body and self and between body and society. Learning to choreograph, the choreographer learns to theorize; learning to dance, the dancer assimilates the body of facts and the structuring of discursive frameworks that permit theorization.

[...]

The emphasis in cultural theory on how events mean extends to an examination of the researcher's own role in determining that meaning. Cultural theory encourages awareness of the researcher's role in identifying, interpreting, and synthesizing evidence; it has experimented with an impressive array of devices designed to signal this awareness to the reader. The reflexive understanding of the relationship between the subject of research and the process of research has special significance for dance scholarship, given the difficulties of documenting dance and of translating dance into written text. The fact that dance vanishes in the moment of its performance, leaving little evidence of its existence, and that its eloquence derives entirely from nonverbal action, illuminate the processes through which it is reconstituted for purposes of research. Dance scholars working to embody these processes in their writing contribute to cultural theory not only their invaluable insights into bodily practices, but also their profound understanding of the project of translating from one cultural domain to another.

The entry "Dance" in Diderot's *Encyclopédie* asserts confidently that dance consists of "regulated movements of the body, jumps, and measured steps performed to the sound of musical instruments or the voice." The entrance of cultural theories into dance research destabilizes such claims by demonstrating multiple, distinct approaches to the interpretation and even the definition of dance. Cultural theory facilitates an examination of a dance's cultural meanings and at the same time focuses attention on the research process itself. By recognizing in the body the ability to signify in different ways, cultural theory offers to dance research a broad repertory of strategies for analyzing dance and a new conception of the relationship between dance and the language that describes it. Applying cultural theory to various dance topics, scholars can elucidate a cultural identity for the dancing body, the dancing individual, and the dancing group. In undertaking such an inquiry, they also position their own bodies as participants in the process of making dance meaningful.

9.3. ANDRÉ LEPECKI AND JENN JOY

Planes of Composition: Dance, Theory and the Global (London: Seagull Books, J2009).

Postmodern dance theory writing is characterized by verbal exuberance: wordplay, neologisms, bizarre juxtaposition, esoteric and often opaque scholarly jargon, and obnoxious-yet-ingenious punctuational/typographical *jeux d'esprit* such as these:

circulate and (ex)change
(re)presentation
(re)sound(ing) tracks
auto(bio)graphic
thINKing DANCE
"The (M)other of Writing"
"Walking/Dancing: an historical (pre)amble"

(W)RAPPED IN ILLUSION

(It is no coincidence that many of these random examples play on the act of writing or recording.) The authors of this reading are literally ebullient: drunk on words and the imagery conjured by the neologism "foamization" to express the bubbling over of ideas, cultures, theories, practices, philosophies, and so on implicit in a postmodernist universe where "All texts are intertexts,"[34] so everything is related to everything.

Another verbal tic of postmodern dance theorists is their infatuation with the idea of *theory* and the word itself, along with *theorist* and *theorize*:

The proliferation of theories also produced a tendency to use the term *Theory* (with a capital *T*) to describe the wealth of conflicting critical theories. In this sense, Theory replaces philosophy as the most abstract and general mode of theoretical discourse. Theory has emerged as an autonomous enterprise in many academic disciplines, giving rise to a tendency to do work in Theory, which engages various critical theories, problems, and concepts, or explores the nature and function of theory itself in the academic disciplines.[35]

Historically, *theory* was used sparingly, discretely, because its parameters were circumscribed. Now it is ubiquitous because it is implicit in every dance or dance-related act and thought. Milner speaks of "post-structural theoretical relativism."[36]

READING 9.3
Lepecki and Joy

PP. VIII–IX

When thinking about dance, dancing, theorizing dance and how these practices respond, move with and are moved by our current political, economic and discursive predicament of a globalized planet, an insight from one of the contributors to this volume, the German philosopher Peter Sloterdijk, is of particular relevance: "The current implementation of networks encircling the entire Earth—along with all its virtual excrescences—does not represent so much, from a structural point of view, a globalization, than a foamization [*écumisation*]."

By displacing the emphasis from the figure of the globe as metaphor for the planetary condition, and replacing it with the bubbling dynamic of foam, Sloterdijk is identifying the demise of all narratives that insist on "a unique integrating hypersphere." Rather, our current condition, where a hyper-mobilization of the planet is under way, primarily fuelled by well-tested colonialist and capitalist policies and dynamics, demands the creation of a political phenomenology of heterogeneities—a theory that acknowledges the reality of the irregular, the proliferation of dynamic eccentricities, and thus challenges the very notion of centre upon which colonial and postcolonial melancholic and neoliberal kineticism gain their organizational and hegemonic forces.

[...]

How to choreograph, or how to improvise, a mobilization of limbs and of thinking (never in opposition to each other, but always already chiasmatically coupled in generative assemblages) that does not fall prey to other forces of mobilization at the service of market acceleration and neo-imperial dislocations? How to dance and how to theorize dancing that explicitly addresses the fact that its grounds are heterogeneous, dynamic, bumpy, bubbling, treacherous, violent, resonant, vibrant and always inventive political terrains? These questions not only challenge dancers and choreographers to reconsider the premises under which they create their dance practices, but they also challenge dance theorists to rethink what may be the adequate analytical and critical tools for these dances.

In this challenge, what needs to be activated is the capacity for discourse to always escape itself, to decentre itself, to misbehave and flee in order to find and forge words, concepts, sites and sentences whose heterogeneity would inform a renewed critical-kinetic effort to revitalize well-established, properly poised theoretical positions. In order for critical dance studies to enter into a dialogue with the political dynamics of the current planetary mobilization, it must hear what the particularities of postcolonial critiques, what the heterogeneous voices of decentred positions and subjectivities, what the forces of critical and neo-Marxist theories, and what the forces animating any philosophical project that replaces ethics for ontology (and that, moreover, ties that ethics to a resisting biopolitics that relaunches, in a pragmatic, empirical way, Spinoza's call to experimentally know "what a body can do") have to add to our understanding of dance today. This is not yet another call for interdisciplinarity but rather a call for the activation of a slightly chaotic, slightly uncontrollable, theoretical foaming, exact and rigorous, poetic and political, dynamic and concrete, as a way to allow for these heterogeneities to become critical imperatives.

9.4. African American Dance Theory II

9.4A. THOMAS F. DEFRANTZ
Dancing Many Drums: Excavations in African American Dance, Studies in Dance History 19 (University of Wisconsin Press, 2002).

9.4B. ANITA GONZALEZ
Black Performance Theory (Durham, NC: Duke University Press, 2014).

Thomas DeFrantz shows the enduring relevance, in the postmodern age, of Robert Farris Thompson's "seminal articulation" of the theoretical elements of West African dance. He traces the steady transmission of Thompson's five-point analysis by dance scholars—among them Dolores Kirton Cayou, Brenda Dixon Gottschild, and Jacqui Malone—unchanged with only minor additions or refinements along the way.[37] Leaving aside, for the moment, "songs and dances of derision," the first four of Thompson's original five points ("percussive concept of performance; multiple meter; apart playing and dancing; [and] call-and-response") are reinterpreted by DeFrantz as "African*isms*" (my emphasis): "insistent rhythmicity, angularity, percussive rupture of underlying flow, [and] individualism within a group dynamic." The word *Africanisms* (like Gottschild's "Africanist") emphasizes the fact that the dance in question is created, performed, and described in a place other than Africa by people whose nationality is not African. This physical distance implies historical difference: questions of memory, interpretation, transmission, translation, subjugation, miscegenation, authenticity, and innovation. Memory, in fact, may be what most separates African American dance from postmodern dance, which places such a high premium on the experimental, the innovative, the unprecedented, the avant-garde.

There is a sixth element from Thompson's writing that DeFrantz includes in his list of Africanisms. In Thompson's book *Flash of the Spirit*, which followed his "Aesthetic of the Cool" article by almost twenty years, he enshrines the concept in Kongo culture of "flash of the spirit" in his repertoire of prediaspora inheritences.[38] Thompson describes "flash of the spirit" as an attribute of a charm (*nkisi*; plural *minkisi*) believed to contain "an inner spark of divinity or soul." *Minkisi* were contained in a vessel, such as a *nkisi*-kettle, that "was even believed to be enlivened by the 'flash of the spirit,' the glitter of a falling star, mystically absorbed . . . . 'so that the *nkisi* will always have life, like the flow of quicksilver, so that it will be swift and moving, like the waters of the ocean, so that the spirit in the charm can merge with the sea and travel far away.'"[39] DeFrantz associates this concept with dance (though Thompson did not) as a kind of transcendent energy "that simultaneously confirms temporal presence and ubiquitous spirituality."

DeFrantz brings Thompson's "theoretical imperatives" decisively into the cultural theory orbit by expanding on "songs and dances of derision." Thompson had explained the "moral function" of the dance of derision in its original African context: "The dance of derision attests that although most West African dances exist as metaphors of right living, some Africans do cheat, steal, and kill."[40] Malone connects the dances of derision in the United States to the cakewalk, "America's first international dance craze" around the turn of the twentieth century, that may have originated with black slaves ridiculing "white folks'" dances—specifically, the grand march (see Reading 8.3a).[41] For DeFrantz, the "metacommentary" that "suggests narratives outside the physical frame of performance" are rooted in the uneradicable collective trauma of the diaspora. In her essay "What Is Black Dance?," Zita Allen answers her title's question: "At the heart of the matter is the history of African descendants, a history with slavery at its core, a history without which this 'black dance' question might never have existed."[42] It is easy to see how DeFrantz would find that the transgressive or subversive nature of dances of derision "most clearly encompassed the political dimension of 'black dance' performance." In other words, dances of derision constitute the component of political conscience and agency in contemporary African American dance.

Both "flash of fire" and "dances of derision" reflect an ethos in African American dance that emphatically rejects and far transcends any notion of a dance performance as mere spectacle, artifact, exhibit, or re-enactment.

In the introduction to *Black Performance Theory*, DeFrantz and Anita Gonzalez present a compressed summary of milestones in African American dance theory in thirty-year leaps, from Hurston to Thompson to coedited volumes of academic essays on "hybridity, public spheres, the postcolonial, queer black sexualities, and de-essentialized identities" in postmodern black performance (2–5). The introduction also contains a three-part dialogue between the two editors: "Parsing Black," "Parsing Performance," and "Parsing Theory," from which Reading 9.4b is excerpted. In "Parsing Black," DeFrantz emphasizes the "Africanist aesthetics" derived from Thompson's taxonomy; Gonzalez emphasizes, instead, the multicultural outreach of poststructural theory: "By way of contrast, I understand black as a response to histories that extend beyond Africa and its aesthetics. . . . Cultural infusions from other parts of the world collect and mingle with the multitude of African performance genres to create a great diversity of styles" (6). In "Parsing Theory," in which both authors explicitly define theory as based on practice, Gonzalez emphasizes the primacy of "subjectivity" (i.e., reflexivity) in African American dance. The brief yet intimate self-identifications prefacing each of their responses manifests the authors' belief that in order to understand their ideas, the reader needs to know exactly where they are coming from.

READING 9.4A
DeFrantz

From *Dancing Many Drums*, "African American Dance: A Complex History" (3–35).

PP. 14–15

. . . [Robert Farris] Thompson had conducted extensive fieldwork in a range of sub-Saharan cultures to arrive at his seminal articulation of pan-African dance and music performance eventually published in the 1966 article "Dance and Culture: An Aesthetic of the Cool." His analysis describes "the dominance of a percussive concept of performance; multiple meter; apart playing and dancing; call-and-response; and, finally the songs and dances of derision." Thompson's work, extended slightly by separate research in the teaching primer *Modern Jazz Dance* by Dolores Kirton Cayou, predicted a third strain of African American dance scholarship that explored theoretical imperatives embedded within dance practice. The documentation of these qualities of motion provided critical linkage between obviously intertwined sacred and social traditions of African American dance performance. Each of these attributes could also be discerned in concert work made by artists involved in the Black Arts movement, although the final attribute—the songs and dances of derision—most clearly encompassed the political dimension of "black dance" performance. In this category, movement provokes metacommentary and suggests narratives outside the physical frame of performance. For many concert artists of the Black Arts movement, the ability of stage dance to refer to experiences well outside the proscenium frame provided the most important connections of their work to contemporary black experience.

These performance characteristics indicated a continuity of aesthetic approaches to dance and music-making in line with the articulation of a "black aesthetic" in the late 1960s. Reconceived in the 1990s by cultural and literary theorists as "Africanist retentions" or "Africanisms," these hallmarks of African-derived performance provide a theoretical framework for the identification and interpretation of diasporic traditions of art-making. Africanisms discernible in concert dance, for example, are qualities of design and execution based on insistent rhythmicity, angularity, percussive rupture of underlying flow, individualism within a group dynamic, and access to a dynamic "flash of the spirit" that simultaneously confirms temporal presence and ubiquitous spirituality. These qualities are not particular movements so much as compositional strategies that may inform any given moment in a dance. As such, they are recurrent aesthetic imperatives that may be employed both by African diaspora artists and, significantly, by others following this tradition. While some scholars have resisted this theoretical approach because of its implication of a narrow and singular "African dance" idiom, the identification of these conceptual traditions has created the most consistent approach to documenting Africanist performance across generations and geographies of African American dancers and choreographers, as well as in work by others, including white Americans, Europeans, and Asians.

READING 9.4B
DeFrantz and Gonzalez

From *Black Performance Theory*, Introduction: "From 'Negro Expression' to "Black Performance'" (1–15).

P. 7

Parsing Theory
[DeFrantz] **Male-Identified Queer High Yellow Duke University:** Theory, in this formation, is the mobilization of practice toward analysis. The taking stock, or noticing, of action to recognize its component parts and its implications, and the extension of that noticing to construct a way to understand, or interpret,

what is happening there. Theory assumes action and practice already in motion; theory might be the realization of that noticing translated into text, or music and motion. Surely theory doesn't have to be written in order to become manifest, but just as surely theory has to be shared among people to be a valuable analytic.

[Gonzalez] **Afro Southern Caribeña now in Ann Arbor:** Theory is not limited to academic or intellectual inquiries. Theories develop through evaluative processes initiated by artists in the moment in which they assess what "works" about a performance. Performance theory can be delivered through a hand gesture or sketch, embedded in a lecture, or disseminated within the pauses of a sound score. Artists articulate thoughtful analyses in a multiplicity of ways. Post-performance discussions easily take the form of active breath or performed actions that comment and expand upon originating concepts, relocating the performance practices within new theoretical contexts. This is theory manifest: an articulate response to a performance. All theory, and certainly the best theory, is subjective—a unique and personal response to the performance act that helps the reader or viewer to perceive in a new or unexpected manner.

9.4C. HALIFU OSUMARE
The Africanist Aesthetic in Global Hip-Hop: Power Moves (New York: Palgrave Macmillan, 2007).

Just as African dance idioms were disseminated via the diaspora to colonial cultures, so too African American dance, especially in its hip-hop dialect, has reciprocally colonized, as it were, global popular culture. Halifu Osumare writes:

Hip-hop culture has become international in breadth and depth, with thousands of cultures throughout the globe having embraced it in various forms. The culture has spawned rap in as many languages as there are ethnic groups, replete with deejay, breakdance and graffiti collectives across the globe. From initial breakdance collectives that mimicked 1980s films like *Flashdance* and *Beat Street* to fledgling local music industries that have become inroads for the U.S. invasion of American multinational music conglomerates, hip-hop culture has not only bolstered a previous rock-music-based U.S. pop culture industry, but also has gained a foothold in the international arena (2).

A central aspect of hip-hop performance, according to Osumare, is the verbal component of rap and call-and-response form, both of which she identifies with the African word *Nommo*:

> Dances done to James Brown's soul music [in this instance, "Please, Please, Please"] become physical manifestations of *Nommo*, the power of the Word. In black cultural production like James Brown's music, the interchangeable dynamics of movement and sound cojoin to form the first principle of an aesthetic that is not merely product, but indeed about *process*, always in motion, always becoming. The African concept of *Nommo* is a principle that emphasizes the changing now, the improvisatory self. [. . .]
>
> The hip-hop slang phrase "word up" . . . unconsciously encompasses the concept of using this primal force called *Nonno*. In the call and response culture of hip-hop music, "word up," or just simply "word," is often used to punctuate a statement just made, as a response to one's own or someone else's calling forth of word energy through the power of voicing; while at other times the phrase is also used as a greeting to a fellow "head" or a recognized member of hip-hop subculture. It seems no coincidence that a vernacular hip-hop slang term is in actuality recognition of the ancient first principle at the root of an African cosmology. (pp. 31–32)

Although Thompson does not mention *Nommo* by name, its connection to his "talking dances," "antiphony," and "dances of derision" is evident. In Reading 9.4c, *Nommo* is shown to have profound theoretical significance for intertextuality in diasporic dance discourse.[43]

READING 9.4C
Osumare

PP. 50–53

Indeed, many of the principles of African aesthetics—*Nommo* word power, polyrhythmic musical structure, trickster rhetorical strategies, and improvisatory subject negotiation—and the dance modes integral to them were once strictly the purview of people of African ancestry. Within the dance complex this consisted of a relaxed torso, bent knees, rhythmically isolating trunk from head to pelvic girdle, complex polyrhythmic patterns that distribute themselves throughout the body, and quick shifts of weight in the feet show the complexity of the musical structure. Aggregately all these dance traits are pivotal to many cultures throughout the African diaspora. These embodied rhythmic "texts" accompany the diasporic music mentioned earlier: Brazilian samba, Cuban rumba, Dominican merengue, Haitian *danse congo*, and Nueva York salsa. The foundations of this dance aesthetic are clearly what drove the twenties Charleston era and what became irreversibly etched as a national mode of American social dance by the fifties R&B/rock-and–roll cross over period. [. . .]

I am most interested in the global implications of this "Afro-Americanization" process as it relates to the embodied Africanist aesthetic along with various forms of marginalizations that already exist throughout the globe. Irrespective of "race," I am curious about the *effects* that polyrhythmic movements of black vernacular dance have on the b-girl in the act of dancing. I contend that there is a physically "democratizing" effect on the body because of various rhythms being distributed throughout the whole body, (carrying two or more rhythms in the hips and shoulders, while another one is going on in the shifting feet). This equality of body parts, as the rhythmic *Nommo* force circulates through them, carries the potential for change in self-perception because of the potential transformation in self-awareness inherent in African-based dance.

[. . .]

Given the United States' unique position in the global marketplace and the particularly American stress on individualism, dance in hip-hop culture, during the later decades of the twentieth century and the beginning of the twenty-first century, has been particularly implicated in the global proliferation of hip-hop. I argue that embodied identities through particular dance moves, first emanating from hip-hop's black and Latino neighborhoods, are now being exported to the global sphere along with particular rap lyrics and deejay beats. [. . .]

In explicating the current exportation of hip-hop dance internationally, current dance theory and Cultural Studies might address the larger implications that are at stake. Dance and American Studies scholar Jane Desmond offers important suggestions for the placement of dance theory and "studies of bodily texts . . . on the agenda of cultural studies." She notes that in so doing, "we can further our understandings of how social identities are signaled, formed, and negotiated through bodily movement." Although not the first to suggest this, Desmond also reminds us that dance, in all of its manifestations of concert, social, and ritual forms, has been sorely neglected by Western epistemology. Yet because of dance's centrality in Africanist aesthetic, bodily movement becomes a "primary, not secondary social 'text'—complex, polysemous, always, already meaningful, yet continuously changing."

Dance has been historically important in enabling African descendants actually to make visible, through the body, processes of political, cultural, and historical arenas that are obviously drawn from the dancer's (and choreographer's) own place within these fields of social enactment. Therefore, skillful practitioners of Africanist dance styles of any ethnicity must view themselves as literally speaking through their bodies in dialogue with the multimetered rhythm. The individual texts embedded within these moment-by-moment improvisatory dances become crucial to hip-hop's mapped discourse across the globe.

Dancer and political scientist Randy Martin augments embodiment theory with concepts of individual imagination and the temporal and ephemeral nature of movement. "Dance is both a bodily practice that figures an imagined world and a momentary materialization through performance of social principles that otherwise remain implicit."[44] If this is a viable definition of the multiple dimensions of dance, purposeful, value-laden movement produced within the already dialogue-based Africanist aesthetic is a critical manifestation of dance as text.

9.4D. NADINE GEORGE-GRAVES
Urban Bush Women: Twenty Years of African American Dance Theater, Community Engagement, and Working It Out (Madison: University of Wisconsin Press, 2010).

Moving from the global to the local, Urban Bush Women is a black feminist dance company founded by dancer, choreographer, and dance educator Jawole Willa Jo Zollar in 1984 in New York City, and now headquartered in Brooklyn. Its website says: "UBW is committed to highlighting the power, beauty and strength of the African Diaspora. Dance from the African continent values the whole body in motion through a sophisticated use of polyrhythm, weight, pelvic and spinal articulation."[45] To call Urban Bush Women a dance company or group does not do it justice. It is more like a living, moving, holistic praise-song to black womanhood. Its members, accepted without regard to age or body type, are predominantly women of color, though male dancers and white women have performed with them. Clearly individuality is prized over uniformity. Nadine George-Graves says that Zollar "wanted to create dances that showed how African Americans perform themselves 'when not in the presence of whites'" (11). Her overarching aims, achieved through the dances themselves and community outreach, are healing, affirmation, and validation.

UBW's "Hair Stories" (2001) is a popular, widely performed multisectional performance piece, a combination of comedy, pantomime, dance, singing, and audience participation. George-Graves describes it this way: "Be it wrapped, braided, twisted, relaxed, curled, or dreadlocked, the constant shifting of preferred styles tells us much about selfhood. *Hair Stories* tells us that black women are sometimes afraid to see the knots, the roots of who they are. . . . What follows is a roller-coaster ride throught the trials and tribulations, sociology, history, and drama that is the relationship black women have with their hair" (described 43–53, here 44). "Hair Stories" is a fine example of Thompson's "songs and dances of derision" as seen through DeFrantz's lens of Africanist political metacommentary.

UBW participated in the annual International Festival of Arts and Ideas in New Haven, Connecticut (also in 2001), as artists-in-residence in the predominantly black Dixwell community. Their six-week residency centered, according to George-Graves, on the themes of black liberation theology, womanist theology, and the interpretation of dance as an embodiment of the Christian belief in "the Word made flesh"; it included "liturgical dance workshops," lecture-demonstrations, children's creative movement workshops, community sings, and choral workshops (188–194). The project culminated in a full-scale presentation: "Dixwell . . . When the Lions Tell History—A Community Collaboration."[46] Both company and community members participated, and the audience is reported to have "roared its approval."[47] While UBW's outreach may appear largely religious in nature, it still resonates with Plato's belief in the role of mimetic dance—the gift of the god Apollo and the Muses—in the moral and ethical well-being of the *polis*, that is, of the city or community "where laws are, or will be in the future, rightly laid down regarding musical education and recreation" (see Reading 1.1).

READING 9.4D
George-Graves

PP. 30–32

A brief examination of one of Urban Bush Women's earlier pieces is helpful for understanding how the stylistic elements discussed so far come together in the choreography. The first section of *The Thirteenth Tribe, Nyabinghi Dreamtime* is an excellent example of much of Urban Bush Women's style, particularly the ways the aesthetic flows between modern dance tradition and African Diaspora cultures. It is based on Zollar's research into Jamaican Rastafarian traditions that combines political protest and resistance with Old Testament teachings. The Nyabinghi ceremony is a Rastafarian rite that lasts anywhere from three to twenty-one days. Rather than re-creating it, as Katherine Dunham might have done, Zollar uses this research to inspire original choreography. The result is an illustration of the Urban Bush Women style (technique blends, pedestrianism, strength, breath, pace, and emotion).[48]

The piece starts with the sound of many feet stomping, ringing out in the darkness. Low lights come up to reveal six dancers dressed simply in sports bras and shorts. They circle their arms around their heads, slap their chests, and lower themselves to the ground.[49] Immediately, a grounded aesthetic is established. One dancer gives a vocal cue, aurally connecting them all, and they all spin on the floor. As a single drum comes in, the dancers rise up and swing both arms around their heads while taking a step and rolling through their chests. The single African drum acts as a call, lifting them from the ground and moving them forward. They pause, sink down in their pliés, and coolly isolate their pelvises by rotating their hips several times. The gestures are not for sale, as Zollar might say, and combining them with the aesthetic of the cool empowers these provocative acts by leaving no doubt that they are not cheap gestures, even if sexualized.[50] They chassé with their legs extended in arabesque, turn with their legs in back attitude, and spin to the floor. From the floor, they move out of a ballet aesthetic by kicking out their feet, spinning, and hopping into splits and low, crouched positions. The choreography continues in this vein for several minutes. Meanwhile, male and female voices emerge softly, chanting, intoning, and moaning. The vocalizations add another layer to the performance that suggests an evocation, a summoning of spirituality and power. Further blending technique, the dancers stand, plié, rond de jambe, reach out, then flex their feet and stomp. With limp upper torsos, they point their feet, extend their legs, and step forward. They spin, jump, slap their arms, roll their shoulders, and drop in the waist. It is a Garth Fagan-like deconstruction of the elements of African Diaspora dance as well as an exploration of lines, shapes, and directions in ballet and modern dance tradition.[51]

At one point, the dancers hang their heads forward, bend at the waist, and swing their arms prosaically. They "step out" of the choreography and walk around in a pedestrian manner popularized by 1960s postmodern dance. Moving separately and no longer dancing, they each go through different sequences of freezes, runs, turns, kicks, and extensions. They give and take weight and support each other in lifts. They then walk around cautiously as if preparing to defend themselves. They move into a line, and each dancer places her arms around the back of the adjacent one. For the remainder of the piece, the dancers share weight, spin, and leap. They move individually and as a unit, alternating smoothly among modern choreography, African steps, and pedestrian running and walking patterns.

Many significant parts of the Urban Bush Women aesthetic are demonstrated in this piece. As a community and ensemble, the performers use breath to control the piece's energy and pace. All of the actions and attitudes are rooted in a cool strength. Emotionally, they charge the space to allow for possession and calm it to allow for personal reflection. They alternate between moving as a group and as individuals by dancing closer together or farther apart. If one or two people break out for a solo or duet, the group supports them. Above all, this dance displays many influences from different African Diaspora traditions (including the storytelling, chanting, singing, and, of course, dances of African, Caribbean, and African American people), as well as European traditions (ballet, modern) and postmodern pedestrianism.

9.4E. PHILIPA ROTHFIELD AND THOMAS F. DEFRANTZ

"Relay: Choreography and Corporeality," *Choreography and Corporeality: Relay in Motion*, ed. Thomas F. DeFrantz and Philipa Rothfield (London: Palgrave Macmillan, 2016), 1–12.

This essay is the introductory first chapter in a collection of essays that are international and intercultural in scope. African American dance is represented but not dominant. However, the similarity of the language here to DeFrantz's and Gonzalez's "parsing" of theory in Reading 9.4b suggests that the overall philosophy of the collection is guided by theoretical principles derived from African American dance studies.

"Relay," as Rothfield and DeFrantz envision it, is just another name for intertextuality, with the crucial distinction that relay is specially adapted to dance by being kineticized. Like "dancing bodies," "relay" moves not only between and among all kinds and levels of texts and contexts, but more essentially, it vibrates constantly, back and forth, within the force field generated between the poles of theory and practice. Though the connection is surely unintentional, the scientific sensibility evoked here might well remind a dance historian of the investigations into the physics of human movement by Samuel Rudolph Behr and John Weaver in the early eighteenth century. The flexibility and fluidity of this type of thinking are surely fostered by African American dance's unique position at the intersection of history, science, culture, and identity— its built-in interdisciplinarity as observed as far back as Katherine Dunham. Even if only by virtue of the hybridity of the name "African American," and the contestation between other names that have been more or less preferred over time (negro, black, Afro-American, African-American with or without the hyphen), African American dance is freighted with issues of searing breadth and immediacy.

READING 9.4E
Rothfield and DeFrantz

PP. 1–3

> . . . *from the moment a theory moves into its proper domain, it begins to encounter obstacles, walls, and blockages which require its relay by another type of discourse . . . Practice is a set of relays from one theoretical point to another, and theory is a relay from one practice to another. No theory can develop without eventually encountering a wall, and practice is necessary for piercing this wall.* (Foucault, "Intellectuals and Power, A Conversation between Michel Foucault and Gilles Deleuze," 206).

The relay does not follow a predetermined pathway. It moves between theory and practice, without privileging either term. The relay is not a structural concept. It is, rather, a form of movement, a manner of thought which enters into and engages a dynamic terrain. The figure of the relay shakes up the notion of theory and practice, opening up both terms to a sense of the encounter. Deleuze and Foucault speak of theory's encounter with practice, and conversely, of the impact of practice upon theory. In so doing, they do not position theory above its encounter with practice. Theory belongs to practice—it is itself a form *of* practice. In short, the relay unsettles the distinction between theory and practice, opening up both terms to a more dynamic and fluid conception of thought.

The notion of a relay draws attention to the formation of lateral relations, felt between theory and practice, and made possible through their serial encounter with one another. These encounters enable theory and practice to move on, to develop, acquire, and accumulate insight. The encounter also underlies the thinking embodied in this collection, which itself arises from a series of encounters staged across multiple locations, cultures, and kinaesthetic contexts. [. . .] These meetings further helped us to imagine our differences of approach and concerns in dance and with dancing bodies. They also helped us think more broadly about how a relay of ideologies binds up and disperses ways to theorise choreography and corporeality. These experiences have evolved into the diversity of ideas contained herein. While they are collected under the proper names of their authors, and arise from the joint history of the group, they express and traverse a series of differences which cannot be situated within a single, overarching conceptual structure. Such is the nature of the relay: it runs in different directions, marking its own territories of thought, generating history out of its successive encounters.

The relay sets theory in motion. Theory avails itself of concepts along the way, concepts which are themselves marked through a series of unfolding events and interactions. The concept is thus indebted to practice. Hierarchical conceptions of theory and practice are only able to conceive of practice in terms of illustration, exemplification, and instantiation. They confine practice to a supporting role. The notion of the relay activates practice, so that it can advance theory. This is why the relay does not signal a retreat into localism. The relay calls for a re-evaluation of the singular case, which may well find itself linked to a theoretical articulation, not as instantiation, but as a *provocateur* of its future theoretical self. Theory for its part takes up specificity, moving practice into a theoretical, conceptual register. The unfolding reciprocity of theory and practice is evident within the work of this volume. While its authors make use of their specific origins and local practices, these are thought through in a theoretical register. Their articulation of situation, itself a manner of practice, is not a mode of illustration, rather the means whereby theory is generated. The conceptual elaboration of these situations is an extension of thought into theoretical terrain.

If theory functions on a conceptual level, there is a sense here of difference within the concept. Philosophy's habit is to assume the stability and identity of concepts, while acknowledging difference only at the level of instantiation. But if we take the notion of mobility seriously, and take on board the idea of a relay between theory and practice, then we might consider the concept itself as less stable and more mobile. If we don't know what a body can do, we might likewise say that we don't know what a concept can do. Thus, the invitation of this collection is to experience the different ways in which concepts are mobilised and put to work, amidst very different concerns, embodied histories, and motivations. Its suggestion is that theory is itself marked, subject to material and corporeal forces, and is itself open to the different milieus that give voice to theory.

9.5.A. SUSAN LEIGH FOSTER

"Dancing and Theorizing and Theorizing Dancing," *Dance [and] Theory*, eds. Gabriele Brandstetter and Gabriele Klein (Bielefeld: transcript Verlag, 2013), 19–32.

9.5.B. P.A.R.T.S. (PERFORMING ARTS RESEARCH AND TRAINING STUDIOS), Directrice: Anne Teresa De Keersmaeker
Training Cycle and Study Guide (2016–2019), PARTS-studyguide-2016-2019.pdf

Jens Richard Giersdorf has written about the development of three new college-level dance programs in the 1980s and 1990s: the Theaterhochschule "Hans Otto" in Leipzig (then the German Democratic Republic [DDR]); the University of Surrey (England); and the University of California-Riverside.[52] All three programs were modernized in various ways, each according to its local priorities. While "archivisation, analysis and choreography" were components in common, the German program in *Tanzwissenschaft* was supplemented by "Marxist-Leninist philosophy, psychology, cultural studies, aesthetics, and art history" (323, 326); and the British program was based on "description, contextualisation, interpretation and evaluation" (329).

Susan Leigh Foster was chair of the dance department at Riverside when their doctoral program in critical dance studies was proposed in 1991 and eventually established. The proposed changes, as Giersdorf describes them:

> ... moved the programme away from the training of dancers, choreographers and dance pedagogues and towards a purely academic endeavour focused on "research and writing about dance" . . . The degree highlighted historical and reconstructive components in its proposal and drew parallels to art history as a study that did not rely on training in artistic practices. This again identified dance studies at Riverside as a theoretical discipline that emphasised the translation of dance into writing and the reconstruction of dance out of its sources as key issues for the PhD. The actuality of the programme, which admitted its first students in 1993, shifted this focus away from analysis, documentation and reconstruction and emphasised theorisations of dance across time and cultures—especially the relationship between dancing and writing as diverse sign systems embedded in social structures. [. . .] The construction of dance as text and the emphasis on logical and scientific categories denaturalise the process of dance making. As a methodology for dance studies, this approach gives the discipline a framework for an equal status in the academy, one comparable to that of art history or theatre studies. (331 and 330)

It is easy see how this program directly implements the principles outlined in Foster's article in the *International Encyclopedia of Dance* (Reading 9.2) and summarized here (Reading 9.5a).

In these academic programs and many others like them, postmodern dance theory has blossomed, and writing based on it has quantitatively ballooned. Students and faculty alike must be actively writing papers, dissertations, and books, and this work must be published because programs survive or perish on the basis of scholarly publication, and up-to-date programs must be structured to support this agenda. Theory is no longer being written by dancers and dancing masters, *encyclopédistes* and lexicographers, *savants*, polymaths, visionaries, idealists, and the occasional splenetic genius, but by academic scholars (admittedly with some practical dance "background") who aspire to the professoriate in order to teach it, in turn, to younger academic scholars.

One such program in the new model is P.A.R.T.S. (Performing Arts Research and Training Studios) in Brussels, established in 1995 and directed by dancer-choreographer Anne Teresa De Keersmaeker, as a pedagogical institution supporting contemporary dance in Belgium.[53] It is international in scope, with faculty drawn from the companies of such luminaries as Trisha Brown, William Forsythe, and Pina Bausch. The training cycle takes three years and encourages a continual cross-fertilization of practice and theory. The course areas are dance technique (ballet and contemporary); dance workshops (improvisation, composition, repertoire, choreography); body studies (yoga, shiatsu, pilates, Feldenkrais, anatomy); theater; music; dance theory; and special projects.

The P.A.R.T.S. theory course description (Reading 9.5b) should be read in comparison to that of Flavia Pappacena at the Accademia Nazionale di Danza in Rome (see Reading 8.6a). The P.A.R.T.S. student is identified as an "autonomous artist," and the program in general emphasizes sociocultural issues and theories. In the Accademia program, "classical dance" appears seven times (eight if you count "dances of the 18th and 19th centuries"), while the P.A.R.T.S. program deals with general historical "paradigms" and "notions." Philosophy and sociology, which include aesthetics, culture, and gender, are highlighted in the P.A.R.T.S. program, while in the Accademia program certain parts of these two sciences may or may not be present or implicit under different rubrics (e.g., "Aesthetics of classical dance"). In P.A.R.T.S., performance analysis is based on critical reflection, while the Accademia program involves analysis, reconstruction, and terminology. Management appears only in the P.A.R.T.S. program; its presence reflects contemporary students' and college administrations' anxiety over career opportunities after the degree, a growing concern in an era when graduates are not guaranteed employment in their chosen field, and schools are challenged to demonstrate positive outcomes to "sell" their services.

These comparisons between programs are not intended to show the superiority of one over the other, but merely to show the radical difference in *Weltanschauung* separating them.

READING 9.5A
Susan Leigh Foster

P. 31

What I want to suggest here is that theory and method are transportable from one subject matter to another, and this is certainly how Dance Studies in the U.S. has developed, borrowing theories and methods from other disciplines, and testing out the applicability and pertinence of those approaches to the subject of dance. Dance has been theorized as a text, as labor, as speech act, as rhetoric, as a form of mobilization, and as an intertextual system of signs, using methods from semiotics, genealogical analysis, and ethnography. We have also borrowed momentum from emerging interdisciplinary studies such as cultural studies, postcolonial studies, critical race studies, studies of sexuality, and diaspora and globalization studies in order to interrogate dance as a practice that generates cultural, ideological, and identificatory meanings. Any of these borrowings opens up certain lines of inquiry at the same time that it occludes others. The field can thus be seen as an ongoing process of inquiry marked by a high degree of reflexivity because the evanescence of dance itself foregrounds the theoretical dimensions of scholarly research by emphasizing the constructed nature of any object of study.

READING 9.5B
P.A.R.T.S.

THEORY

An autonomous artist must be able to reflect autonomously, to use his/her critical capacities. The theory classes offer information about art, performance, social and cultural theories. How can concepts help to get a grip on basic issues such as communication, theatricality and performance, subjectivity, the relation between art and society?

The classes aim to stimulate reflection about one's current and future practice on the one hand, and the place of art/dance in our culture and society on the other. They do not offer an academic or encyclopedic overview of theory, but an introduction to thinking and reflection.

I. DANCE HISTORY

The course treats the main paradigms of the history of Western theatrical dance. Within each period, a number of historical cases (choreographers, forms, styles) are unfolded with the help of theoretical notions such as body, figure, spectacle, avant-garde, the sublime, expression, ritual, simulacrum, musicality and dance, thinking-concept-movement, spectatorship and participation.

In the 1st year an additional seminar is spent on contextualising the early work of Anne Teresa De Keersmaeker, linked to the composition workshop that works on this theme. In addition to the Trisha Brown repertory workshop in the 2nd year, there is also a short seminar contextualising her work.

[schedule and faculty details]

2. PHILOSOPHY

In the 1st and 2nd year, the philosophy course offers an introduction into modern Western philosophy, seen from different perspectives such as the political, the ethical, and the aesthetical.

Next to the classes, students also have the task to write a paper, with every year a different stage in its development.

[schedule and faculty details]

3. SOCIOLOGY

In the 1st year, the introduction discusses basic concepts such as class, role, social ritual, institution, institutional differentiation, rationalisation, and also refers to classical sociological approaches and topics, such as the individual and consciousness as a black box, or theories of globalisation.

In the 2nd year, the sociology course focuses on the cultural field, through an institutional analysis of the structure and evolution of the Western art system. Another course in the 2nd year focuses on gender theories.

[schedule and faculty details]

4. PERFORMANCE ANALYSIS

In the performance analysis classes, students develop a vocabulary to discuss performances they have seen live or on video, both contemporary and historical works. The goal is to refine their reflection and discussion of art works, to go resolutely beyond "liking" or "not-liking" as the start of an analysis of an artwork.

In the 1st and 2nd year, students also write a short paper reflecting on performances they have seen.

[schedule and faculty details]

5. ART HISTORY

This course offers an introduction into visual arts and its [*sic*] history.

[schedule and faculty details]

6. TOPICAL SEMINARS

In the 3rd year, theory becomes even more a practice of reading, thinking and discussing. Theory is approached as theory, but the content of the seminars can be very diverse, ranging from very abstract concepts to concrete political or social issues, from themes that are very far from the arts to topics that deal with the relation between art and society.

In 2015–6, seminars deal with topics such as artistic versus political activism, methodologies of making work, queer theory, the bible, technologies of the self [etc.].

[schedule and faculty details]

7. MANAGEMENT

In the "management" course, students learn to know and discuss about important elements of the organisation of professional life, such as production, organisation, touring, co-production, partnerships and curating, but also about time management, public funding.

[schedule and faculty details]

9.6A. KENT DE SPAIN
"Resisting Theory: The Dancing Body and American Scholarship," *Society of Dance History Scholars Proceedings: Thirtieth Annual Conference Co-sponsored with CORD, Centre national de la danse, Paris, France, June 21–24, 2007* (Society of Dance History Scholars, 2007), 59–64.

9.6B. JANET LANSDALE
"A Tapestry of Intertexts: Dance analysis for the twenty-first century," *The Routledge Dance Studies Reader*, ed. Alexandra Carter and Janet O'Shea, 2nd ed. (London: Routledge, 2010), 158–167.

At the 2007 conference at the Centre national de la danse in Paris-Pantin, on the theme: "Repenser pratique et théorie/Rethinking Theory and Practice" (see also Reading 8.6b), the majority of the papers reflected three mutually reinforcing trends: the historical dimension was shallow; the theoretical dimension manifested a preference for strategies incompatible with historical repertoires; and the traditional theory-practice dyad was upended by a phenomenon still unfamiliar or uncomfortable to many attendees: postmodern dance theory.

Kent De Spain offers a remarkably jargon-free and balanced appraisal of the pros and cons of postmodern dance theory (Reading 9.6a). He provides a sense of the historical background needed to understand why and how cultural theory (see Reading 9.2) rejected traditional dance theory to underpin postmodern dance theory; how, because of all the contingent interdisciplinarity involved, critical theory is particularly vulnerable to ambiguity, cultural prejudices, and individual agendas; and how poststructuralism privileges the "linguistic gloss" or "linguistic construct." De Spain asks, in effect, whether "cultural theory" is a viable approach to dance theory.

The same ominous feeling of doubt and anxiety, using images of aggression and oppression, is expressed in the passage from Janet Lansdale (Reading 9.6b), an extrapolation of the consequences of intertextuality. Where De Spain talks about conflict and choosing sides, Lansdale talks about colonization of "an unsuspecting victim," and "choices made, in this treacherously open poststructuralist field."

READING 9.6A
Kent De Spain

PP. 59–60

Over the course of the past 20 years or so, dance theory has come into its own as a legitimate field of study, one that even has the potential to contribute unique ideas and approaches to other areas of academic discourse. Much of the development, I think, can be attributed to the work of broadly educated dance scholars adopting and adapting critical paradigms from other fields to the demands of studying dance art and practice. Critical theory, cultural studies, and a handful of "isms" have helped dance see itself more intimately contexted in relation to the reflection and production of cultural meanings. As pre-jailbird Martha Stewart might have said, "That's a good thing." But (and isn't there always a "but"?) postmodern theory has taught us to be sensitive to the negative spaces. Presence implies absence. Action implies agency for some and not for others. Well-intentioned power still looks like power to the powerless. So I have a few things to say regarding the dark side of theory, not to halt the "progress" of dance studies in any way, just to make sure that as we step forward we continue to recognize who/what we might be stepping upon.

Postmodernism has revealed to us the breakdown of the historicized, centralized, positivist point of view, and I do not think that many of us miss it. We have seen the dance history we thought we knew deconstructed and reconstructed repeatedly in the shifting politics of discourse. We have learned a new set of values, values that relate to the relativistic, fragmented, and subjective margins. And we have even learned to see the fragments in ourselves, and to notice our own marginality within specific cultural or social contexts. What we have not been quite as quick to recognize (we know it, but do we really *know* it?) is the hegemonic nature of discourse itself. In the self-perpetuating rush to produce and publish, and in the dance field's chip-on-my-shoulder need to keep up with the theoretical Joneses, I sometimes fear that we are in danger of losing track of the unique values which make dance a human art/practice worthy of such intense study. So, by working from the general to the specific, I want to take this opportunity to explore just a few of the ramifications of theoretical discourse in dance.

My first concern is with theory itself. In science, theories are ideas offered up as a way of explaining phenomena, something to be tested and proven/disproven. In critical studies, theories are not so much "proved" as "approved of" through the success (relevance, notoriety, etc.) of a particular line of discourse within a discipline, or across disciplines. But whether scientific or critical, I see theories more like "strange attractors" (an idea from the study of chaotic systems), images/ideas that have a kind of gravitational pull, allowing the turmoil of our thoughts and experiences to coalesce in structured ways. As such, theories must be seen as both invaluable and insidious.

Our experiences are both synchronic and diachronic: synchronic because of the simultaneous, multichannel, only partially integrated, nature of exteroceptic and interoceptic sensation; diachronic because of the inescapably linear flow of human time, with its anticipations, presence/absence, and reflections. Without organizing structures, our experiences would simply overwhelm us. And that is why we cannot afford to treat theories as mere explanations of experiential phenomena. Theories, as cultural and personal products, interact with experience at a much deeper level, which is why I once wrote that, "Theories are the stories we tell ourselves to make our experiences match our values." The first step toward responsible discourse is to maintain the liminality of both our values and our changing theoretical foundations to increase awareness of how what we experience of dance has already been shaped by theory before we can begin to reflect on it.

My next area of concern is "postmodern" theory. As we in the industrialized West recognized the disintegration of our modernist paradigm, and the breakdown of ideals such as "progress" and "history" and "pure art," we needed to find ways to understand the world as newly constituted (or, if we step out from behind the shadow of the passive voice, we might say that we needed to constitute the new world). In particular, we needed to recognize (establish) where we stood in relation to the ever growing, ever fragmenting, cultural periphery. With all the best of intentions, we began to explore issues of marginalization and agency, the "male gaze," desire, and postcolonialism. And we began to understand that "truth" looks different depending on whether you are holding the weapon or facing it (regardless of whether that weapon is military, economic, or cultural). Lumping theory into one big category and critiquing it would seem to do a disservice to "good" theory or, at least, "well-intentioned" theory. But we in the West have a long history of good intentions gone awry: the Inquisition; Manifest Destiny; the "White Man's Burden"; "Better Dead Than Red," and now, of course, "Spreading Freedom and Democracy Around the World."

When we finally recognized that the modernist umbrella was not big enough to cover the expanding periphery (the periphery was not really expanding, we just became better at seeing it), we simply began to construct a larger umbrella: postmodern theory. On its surface, postmodern theory carves out a discursive space for alterity, both within and beyond the margins of the dominant culture. And from the viewpoint of dominant culture that is exactly what postmodern theory does. But postmodern theory is also an (mostly) unconscious academic project, launched from within the cultures that dominate the production and distribution of theoretical discourse, to reestablish intellectual/theoretical hegemony over a fragmenting world. By confessing our sins as members of a dominant colonialist culture, we have granted ourselves the absolution of our newfound enlightenment. We have politely granted the marginalized a new theoretically empowered space at the margins (marginality has even developed its own sort of cultural cachet) without either ceding them actual power or leaving them the hell alone. To hand someone agency simply reinforces your power to take it away. And to theorize someone as a victim of marginalization can deny or undermine his or her own experienced sense of resistance and agency.

pp. 63–64

. . . We talk about cultural products—in this case dances—as if each were a "thing" unto itself that if looked at closely enough could be solved like a puzzle. But this only works at the macro level, where a piece such as "The Four Temperaments" is simply a linguistic gloss for a constantly shifting cultural construct, an open set of experiences and interpretations organized around and stimulated by a recognizably similar set of movements and sounds.[54] But the closer you try to get to "The Four Temperaments" the more it disappears from view. Different performances experienced by different people holding different values and theoretical constructs lead to different and sometimes incompatible interpetations. Linguistic communication demands that we find a way to refer to the objects and processes within our culture, but language loses some of its cockiness at the level of specific embodied experience.

And make no mistake, language is at the crux of the issues I am questioning here—the power of language in the continuing efforts on the part of social science and critical theorists to encapsulate/analyze/theorize the "representation" and "desire" and "agency" and the like in media and the performing arts. While such theory might be useful in the intellectualization of experience, it does not, I believe, contribute more to embodied experience than it takes away. Linguistic constructs can act as a gloss for what is an inherently complex and downright messy somatic experience. In my view, somatic experience is our primary investigatory tool in our relationship with cultural constructs. The cultural power of a linguistic gloss has a tendency to make us shortcut experiential investigation and accept an area of experience ("desire," for example) as "understood" or, at least, "understandable" instead of fully dancing the cultural resistance and complexity of individual somatic differences. Of course, all experience is culturally mediated. But by the same token, all culture is experientially mediated. The interaction and interpenetration of culture and experience is the ground upon which we develop "desire" and "agency."

Over the years, we theorists have been, and are still, engaged in a continually developing process of "writing the dancing body." But did anyone bother to ask the body if it wanted to be written? We have honed our linguistic and analytical skills to the point where we can read intertexts on the fly, but we have failed to notice that all of those texts are linguistic constructs while the dancing body is speaking in another kind of language altogether. We have gone from a time when we could hardly speak about the body, right past the body, to a place where we can't seem to shut up about the body. At least too little to say somehow acknowledged the difficulty in speaking from/about embodied somatic experience. Too much to say seems too often to ignore embodied experience altogether. Instead of writing the body, we are speaking for it. Feminist theory asked us to become aware of our tendency to view the body as object. Why is treating someone else's body as text more politically acceptable than treating that same body as object? Theory, in its own will to power, has shown no qualms and even no awareness that it has appropriated the dancing body towards the accomplishment of its own agenda. Not only are dance and dance theory not the same thing, but more and more I see their values and intentions in conflict. The day may come when we are forced to take up sides. Literally and figuratively, where do you stand?

I know where I stand. [I take off my shirt here to reveal a T-shirt that says: "My Body is Not Your Text."] I just hope I'm not too late.

READING 9.6B
Janet Lansdale

p. 166

The intertextual point is that the texts relevant to any dance bear traces from the immediate present, as well as the supposedly dead past. If it is obvious that "all texts contain traces of other texts," a more sophisticated version of this idea focuses on "the interactions between texts, producers or texts and their readers' lifeworlds." How the spectator, or reader, contributes his or her own intertexts to "create" the work (in a highly specific sense) is also the subject of debate. My choices figure here: yours would change the narrative. In consequence, interpretations can be defended yet still be fluid. Paradoxically it allows the reader to "create the text" and simultaneously to "read the text as it wishes to be read." Hence it is "a tool which cannot be employed by readers wishing to produce stability and order, or wishing to claim authority over the text or other critics."

In summary, the application of particular theories to analysis of dance, music and theatre is not without difficulty. Choice can appear to be arbitrary at one extreme, or to be an attempt to colonise an unsuspecting victim at the other. What the rationale might be for choosing any particular theory is exposed to question, requiring the writer to answer whether it is driven by random choice, historical tradition, an argument about theory, current fashion or personal inclination. The process of choosing, and the validity and appropriateness of choices made, in this treacherously open post-structuralist field becomes fundamentally the issue.

9.7. GABRIELE BRANDSTETTER

"Dis/Balances. Dance and Theory," *Dance [and] Theory*, eds. Gabriele Brandstetter and Gabriele Klein (Bielefeld: transcript Verlag, 2013), 197–210.

We end with history.

It isn't often one sees a contemporary dance theorist talk about the history of dance theory—and even less so of its pre-1900 history. To answer broad questions like these: "What are the generalizing, analytical, reflexive dimensions which distinguish a theory of art in the narrower sense? And in what way, others will ask, would one associate dancing, not in the sense of a staged performance, but as a kind of movement in other social contexts, intermingled with theories and discourses?" (198), Gabriele Brandstetter embarks on "a brief excursion into the history of theories of dance; proceeding from the notion that dance has always—in practice—incorporated theory/theories" (200). She delves all the way back, in fact, to Johann Pasch at the beginning of the eighteenth century. Her quotation from Pasch has already appeared in this book (see Reading 4.2), and Gottfried Taubert (Reading 4.3) repeated the same passage.

Brandstetter cites Pasch's words as emblemmatic of a traditional conception of dance as a dynamic interaction between theory and practice; this interaction Brandstetter calls *praxeology*, apparently her own coinage, which she defines as "theoretically 'informed' praxis" that "would create a balance" between the two sides of the equation (198). Praxeology is confronted and negated by a "resistance to theory," a term that she dates to the work of Paul de Man,[55] although she recognizes that the concept itself originated in the second half of the eighteenth century with the paradigm change, introduced by Cahusac and Noverre, "between the idea of dancing as a 'learned art' and that of movements designed to 'touch the feelings'"—and effecting, in other words, a kind of body-mind "caesura." In postmodern dance and dance theory, Brandstetter, perhaps optimistically, sees a cycling back to the praxeological ideal through the "self-reflectivity" of dancers who theorize about their own work.[56]

It should be recognized that "self-reflectivity" and praxeology essentially perform the same function as what Pasch and Taubert called *executio*, or the theory of practice. We have seen the theory of practice returning, since Plutarch, in the work of Sulzer, Despréaux, Blasis, Adice, Giraudet, Graham, and here in Brandstetter's praxeology. The equivalence of *executio*, the theory of practice, and praxeology is made perfectly explicit by Gabriele Klein:

Dance theory, so the implicit and sometimes explicit assumption of these texts [suggests], can only be conceived as a theory of practice, as a theory, which does not exclusively or primarily concentrate on a product, but also—and foremost—on a process, i.e. by reflecting the methods used and the forms of collaboration. Dance theory is thus only conceivable in the context of a form of dance studies that defines itself as an empirical science (*Erfahrungswissenschaft*), as a "science of reality," as a "practical science." Dance theory, and this is the second premise, should be generated by the experience-guided reflection of artistic practice. Dance theory thus lies somewhere "in-between," in a realm between artistic and scientific practices and their respective forms and methods of reflection. From this perspective, it is simultaneously the premise, instrument and effect of artistic practice.[57]

In the grand scheme of Pasch and Taubert, however, *executio* is only the bottom rung of the theoretical "stepladder to all the virtues" that ascends ultimately to piety.[58] Praxeology and self-reflectivity, therefore, represent an impoverishment of Pasch's original concept, in consequence of which the whole ethical-moral superstructure of Pasch's and Taubert's scheme vanishes, and with it, the rhetorical and spiritual language of dance is depleted.

On the other hand, a dance theory based on *executio* offers a fascinating proposition (despite Brandstetter's protestation of "no 'utilization' or illustration of theorems" in praxeology): the possibility for a dance to embody theory, as it were, in the flesh—the chance to directly experience dance as a revelation of theory. Yvonne Rainer's "Trio A" does precisely this, even if its deliberate drabness and inexpressivity embody, sadly, only theory's clichéd reputation for arid braininess. A more encouraging example is Anne Teresa De Keersmaeker's "Violin Phase" (1982), titled after Steve Reich's minimalist composition to which it is set. She identifies this fully achieved dance—astonishingly—as "part of my very first piece" (see Fig. 9.1).[59] A wide, perfect circle and its center

Figure 9.1. (and cover). Anne Teresa De Keersmaeker (choreographer and dancer), "Violin Phase," performed at the Museum of Modern Art, New York (2011, © Max Vadukul).

point are traced on a thin layer of white sand covering the dance floor. A single female dancer (De Keersmaeker herself), wearing a simple shift resembling 1920s tennis whites, more athletic than balletic, stands on the circumference, rotating her torso to make her arms swing from side to side; then, continuing this motion, she begins to step around the circle. With each swaying step she kicks up enough sand to leave a shallow curved groove, which when seen from above resembles the sign for a *pas marché* in Beauchamps-Feuillet notation, thus giving the appearance that the dancer is inscribing her own choreography in the sand (compare with Fig. 4.1); the performance has been described as "a type of drawing in itself."[60] After several revolutions, the linear circle is softened into the outline of a blossom, which the dancer starts crisscrossing diagonally. First the sign of a cross is formed, but as the crossings continue, the spaces within the quadrants are gradually filled and the steps become increasingly impetuous, until at the abrupt end the dancer is standing in the center of a mandala.[61]

Reich's music is melodically repetitious and constant in tempo. The dancer's steps seem more or less in time with the music at first (a right and left step to each repetition of the theme), but as the music gradually becomes more complex, the music–step relation becomes more blurred and the less it seems to matter.

There is a kind of dance theory geneology embodied in this dance, and extending well back before Johann Pasch. The Renaissance Italian elements of *misura, memoria, maniera, tempo, compartimento di terreno,* and *agilitade* are present in abundance; in particular, the dancer's air of casual, wanton abandon connects the Italians' *aere, fantasmate,* and *acidentia* with postmodern pedestrianism. The dancer's long stride and outspread arms resemble Laban's figure in a tetrahedron (see Fig. 8.1). The idea of this dance as a "type of drawing" invokes the principle of *dessein* espoused by Hardouin, Cahusac, and Adice. The actual shape of the dancer's *pas marché* is, plausibly, the invention of Pierre Beauchamps, who was Pasch's teacher.[62] Pasch, who introduced the "theory of practice" (the prototype of Brandstetter's praxeology), was in turn the teacher of Gottfried Taubert. Taubert extended Pasch's theory toward metaphysical transcendence through ethics and piety. But we should remember that it was Plato, after all, who first perceived the metaphysical dimension of dance, which is expressed in De Keersmaeker's final revelation of a mandala.

If ever a dance was made to prove a theorem, this is it, and it does its job with verve and brio and aesthetic delight.

READING 9.7
Gabriele Brandstetter

PP. 200–202

According to a conception of the relationship between dance and theory—which, though still relevant today, has undergone several versions in the history of dance—theory is implicit in dance and dancing. The balance of a relation between these two aspects—dance theory and dance practice—is thus relegated to the actions of dancing and choreographing. Thus a *praxeology* of dance in the sense mentioned above does not mean an understanding of dance as "applied theory," [because] there is no "utilization" or illustration of theorems. It refers rather to what might be called an extended concept of dance, which does not confine the practice, the action or, yes, the "work" of dancing to the performance of a dance, but sees it as a dynamic process. By the nature of things the historical concepts of such a praxeological understanding of dance are subject—in the context of art—to great social and political changes. A comparative study of such concepts in, say, the 18th, 19th and 20th/21st centuries would have to pursue the change of paradigm of such involvements of theory *in* dance, for example, on the basis of criteria that would shed light on the relevant understanding of bodily movement, gender and space as well as the representational contexts and models of the "order of knowledge." In the 18th century, in the period of transition from the Enlightenment to a "sentimental," expression-oriented conception of (dance) movement (in the sense of "movere"[63]), such a change of paradigm clearly manifests itself in the opposition between the idea of dancing as a "learned art" and that of movements designed to "touch the feelings." In his treatise *Beschreibung wahrer Tanz-Kunst* (Description of a True Art of Dancing, 1707) the Leipzig dancing and fencing master Johann Pasch wrote:

> The true art of dancing is in *theoria* a science that sets or gives nature's urge towards more than highly necessary or joyful movement (*per disciplinas philosophicas*) such rules as enable the movement to be performed in *praxi* (*in specie per disciplinas mathematicas*) rationally and also naturally and humanly and used for one purpose or another. (Pasch 1978: 16)[64]

Since the mid-18th century such an understanding of dance, which is "in *theoria* a science" (ibid.), as a regulator of an (aesthetic) upbringing in and through movement,[65] has confronted a concept of dance as an art of expression. A *resistance to theory* (de Man 1986) manifests itself *inter alia* in relegating the disciplining function of a *theoria* as an ordering of our knowledge of dancing and "shifting" the momentum of the movement into the relation to and through the (non-regulatable) expression. The claim of a non-artificial art of dance movement as understood by Gasparo Angiolini, Jean-Georges Noverre and Friedrich Schiller consists in touching the feelings of the spectator.

A leap into the modern phase in the history of dance is marked by a clear break in the relationship between the theory and practice of dance. If the 18th century models that defined "dance" itself as a form of "*theoria*" (Pasch) were still variants of a systematic and rational concept of the nature of human beings and their environment, by the beginning of the 20th century general narrative theories of dance were becoming obsolete. For this very reason in this period of social, media and aesthetic upheavals a clear caesura, a dividing line between dance theory and practice is no longer even discernible. As in 20th century *theatre*, new concepts and aesthetics of dance succeed each other at ever shorter intervals in the history of dance: In the end it is the scientific and philosophical findings about movement on the one hand and the concepts of influential dance practitioners on the other that mutually influence each other—see the researches of Hermann von Helmholtz, the philosophy of Henri Bergson, or the dance and choreographical concepts of Rudolf von Laban and as well the body and movement theories of the great phenomenological philosophers Edmund Husserl and Maurice Merleau-Ponty. The reflection takes place in dance itself. Highly variegated models of self-reflectivity mark the dance of the avant-garde and the multifarious character of the dance and performance scene from the 1960s to today's contemporary dance. It would take us too far afield to broach all this here even in summary fashion. It should be noted, however, that this "implication" (enfolding) of theory *in* dance refers not only to a—however defined—self-reflectivity of the performers' own modes of presentation. Even the processes of production, the work of drafting and rehearsing, the media, the (self-) promotion discourses are part of a praxeological, a theoretically "informed" form of contemporary dance: Where should we seek the caesura between theory and dance (praxis) here? It may be significant that the im-balance itself is ironically overplayed, e.g. by the fact that the endless discourse, the blurb, the project description and literary reviews are calmly incorporated in the dance production as a textual supplement in the form, for example, of *self-interviews*, which a number of contemporary dancers and choreographers— e.g. Frédéric Gies, Jefta van Dinther, Mette Ingvartsen, Alice Chauchat, Isabelle Schad, Xavier Le Roy—have declared to be a genuine element of their artistic work.[66] The relationship between dance and theory is one that has to be perpetually renegotiated in frictions and disruptions.

NOTES

1. Gertrude Stein (1874–1946), "Composition as Explanation" (1925), first presented as a lecture at Cambridge and Oxford Universities in 1926; https://www.poetryfoundation.org/resources/learning/essays/detail/69481.

2. Mary Wigman (1886–1973): "Die Rede über Tanz hat mit Tanz nichts zu tun," quoted in Gabriele Klein and Christa Zipprich, "Tanz Theorie Text: Zur Einführung," Gabriele Klein and Christa Zipprich, eds., *Tanz Theorie Text*, Jahrbuch Tanzforschung 12 (Münster: LIT Verlag, 2002), 1. I have not found an original source of this quotation.

3. David Daniel, "A Conversation with Suzanne Farrell," *Reading Dance*, 566. The interview was first printed in 1978–1979.

4. Anna Sokolow (1910–2000), "The Rebel and the Bourgeois," *The Modern Dance: Seven Statements of Belief*, ed. Selma Jeanne Cohen (Middletown, CT: Wesleyan University Press, 1966), 29.

5. Pina Bausch (1940–2009), *Pina Bausch: entretiens avec . . .* , Mot pour Mot, ed. Philippe Noisette (Paris: Van Dieren Éditeur, 1997), 9: ". . . je réfuse les systèmes."

6. Merce Cunningham, "The Impermanent Art," *Seven Arts* 3, ed. Fernando Puma (Indian Hills, CO: The Falcon's Wing Press, 1955), 70–71; quoted in Jack Anderson, *Ballet & Modern Dance: A Concise History*, 2nd ed. (Princeton, NJ: Dance Horizons, 1992), 201.

7. Reprinted with the kind permission of the Merce Cunningham Trust. An excerpt appears at https://www.mercecunningham.org/the-work/writings/on-composing-a-dance/.
    The entire article was reprinted in Cohen, *Dance as a Theatre Art*, 198–204.

8. Doris Humphrey (1895–1958), *The Art of Making Dances* (1959), quoted in Anderson, *Ballet & Modern Dance*, 197.

9. Jill Johnston, "Which Way the Avant Garde?," *The New York Times* (August 11, 1968), D24.

10. Based on Sally Banes, *Writing Dancing in the Age of Postmodernism* (Hanover, NH: Wesleyan University Press, 1994), 207–26; and Nancy Reynolds and Malcolm McCormick, *No Fixed Points: Dance in the Twentieth Century* (New Haven, CT: Yale University Press, 2003), 422–423.

11. Reynolds and McCormick, *No Fixed Points*, 423.

12. This entire paragraph is based on Daniel M. Callahan, "The Gay Divorce of Music and Dance: Choreomusicality and the Early Works of Cage-Cunningham," *Journal of the American Musicological Society* 71, no. 2 (Summer 2018): 439–525. Terry Teachout, "Pale Horse, Pale Rider," in Robert Gottlieb, ed., *Reading Dance* (New York: Pantheon Books, 2008), 481, calls Cunningham and Cage's minimal choreomusicality and their aleatoric method "two of the most absurdly rigid theories ever foisted upon a dance audience" (481).

13. Yvonne Rainer, "A.Trio," https://www.youtube.com/watch?v=8NG1Q46gTMU&list=PLVALBxbrx-SYI1GNUIvqUGQSVUFKqVniJ&index=2.

14. Jane Jacobs, *The Death and Life of Great American Cities* (1961), a landmark work on urban planning, quoted in Thomas J. Lax, "Allow me to begin again," *Judson Dance Theater: The Work is Never Done* (New York: The Museum of Modern Art, 2018), 21. Pedestrianism will also be cited as a "major element" of postmodern African American dance; see Reading 9.4a.

15. Rainer, "A Quasi Survey of Some 'Minimalist' Tendencies in the Quantitatively Minimal Dance Activity Midst the Plethora, or an Analysis of *Trio A*," *Minimal Art: A Critical Anthology*, ed. Gregory Battcock (New York: E. P. Dutton, 1968), 263–273.

16. Reynolds and McCormick, *No Fixed Points*, 404–405. See also Ramsay Burt, *Judson Dance Theater: Performative Traces* (London: Routledge, 2006), 75–84.

17. See Reading 8.4.

18. A reference to Andy Warhol's inflated silver pillows used as a scenic element in Cunningham's *RainForest* (1968).—Ed.

19. The title of the dance Cunningham is describing here is "Story" (1963).—Ed.

20. See the review by Marian Smith in the *Journal of the American Musicological Society* 54, no. 1 (Spring 2001), 175–176, 185.

21. Ingrid Brainard, Sandra Noll Hammond, and Kennetha R. McArthur, "Technical Manuals," *International Encyclopedia of Dance*, vol. 6, 121–129.

22. Brainard, s.v. "Technical Manuals," 121.

23. Randy Martin, *Critical Moves: Dance Studies in Theory and Politics* (Durham, NC: Duke University Press, 1998), 37.

24. Carroll, "Dance," 591.

25. http://en.wikipedia.org/wiki/Dance_theory.

26. *International Encyclopedia of Dance*, vol. 4, 360–379.

27. Reprinted with the kind permission of Oxford University Press.

28. Andrew Milner, *Contemporary Cultural Theory* (London: UCL Press, 1994), 78–79.

29. Roland Barthes, *L'empire des signes* (Geneva: Éditions Albert Skira, 1970), 66: "Le signe est une fracture qui ne s'ouvre jamais que sur le visage d'un autre signe."

30. Roland Barthes, "(Théorie du) texte," *Oeuvres complètes*, vol. IV 1972–1976 (Paris: Éditions du Seuil, 2002), 455; originally published in the *Encyclopaedia Universalis*, vol. XV (1973). The *Encyclopaedia Universalis*, according to its webpage (http://www.encyclopaedia-universalis.fr/), is a generalist encyclopedia equivalent to the *Encyclopaedia Britannica*.

31. Michel Foucault, *Power/Knowledge: Selected Interviews and Other Writings 1972–1977*, ed. Colin Gordon (New York: Pantheon Books, 1980), 126; quoted in Milner, *Contemporary Cultural Theory*, 91.

32. Barthes, "La littérature comme mathésis," *Roland Barthes par Roland Barthes*, Écrivains de toujours 96 (Paris: Seuil, 1975), 123.

33. *Encyclopédie*, vol. IV (1751), 623, and restated later with slight differences in Cahusac's *La danse ancienne et moderne*, vol. I, xii; cf. text in Reading 5.4. As is conventional in an encyclopedia, neither source is cited by Foster.

34. Gottschild, *Digging the Africanist Presence*, 3.

35. Douglas Kellner, "Critical Theory," *New Dictionary of the History of Ideas*, ed. Maryanne Cline Horowitz (New York: Charles Scribner's Sons, 2005), vol. 2, 507–511. *Gale Virtual Reference Library*, http://link.galegroup.com/apps/doc/CX3424300178/GVRL?u=29002&sid=GVRL&xid=17ad8b67.

36. Milner, *Contemporary Cultural Theory*, 103.

37. Jacqui Malone, *Steppin' on the Blues* (Urbana: University of Illinois Press, 1996), 11–18.

38. Robert Farris Thompson, *Flash of the Spirit: African and Afro-American Art and Philosophy* (New York: Vintage Books, 1983), 117–124. Kongo culture refers to the civilization in west Africa known in the colonial era as the Belgian Congo, and now as the Democratic Republic of Congo.

39. Thompson, *Flash of the Spirit*, 124 and 122; internal quotes from Lydia Cabrera, *El Monte: Igbo Fina Ewe Orisha, Vititinfinda* (Havana: Ediciones C. R., 1954).

40. Thompson, "An Aesthetic of the Cool," 95, 98.

41. Malone, *Steppin' on the Blues*, 18, 41, 71–72, and photo opposite p. 90.

42. Zita Allen, "What Is Black Dance?," in *The Black Tradition in American Modern Dance* (pamphlet produced for the American Dance Festival, 1991–1992 season, c. WNET 2017), https://www.thirteen.org/freetodance/behind/behind_blackdance3.html.

43. There is no apparent linguistic relationship between *Nommo* (also spelled *Nonno* by Osumure) and the Greek word *nomes* used by Aristotle (see Reading 1.2), although there is a coincidental one.

44. Osumare's footnote 78 (187) is quoted here:

Randy Martin, *Critical Moves: Dance Studies in Theory & Politics* (Durham, NC: Duke University Press, 1998), 109. Martin also makes significant contributions to the theoretical understanding of how bodily movement as a part of the experiential world, as opposed to mere theoretical reflection, might shed more light on the relationship of theory and practice: "The distinction between theory—the effort to grasp something whole in order to reflect on it, as if from the outside—and practice—the experiential engagement with something as if from within the process of doing it— retains some utility only if reflection and experience are not treated as sep- arable acts but as two interconnected movements of the same activity" (5).

45. https://www.urbanbushwomen.org/about-ubw/.

46. Jennifer Dunning, "Jawole Willa Jo Zollar," *Fifty Contemporary Choreographers*, ed. Martha Bremser and Lorna Sanders, 2nd ed. (London: Routledge, 2011), 374.

47. Kate Mattingly Moran, review "Dancing the Voice of the People," *Dance Magazine* 75, no. 10 (October 2001): 100–101.

48. George-Graves adds playfulness, vocalization (with "a nommo force," 33), and energy (35). "Technique blends" refers to the mixture of African American and classical ballet terms and gestures. For pedestrianism, see Reading 9.1.—Ed.

49. "Slap their chests" and (below) "slap their arms": see Thompson: "a striking of one part of the body against another" (Reading 8.3c).—Ed.

50. "Aesthetic of the cool," from Thompson, is defined by George-Graves as "an African Diaspora performance trope that calls for discipline and con- trol during even the most chaotic moments" (28). "Not for sale": selling is associated with "pelvic thrust," "freedom of loose hips," and "isolat[ing] the rib cage or shoulders"; it "bespeaks a culture still fraught with representations of oversexed women of color" (George-Graves, 14–16).—Ed.

51. Garth Fagan (b. 1940), Jamaican-born modern dance choreographer.—Ed.

52. Jens Richard Giersdorf, "Dance Studies in the International Academy: Genealogy of a disciplinary formation," *The Routledge Dance Studies Reader*, ed. Alexandra Carter and Janet O'Shea, 2nd ed. (Abingdon: Routledge, 2010), 319–334.

53. This paragraph is paraphrased from the P.A.R.T.S. *présentation* page: http:// www.parts.be/fr/presentation (site no longer accessible). Reading 9.5b based on https://www.parts.be/training-cycle.

54. "The Four Temperaments" is a ballet by George Balanchine (first performed 1946, music by Paul Hindemith).—Ed.

55. Brandstetter cites Paul de Man, *The Resistance to Theory* (Minneapolis: University of Minnesota Press, 1986).

56. "Self-reflectivity" is Brandstetter's redundant version of reflexivity/ reflectivity.

57. Gabriele Klein, "Dance Theory as a Practice of Critique," *Dance [and] Theory*, eds. Gabriele Brandstetter and Gabriele Klein (Bielefeld: transcript Verlag, 2013), 138.

58. Taubert, "Vorrede," 23; also Tilden Russell, *Theory and Practice in the Eighteenth Century: The German-French Connection*, Studies in Seventeenth- and Eighteenth-Century Art and Culture (Newark: University of Delaware Press; Rowman & Littlefield, 2017), 168–169.

59. Anne Teresa De Keersmaeker et al. *Work/Travail/Arbeid*, 4 vols. (Brussels: WIELS, Mercatorfonds & Rosas, 2015), vol. 1, 35. "Violin Phase," Anne Teresa De Keersmaeker (choreographer and dancer), performed at the Museum of Modern Art, New York (2011, © Max Vadukul). For a video of this dance, performed outdoors and filmed in color, see https://www. youtube.com/watch?v=i36Qhn7NhoA (dir. Thierry De Mey, © Herman Sorgeloos, 2001).

60. Brian Dillon, "The Curve of Time," *Work/Travail/Arbeid*, vol. 3, 54.

61. Dillon's "The Curve of Time" includes twelve overhead video stills (2001) taken from directly above the center of the circle and showing the progressive stages of completion within it (50–51); he also reproduces twelve choreographic figures drawn by De Keersmaeker, showing various paths by which the final pattern is revealed (56–60).

62. "Plausibly," because we do not know how much of Beauchamps-Feuillet was Beauchamps's contribution, and how much was Feuillet's.

63. *Movere* (to move, in Latin) can be construed as referring either to physical motion or to the passions. Brandstetter seems to imply the latter.—Ed.

64. Brandstetter cites the 1978 facsimile edition of Pasch's 1707 publication. Her translation of this paragraph should be compared with that in Reading 4.2.—Ed.

65. "It is a concept of dance which even Plato regarded as the regulator of a physically healthy upbringing: somewhere between military exercises and disciplined actions in the public sphere."—Brandstetter's note.

66. Rudi Laermans, *Moving Together: Theorizing and Making Contemporary Dance* (Antennae: Valiz, 2015), also frequently uses this device.—Ed.

Appendix: Table of Dance Periodization

Dates/Century	Chapter	Name		
360 BCE–450 CE	1	Antiquity		
450–1450		Middle Ages		
1450–1600	2	Renaissance		
		Dance Practice	**Dance Theory**	**Music**
17th century	3	"Long Baroque"	Baroque	Baroque
1700–1721	4	"Long Baroque"	Enlightenment	Galant
18th century	5	"Long Baroque"	Enlightenment	Classic
18th century	6	"LongBaroque"/ pre-Romantic	Enlightenment/ pre-Romantic	High Classic/ pre-Romantic
19th century	7	Romantic		
20th century	8	Modern		
mid-20th– 21st centuries	9	Postmodern		

Bibliography

PRIMARY SOURCES

Adice, G. Léopold. BnF, Bibliothèque-musée de l'opéra, B-61(1), Gallica 311742d.

Adice, G. Léopold. BnF, Bibliothèque-musée de l'opéra, B-61(2), Gallica 312027q.

Adice, G. Léopold. BnF, Bibliothèque-musée de l'opéra, B-61(3), Gallica 311971p.

Adice, G. Léopold. BnF, Bibliothèque-musée de l'opéra, B-61(4), Gallica 3119722.

Adice, G. Léopold. " 'Grammaire et Théorie chorégraphique' and Other Writings."
Mss., Paris: Bibliothèque nationale de France, Bibliothèque-musée de l'opéra,
B-61 (1–5).

Adice, G. Léopold. *Théorie de la gymnastique de la danse théâtrale*. Paris: Imprimerie
centrale de Napoléon Chaix et Cie., 1859.

Arbeau, Thoinot. *The Book on the Art of Dancing*. Translated by Madeleine
Inglehearn and Peggy Forsyth. London: Dance Books, 1981.

Arbeau, Thoinot. *Orchesographie, Metode, et Teorie*. Lengres: Iehan des Preyz,
1591. Facs. ed. Geneva: Editions Minkoff, 1972.

Arbeau, Thoinot. *Orchesography* (1589). Translated by Mary Stewart Evans.
New York: Dover, 1967.

Aristotle. *Metaphysics*, Books I–IX. Translated by Hugh Tredennick. Loeb
Classical Library 271. Cambridge, MA: Harvard University Press, 1933.
https://www.loebclassics.com/view/LCL271/1933/volume.xml.

Aristotle. *Nicomachean Ethics*, rev. ed. Translated by H. Rackham. Loeb Classical
Library 73. Cambridge, MA: Harvard University Press, 1934. https://www.
loebclassics.com/view/LCL073/1926/volume.xml.

Aristotle. *Physics*, vol. II. Translated by Philip H. Wicksteed and Francis
M. Cornford. Loeb Classical Library 255. Cambridge, MA: Harvard University
Press, 1934. https://www.loebclassics.com/view/LCL255/1934/volume.xml.

Aristotle. *Poetics*. Edited and translated by Stephen Halliwell, 27–141. Loeb
Classical Library 199. Cambridge, MA: Harvard University Press, 1995.
https://www.loebclassics.com/view/LCL199/1995/volume.xml.

Aristotle. *Posterior Analytics*. Translated by Hugh Tredennick. Loeb Classical Library 391. Cambridge, MA: Harvard University Press, 1960. https://www.loebclassics.com/view/LCL391/1960/volume.xml.

Behr, Samuel Rudolph. *Andere Theil der Tantz-Kunst, oder Ausgesiebete Grillen*. Leipzig: Christoph Heydler, 1703.

Behr, Samuel Rudolph. *Anleitung zu einer wohlgegründeten Tantz-Kunst*. Leipzig: Christoph Heydler, 1703.

Behr, Samuel Rudolph. *L'Art de bien danser, Die Kunst wohl zu Tantzen*. Leipzig: Martin Fulde, 1713. Facs. ed. Munich: Heimeran Verlag, 1977.

Behr, Samuel Rudolph. *Wohlgegründete Tantz-Kunst*, 3rd expanded and improved ed. Leipzig: Joh. Heinichens Wittwe, 1709.

Blasis, Charles. *The Code of Terpsichore: The Art of Dancing. Comprising Its Theory and Practice, and a History of Its Rise and Progress, from the Earliest Times*, 2nd ed. Translated by R. Barton. London: Edward Bull, 1831.

Blasis, Charles. *An Elementary Treatise upon the Theory and Practice of the Art of Dancing*. Translated by Mary Stewart Evans. New York: Dover, 1968.

Blasis, Charles. *Manuel complet de la danse*. Translated by M. Barton. Paris: Librairie Encyclopédique de Roret, 1830.

Blasis, Charles. *Nouveau manuel complet de la danse ou traité théorique et pratique de cet art*, new ed. Paris: Librairie Encyclopédique de Roret, 1866.

Blasis, Charles. *Traité élémentaire, théorique et pratique de l'art de la danse*. Milan: Joseph Beati et Antoine Tenenti, 1820. Facs. ed. Bologna: Arnaldo Forni Editore, 2002.

Bourgeois, Edmond. *Traité pratique et théorique de la danse*. Paris: Garnier Frères, 1909?.

Brandstetter, Gabriele. "Dis/Balances. Dance and Theory." In *Dance [and] Theory*, edited by Gabriele Brandstetter and Gabriele Klein, 197–210. Bielefeld: transcript Verlag, 2013.

Cahusac, Louis de. *La danse ancienne et moderne ou traité historique de la danse*. 3 vols. La Haye: Jean Neaulme, 1754.

Cahusac, Louis de. "Danse." In *Encyclopédie, ou, dictionnaire raisonné des sciences, des arts et des métiers*, edited by Denis Diderot and Jean le Rond D'Alembert, vol. IV, 623–629 (Paris: Briasson, Le Breton, Faulche, 1751).

Caroso, Fabritio. *Nobiltà di Dame . . . Nuouamente dal proprio Auttore corretto, ampliato di nuoui Balli, di belle Regole, & alla perfetta Theorica ridotto* (Venice: il Muschio, 1600). Modern ed. *Courtly Dance of the Renaissance: A New Translation and Edition of the "Nobiltà di Dame" (1600)*. Translated and edited by Julia Sutton. New York: Dover, 1995.

Cayou, Dolores Kirton. *Modern Jazz Dance*. Palo Alto, CA: Mayfield, 1971.

Compan, [C.]. *Dictionnaire de Danse*. Paris: Chez Cailleau, 1787. Facs. ed. Geneva: Minkoff, 1979.

Cornazano, Antonio. *The Book on The Art of Dancing*. Translated by Madeleine Inglehearn and Peggy Forsyth. London: Dance Books, 1981.

Cornazano, Antonio. "Il 'libro dell'arte del danzare' di Antonio Cornazano." Edited by C. Mazzi. *La Bibliofilia* XVII, no. 1 (April 1915): 1–30.

Cunningham, Merce. "The Impermanent Art." In *Seven Arts* 3, edited by Fernando Puma, 70–71. Indian Hills, CO: The Falcon's Wing Press, 1955.

Cunningham, Merce. "Two Questions and Five Dances." *Dance Perspectives* 34 (Summer 1968): 46–53.

DeFrantz, Thomas, ed. *Dancing Many Drums: Excavations in African American Dance*. Studies in Dance History 19. Madison: University of Wisconsin Press, 2002.

DeFrantz, Thomas, and Anita Gonzalez, eds. *Black Performance Theory*. Durham, NC: Duke University Press, 2014.

De Keersmaeker, Anne Teresa. "Violin Phase," a choreography by Anne Teresa De Keersmaeker, © Herman Sorgeloos. Picture made during the recording of the film *Fase, Four Movements to the Music of Steve Reich* by Thierry De Mey. https://www.youtube.com/watch?v=i36Qhn7NhoA.

De Spain, Kent. "Resisting Theory: The Dancing Body and American Scholarship." *Society of Dance History Scholars Proceedings*, 59–64.

Despréaux, Jean-Étienne. "Danse-Ecrite, ou Terpsi=Coro=Graphie, ou nouvel Essai de Théorie de la Danse, par J. E. Despréaux." Ms. Paris: Bibliothèque-Musée de l'Opéra, Fonds Deshayes F-Des P 4, 1815.

Despréaux, Jean-Étienne. *Mes passe-temps: Chansons suivies de L'art de la danse, Poëme en quatre chants, Calqué sur l'Art Poétique de Boileau Despréaux.* 2 vols. Paris: author, 1806.

Domenico da Piacenza. *De arte saltandi & choreas ducendi/Dela arte di ballare et danzare*. Ms., Paris: Bibliothèque nationale, fonds Ital. 972 (between 1452 and 1465); modern ed. Smith, *Fifteenth-Century Dance and Music*, vol. I, 8–67.

Dufort, Giambatista. *Trattato del ballo nobile*. Naples: Felice Mosca, 1728. Facs. ed. Westmead: Gregg, 1972.

Dunham, Katherine. "The Negro Dance." *Negro Caravan: Writings by American Negroes*. Edited by Sterling A. Brown, Arthur P. Davis, and Ulysses Lee, 990–1000. New York: Dryden Press, 1941.

Ebreo, Guglielmo, of Pesaro. *De pratica seu arte tripudii* [1463]/*On the Practice or Art of Dancing*. Translated by Barbara Sparti. Oxford: Oxford University Press, 1993.

Ferriol y Boxeraus, Bartholome. *Reglas utiles para los aficionados a danzar*. Capoa [Capua]: Joseph Testore, 1745.

Feuillet, Raoul Auger. *Chorégraphie ou l'art de décrire la dance* and *Recueil de dances*. Paris: author, 1700. Facs. ed. New York: Broude Brothers, 1968.

Feuillet, Raoul Auger. *Chorégraphie ou l'art de décrire la danse*, 2nd ed., augmentée. Paris: author, 1701. Facs. ed. Bologna: Arnoldo Forni Editore, 1983.

Feuillet, Raoul Auger. "Traité de la cadance." In *Recüeil de dances contenant un tres grand nombres [sic], des meillieures entrées de ballet de Mr. Pecour*. Paris: author, 1704. Facs. ed. Westmead, Hants.: Gregg, 1972.

Foster, Susan Leigh. "Dancing and Theorizing and Theorizing Dancing." *Dance [and] Theory*. Edited by Gabriele Brandstetter and Gabriele Klein, 19–32. Bielefeld: transcript Verlag, 2013.

Foster, Susan Leigh. "New Areas of Inquiry." *International Encyclopedia of Dance* 4: 376–379.

Franco, Susanne. "Re-Thinking 'Practice' and 'Theory' from an Italian Perspective." *Society of Dance History Scholars Proceedings*, 122–125.

Gallini, Giovanni-Andrea. *A Treatise on the Art of Dancing*. London: author, 1772.

George-Graves, Nadine. *Urban Bush Women: Twenty Years of African American Dance Theater, Community Engagement, and Working It Out*. Madison: University of Wisconsin Press, 2010.

Giraudet, Eugène. *La danse, la tenue, le maintien l'hygiène & l'éducation*, 55th ed. Paris: author, [1897 or later].

Giraudet, Eugène. *Traité de la danse*, 7th ed. Paris: Imprimerie A. Ventin, [1894 or later].

Giraudet, Eugène. *Traité de la danse; Tome II: Grammaire de la danse et du bon ton à travers le monde et les siècles depuis le singe jusqu'à nos jours*. Paris: author, 1900.

Gottschild, Brenda Dixon. *Digging the Africanist Presence in American Performance: Dance and Other Contexts*. Contributions in Afro-American and African Studies 179. Westport, CT: Greenwood Press, 1996.

Goussier, Louis-Jacques. "Choréographie." *Encyclopédie ou Dictionnaire raisonné*, vol. III (1751): 367–373.

Graham, Martha. "A Modern Dancer's Primer for Action." In *Dance: A Basic Educational Technique*, edited by Frederick Rand Rogers, 178–187. New York: The Macmillan Company, 1941.

Grocheio, Johannes de. *Concerning Music*, 2nd ed. Translated by Albert Seay. Colorado Springs: Colorado College Music Press, 1974.

Grocheio, Johannes de. *De musica*. In *Die Quellenhandschriften zum Musiktraktat des Johannes de Grocheio*, edited by Ernst Rohloff. Leipzig: VEB Deutscher Verlag für Musik, 1972.

Guest, Ann Hutchinson. *Choreo-Graphics; A Comparison of Dance Notation Systems from the Fifteenth Century to the Present.* New York: Gordon and Breach, 1989.

Guillemin. *Chorégraphie, ou l'art de décrire la danse.* Paris: L'auteur, Petit, 1784.

Hardouin, Pierre-Alexandre. *Phénomène imprévu, ou La Danse en déroute.* Caen: 1748; Rouen Bibliothèque municipale, Mt p 4848-3.

Hardouin, Pierre-Alexandre. "premier Moyen, portrait du Maitre" Ms: Caen, Archives départementales du Calvados, Fonds Médor, Cote 2E697.

H'Doubler, Margaret N. *Dance: A Creative Art Experience.* New York: F. S. Crofts and Company, 1940.

H'Doubler, Margaret N. *The Dance and Its Place in Education.* New York: Harcourt, Brace and Company, 1925.

H'Doubler, Margaret N. *A Manual of Dancing: Suggestions and Bibliography for the Teacher of Dancing.* Madison, WI, 1921.

Hurston, Zora Neale. *The Complete Stories.* New York: Harper Perennial Modern Classics, 2009.

Hurston, Zora Neale. *Zora Neale Hurston: Folklore, Memoirs, and Other Writings.* Edited by Cheryl A. Wall. New York: The Library of America, 1995.

Laban, Rudolf [von]. *Gymnastic und Tanz*, 6th ed. Oldenburg: Gerhard Stalling Verlag, 1926.

Laban, Rudolf [von]. *Modern Educational Dance*, 2nd, rev. ed. Translated by Lisa Ullmann. London: Macdonald & Evans, 1963.

Laban, Rudolf [von]. *Principles of Dance and Movement Notation.* New York: Dance Horizons, 1956.

Laban, Rudolf [von]. *Die Welt des Tänzers.* Stuttgart: Walter Seifert, 1920.

Laban, Rudolf [von], and F. C. Lawrence. *Effort: Economy in Body Movement*, 2nd ed. Boston: Macdonald and Evans Limited, 1974.

Lansdale, Janet. "A Tapestry of Intertexts: Dance Analysis for the Twenty-First Century." In *The Routledge Dance Studies Reader*, edited by Alexandra Carter and Janet O'Shea, 2nd ed., 158–167. London: Routledge, 2010.

Lauze, F[rançois] de. *Apologie de la danse by F. De Lauze* (1623). Facs. ed. Geneva: Minkoff, 1977. Translated by Joan Wildeblood. London: Frederick Muller, 1952.

Lepecki, André, and Jenn Joy, eds. *Planes of Composition: Dance, Theory and the Global.* London: Seagull Books, 2009.

Louis, Murray. "Forward Is Not Always Going Ahead." *Dance Perspectives* 38 (Summer 1969): 28–33.

Lucian. "The Dance [*Peri Orcheseos*]." In *Lucian*, vol. 5, translated by A. M. Harmon, 209–289. Loeb Classical Library 302. Cambridge, MA: Harvard

University Press, 1936. https://www.loebclassics.com/view/LCL302/1936/volume.xml.

Magri, Gennaro. *Trattato teorico-prattico di Ballo*. Naples: Vincenzo Orsino, 1779. Repr. ed. *Theoretical and practical treatise on dancing*. Translated by Mary Skeaping with Anna Ivanova and Irmgard E. Berry; edited by Irmgard E. Berry and Annalisa Fox. London: Dance Books, 1988.

Menestrier, Claude-François. *Des Ballets anciens et modernes selon les regles du theatre*. Paris: René Guignard, 1682. Facs. ed. Geneva: Minkoff, 1972.

Nikolais, Alwin. "Choreosonic Music of the New Dance Theatre of Alwin Nikolais" (cacophonic 10ACKLP).

Nikolais, Alwin. *nik: a documentary*. Edited by Marcia B. Siegel. *Dance Perspectives* 48 (Winter 1971).

Nikolais, Alwin, and Murray Louis. *The Nikolais/Louis Dance Technique: A Philosophy and Method of Modern Dance*. New York: Routledge, 2005.

Noverre, His Circle, and the English Lettres sur la Danse. Edited by Michael Burden and Jennifer Thorp. The Wendy Hilton Dance & Music Series 19. Hillsdale, NY: Pendragon Press, 2014.

Noverre, Jean-Georges. *Letters on Dancing and Ballets* [1803 ed.]. Translated by Cyril W. Beaumont. London: author, 1930.

Noverre, Jean-Georges. *Lettres sur la danse et sur les ballets*. Lyon: Aimé Delaroche, 1760.

Noverre, Jean-Georges. *Lettres sur la danse et sur les ballets et les arts* (1803). Edited by Flavia Pappacena. Lucca: Lim Editrice, 2012.

Noverre, Jean-Georges. *Lettres sur les arts imitateurs en général, et sur la danse en particulier*. 2 vols. Paris: Léopold Collin; La Haie: Immerzeel, 1807.

Noverre, Jean-Georges. *The Works of Monsieur Noverre Translated from the French*. Translated by Joseph Parkyns MacMahon. 3 vols. London, 1782.

Osumare, Halifu. *The Africanist Aesthetic in Global Hip-Hop: Power Moves*. New York: Palgrave Macmillan, 2007.

Pappacena, Flavia. "Accademia Nazionale de Danza, Elenco dei Nuovi Codici, Ambiti Disciplinari, Settore Disciplinari, Declaratorie e Campi Disciplinari di Competenza." n.d.

P.A.R.T.S. Training Cycle and Study Guide (2016–2019). http://www.parts.be/fr/presentation. http://www.parts.be/fr/curriculum-training#theory.

Pasch, Johann. *Beschreibung wahrer Tanz-Kunst*. Frankfurt: Wolfgang Michahelles und Johann Adolph, 1707. Facs. ed. Leipzig: Zentralantiquariat der DDR; Munich: Heimeran Verlag, 1978.

Plato. *Laws*. Book II. Translated by R. G. Bury. Loeb Classical Library 187. Cambridge, MA: Harvard University Press, 1984. https://www.loebclassics.com/view/LCL187/1926/volume.xml.

Plutarch. *Moralia*, vol. IX. Translated by Edwin L. Minar, Jr., F. H. Sandbach, and W. C. Helmbold. Loeb Classical Library 425. Cambridge, MA: Harvard University Press, 1961. https://www.loebclassics.com/view/LCL425/1961/volume.xml.

Rainer, Yvonne. "A.Trio." https://www.youtube.com/watch?v=8NGiQ46gTMU&list=PLVALBxbrx-SYIiGNUIvqUGQSVUFKqVniJ&index=2.

Rainer, Yvonne. "A Quasi Survey of Some 'Minimalist' Tendencies in the Quantitatively Minimal Dance Activity Midst the Plethora, or an Analysis of *Trio A*." In *Minimal Art: A Critical Anthology*, edited by Gregory Battcock, 263–273. New York: E. P. Dutton, 1968.

Rainer, Yvonne. "Some Retrospective Notes on a Dance for 10 People and 12 Mattresses Called 'Parts of Some Sextets,' Performed at the Wadsworth Atheneum, Hartford, Connecticut, and Judson Memorial Church, New York, in March, 1965." *The Tulane Drama Review* 10, no. 2 (Winter 1965): 168–178.

Rohloff, Ernst. *Die Quellenhandschriften zum Musiktraktat des Johannes de Grocheio*. Leipzig: VEB Deutscher Verlag für Musik, 1972.

Rothfield, Philipa, and Thomas F. DeFrantz. "Relay: Choreography and Corporeality." In *Choreography and Corporeality: Relay in Motion*, edited by Thomas F. DeFrantz and Philipa Rothfield. London: Palgrave Macmillan, 2016.

Saint-Léon, Arthur. *La Sténochorégraphie*. Paris: author and Brandus & Cie., 1852. Facs. ed. by Flavia Pappacena. Lucca: Libreria Musicale Italiana, 2006.

Society of Dance History Scholars. Call for Papers: "Re-Thinking Practice and Theory: International Symposium on Dance Research." dp-colloquerpt-juin07.pdf.

Society of Dance History Scholars Proceedings: Thirtieth Annual Conference Co-sponsored with CORD, Centre national de la danse, Paris, France 21–24 June 2007. Society of Dance History Scholars, 2007.

Sulzer, Johann George. *Allgemeine Theorie der Schönen Künste*, vol. II. Leipzig: M. G. Weidmanns Erben und Reich, 1775.

Taubert, Gottfried. "Kurtzer Entwurff Von Der Zuläßigkeit des sowol natürlichen als künstlichen Tantz-*Exercitii*." Ms.: St. Petersburg, National Library of Russia, German. Q. XI. No. 2, n.d. (between ca. 1729 and 1746).

Taubert, Gottfried. *Rechtschaffener Tantzmeister*. Leipzig: Friedrich Lanckischens Erben, 1717. Facs. ed. Leipzig: Zentralantiquariat der DDR, and Munich: Heimeran Verlag, 2 vols., 1976. Translated and edited by Tilden Russell. *The Compleat Dancing Master*, 2 vols.

Thompson, Robert Farris. "An Aesthetic of the Cool: West African Dance." *African Forum* 2, no. 2 (Fall 1966): 85–102.

Weaver, John. *Anatomical and Mechanical Lectures upon Dancing*. London: J. Brotherton and W. Meadows, 1721. Facs. ed. Ralph: 861–1031.

Weaver, John. *An Essay Towards an History of Dancing*. London, J. Tonson, 1712. Facs. ed. Ralph: 391–672.

Weaver, John. *The History of the Mimes and Pantomimes*. London, 1728. Facs. ed. Ralph: 677–732.

Weaver, John. *Orchesography. Or, the Art of Dancing*. London: H. Meere, 1706. Facs. eds. Westmead, Hants.: Gregg, 1971; Ralph: 175–285.

Weaver, John. *A Small Treatise of Time and Cadence in Dancing*. London: H. Meere, 1706. Facs. eds. [bound with *Orchesography*]. Westmead, Hants.: Gregg, 1971; Ralph: 361–372.

Weaver, John. *The Spectator* 334 (March 24, 1712). Facs. ed. Ralph: 381–383.

Zorn, Friedrich Albert. *Grammar of the Art of Dancing: Theoretical and Practical*. Translated by Benjamin P. Coates and edited by Alfonso Josephs Sheafe. Boston: International Publishers, 1920.

OTHER SOURCES

Acta eruditorum anno MDCLXXXIII. Leipzig: J. Grossius & J. P. Gletitschius, 1683.

Alberti, Leon Battista. *On Painting*, rev. ed. Translated and edited by John R. Spencer. New Haven, CT: Yale University Press, 1966.

Alberti, Leon Battista. *On Painting and on Sculpture: The Latin Texts of* De pictura *and* De Statua. Edited and translate by Cecil Grayson. London: Phaidon, 1972.

Albertieri, Luigi. *The Art of Terpsichore: An Elementary, Theoretical, Physical, and Practical Treatise of Dancing*. New York: G. Ricordi & Co., 1923.

Allen, Zita. "What Is Black Dance?" *The Black Tradition in American Modern Dance*. Pamphlet produced for the American Dance Festival, 1991–1992 season, c. WNET 2017. https://www.thirteen.org/freetodance/behind/behind_blackdance3.html.

Alter, Judith B. *Dance-Based Dance Theory*, New Studies in Aesthetics 7. New York: Peter Lang, 1991.

Anderson, Jack. *Ballet & Modern Dance: A Concise History*, 2nd ed. Princeton, NJ: Dance Horizons, 1992.

Anonymous. "Criton, ou de la grace et de la beauté," In *Les Graces*, 169–256. Paris: Laurent Prault, and Bailly, 1759.

Anonymous. *Notice des livres de la bibliothèque de feu M. J.-E. Despréaux*. Paris: Olivier, Royer, and Brunet, 1820.

Baltzly, Dirk. "Stoicism." *Stanford Encyclopedia of Philosophy*. https://plato.stanford.edu/entries/stoicism/ (2018). Accessed October 29, 2018.

Banes, Sally. *Writing Dancing in the Age of Postmodernism*. Hanover, NH: Wesleyan University Press, 1994.

Barbier, Antoine-Alexander. *Dictionnaire des ouvrages anonymes et pseudonymes*, 2nd ed., vol. I. Paris: Barrois L'ainé, 1822.

Barocktanz/La danse baroque/Baroque Dance. Edited by Stephanie Schroedter, Marie-Thérèse Mourey, and Giles Bennett. Hildesheim: Georg Olms Verlag, 2008.

Baron, A. *Lettres et entretiens sur la danse*. Paris: Dondey-Dupré père et fils, 1824.

Barthes, Roland. *L'empire des signes*. Geneva: Éditions Albert Skira, 1970.

Barthes, Roland. *Roland Barthes par Roland Barthes*. Écrivains de toujours 96. Paris: Seuil, 1975.

Barthes, Roland. "(Théorie du) texte." *Oeuvres complètes*, vol. IV 1972–1976, 443–459. Paris: Éditions du Seuil, 2002; originally published in the *Encyclopaedia Universalis*, vol. XV (1973).

[Bausch] *Pina Bausch: entretiens avec . . .*, Mot pour Mot. Edited by Philippe Noisette. Paris: Van Dieren Éditeur, 1997.

Baxandall, Michael. *Painting and Experience in Fifteenth-Century Italy*, 2nd ed. Oxford: Oxford University Press, 1988.

Beaumont, Cyril W. *A Bibliography of Dancing*. New York: Benjamin Blom, 1963.

Beaumont, Sir Harry. (*nom de plume* of Joseph Spence). *Crito: or, A Dialogue on Beauty*. Dublin: George Faulkner, 1752.

Beauzée, Nicolas, and Jacques-Philippe-Augustin Douchet. "Grammaire." *Encyclopédie* 7: 841–847.

Berchoux, J. *La danse, ou les dieux de l'opéra*. Paris: Giguet det Michaud, 1806.

Black, Daniel. *Embodiment and Mechanisation: Reciprocal Understandings of Body and Machine from the Renaissance to the Present*. Farnham, Surrey: Ashgate, 2014.

Blomkvist, Magnus. "François de Lauze und seine 'Apologie de la danse' (1623)." *Tanz und Bewegung in der barocken Oper: Kongressbericht Salzburg 1994*, edited by Sybille Dahms and Stephanie Schroedter, 31–43. Innsbruck and Vienna: Studien Verlag, 1996.

Bongiovanni, Salvatore. "Magri in Naples: Defending the Italian Dance Tradition." In *The Grotesque Dancer on the Eighteenth-Century Stage*, translated by Bruce Alan Brown, 33–61.

Bonin, Louis. *Die Neueste Art zur Galanten und Theatralischen Tantz-Kunst*. Frankfurt: Joh. Christoff Lochner, 1712. Facs. ed. Berlin: Edition Hentrich, 1996.

Bonnet, Jacques. *Histoire générale de la danse sacrée et profane*. Paris: Chez d'Houry fils, 1723.

Borassatti, Giustiniano. *Il Gimnasta in pratica, ed in teorica*. Venice, 1753.

Borelli, Giovanni. *De motu animalium*, 2 vols. Rome: Angelo Bernabò, 1680–1681.

Bourassa, Dominique. "Terpsichore in the Spotlight of the *Lumières*: Dance in the Classification of Knowledge During the Age of Reason." Unpublished paper, read at the 20th Annual Oxford Dance Symposium. New College, Oxford, April 2018.

Brainard, Ingrid, Sandra Noll Hammond, and Kennetha R. McArthur. "Technical Manuals." *International Encyclopedia of Dance* 6 (1998): 121–129.

Brandstetter, Gabriele, and Gabriele Klein, eds. *Dance [and] Theory*. Bielefeld: transcript Verlag, 2013.

Burden, Michael, and Jennifer Thorp, eds. *Ballet de la Nuit: Rothschild B1/16/6*. The Wendy Hilton Dance & Music Series 15. Hillsdale, NY: Pendragon Press, 2009.

Burke, Edmund. *A Philosophical Enquiry into the Origin of Our Ideas of the Sublime and Beautiful* [1st ed. 1757]. Edited by James T. Boulton. Notre Dame, IN: University of Notre Dame Press, 1958.

Burt, Ramsay. *Judson Dance Theater: Performative Traces*. London: Routledge, 2006.

Callahan, Daniel M. "The Gay Divorce of Music and Dance: Choreomusicality and the Early Works of Cage-Cunningham." *Journal of the American Musicological Society* 71, no. 2 (Summer 2018): 439–525.

Carroll, Noël. "Dance." In *The Oxford Handbook of Aesthetics*, edited by Jerrold Levinson, 583–593. Oxford: Oxford University Press, 2003.

Carter, Alexandra, and Janet O'Shea, eds. *The Routledge Dance Studies Reader*, 2nd ed. London: Routledge, 2010.

Cassidy, James P. *A Treatise on the Theory and Practice of Dancing*. Dublin: William Folds, 1810.

Castelli, Patrizia. "Il moto aristotelico e la 'licita scientia.' Guglielmo Ebreo da Pesaro e la speculazione sulla danza nel XV secolo." In Patrizia Castelli, Maurizio Minguardi, and Maurizio Padovan, *Mesura et arte del danzare: Guglielmo Ebreo da Pesaro e la danza nelle corti italiane del XV secolo*, 35–57. Pesaro: Commune di Pesaro, 1987.

Clark, VèVè A., and Sara E. Johnson. *Kaiso! Writings by and about Katherine Dunham*. Madison: University of Wisconsin Press, 2005.

Cohen, Selma Jeanne. *Dance as a Theatre Art: Source Readings in Dance History from 1581 to the Present*. New York: Harper & Row, 1974.

Copeland, Roger, and Marshall Cohen, eds. *What is Dance? Readings in Theory and Criticism*. Oxford: Oxford University Press, 1983.

d'Albert, Charles. *Dancing. Technical Encyclopaedia of the Theory and Practice of The Art of Dancing*. London: author, 1913–1914.

d'Albert, Charles. *The Encyclopedia of Dancing*, revised ed. London: T. M. Middleton & Co., 1920.

"Dance Theory." *Wikipedia*. http://en.wikipedia.org/wiki/Dance_theory. Accessed December 5, 2014.

Daniel, David. "A Conversation with Suzanne Farrell." *Reading Dance*: 556–569.

Dee Das, Joanna. "Katherine Dunham (1909–2006)." Dance Heritage Coalition (2012). http://www.danceheritage.org/treasures/dunham_essay_deedas.pdf. Accessed June 18, 2018.

DeFrantz, Thomas F. Untitled video demonstration of buck and wing. https://www.youtube.com/watch?v=A34OD4eAr7o. Accessed August 5, 2018.

De Keersmaeker, Anne Teresa, et al. *Work/Travail/Arbeid*. 4 vols. Brussels: WIELS, Mercatorfonds & Rosas, 2015.

Denby, Edwin. *Dance Writings and Poetry*. Edited by Robert Cornfield. New Haven, CT: Yale University Press, 1998.

Descartes, René. *Musicae compendium* (1618). Translated by Thomas Harper. *Renatus Descartes Excellent Compendium of Musick*. London: Thomas Harper, 1653.

Descartes, René. *Observationes de passionibus animae*, new ed. Hanover: Nicolaus Foerster, 1707.

[Despréaux]. *Notice des livres de la bibliothèque de feu M. J.-E. Despréaux*. Paris: Olivier, Royer, and Brunet, 1820.

Desrat, G. *Traité de la danse*, new ed. Paris: H. Delarue et Cie., n.d. [190?].

Diderot, Denis. "Art." *Encyclopédie* I: 713–719.

Diderot, Denis. "Entretiens sur *Le fils naturel*." In *Oeuvres complètes de Diderot*, edited by J. Assézat, 134–168. Paris: Garnier Frères, 1875. Repr. ed. Nendeln: Kraus, 1966, vol. VII, third *entretien*.

Diderot, Denis, and Jean le Rond D'Alembert, eds. *Encyclopédie, ou, dictionnaire raisonné des sciences, des arts et des métiers*, 17 vols. Paris: Briasson, Le Breton, Faulche, 1751–1765.

Dillon, Brian. "The Curve of Time." *Work/Travail/Arbeid* 3: 45–55.

Dunning, Jennifer. "Jawole Willa Jo Zollar." In *Fifty Contemporary Choreographers*, 2nd ed. Edited by Martha Bremser and Lorna Sanders, 370–375. London: Routledge, 2011.

Fabbricatore, Arianna Beatrice. *La Querelle des Pantomimes: Danse, culture et société dans l''Europe des Lumières*. Rennes: Presses universitaires de Rennes, 2017.

Fernandes, Ciane. *The Moving Researcher: Laban/Bartenieff Movement Analysis in Performing Arts Education and Creative Arts Therapies*. London: Jessica Kingsley, 2015.

Foucault, Michel. *Power/Knowledge: Selected Interviews and Other Writings 1972–1977*. Edited by Colin Gordon. New York: Pantheon Books, 1980.

Fumaroli, Marc. *When the World Spoke French*. Translated by Richard Howard. New York: New York Review of Books, 2011.

Furetière, Antoine. *Dictionaire universel*. La Haye: Arnout & Reinier Leers, 1690.

Gager, John G. *Curse Tablets and Binding Spells from the Ancient World*. New York: Oxford University Press, 1992.

Giersdorf, Jens Richard. "Dance Studies in the International Academy: Genealogy of a disciplinary formation." In *The Routledge Dance Studies Reader*, 2nd ed., edited by Alexandra Carter and Janet O'Shea, 319–334. Abingdon: Routledge, 2010.

Glon, Marie. "Les lumières chorégraphiques: Les maîtres de danse européens au coeur d'un phénomène éditorial (1700–1760)." Unpublished doctoral thesis. Paris: École des Hautes Études en Sciences Sociales, 2014.

Glück, Marliese. "Courante." In *Die Musik in Geschichte und Gegenwart*, edited by Ludwig Finscher, cols. 1029–1035 (Kassel, Basel: Bärenreiter, 1995).

Goellner, Ellen W., and Jacqueline Shea Murphy. "Introduction: Movement Movements." In *Bodies of the Text: Dance as Theory, Literature as Dance*, edited by Ellen W. Goellner and Jacqueline Shea Murphy, 1–18. New Brunswick, NJ: Rutgers University Press, 1995.

Gottlieb, Robert. "Balanchine's Dream." *Vanity Fair* (December 1998). https://www.vanityfair.com/culture/1998/12/george-balanchine-new-york-city-ballet-history.

Gottlieb, Robert, ed. *Reading Dance*. New York: Pantheon Books, 2008.

Les Graces. Paris: Laurent Prault, and Bailly, 1759.

Graham, Martha. *Blood Memory*. New York: Doubleday, 1991.

Graham, Martha. *The Notebooks of Martha Graham*. New York: Harcourt Brace Jovanovich, 1973.

Guest, Ann Hutchinson. *Choreo-Graphics: A Comparison of Dance Notation Systems from the Fifteenth Century to the Present*. New York: Gordon and Breach, 1989.

Guillemin, *Chorégraphie, ou l'art de décrire la danse*. Paris: L'auteur, Petit, 1784.

Habermas, Jürgen. *The Theory of Communicative Action*, vol. 2. Translated by Thomas McCarthy. Boston: Beacon Press, 1987.

Hall, Fernau. "Dance Notation and Choreology." In *What Is Dance? Readings in Theory and Criticism*, edited by Roger Copeland and Marshall Cohen, 390–399. Oxford: Oxford University Press, 1983.

Hammond, Sandra Noll. "Ballet's Technical Heritage: The Grammaire of Léopold Adice." *Dance Research: The Journal of the Society for Dance Research* 13, no. 1 (Summer 1995): 33–58.

Harris-Warrick, Rebecca, and Bruce Alan Brown, eds. *The Grotesque Dancer on the Eighteenth-Century Stage: Gennaro Magri and His World*. Madison: University of Wisconsin Press, 2005.

Heiter, Gerrit Berenike. "*Il Gimnasta* (1751–1756): Acrobatic Performances in Connnection with Other Theatrical Performances." Unpublished paper: 20th Annual Oxford Dance Symposium, New College, Oxford, 2018.

Heiter, Gerrit Berenike. "Tanz in Stich und Typen—Exemplarrecherche zu Gottfried Tauberts *Rechtschaffenem Tantzmeister.*" In *Gottfried Tauberts "Rechtschaffener Tantzmeister" (Leipzig 1717): Kontexte—Lektüren—Praktiken,* edited by Hanna Walsdorf, Marie-Thérèse Mourey, and Tilden Russell, 211–253. *Cadences—Writings on the History of Dance and Music,* Bd. 2. Berlin: Frank & Timme, 2019.

Hilton, Wendy. "A Dance for Kings: The 17th-Century French *Courante.*" *Early Music* 5, no. 2 (1977): 160–172.

Hogarth, William. *The Analysis of Beauty* [1753]. Edited by Ronald Paulson. New Haven, CT: Yale University Press, 1997.

Hoyt, Nellie S., and Thomas Cassirer. *Encyclopedia Selections.* The Library of Liberal Arts. Indianapolis: Bobbs-Merrill, 1965.

Hurston, Lucy Anne, and the Estate of Zora Neale Hurston. *Speak, So You Can Speak Again: The Life of Zora Neale Hurston.* New York: Doubleday, 2004.

Institut de France, *Le Dictionnaire de l'Académie française,* 6th ed. Paris: Firmin Didot Frères, 1835.

International Encyclopedia of Dance. 6 vols. Edited by Selma Jeanne Cohen. New York: Oxford University Press, 1998.

Jacotot, Sophie. "Les 'théories' de danses nouvelles en France dans l'entre-deux-guerres: quelles sources ces documents constituent-ils pour la connaissance des pratiques dansées?" *Society of Dance History Scholars Proceedings,* 502–507.

Jeschke, Claudia. *Tanzschriften: Ihre Geschichte und Methode.* Bad Reichenhall: Comes Verlag, 1983.

Johnston, Jill. "Which Way the Avant Garde?" *The New York Times* (August 11, 1968): D24.

Kappeler, Annette, Jan Lazardzig, and Nicola Gess. "Claude-François Ménestrier's Theories on Festivals and Performing Arts Encompassed by an Overarching Image Philosophy: An Introduction." In *Images d'action: Claude-François Ménestrier's Theoretical Writings on Festivals and Performing Arts: Translation and Commentary,* 11–26. Leiden: Wilhelm Fink, 2018.

Kappeler, Annette, Jan Lazardzig, and Nicola Gess, eds. *Images d'action: Claude-François Ménestrier's Theoretical Writings on Festivals and Performing Arts: Translation and Commentary.* Leiden: Wilhelm Fink, 2018.

Kellner, Douglas. "Critical Theory." *New Dictionary of the History of Ideas,* edited by Maryanne Cline Horowitz, vol. 2, pp. 507–511. New York: Charles Scribner's Sons, 2005. *Gale Virtual Reference Library,* http://link.galegroup.com/apps/doc/CX3424300178/GVRL?u=29002&sid=GVRL&xid=17ad8b67.

Kirstein, Lincoln. *Four Centuries of Ballet: Fifty Masterworks.* New York: Dover, 1984.

Klein, Gabriele. "Dance Theory as a Practice of Critique." In *Dance [and] Theory*, edited by Gabriele Brandstetter and Gabriele Klein, 137–149. Bielefeld: transcript Verlag, 2013.

Klein, Gabriele, and Christa Zipprich. "Tanz Theorie Text: Zur Einführung." In *Tanz Theorie Text*, edited by Gabriele Klein and Christa Zipprich, 1–14. Jahrbuch Tanzforschung 12. Münster: LIT Verlag, 2002.

Laermans, Rudi. *Moving Together: Theorizing and Making Contemporary Dance*. Antennae: Valiz, 2015.

Larousse, Pierre. "Compan, Charles." In *Grand dictionnaire universel du XIXe siècle*, vol. IV, 770. Paris: Administration du Grand Dictionnaire universel, 1869.

Lancelot, Francine. *La Belle Dance*. Paris: Van Dieren, 1996.

Lawler, Lillian B. *The Dance in Ancient Greece*. London: Adam & Charles Black, 1964.

Lax, Thomas J. "Allow Me to Begin Again." In *Judson Dance Theater: The Work Is Never Done*, 14–25. New York: The Museum of Modern Art, 2018.

Lecointe, John. *An Apology for Dancing*. Translated by J. Peyton. London: J. Kippax, 1752.

Lecomte, Nathalie. *Entre cours et jardins d'illusion: Le ballet en Europe (1515–1715)*. Pantin: Centre national de la danse, 2014.

Lester, Joel. *Compositional Theory in the Eighteenth Century*. Cambridge, MA: Harvard University Press, 1992.

Lettres patentes du Roi, pour l'établissement de l'Académie royale de danse en la Ville de Paris. Verifiées en Parlement le 30. Mars 1662. Paris: Pierre le Petit, 1663.

Levinson, André. "The Spirit of the Classic Dance." In *Reading Dance*, edited by Robert Gottlieb, 412–418. New York: Pantheon Books, 2008.

Levinson, Jerrold, ed. *The Oxford Handbook of Aesthetics*. Oxford: Oxford University Press, 2003.

Liddell, Henry George, and Robert Scott. *An Intermediate Greek-English Lexicon*, 7th ed. Oxford: Oxford University Press, 1961.

Little, Meredith Ellis, and Carol G. Marsh. *La Danse Noble: An Inventory of Dances and Sources*. Williamstown: Broude Brothers, 1992.

Littré, Emile. *Dictionnaire de la langue française*. Paris: Librairie Hachette et Cie., 1873–1874.

Lloyd, Margaret Lloyd. Review: "A Study in Dance Theory." *The Christian Science Monitor* (September 28, 1940): 5.

Lorin, André. "Livre de contredance presenté au roy." Ms., Paris: Bibliothèque nationale, Mss. Fr. 1697; gallica.bnf.fr/ark:/12148/btv1b90600978.

Louison-Lassablière, Marie-Joëlle. "Une discipline en gestation: L'Orchestique." In *L'Encyclopédie ou la création des disciplines*, edited by Martine Groult, 153–166. Paris: CNRS Éditions, 2003.

Louison-Lassablière, Marie-Joëlle. *Études sur la danse: De la Renaissance au siècle des Lumières*. Paris: L'Harmattan, 2003.

Maletic, Vera. *Body-Space-Expression: The Development of Rudolf Laban's Movement and Dance Concepts*. Berlin: Mouton de Gruyter, 1987.

Malkin, Mary Ann O'Brian. *Dancing by the Book: A Catalogue of Books 1531–1804*. New York: Author, 2003.

Malone, Jacqui. *Steppin' on the Blues*. Urbana: University of Illinois Press, 1996.

Manning, Susan. "Key Works, Artists, Events, Venues, Texts: Black Dance on U.S. Stages in the 20th Century." Black Arts Initiative, bai.northwestern.edu/wp-content/uploads/2012/08/Black-Dance-Timeline.docx.

Martin, Gabriele. *Bibliotheca Bultelliana: seu Catalogus librorum Bibliothecae V. Cl. D. Caroli Bulteau*. Paris: Petrus Giffart and author, 1711.

Martin, Randy. *Critical Moves: Dance Studies in Theory and Politics*. Durham, NC: Duke University Press, 1998.

Martinet, J. J. *Essai ou principes élémentaires de l'art de la danse*. Lausanne: Monnier et Jacquerod, 1797.

Mathiesen, Thomas J. "Aristides Quintilianus." *Grove Music Online*. http://www.oxfordmusiconline.com/subscriber/article/grove/music/01244?q=Aristides+Quintilianus&search=quick&pos=1&_start=1#F010731.

Mattheson, Johann, *Der vollkommene Capellmeister*. Hamburg: Christian Herold, 1739.

McGee, Timothy J. "Medieval Dances: Matching the Repertory with Grocheio's Descriptions." *The Journal of Musicology* VII, no. 4 (Fall 1989): 498–517.

Méreau. *Réflexions sur le maintien et sur les moyons d'en corriger les defauts*. Gotha: Mevius & Dieterich, 1760.

Meyer, F. Herm. "Die geschäftlichen Verhältnisse des deutschen Buchhandels im achtzehnten Jahrhundert." *Archiv für Geschichte des Deutschen Buchhandels* V (1880): 175–255.

Milner, Andrew. *Contemporary Cultural Theory*. London: UCL Press, 1994.

Moore, Lillian. *Images of the Dance: Historical Treasures of the Dance Collection 1581–1861*. New York: The New York Public Library, 1965.

Moran, Kate Mattingly. Review "Dancing the Voice of the People." *Dance Magazine* 75, no. 10 (October 2001): 100–101.

Moroda, Derra de. *Derra de Moroda Dance Archives, The Dance Library: A Catalogue*. Edited by Sybille Dahms and Lotte Roth-Wölfle. Munich: Robert Wölfle, 1982.

Mourey, Marie-Thérèse. "Kultur und Identität, Theologie und Anthropologie: Gottfried Taubert im Kontext des frühen 18. Jahrhunderts." In *Gottfried Tauberts "Rechtschaffener Tantzmeister" (Leipzig 1717): Kontexte—Lektüren— Praktiken*, edited by Hanna Walsdorf, Marie-Thérèse Mourey, and Tilden

Russell. *Cadences—Writings on the History of Dance and Music*, Bd. 2. Berlin: Frank & Timme, 2019.

Nikolais, Alwin. "Choreosonic Music of the New Dance Theatre of Alwin Nikolais," LP recording (cacophonic 10ACKLP), 1959.

Osumare, Halifu Osumare. "Dancing the Black Atlantic: Katherine Dunham's Research-to-Performance Method." *AmeriQuests* 7, no. 2 (September 2010).

The Oxford Annotated Apocrypha, revised standard version. Edited by Bruce M. Metzger. New York: Oxford University Press, 1965.

Page, Christopher. "Grocheio [Grocheo], Johannes de." *Grove Music Online.* https://doi.org/10.1093/gmo/9781561592630.article.14359 (2001).

Palmer, Donald D. *Structuralism and Poststructuralism for Beginners*. New York: Writers and Readers, 1997.

Panckoucke, Charles-Joseph, ed. *Encyclopédie méthodique par ordre des matières. Encyclopédie méthodique. Arts académiques. Équitation, escrime, danse, et art de nager.* Paris: Chez Panckoucke, and Liège: Chez Plomteux, 1786.

Pappacena, Flavia. "*Danse écrite ou La Terpsi-choro-graphie ou Nouvel Essay de Theorie de la dans.*" Manuscript dated 1813 by Jean-Étienne Despréaux kept at the Bibliothèque of the Paris Opéra. *Society of Dance History Scholars Proceedings*, 496–501.

Pappacena, Flavia. "The Sténochorégraphie in the Context of the Experimentations of the 18th and 19th Centuries." In *Arthur Saint-Léon*, Sténochorégraphie, edited by Flavia Pappacena, 61–71. *Chorégraphie* 4 (Rome: LIM, 2006).

Pappacena, Flavia. "La 'Terpsi-choro-graphie' di J.-E. Despréaux (1813): la trasformazione della notazione coreutica fra il XVIII e il XIX secolo." *Chorégraphie: Studi e richerche sulla danza* 4, no. 7 (1996): 23–50.

Pauli, Charles. *Elemens de la danse.* Leipzig: Ulr. Chret. Saalbach, 1756.

Peacock, Francis. *Sketches Relative to the History and Theory, but More Especially to the Practice of Dancing*. Aberdeen: J. Chalmers & Co., 1805.

Peponi, Anastasia-Erasmia. "Aristotle's Definition of Dance." In *Choreutika: Performing and Theorising Dance in Ancient Greece*, edited by Laura Gianvittorio, 215–243. Pisa: Fabrizio Serra Editore, 2017.

Price, Curtis. "Music, Style and Society." In *Music and Society: The Early Baroque Era*, edited by Curtis Price, 1–22. Englewood Cliffs, NJ: Prentice Hall, 1993.

Ralph, Richard. *The Life and Works of John Weaver*. New York: Dance Horizons, 1985.

Rameau, Pierre. *Le Maître à danser.* Paris: Chez Jean Villette, 1725. Facs. ed. New York: Broude Brothers, 1967.

Ravelhofer, Barbara, ed. *B. de Montagut: Louange de la danse*. Renaissance Texts from Manuscript 3. Cambridge: RTM Publications, 2000.

Répertoire international des sources musicales (RISM). Series B III, *The Theory of Music*, vols. I–VI. Edited by Joseph Smits van Waesberghe, Peter Fischer, Michel Huglo, et al. Munich-Duisberg: G. Henle Verlag, 1961–2003.

Reynolds, Nancy, and Malcolm McCormick. *No Fixed Points: Dance in the Twentieth Century*. New Haven, CT: Yale University Press, 2003.

Robinet, Jean-Baptiste, ed. *Supplément à l'Encyclopédie, ou Dictionnaire raisonné des sciences, des arts et des métiers*. Amsterdam: M. M. Rey, 1776.

Ross, Janice L. "Margaret Newell H'Doubler (1889–1982)." *100 Dance Treasures*. Dance Heritage Coalition. http://www.danceheritage.org/treasures/hdoubler_essay_ross.pdf.

Rousseau, Jean-Jacques. *Du contract social*. Amsterdam: Chez Marc Michel Rey, 1762.

Rousseau, Jean-Jacques. *Dictionnaire de musique*. Paris: Chez la Veuve Duchesne, 1768.

Russell, Tilden. *The Compleat Dancing Master: A Translation of Gottfried Taubert's Rechtschaffener Tantzmeister (1717)*, 2 vols. New York: Peter Lang Publishing, 2012.

Russell, Tilden, and Dominique Bourassa. *The Menuet de la cour*. Terpsichore Tanzhistorische Studien 4. Hildesheim: Georg Olms Verlag, 2007.

Russell, Tilden. *Theory and Practice in the Eighteenth Century: The German-French Connection*. Studies in Seventeenth- and Eighteenth-Century Art and Culture. Newark: University of Delaware Press, 2017.

Schroedter, Stephanie. "Dance-Music-Theatre in the Shadow of Plato and Aristotle—Claude-François Ménestrier's Reception of Ancient Philosophers in His Dance Poetics." In *Images d'action: Claude-François Ménestrier's Theoretical Writings on Festivals and Performing Arts: Translation and Commentary*, edited by Annette Kappeler, Jan Lazardzig, and Nicola Gess, 447–457. Leiden: Wilhelm Fink, 2018.

Schroedter, Stephanie. "The Practice of Dance at the Crossroad between Pragmatic Documentation, Artistic Creativity and Political Reflection: Sources of the Theatrical Dance of the Early 19th Century." *Society of Dance History Scholars Proceedings*, 508–514.

Schroedter, Stephanie. *Vom "Affect" zur "Action"; Quellenstudien zur Poetik der Tanzkunst vom späten Ballet de Cour bis zum frühen Ballet en Action*. Würzburg: Königshausen & Neumann, 2004.

Smith, A. William. *Fifteenth-Century Dance and Music*. 2 vols. Dance and Music Series 4. Stuyvesant, NY: Pendragon Press, 1995.

Smith, Marian. "Review of the *International Encyclopedia of Dance*." *Journal of the American Musicological Society* 54, no.1 (Spring 2001): 174–191.

Smits van Waesberghe, Joseph. *Musikerziehung.* Musikgeschichte in Bildern III/3. Leipzig: VEB Deutscher Verlag für Musik, 1969.

Society of Dance History Scholars. "Call for Papers." dp-colloquerpt-juin07.pdf.

Society of Dance History Scholars Proceedings: Thirtieth Annual Conference Co-sponsored with CORD, Centre national de la danse, Paris, France 21–24 June 2007. Society of Dance History Scholars, 2007.

Sokolow, Anna. "The Rebel and the Bourgeois." *The Modern Dance: Seven Statements of Belief,* edited by Selma Jeanne Cohen, 29–37. Middletown, CT: Wesleyan University Press, 1966.

Stein, Gertrude. "Composition as Explanation." 1925. https://www.poetryfoundation.org/resources/learning/essays/detail/69481.

Stearns, Marshall, and Joan Stearns. *Jazz Dance: The Story of American Vernacular Dance.* New York: Schirmer, 1979.

Tanz und Bewegung in der barocken Oper; Kongreßbericht Salzburg 1994. Edited by Sybille Dahms and Stephanie Schroedter. Vienna: Studien Verlag, 1996.

Teachout, Terry. "Pale Horse, Pale Rider" (1994). In *Reading Dance,* edited by Robert Gottlieb, 479–487. New York: Pantheon Books, 2008.

Théleur, E. A. *Letters on Dancing.* London: Sherwood & Co., 1832. Facs. ed. *Studies in Dance History* II/1. Society of Dance History Scholars, 1990.

Thompson, Robert Farris. *African Art in Motion.* Berkeley: University of California Press, 1974.

Thompson, Robert Farris. *Flash of the Spirit: African and Afro-American Art and Philosophy.* New York: Vintage Books, 1983.

Tucker, Earl. "Snake Hips." Video. www.youtube.com/watch?v=7U4ww-MmAY4. Accessed August 17, 2018.

Uji, Charles, and Tijime Justin Awuawuer. "Towards the Theories and Practice of the Dance Art." *International Journal of Humanities and Social Science* 4, no. 4 (Special Issue on Contemporary Issues in Social Science, February 2014): 251–259.

Ullman, Lisa, compiler. *A Vision of Dynamic Space.* London: Laban Archives and The Falmer Press, 1984.

Urban Bush Women website: https://www.urbanbushwomen.org/about-ubw/.

Vitruvius [Marcus Vitruvius Pollio]. *The Ten Books of Architecture.* Translated by Morris Hicky Morgan. Cambridge, MA: Harvard University Press, 1926.

Walker, Alice. "In Search of Zora Neale Hurston." *Ms. Magazine* (March 1975): 74–89.

Walsdorf, Hanna, Marie-Thérèse Mourey, and Tilden Russell, eds. *Gottfried Tauberts "Rechtschaffener Tantzmeister" (Leipzig 1717): Kontexte—Lektüren—Praktiken,* ed. Hanna Walsdorf, *Cadences—Writings on the History of Dance and Music,* Bd. 2. Berlin: Frank & Timme, 2019.

Weiss, Piero, and Richard Taruskin. *Music in the Western World: A History in Documents*. New York: Schirmer Books, 1984.

Wellesz, Egon. "Musicology." In *Grove's Dictionary of Music and Musicians*, 3rd ed., edited by H. C. Colles, 455–462. *Supplementary Volume*. New York: The Macmillan Company, 1940.

Winter, Marian Hannah. *The Pre-Romantic Ballet*. London: Pitman, 1974.

Woitas, Monika. "Das 'aufgeklärte' Ballett oder Aspekte einer ästhetisch-dramaturgischen Kontroverse zu Beginn des 18. Jahrhunderts." *Tanz und Bewegung in der barocken Oper*, 67–83.

Index

For the benefit of digital users, indexed terms that span two pages (e.g., 52–53) may, on occasion, appear on only one of those pages.

Figures and boxes are indicated by *f* and *b* following the page number